Harvard Studies in East Asian Law

Contemporary Chinese Law: Research Problems and Perspectives

The Harvard Law School, in cooperation with Harvard's East Asian Research Center, the Harvard-Yenching Institute, and scholars from other institutions, has initiated a program of training and research designed to further scholarly understanding of the legal systems of China, Japan, Korea, and adjacent areas. Accordingly, Harvard University Press has established a new series to include scholarly works on these subjects. The editorial committee consists of Jerome Alan Cohen (chairman), John K. Fairbank, L. S. Yang, and Donald Shively.

Contemporary Chinese Law:
Research Problems and Perspectives

Edited by Jerome Alan Cohen

With Contributions by

Harold J. Berman
Hungdah Chiu
Jerome Alan Cohen
David Finkelstein
George Ginsburgs
Dan F. Henderson

Tao-tai Hsia
Victor H. Li
Stanley Lubman
Marinus J. Meijer
Richard M. Pfeffer
Yasuhei Taniguchi

Harvard University Press
Cambridge, Massachusetts
1970

To the memory of

Joseph R. Levenson
Sather Professor of History
University of California (Berkeley)

whose original perspectives and imaginative
insights did so much to enlarge our
vision of contemporary China.

Acknowledgments

The Subcommittee on Chinese Law, consisting of Dan F. Henderson, Clarence Morris, and Jerome Alan Cohen, is grateful to the Joint Committee on Contemporary China, to its sponsors — the Social Science Research Council and the American Council of Learned Societies — and to the Ford Foundation for their support of its work. We especially appreciate the untiring and wise counsel of Bryce Wood of the S.S.R.C., who has guided the Subcommittee's activities from the outset. We also wish to thank Lois Dougan Tretiak for her valuable assistance in editing this volume for publication and Mrs. Bertha Ezell for her skilled typing of the bulk of the manuscript.

Contents

Tables

Contemporary Chinese Law:
Research Problems and Perspectives

Abbreviations

CFYC	*Cheng-fa yen-chiu* (Political-legal research)
FH	*Fa-hsüeh* (Legal studies)
FKHP	*Chung-hua jen-min kung-ho-kuo fa-kuei hui-pien* (Collection of laws and regulations of the People's Republic of China), 13 vols.
FLHP	*Chung-yang jen-min cheng-fu fa-ling hui-pien* (Collection of laws and decrees of the Central People's Government), 7 vols.
JMJP	*Jen-min jih-pao* (People's daily), Peking
KMJP	*Kuang-ming jih-pao* (Kuangming daily), Peking
NFJP	*Nan-fang jih-pao* (Southern daily), Canton
SCMP	*Survey of China Mainland Press* (translations by the American Consulate General Press Monitoring Unit, Hong Kong)
SGP	*Sovetskoe gosudarstvo i pravo* (Soviet state and law)

Introduction

Jerome Alan Cohen

Whatever else the 1960's may be remembered for — the proliferation of macroweapons, microstates or miniskirts — historians of the decade might allot a footnote to the more modest, but less disconcerting, proliferation of English language studies of Chinese law. Over thirty years ago a survey of then recent research on Chinese law revealed "an increased interest on the part of Chinese, Japanese, and Western scholars." [1] The author noted that, although "[t]he amount of work achieved . . . constitutes as yet but a slight beginning in what is still a largely unworked field," it "clearly indicates the potential contributions which further researches can make to our understanding of the evolution of Chinese social, economic and political life and institutions." No one rose to dispute the author's conclusion that Chinese law offers "a rich source from which to derive a more realistic appraisal of the forces actually at work in Chinese society at different epochs." Yet — except in Japan and the Soviet Union, where scholars of things Chinese received additional stimulus from the adventitious circumstances of international politics — the cumulative impact of the Sino-Japanese War, World War II, the Chinese Civil War, and the triumph of Communism slowed the development of what had been a promising academic field. [2]

Note: An earlier version of the first part of this introduction appeared in the *Journal of Asian Studies*, 27, no. 3 (May 1968), 475–483.

1. Cyrus H. Peake, "Recent Studies on Chinese Law," *Political Science Quarterly*, 52 (1937), 117.

2. Although, as Mr. Taniguchi points out in his contribution to this volume, Japanese scholars were virtually precluded from studying Communist Chinese law until the establishment of the People's Republic of China in 1949, political conditions prior to that time had enhanced their opportunities to engage in research on pre-Communist law and customs. In footnote 2 of his chapter Mr. Taniguchi lists several Japanese bibliographies of postwar Japanese scholarship on Chinese law. For relevant bibliographies in Western languages, see John K. Fairbank and Masataka Banno, *Japanese Studies of Modern China* (Rutland, Vt., and Tokyo: C. E. Tuttle,

For almost a generation English language research in Chinese law lay in the doldrums. In Great Britain, although there were occasional publications during this period,[3] no work comparable to that previously done by Staunton, Alabaster, or Jamieson appeared.[4] Nor, apart from Roscoe Pound,[5] did the United States produce successors to Americans who, in the course of assisting China to develop modern law schools and legal institutions during the late nineteenth and early twentieth centuries, had published a variety of studies and reports on Chinese law.[6] Moreover, Chinese lawyers with Western training, who had begun to add to our understanding of their country's legal heri-

1955), pp. 73–80; and "Japanisches Schrifttum zum Recht der Volksdemokratien Asiens," *Osteuropa Recht*, 6 (1960), 303–305; and Hisashi Uchida, "Japanisches Schrifttum zum Recht der Ostblockstaaten," *Osteuropa Recht*, 9 (1963), 239–264.

The impressive achievements of Soviet scholarship on Communist Chinese law during the 1950's are listed in the bibliography contained in Mr. Ginsburgs's contribution to this volume.

3. See, e.g., Maurice Freedman, *Chinese Family and Marriage in Singapore* (London: Her Majesty's Stationery Office, 1957); "Colonial Law and Chinese Society," *Journal of the Royal Anthropological Institute*, 80 (1950), pts. 1 and 2; and "The Penhas Case: Mixed and Unmixed Marriage in Singapore," *The Modern Law Review*, 16 (1953), 366; D. E. Greenfield, "Marriage by Chinese Law and Custom in Hong-kong," *International and Comparative Law Quarterly*, 7 (1958), 437–451; Henry McAleavy, "Dien in China and Vietnam," *Journal of Asian Studies*, 17 (1958), 403–415; and Denis Twitchett, "The Fragment of the T'ang Ordinances of the Department of Waterways Discovered at Tunhuang," *Asia Major*, n.s., 6 (1957), 23–79; and "The Fan Clan's Charitable Estate, 1050–1760," in *Confucianism in Action*, ed. David S. Nivison and Arthur F. Wright (Stanford: Stanford University Press, 1959).

4. George T. Staunton, *Ta Tsing Leu Lee, Being the Fundamental Laws . . . of the Penal Code of China* (London, 1810); Ernest Alabaster, *Notes and Commentaries on Chinese Criminal Law* (London, 1899); "Notes on Chinese Law and Practice Preceding Revision," *Journal of the North China Branch, Royal Asiatic Society*, n.s., 37 (1906), 83–149; "Dips into an Imperial Law Officer's Compendium," *Monumenta Serica*, 2 (1936), 426–437; and George Jamieson, *Chinese Family and Commercial Law* (Shanghai: Kelly and Walsh, 1921).

5. In 1946, ten years after his retirement as Dean of Harvard Law School, Pound, at the age of seventy-five, became adviser to the Ministry of Justice of the Republic of China for two years. See Roscoe Pound, *Some Problems of the Administration of Justice in China* (Nanking: National Chengchi University, 1948); "The Chinese Constitution," *New York University Law Quarterly Review*, 22 (1947), 194–232; "Progress of the Law in China," *Washington Law Review*, 23 (1948), 345–362; "Comparative Law and History as Bases for Chinese Law," *Harvard Law Review*, 61 (1948), pp. 749–762; and "The Chinese Civil Code in Action," *Tulane Law Review*, 29 (1955), 277–291.

6. See, e.g., W. A. P. Martin, *Traces of International Law in Ancient China* (n.p., 1881); T. R. Jernigan, *China in Law and Commerce* (New York: Macmillan, 1905); R. T. Bryan, Jr., *An Outline of Chinese Civil Law* (Shanghai: Commercial Press, 1925); W. W. Blume, "Christian Legal Education in China," *China Law Review*, 1 (1922–1924), 131–134; and "Legal Education in China," *ibid.*, pp. 305–311; and C. S. Lobingier, "The Corpus Juris of New China," *Tulane Law Review*, 19 (1945), 512–552, which lists that author's numerous prewar essays.

tage,[7] seem increasingly to have been diverted from this pursuit.[8]

If one looked to the continent for consolation, the situation was little better, except in the Netherlands. Shortly after World War II, a number of Dutch scholars renewed the Leiden school's distinguished tradition of law and sinology and, ironically, produced some of the best writing that has appeared in English.[9] However, in postwar France the impressive precedents that had been set by Philastre, Hoang, Pelliot, Deloustal, Boulais, Maspéro, Escarra,[10] and others inspired few emulators.[11] And Karl Bünger's[12] departure to diplomacy in the early 1950's deprived postwar Germany of its foremost specialist

7. See, e.g., John C. H. Wu, *The Art of Law* (Shanghai: Commercial Press, 1936); Boyer P. H. Chu, *Commentaries on the Chinese Civil Code* (Shanghai, 1935); and F. T. Cheng, *The Chinese Supreme Court Decisions* (Peking: Commission on Extraterritoriality, 1922).

8. For sporadic exceptions, see Chao-lung Yang, "Powers of Chinese Courts," *Vanderbilt Law Review*, 1 (1947), 16–46; Yu Kwei, "Some Judicial Problems Facing China," *Washington Law Review*, 23 (1948), 363–374; Tien-hsi Cheng, "The Development and Reform of Chinese Law," *Current Legal Problems*, 1 (1948), 170–187; Chiyen Chen, "The Foster Daughter-In-Law System in Formosa," *American Journal of Comparative Law*, 6 (1957), 302–314; and Chin-sui Liu, "The Chinese Council of Grand Justices," *American Journal of Comparative Law*, 7 (1958), 402–408.

9. See especially Marinus J. Meijer, *The Introduction of Modern Criminal Law in China* (Batavia [Jakarta]: De Unie, 1949); M. H. van der Valk, *Interpretations of the Supreme Court at Peking, Years 1915 and 1916* (Batavia [Jakarta]: Sinological Institute, Faculty of Arts, University of Indonesia, 1949); and *Conservatism in Modern Chinese Family Law* (Leiden: Brill, 1956); A. F. P. Hulsewé, *Remnants of Han Law*, vol. 1 (Leiden: Brill, 1955); Robert H. Van Gulik, *T'ang-yin-pi-shih*, "*Parallel Cases from under the Pear-tree*" (Leiden: Brill, 1956).

10. P. L. F. Philastre, *Le Code annamite: Études sur le droit annamite et chinois*, 2 vols. (Paris, 1876; 2nd ed., 1909); Pierre Hoang, *Notions techniques sur la propriété en Chine* (Shanghai, 1897); and *Le Mariage chinois au point de vue légal* (Shanghai, 1898); Paul Pelliot, "Notes de bibliographie chinoise, II: Le Droit chinois," *Bulletin de l'École Française d'Extrême Orient*, 9 (1909), 123–152; Raymond Deloustal, "La justice dans l'ancien Annam," *Bulletin de l'École Française d'Extrême Orient*, vols. 8–13 (1908–1913); vol. 19 (1919); vol. 22 (1922); Guy Boulais, *Manuel de code chinois* (Shanghai: Imprimerie de la mission catholique, 1924); Henri Maspéro, "Le Serment dans la procédure judiciaire de la Chine antique," *Mélanges chinois et bouddhiques*, 3 (1934–1935), 257–317; and Jean Escarra, *Le Droit chinois* (Peking: Vetch, 1936). This work has been translated into English: Gertrude R. Browne, tr., *Chinese Law* (Seattle: Works Progress Administration, 1936), reprinted (xerox) (Cambridge, Mass., 1961). For other useful work by Escarra, see, e.g., "Western Methods of Researches into Chinese Law," *Chinese Social and Political Science Review*, 8 (1924), 227–248.

11. For happy exceptions, see Étienne Balazs, *Le Traité juridique du "Souei-chou"* (Leiden: Brill, 1954); and Jacques Gernet, "La Vente en Chine d'après les contrats de Touen-houang (IXe–Xe siècles)," *T'oung Pao*, 45 (1957), 295–391.

12. Dr. Bünger's contributions to the study of both contemporary and traditional law can readily be appreciated by consulting Frank L. Gniffke, "German Writings on Chinese Law: An Annotated, Classified Bibliography of German Language Materials on the Chinese Legal System and Chinese International Law Through 1968," *Osteuropa Recht*, 15 (1969), 191–233.

in Chinese law, although scattered works by others kept alive the flame.[13]

Renewed Interest in Chinese Law

This bleak Western picture began to brighten in the early 1960's with the publication by nonlawyers of a number of important books in English relating to premodern Chinese law. Although not explicitly focussed on the legal system, Kung-chuan Hsiao's *Rural China: Imperial Control in the Nineteenth Century*[14] proved to be a mine of information on the actual functioning of informal and formal legal processes. Shortly thereafter, T'ung-tsu Ch'ü published a revised and improved English version of his earlier Chinese text, *Law and Society in Traditional China*, which analyzed the relation of premodern substantive law to China's ideology, social structure and value system.[15] This was followed in 1962 by Ch'ü's *Local Government in China Under the Ch'ing*,[16] a detailed study of the personnel and procedures of the basic level organization for administering the substantive law. In the very same year Sybille van der Sprenkel produced *Legal Institutions in Manchu China*,[17] a well written synthesis of existing learning that, despite its sociological disclaimer of legal competence, might well have been subtitled "What every young lawyer should know about traditional Chinese law." In addition Denis Twitchett's *Financial Administration Under the T'ang* shed new light on the formative epoch of the traditional system.[18]

Even more encouraging in terms of the long range development of the field has been the recent realization by American law faculties that the study of Chinese law is too important to be left exclusively to nonlawyers — a position that sinologists had been unsuccessfully urging for years. Not only have law schools in this country begun to support research in Chinese law, but, more significantly, in view of the

13. See *ibid.*, especially the works of Eduard J. M. Kroker and Bernhard Corinth.
14. Kung-chuan Hsiao, *Rural China: Imperial Control in the Nineteenth Century* (Seattle: University of Washington Press, 1960).
15. T'ung-tsu Ch'ü, *Law and Society in Traditional China* (Paris and The Hague: Mouton, 1961).
16. T'ung-tsu Ch'ü, *Local Government in China Under the Ch'ing* (Cambridge, Mass.: Harvard University Press, 1962).
17. Sybille van der Sprenkel, *Legal Institutions in Manchu China* (London: University of London, Athlone Press, 1962).
18. Denis Twitchett, *Financial Administration Under the T'ang* (Cambridge, Eng.: Cambridge University Press, 1963).

strong teaching emphasis in American legal education, they have also begun to introduce courses in Chinese law into their curricula. In 1960 no American law school offered instruction in this subject. By 1969 it was being taught in the law schools of Boston University, the University of California (Berkeley), George Washington University, Harvard University, the University of Indiana, the University of Michigan, the University of Pennsylvania, the University of Washington, and Washington University (St. Louis). Columbia, N.Y.U., and Yale have also experimented in this area, and other institutions are preparing to do the same. Given the practical orientation that is traditional in our law schools, this is a remarkable development. To be sure, some of the impetus for it has derived from considerations of the "know-thine-enemy" sort, and occasionally one has the feeling that, just as every nation that aspires to great power status must have an atomic bomb, so too every aspiring law school must have a Chinese law course, if only to appear among the avant-garde on the next trip to the Ford Foundation. However, one need not seek ulterior motives. As Max Weber demonstrated long ago, the Chinese legal experience has much to contribute to the study of both law and the processes of modernization, and American law schools are becoming increasingly aware of the relevance of history, the social sciences, and area studies to the intellectual perspectives that will be required by lawyers who will be practicing in the twenty-first century. Moreover, as a growing number of law firms and government agencies have come to recognize, various aspects of contemporary Chinese law relate to what law graduates now do, in both public and private professional capacities.[19]

This belated interest of American law schools in Chinese law is now

19. See, e.g., Kristovich, Public Administrator v. Shu Tong Ng, 228 California Appellate 2d 160 (1964), certiorari denied by the United States Supreme Court, 381 U.S. 902 (1965); and Louknitsky v. Louknitsky, 123 California Appellate 2d 406 (1954); these were, respectively, an inheritance case and a divorce case in which, had expert testimony on Chinese law been produced, it would have facilitated enlightened judicial decision-making. See also Gabriele Crespi Reghizzi, "Legal Aspects of Trade with China: The Italian Experience," Harvard International Law Journal, 9 (Winter, 1968), 85–139; Victor H. Li, "Legal Aspects of Trade with Communist China," Columbia Journal of Transnational Law, 3 (1964), 57–71. In negotiating the recent treaty on outer space, one of the frustrations experienced by members of the American delegation to the United Nations arose from the inability to find within the United States Government someone trained in both law and Chinese studies who could verify the accuracy of the Chinese version of the treaty, which had been prepared by the U.N. Secretariat. The United States finally had to rely on the approval of the delegation of the Republic of China.

beginning to have an impact upon scholarship. Law-trained people, some of whom are Chinese, have already published a substantial number of articles. Because legal scholarship is customarily concerned with current problems, because foundation grants are often readily available for studies of Communism, and because the requirements for research in legal history are formidable, most of these articles deal with the People's Republic of China (PRC). There have been studies of legal institutions and procedures,[20] criminal law,[21] civil law,[22] public international law,[23] legal aspects of international

20. See David C. Buxbaum, "Preliminary Trends in the Development of the Legal Institutions of Communist China and the Nature of the Criminal Law," *International and Comparative Law Quarterly*, 11 (1962), 1–30; Jerome A. Cohen, "The Criminal Process in the People's Republic of China: An Introduction," *Harvard Law Review*, 79 (1966), 458–533; and "The Chinese Communist Party and 'Judicial Independence': 1949–1959," *Harvard Law Review*, 82 (1969), 967–1006; Gene T. Hsiao, "Communist China: Legal Institutions," *Problems of Communism*, 14 (1965), 112–121; Luke T. Lee, "Chinese Communist Law: Its Background and Development," *Michigan Law Review*, 60 (1962), 439–472; George Ginsburgs, "Theory and Practice of Parliamentary Procedure in Communist China: Organizational and Institutional Principles," *University of Toronto Law Journal*, 15 (1963), 1–48; G. Ginsburgs and Arthur Stahnke, "The Genesis of the People's Procuratorate in Communist China, 1949–1951," *China Quarterly*, no. 20 (1964), pp. 1–37, and "The People's Procuratorate in Communist China: The Period of Maturation, 1951–54," *China Quarterly*, no. 24 (1965), pp. 53–91; see also Victor H. Li, Book Review, *Michigan Law Review*, 67 (1968), 179–212.
21. See the articles by Buxbaum, Cohen, Hsiao, Lee, Li, and Ginsburgs and Stahnke cited in note 20; also David C. Buxbaum, "Horizontal and Vertical Influences upon the Substantive Criminal Law in China: Some Preliminary Observations," *Osteuropa Recht*, 10 (1964), 31–51; Tao-tai Hsia, "Justice in Peking: China's Legal System on Show," *Current Scene*, 5 (1967), 1–12; Fu-shun Lin, "Communist China's Emerging Fundamentals of Criminal Law," *American Journal of Comparative Law*, 13 (1964), 80–93; and Lung-sheng Tao, "The Criminal Law of Communist China," *Cornell Law Quarterly*, 52 (1966), 43–68.
22. See Gene T. Hsiao, "The Role of Economic Contracts in Communist China," *California Law Review*, 53 (1965), 1029–60; Richard M. Pfeffer, "The Institution of Contracts in the Chinese People's Republic," *China Quarterly*, no. 14 (1963), pp. 153–177, and no. 15 (1963), pp. 115–139; and "Contracts in China Revisited, with a Focus on Agriculture, 1949–63," *China Quarterly*, no. 28 (1966), pp. 106–129.
23. See Hungdah Chiu, "Communist China's Attitude Toward International Law," *American Journal of International Law* (hereafter *AJIL*), 60 (1966), 245–267; "The Theory and Practice of Communist China with Respect to the Conclusion of Treaties," *Columbia Journal of Transnational Law*, 5 (1966), 1–13; "Communist China and the Law of Outer Space," *International and Comparative Law Quarterly*, 16 (1967), 1135–38; "Certain Legal Aspects of Communist China's Treaty Practice," *Proceedings of the American Society of International Law* (hereafter *Proceedings*) (1967), 117–126; and "Communist China's Attitude Toward the United Nations: A Legal Analysis," *AJIL*, 62 (1968), 20–60; Jerome A. Cohen, "Chinese Attitudes Toward International Law — and Our Own," *Proceedings* (1967), 108–116 reprinted in this volume; R. Randle Edwards, "The Attitude of the People's Republic of China Toward International Law and the United Nations," *Papers on China*, 17

trade,[24] and problems of research methodology.[25] But even lawyers preoccupied with the present want to know how it got that way and how to evaluate it. Thus there is a growing interest in studying the traditional legal system and non-Communist efforts to modernize it.[26] Very recently, the pace of book publication has quickened, largely but not exclusively as a result of law school programs. After collaborating for six years in a course at the University of Pennsylvania Law School, a distinguished sinologist, Derk Bodde, and a distinguished legal scholar, Clarence Morris, have produced a major work, *Law in Imperial China*.[27] This volume of commentary and translated cases presents the most comprehensive analysis of the Ch'ing dynasty's judicial process yet to appear in the West and also serves as an excellent vehicle for classroom discussion. My own teaching materials on Communist sanctioning processes have been published,[28] as has Shao-chuan Leng's study of the evolution of Communist judicial institutions.[29] Fortunately, research aids are also gradually emerging. Fu-shun Lin has compiled a bibliography of English language sources

(Harvard University, 1963), 235–271; Tao-tai Hsia, "Settlement of Dual Nationality Between Communist China and Other Countries," *Osteuropa Recht*, 11 (1965), 27–38; Douglas Johnston, "Treaty Analysis and Communist China: Preliminary Observations," *Proceedings* (1967), 126–134; and Luke T. Lee, "Treaty Relations of the People's Republic of China: A Study of Compliance," *University of Pennsylvania Law Review*, 116 (1967), 244–314. For an interesting article by a political scientist, see Shao-chuan Leng, "Communist China's Position on Nuclear Arms Control," *Virginia Journal of International Law*, 7 (1966), 101–116.

24. See articles by Crespi Reghizzi and Li, note 19, and Gene T. Hsiao, "Communist China's Foreign Trade Organization," *Vanderbilt Law Review*, 20 (1967), 303–319; and "Communist China's Trade Treaties and Agreements," *Vanderbilt Law Review*, 21 (1968), 623–658.

25. Jerome A. Cohen, "Interviewing Chinese Refugees: Indispensable Aid to Legal Research on China," *Journal of Legal Education*, 20 (1967), 33–62, reprinted in this volume.

26. See Jerome A. Cohen, "Chinese Mediation on the Eve of Modernization," *California Law Review*, 59 (1966), 1201–26; David C. Buxbaum, "Horizontal and Vertical Influences," note 21, and "Chinese Family Law in a Common Law Setting," *Journal of Asian Studies*, 25 (1966), 621–644; Herbert H. P. Ma, "The Chinese Control Yuan: An Independent Supervisory Organ of the State," *Washington University Law Quarterly* (1963), 401–426; and Wen Yen Tsao, "The Chinese Family from Customary Law to Positive Law," *Hastings Law Journal*, 17 (1966), 727–765. For an historian's analysis of some Ch'ing judicial decisions, see Judy F. Harrison, "Wrongful Treatment of Prisoners: A Case Study of Ch'ing Legal Practice," *Journal of Asian Studies*, 23 (1964), 227–244.

27. Derk Bodde and Clarence Morris, *Law in Imperial China* (Cambridge, Mass.: Harvard University Press, 1967).

28. Jerome A. Cohen, *The Criminal Process in the People's Republic of China, 1949–1963: An Introduction* (Cambridge, Mass.: Harvard University Press, 1968).

29. Shao-chuan Leng, *Justice in Communist China* (Dobbs Ferry, New York: Oceana Books, 1967).

8 | Introduction

on Chinese law.[30] Along with an essay on the administration of justice in the People's Republic, Tao-tai Hsia has published a list of its 1949–1963 legislation and of legal articles from mainland periodicals.[31] The Harvard Law School Library's *Preliminary Union List of Materials on Chinese Law* has now appeared,[32] as has a valuable calendar of China's treaties compiled by Douglas Johnston and Hungdah Chiu.[33]

British and continental lawyers have not attempted to duplicate this American "great leap forward," but promising developments are under way in a number of countries. In Britain, the noted anthropologist Maurice Freedman has become increasingly interested in legal problems,[34] and Anthony Dicks, a barrister, has joined the law faculty of Cambridge University; it is to be hoped that he will help to fill the void created by the untimely passing of Henry McAleavy.[35] In the Netherlands, M. H. van der Valk has maintained a steady output of informative articles in English,[36] and Marinus Meijer and A. F. P. Hulsewé are preparing volumes on the Communist and Han periods, respectively. There has been a marked increase in German language publications, especially on traditional law.[37] Scholars at the Uni-

30. Fu-shun Lin, *Chinese Law, Past and Present* (New York: East Asian Institute, Columbia University, 1966).

31. Tao-tai Hsia, *Guide to Selected Legal Sources of Mainland China* (Washington, D.C.: Library of Congress, 1967).

32. Harvard Law School Library, *Preliminary Union List of Materials on Chinese Law* (Cambridge, Mass.: Harvard University Press, 1968). This volume was sponsored by the Joint Committee on Contemporary China's Subcommittee on Chinese Law, whose origin and activities are discussed below.

33. Douglas Johnston and Hungdah Chiu, *Agreements of the People's Republic of China, 1949–1967: A Calendar* (Cambridge, Mass.: Harvard University Press, 1968).

34. See, *e.g.*, Maurice Freedman, "Chinese Family Law in Singapore: The Rout of Custom," in J. N. D. Anderson, ed., *Family Law in Asia and Africa* (London: Allen and Unwin, 1968), pp. 49–72; and "The Family in China, Past and Present," *Pacific Affairs*, 34 (1961–62), 323–336.

35. Until his death Professor McAleavy continued to include articles on law among his varied interests. See, *e.g.*, "The People's Courts in Communist China," *American Journal of Comparative Law*, 11 (1962), 52–65; "Some Aspects of Marriage and Divorce in Communist China," in J. N. D. Anderson, ed., *Family Law in Asia and Africa* (London: Allen and Unwin, 1968), 73–89; and "Chinese Law in Hong Kong: The Choice of Sources," in J. N. D. Anderson, ed., *Changing Law in Developing Countries* (London: Allen and Unwin, 1963), 258–269.

36. See M. H. van der Valk, "Voluntary Surrender in Chinese Law," *Law in Eastern Europe*, 14 (1967), 359–394; "Movables and Immovables and Connected Subjects in Chinese Law," *Law in Eastern Europe*, 7 (1963), 167–206; "[The Law of Inheritance in] China," *Law in Eastern Europe*, 5 (1961), 297–364; "Security Rights in Communist China," *Osteuropa Recht*, 9 (1963), 210–235.

37. See the many titles in Gniffke, "German Writings on Chinese Law," note 12.

versité Libre de Bruxelles have produced several works.[38] Also, a young Italian, Gabriele Crespi Reghizzi, has begun to introduce the subject of contemporary Chinese law in his country.[39] And, fortunately, France's establishment of diplomatic relations with Mainland China has at least spurred French scholars of international law to action;[40] moreover, sinological research in legal history has not entirely disappeared.[41]

Cooperative Efforts to Meet Common Problems

Those who have engaged in this recent flurry of activity have encountered common problems. Not surprisingly, the most immediate and intractable of these is the translation of Chinese legal terms. Anyone who has ever attempted to render provisions of the Ch'ing Code into English has confronted as exasperating a challenge as is known to legal scholarship. Ernest Alabaster, for example, long ago warned that, while there were a vast number of resemblances between Chinese and Western legal systems, there were very few real analogies. It was, therefore, dangerous, he maintained, to apply foreign legal terms to Chinese law; to do so "clothes the language artificially and gives it a baboon-like look." [42] Yet it is difficult, to say the least, for lawyers to escape their own language, the indispensable system of specialized communication that constitutes the very bond of their profession. Is it any wonder that one who seeks an English version of the Ch'ing Code still must turn to Staunton's monumental, but flawed and incomplete, 1810 translation?

Because those who modernized Chinese law in the first half of the

38. See Marthe Engelborghs-Bertels and René Dekkers, *La République populaire de Chine, cadres institutionnels et réalisations. I: L'histoire et le droit* (Bruxelles: Centre d'études des pays de l'Est, Université Libre de Bruxelles, 1963); Engelborghs-Bertels, "L'Assimilation de l'esprit du droit occidental en Chine," *Co-existence*, 4 (1967), 77–93; Dekkers, "La vie juridique," in *Le Régime et les institutions de la république populaire chinoise* (Bruxelles: Centre d'études des pays de l'Est, Université Libre de Bruxelles, 1960), pp. 56–58.

39. See Gabriele Crespi Reghizzi, "Lo Studio Del Sistema Guiridico Cinese Contemporaneo," *L'Est*, no. 3 (1967), pp. 165–205; and "Diritto Cinese E Rivoluzione Culturale," *Rivista Di Diritto Civile*, 13 (1967), 301–305. Also recall the article by Crespi Reghizzi, note 19.

40. See Jean Beauté, *La République populaire de Chine et le droit intérnational* (Paris: Pedone, 1964).

41. See Françoise Aubin, "Index de 'Un code des Yuan' de P. Ratchnevsky," *Mélanges publiés par l'Institut des Hautes Études Chinoises*, 2 (1960), 423–515.

42. Ernest Alabaster, "Notes on Chinese Law and Practice Preceding Revision," *Journal of the North China Branch, Royal Asiatic Society*, n.s., 37 (1906), 139–141.

twentieth century drew heavily upon continental civil law models, both directly and via Japan, the task of translating Republican terminology into continental languages is somewhat less frustrating than that of dealing with Ch'ing materials. For Anglo-Americans the problems resemble the familiar and more manageable ones of seeking linguistic analogies between the common and civil law systems.[43]

The advent of Communism, however, has further complicated the terminological situation. Although the Soviet legal system is itself a member of the civil law family, the effort to adapt it to Chinese conditions led to the creation of many new Chinese legal and institutional terms for which Western equivalents must be devised. Moreover, although the Communists have retained many Republican terms, they sometimes attach new meanings to them. They have also tended to resurrect certain traditional terms that had fallen into disuse during the Republican era, but again one must be alert to the extent to which the content of these terms has been modified. Finally, because the Chinese Communists have striven to simplify bourgeois legal language and to minimize the training and role of legal experts, their legal terminology often seems loose and opaque, at least in comparison with that of the Republic, if not with that of the Ch'ing.

As a first step in assisting the development of Chinese legal studies, in early 1963 the Joint Committee on Contemporary China of the American Council of Learned Societies and the Social Science Research Council provided support for the compilation of a Chinese-English dictionary of Communist legal and institutional terms. It was recognized, of course, that at this early stage of scholarship on the People's Republic one could not hope for a dictionary that would capture all the varieties and subtleties of meaning of certain terms and embrace all terms which in the current context ought to be deemed "legal." These refinements would have to await careful analysis of particular legal problems. One could hope, however, for a working tool that would be of substantial help not only to Western lawyers brash enough to grapple with a language for which there is no contemporary law dictionary, but also to all students of Chinese Communist affairs, including government experts and even Chinese

43. Building on earlier versions, the Law Revision Planning Group of the Council for United States Aid of the Republic of China has published very good English translations of the basic legislation in force on Taiwan today and has thereby done a great deal to alleviate problems of coping with Republican terminology. See *Laws of the Republic of China*, first series (Taipei, 1961), second series (Taipei, 1962).

lawyers on both sides of the Bamboo Curtain.[44] At the very least, such a tool could be expected to promote standardization of many English equivalents and to direct scholarly attention to the troublesome problems of substance that often must be dealt with before a translation can be deemed suitable. Fortunately, Philip R. Bilancia, now of New York's New School for Social Research, was willing to leave the practice of law to undertake principal responsibility for this large enterprise, and, after more than six years of painstaking effort, he has completed the first draft of a manuscript that runs well over a thousand pages. With the aid of other scholars in this field, he is currently revising the manuscript for publication. Preliminary indications suggest that the dictionary will vindicate its promise.

The Joint Committee did not content itself with the dictionary project, but took steps to foster a broader program of research and interchange of ideas relating to Chinese law. In 1965 it appointed a Subcommittee on Chinese Law, whose major mandate was to plan a series of conferences designed to enhance cooperation among researchers in this country and abroad. Support for these conferences was provided by the Ford Foundation, through the SSRC.

The first conference, designated "Chinese Communist Law: Tools for Research," was convened May 27–30, 1967. Its thirty participants, who came from six countries, represented the disciplines of law, political science, sociology, history, and sinology. They met to discuss papers that survey the range of accessible legal materials, the possibilities of supplementing information from published sources with that derived from refugee interviewing, the historical development of modern Chinese legal terminology and the translation problems encountered by specialists in various topics, the data and insights to be acquired from resort to Japanese, Soviet, and Nationalist Chinese studies of Communist Chinese law, and the perspectives offered by sophisticated application of comparative and sociological methodology. This volume presents the fruits of that conference.

Highlights of the Volume

"How does one learn about law in Communist China? What research materials are available? Is the language a great obstacle? Is

44. For discussion of inadequacies in the translations of legal materials published by both Peking's Foreign Languages Press and agencies of the United States Government, see Jerome A. Cohen, review of A. P. Blaustein, *Fundamental Legal Documents of Communist China*, in *Yale Law Journal*, 72 (1963), 838, 842.

the Chinese system very different from ours? How does it compare with the Soviet system?" These are the questions most frequently asked by interested laymen, students, lawyers, and scholars. This volume seeks to answer the first three questions and to indicate some of the problems involved in the continuing effort to answer the others. The following brief comments on each chapter do not by any means do them justice or even sum them up, but merely introduce the authors and suggest the dimensions of their contributions.

In the first chapter Mr. Hsia, who is Chief of the Far Eastern Law Division of the Library of Congress, delineates the paucity of published primary sources for research in Communist Chinese law. After offering a statistical overview of the PRC's books on law, he evaluates the quality of the relevant monographic, periodical, and newspaper literature. He then describes the state of the Chinese law schools and research institutions that are, at least in principle, supposed to provide most of the intellectual nourishment for the evolution of the legal system. He concludes with a discussion of Nationalist Chinese works on law in the People's Republic and includes in an appendix a useful note on Nationalist holdings of Communist legal publications.

The increasingly troublesome problems of obtaining documentation concerning contemporary legal developments have led to a search for other sources of information. The next two chapters examine the potentialities of interviewing former residents of the PRC. My own essay relates experiences involved in conducting intensive interviews with thirty-eight emigrés during 1963–64 and appraises the importance and the limitations of this mode of research. This is complemented by Victor Li's account of how, two years later, he went to Hong Kong not to interview a relatively small number of especially knowledgeable people in depth but to experiment with methods of acquiring data from a great many ordinary refugees. He discusses the problems and prospects of finding a large number of reliable and cooperative informants, of attempting to construct from them a "sample" that might be representative of the mainland population, of administering questionnaires to persons unacquainted with this research technique, and of recruiting and training assistants to help with interviewing. The fact that Mr. Li, who has subsequently joined the faculty of the Columbia University Law School, conducted his interviews as a student rather than as a professor and as a person of Chinese descent rather than as a Caucasian adds significance to his verification of many of my earlier observations on the general feasibility of interviewing.

Mr. Li also notes how interviewing brought home to him the full difficulty of finding English and Chinese terms of equivalent meaning. He discovered, for example, that today the word "dispute" has broader and less formal connotations than its common Chinese counterpart *chiu-fen*, which to many refugees implies a rather high degree of conflict. In order to stimulate research that would move our understanding of Communist legal language beyond the tentative definitions of the draft dictionary being compiled by Mr. Bilancia, a number of experts were asked to prepare papers on linguistic problems encountered in their work. They produced four chapters that tell us much about the origins, development, and contemporary meaning of Chinese terminology in the fields of international law, criminal law, and civil law. Although the titles of these chapters may seem forbidding to the nonlawyer, their "technical" subjects should actually prove to be of interest to students of China in both the social sciences and the humanities, who confront many similar problems. Moreover, the topics discussed, far from being "merely academic," are often matters of concern to foreign ministries that must interpret events in China and negotiate with Chinese officialdom.

Problems of translating legal terms have plagued the conduct of Sino-Western relations at least since 1689, when the Russian, Latin, and Chinese texts of the Treaty of Nerchinsk reflected widely divergent versions of what the parties had agreed to concerning the punishment of criminals. In some negotiations, of course, inaccurate translation may have been intentionally resorted to as a compromise that postponed resolution of a delicate question or as a device that saved face for one side or both. In other cases, however, discrepancies were undoubtedly the product of genuine linguistic confusion. Even in our own day, as Mr. Chiu illustrates, there have been instances when Western-trained Chinese diplomats, although sensitive to the legal implications of alternative translations, have nevertheless failed to devise appropriate Chinese equivalents for Western terms, with embarrassing consequences for their government; translation problems that have been perceived during negotiations have sometimes constituted substantial obstacles to diplomatic achievement. Indeed, it is sobering to recall that disputes during both the negotiation and the implementation of the only significant bilateral agreement ever made between the United States and Communist China — the 1955 "agreed announcement" on the exchange of civilians — centered upon the meaning to be assigned to key terms in the English and Chinese texts.[45] Scholarship such as that of Mr. Chiu, who has served on the faculty of National Taiwan University and is a research associate at Harvard Law School, should help to prevent future linguistic misunderstanding.

International law was the vehicle that introduced modern Western legal concepts and their linguistic symbols into China. Soon after an American missionary and his Chinese associates translated the leading textbook of the day into Chinese in 1864, it was imported into Japan and added to the ferment that was already taking place in that country over the need to modernize its entire legal system. By the turn of the century, Japan's remarkable success in adapting Western law to local circumstances, and the major contribution that this appeared to make to the nation's power, transformed Japan from China's student to its teacher. Dan F. Henderson of the University of Washington Law School, a specialist in Japanese law, describes how Japan helped to introduce knowledge of Western domestic law to China by training Chinese students in Japanese universities, by cooperating in the arduous task of translating the new legal learning from Japanese to Chinese, and by sending law teachers and legal advisers to China. He analyzes the complexities of forging modern Chinese legal terms and law codes and, by means of a statistical comparison of legal vocabulary found in the criminal law of Japan and China up to and including the Communist period, he illustrates the lasting influence of Japan's early twentieth-century contribution.

This quantitative assessment of the language of the PRC's criminal law is followed by a wide-ranging and sensitive qualitative assessment by David Finkelstein, the Ford Foundation's resident expert on China. He examines the extent to which the Communists have created rather than inherited the vague terminology they employ in the administration of justice and the extent to which they have benefitted from, rather than been handicapped by, terminological uncertainties. One can infer from his essay that correct understanding of criminal law terminology can sometimes have an

45. See Robert B. Ekvall, *The Faithful Echo* (New York: Twayne, 1960), chap. 12; and Kenneth T. Young, *Negotiating with the Chinese Communists: The United States Experience, 1953–1967* (New York, Toronto, London, Sydney: McGraw-Hill, 1968), chap. 3.

important bearing upon political analysis. For example, whether a deposed leader is said to have been "led" rather than "dragged" through the streets may be of only marginal interest to political observers, but it may not be stretching a point to read political significance into whether he was "taken away" or "arrested." "Arrest" indicates incarceration by representatives of the Ministry of Public Security. If the leader was "taken away," however, it suggests that "the masses" may be incarcerating major figures and alerts the observer to the possibility that those in power may no longer regard the public security agency as a reliable instrument of their will, a situation which would raise grave doubts about the stability of the regime. Yet Mr. Finkelstein's emphasis on the imprecise way in which the Chinese Communists employ many legal terms should warn the unwary that it is easy to be misled by the use of one term rather than another.

The case study by Mr. Meijer, a Dutch scholar-diplomat who has long served in East Asia, makes it clear that imprecision is not unknown to the PRC's civil law. His interesting exegesis on the word *ying* as used in Article 6 of the Marriage Law illustrates the research and analysis that often must precede accurate translation of even a single term. In what is really an exercise in the construction of an important Chinese statute, he views his subject against the background of the marriage policies and practices of traditional China, the Nationalist regime and the various pre-1949 Chinese Communist governments, as well as the changing model that Soviet law has held out to the Chinese comrades.

After finding published and human sources relating to a given aspect of Chinese law and after learning to cope with the linguistic obstacles to understanding them, one who engages in the comparative study of law then confronts his most difficult problem: what use, after all, should he make of the information so assiduously acquired? What is its significance in relation to the Chinese legal system as a whole and to the political, social, economic, historical, and cultural matrix in which that system operates? Can Chinese legal phenomena be compared in any meaningful way to those of legal systems that operate in vastly different settings? The next three chapters suggest approaches to these problems in the context of civil, criminal, and international law, respectively.

In his discussion of civil law, particularly contract law, Stanley

Lubman, a member of the law faculty of the University of California at Berkeley, emphasizes the differences that exist between Western and Chinese legal institutions and argues against what he claims to be the assumption of others — that China has contract law readily comparable to that of developed legal systems. Chinese law, he maintains, too actively serves political ends and is too intimately bound up with administration to enjoy the relative autonomy that we normally associate with law. Chinese contracts, and the modes of settling disputes that arise under them, are too flexible to be regarded as the analogues of institutions that bear the same titles in Western countries. After telling us much about the role that contracts of various kinds play in the Chinese economy, Mr. Lubman concludes by calling for more extensive application of the functional approach to the study of Chinese legal institutions, in an effort to clarify our understanding of the purposes and values that those institutions serve in China's distinctive legal culture.

Richard M. Pfeffer, a lawyer and assistant professor of political science at Johns Hopkins University, also advocates the functional approach. Yet, drawing on recent advances in both the sociology of organizations and the sociology of law, he is far more sanguine than Mr. Lubman about the feasibility of comparing Chinese and American legal institutions. While recognizing the important differences in the criminal processes of these two countries, he demonstrates that a systematic and evenhanded investigation of the actual operation of the law reveals more similarities than we Americans might care to acknowledge. His thesis is irrefutable: those who compare our ideals with foreign realities engage in rhetoric rather than scholarship.

That some American authorities on international law fail to perceive the distinction, choosing instead to adhere to the "do as we say, not as we do" approach, is one of the themes of my chapter on Chinese attitudes toward international law. Explicit comparison of the behavior of the United States with that of the PRC is necessary not only in the interests of fairness and of formulating generalizations concerning the extent to which great or near-great powers practice as well as preach international law, but also because Peking's international conduct, like Washington's, is influenced in part by how others play the game. The essay also stresses the need to place the PRC's record — and that of its Nationalist rival — in the context of China's recent "century of humiliation," which has motivated all Chinese patriots to strive to attain equality for their country.

As useful as comparisons of Chinese and American law may be, scholars who give an exclusively Sino-American cast to their search for research perspectives indulge in a sophisticated form of ethnocentrism. There are, of course, other great national legal systems, and virtually all of them afford more plausible opportunities for comparison with China than does our own. The two countries that appear to offer students of Chinese law the most interesting comparative insights are the Soviet Union and Japan; the former because of its half century of innovation with a supposedly new type of law and because of the profound influence that this exerted over Communist Chinese thought and institutions from the founding of the earliest revolutionary bases until the close of the PRC's first decade; and the latter because of the similarities between its premodern neo-Confucian legal culture and that of traditional China and because of the role that Japan subsequently played in the modernization of pre-Communist Chinese law. It is undoubtedly more than coincidence that scholarship on Chinese law flourished in these two countries during the decade of the 1950's while elsewhere it remained in the doldrums. In these circumstances it seemed desirable to ask specialists in Soviet and Japanese law to undertake essays that would describe how scholars in those countries have viewed China's legal development and that would facilitate access to their writing.

Yasuhei Taniguchi, of the law faculty of Kyoto University, offers an enlightening introduction to Japanese research on contemporary China and the political currents that play upon it. He surveys the reasons for the popularity of studies of Communist Chinese law, the sympathetic Marxist orientation of Japanese writers in this field, and the impact upon their outlook of the bitter Sino-Soviet quarrel. His assessment of the quality of their work reveals the impressionistic and naive content of much of it, but indicates its value in providing information and interpretation that might otherwise be unavailable to the academic community. Both sets of characteristics are especially apparent in the reports of groups of Japanese lawyers who have had some unusual opportunities to learn about Chinese law in the course of brief visits to the mainland.

Harold J. Berman of the Harvard Law School faculty, who is well known for his studies of the Soviet legal system, sketches the evolution of Soviet views of Chinese law from the scholarly publications of the middle fifties, which "glowed with the pride of parenthood," to the polemical denunciations of the middle sixties, which attacked the Chinese for gross violations of "socialist legality." This changing Soviet attitude was of course an outgrowth of the overall deterioration of Sino-Soviet relations, but it particularly reflected the dramatic events of 1957–1958 in China that led to the rejection of the Soviet legal model and the equally dramatic, yet more encouraging, events in Russia that have been encapsulated under the rubric of "de-Stalinization." Mr. Berman also points out that in the 1957–1960 period, when Soviet publications began to display impatience and uncertainty about developments in China, some articles in legal journals nevertheless described in considerable detail a variety of Chinese experiments that were designed to enlist the masses in the administration of justice. Noting that in this same period the Communist Party of the Soviet Union revived its own earlier experiments of this nature, he endorses an hypothesis that appears to be gaining support among students of law in the Communist world (see also the following chapter by Mr. Ginsburgs) — that this revival of Soviet interest in forms of participation by the masses quite possibly represented an effort to keep up with the Chinese on the long march toward true Communism's withering of the state. In addition to introducing the changing Soviet image of Chinese law, Mr. Berman calls attention to the Soviet legal system's unique melding of Western and non-Western legal traditions and to its potentialities for serving comparatists as a link between the West and China. Soviet law, he tells us, "is an illegitimate son of Western law, now grown to maturity, and Chinese law is a wayward daughter of Soviet law, still walking the streets."

Our final chapter, by George Ginsburgs of the graduate faculty of the New School for Social Research, contains an interesting commentary on Soviet publications concerning Chinese law and a bibliography of relevant books, pamphlets, and journal articles. Mr. Ginsburgs, a prolific scholar of Soviet affairs who has devoted an increasing portion of his efforts to China, indicates that Soviet writers on Chinese law have been genuine Stakhanovites, exceeding the total output of all the other foreign scholars of the world together, that they have shown far greater interest in the Chinese legal system than in that of any of the other "sister socialist states," that the overwhelming majority of their publications relate to law's role in the organization and exercise of political power, and that the number of publications has dropped very sharply since 1962.

Plainly enough, these essays on the study of contemporary Chinese law constitute merely the first word on the subject — not the last. Because most of the contributors to the volume are relatively young men and because they represent a rapidly increasing group, we can be confident that more help is on the way.

1 Chinese Legal Publications: An Appraisal

Tao-tai Hsia

With the hope of alleviating some of the difficulties which students of Chinese law encounter in gathering research materials, I herein provide a quantitative survey of the annual output of Communist Chinese legal monographs, a brief description of some little-known but important Chinese law books, an analysis of periodical literature on law, some information on newspapers as a source of legal literature, a discussion of legal education and research institutions in China, and a list of Nationalist Chinese writings on Communist Chinese law.

Introduction

First, however, a few general observations on Chinese legal monographs are in order.

Publishers of Legal Works

The publishing house in China which is concerned primarily with legal publications is the Legal Press (Fa-lü ch'u-pan-she), established in March, 1955. According to reports published in *Cheng-fa yen-chiu* (Political-Legal Research), the main tasks of the Legal Press are:

> to rely on the writings and translated resources of various political-legal government organs, institutions of higher learning, and other social organizations; to compile, translate, and publish the books of Marxist-Leninist legal theories dealing with the state and historical studies of the state, the books on theory and practice of political-legal work, reference materials regarding laws and decrees, textbooks to be used in political-legal institutions of higher learning, and the popular reading materials and journals concerning the state and the law.[1]

1. *CFYC*, no. 2 (1955), p. 11.

The annual work report of the Chinese Political-Legal Association, issued in 1956, showed that in the nine month period from March to December, 1955, 49 titles were published by the Legal Press and a total of 2,300,000 copies of books were printed for all titles.[2]

Other publishers of legal works include the Chinese People's University Press; people's presses in Peking and in other local areas; the Masses' Press; Finance Press; Monetary Affairs Press; and the Finance and Economics Press.

Translated Legal Works

Nearly one-half of Communist Chinese legal monographs are translations from Soviet legal publications. Before the Sino-Soviet rift developed, Soviet law professors were frequently invited to China to teach. Some of these Soviet scholars prepared teaching materials especially for the use of Chinese students, and these have been translated into Chinese by various teaching and research offices located in China's law schools. In 1956, the year for which the Chinese legal publication figure is the highest, 75 of the 122 legal monographs published that year were translations, practically all from Russian. In recent years, the deterioration of relations between the two countries has been accompanied by a drastic reduction in the number of Chinese translations from Soviet works, including legal titles.

Popular Works for Mass Consumption

Among the approximately six hundred legal titles published during the years 1949–1966, a large number were small pamphlets written in simple, conversational language and designed to familiarize the masses with some newly promulgated laws, decrees, and other legal documents. Many of them, on the same subject matter (for instance, marriage law, land law, and the constitution) but published by different provincial presses, are almost identical, both in title and in content.

Certificated Publications

The legal publications of greatest interest to legal scholars outside Communist China are probably the "certificated" publications. These are issued for restricted internal circulation and are available only to authorized personnel, who must have certificates in order to obtain

2. CFYC, no. 2 (1956), p. 2.

them. Two examples of certificated legal titles published in 1958 are *Chung-kuo kuo-chia ho fa-ch'üan li-shih ts'an-k'ao tzu-liao* [*Ti-san-tz'u kuo-nei ko-ming chan-cheng shih-ch'i chieh-fang-ch'ü ti cheng-ts'e fa-ling hsüan-chi*] (Reference materials on the history of Chinese state and legal power [Collection of selected policies, laws and decrees of the liberated areas during the period of the third revolutionary civil war]), compiled by Chung-kuo jen-min ta-hsüeh kuo-chia ho fa-ch'üan li-shih yen-chiu-shih (Office of teaching and research on the history of state and legal power of the Chinese People's University); and *Chung-hua jen-min kung-ho-kuo min-shih su-sung ts'an-k'ao tzu-liao* [*Ti-i chi*] (Collection of reference materials on the civil procedure of the People's Republic of China [Part I]), compiled by Chung-kuo jen-min ta-hsüeh shen-p'an-fa chiao-yen-shih (Teaching and research office of trial law of the Chinese People's University).

Collective Authorship

Due to fear of committing ideological errors and to the severe political climate in which he works, a legal scholar in Communist China is often reluctant to have his work published under his name as the sole author. Therefore, very few books of substance are listed under single authorship. Substantial legal works are usually prepared by a group of people and published under the name of their office. *Chung-hua jen-min kung-ho-kuo hun-yin-fa chi-pen wen-t'i* (Basic problems concerning the marriage law of the People's Republic of China), published in 1958, was written by more than four hundred collaborators, including the faculty members of the Office of Teaching and Research on Civil Law and the students of the department of law of the Chinese People's University. Another, *Jen-min ssu-fa kung-tso shih wu-ch'an chieh-chi chuan-cheng ti jui-li wu-ch'i* [*k'o-hsüeh yen-chiu yüeh-chin ts'ung-shu*] (People's judicial work is the sharp weapon of the proletariat dictatorship [scientific leap forward series]), also published in 1958, was written collectively by a group consisting of all faculty members of the Office of Teaching and Research on Trial Law and a large number of students of the department of law of the Chinese People's University. Several textbooks on civil law, criminal law, the constitution, and state and law, published in 1957 and 1958 (some of which will be discussed in the following section) have also been issued under the collective authorship of the respective teaching and research offices of the Central Political-Legal Cadre School.

Formally Printed Textbooks and Constantly Revised Teaching Materials

An extremely small number of printed textbooks on civil law, criminal law, and other subjects was published either during or immediately after the Hundred Flowers period. Because of the fluid state of law in China caused by the absence of codes and the frequent changes in party line, the research value of these dated treatises is necessarily limited. Influenced by the Hundred Flowers experience, Chinese Communist authorities apparently have found it inadvisable to allow jurists to describe the ever-changing legal system in a publication as lengthy and durable as a formally printed textbook. To my knowledge, since 1959 no law textbooks comparable to those published in the 1957–1958 period nor revised editions of the 1957–1958 works have been printed.[3] Another indication of the limited value of these treatises is that one very rarely finds them cited in Chinese law journals.

For use in the classroom, Chinese law schools probably rely principally upon mimeographed materials rather than formally printed texts; this type of legal publication is not included in national bibliographies, nor in Table 1.1. A former political-legal cadre whom I met in Hong Kong estimated that as much as 80–90 percent of the materials used in Chinese law schools is not formally printed; therefore, one may assume that the research value of this mimeographed material is higher than that of the printed. However, this material is not available outside the law schools. An outline of such mimeographed materials is found in *Chiao-hsüeh yü yen-chiu* (Teaching and research), a pedagogical journal of the Chinese People's University. This rarely published first draft outline of a course in criminal law was compiled by the Office of Teaching and Research of Criminal Law of the Chinese People's University, Peking, and issued

3. Two of these 1957–58 works, the *Chung-hua jen-min kung-ho-kuo hsing-fa tsung-tse chiang-i* (Lectures on the general principles of the criminal law of the People's Republic of China), published in 1957, and *Chung-hua jen-min kung-ho-kuo min-fa chi-pen wen-t'i* (Basic problems in the civil law of the People's Republic of China), published in 1958, have been translated into English by the Joint Publications Research Service of the U.S. Department of Commerce.

Table 1.1. Yearly Output of Communist Chinese Monographs in Category 6 — State and Law, and Legal Science — Original Works and (Numbers in Boldface) Translations.

Communist Chinese library classification	1949	1950	1951	1952	1953	1954	1955	1956	1957	1958	1959	1960	1961[a]	1962[b]	1963	1964	1965[b]	1966[b]	Total
6(1) Marxist-Leninist theories	1		1	2	2,**2**	3,**5**	3,**2**	7,**1**	5,**3**	4				1					22,**20**
6(2) Bourgeois[e]							1,**1**	1,**1**		**2**			1	1					4,**5**
6(3) History[d]	1					2			4,**1**	2,**1**	1								9,**3**
61 State law				1,**1**	4	1													5,**3**
611 PRC			1	2	21	21	12	5	3	2	1			2	1				72
612 USSR	**2**		**1**	**2**	1,**4**	1,**6**	**5**	**2**											2,**22**
613 Other socialist countries					**3**		**1**	**1**				**1**							**6**
614 Other countries												**1**							**1**
62 Administrative law																			
621 PRC		3	2	1	1	5	3	15	24	4	3		1			2			64
622 USSR		**1**			**2**			**1**	**1**	**1**									**6**
63 Fiscal law																			
631 PRC						2	2	3	8	2									17
632 USSR								**2**	**1**										**3**
64 Civil law																			
641 PRC			1						1	1									3
642 USSR		**1**	**1**			**1**	**2**	**10**	**7**	**2**					**1**				**25**
643 Other socialist countries								**1**	**1**										**2**
644 Other countries								**1**											**1**
65 Labor law																			
651 PRC	1	1	1	2	1	3	4	2	6	1			1						23
652 USSP.			**1**		**1**			1,**6**	**2**										1,**10**
653 Other socialist countries			**1**																**1**
66 Land law																			
661 PRC		1							1										2
662 USSR																			
663 Other socialist countries						**1**													**1**

67 Regulations of the people's communes and law of collective farms

	C1	C2	C3	C4	C5	C6	C7	C8	C9	C10	C11	C12	Total
671 PRC[e]										2	11	1	14
672 USSR[f]										1	1,7	4	1,12
673 Other socialist countries[e,f]											4	2	6
68 Marriage law													
681 PRC					3	8	5	11	4	2	4	3	40
682 USSR[g]							1	1	1,1	1	1	1	1,6
683 Other socialist countries[g]												1	1
69 Criminal law													
691 PRC								1	1	1	4	2	8
692 USSR								2	1	6	4	1	14
693 Other socialist countries										4	2	1	7
694 Other countries										1	2	1	4
610 Judiciary law													
6101 Judicial systems													
61011 PRC			1	1	1	2	5	6	6	14	3	4	43
61012 USSR	2	4	2		6	9	1,12	6					1,41
61013 Other socialist countries										1	1		2
6102 Law of civil procedure													
61021 PRC								2	3	1			6
61022 USSR							2	2	3	5	2		14
61023 Other socialist countries											1		1
6103 Law of criminal procedure													
61031 PRC													
61032 USSR							2	5	7	1	1	1	17
61033 Other socialist countries										1	5		6
6104 Medical jurisprudence and judicial psychiatry	1,1	2,1	1,1	1									5,3
6105 Criminology (criminal investigation)		1	1,1	1,1	3	1,1							2,6
TOTAL	1	7	15	11	21	40	46	47	53	69	15	9	346
	4	**11**	**11**	**9**	**14**	**36**	**75**	**55**	**14**	**11**	**1**		**248**

a Bibliographic information unavailable
b Bibliographic information incomplete
c Includes criticism
d Includes history of doctrines of law
e Regulations of agricultural producers' cooperatives
f Law of collective farms
g Includes law of family and guardianship

in June 1958. It is an accurate indication of the type of materials (although they are undergoing constant revision) used in Communist Chinese law schools. A translation of the outline appears below as Appendix I.

Quantitative Survey

The yearly output of Communist Chinese legal monographs is shown in Table 1.1, prepared from the information contained in two major national bibliographies: *Ch'üan-kuo tsung-shu-mu* (National bibliography of China)[4] and *Ch'üan-kuo hsin shu-mu* (New national bibliography of China). The former is a yearly publication while the frequency of the latter varies — it has appeared twice monthly in some years and three times a month in others.

In preparing the statistical table, I used the issues of *Ch'üan-kuo tsung shu-mu* for 1949–1958, and all issues of *Ch'üan-kuo hsin shu-mu* currently held by the Library of Congress. All issues of 1961, issues 1–8 of 1962, 10–14 and 17 of 1965, and the tenth and subsequent issues of 1966 of *Ch'üan-kuo hsin shu-mu* were unavailable at the time of this writing. An examination of new works advertised in the Mainland Chinese newspapers suggests that extremely few legal titles were published during the period covered by the missing issues of the *Ch'üan-kuo hsin shu-mu*. Despite this gap in the availability of bibliographic information on Chinese legal publications, Table 1.1 presents an overall quantitative survey of the legal monographs of the Peking regime.

In the table, the publications are grouped together under broad subject headings which were adopted in the Classification Schedule of the Chinese People's University.[5] The numerals before these subject headings are also those used in the schedule. Works on international law are not included in Table 1.1 since the official Chinese classification schedule does not classify international law under the heading, State and Law and Legal Science.

The most productive years in legal publishing in China were 1956

4. For a detailed description of this bibliography, see Chang Chao, "A Recommendation and Study of the National Bibliography of China," *Chiao-hsüeh yü yen-chiu* (Teaching and research), no. 11 (1956), pp. 31–34.

5. For a description of the Classification Schedule, see Chung-kuo jen-min ta-hsüeh t'u-shu-kuan (Library of Chinese People's University), *T'u-shu fen-lei fa* (Classification schedule), 4th ed. (Peking, 1962), pp. 1–30.

(122 titles, including 75 titles of translations) and 1957 (108 titles, including 55 titles of translations). These were the years of the "Hundred Flowers" — the period during which thought control was relaxed in China. The number of legal publications did not decrease drastically in the months immediately after the end of the liberalization period; however, the Party at that time was intent on publishing anti-rightist works. In so doing, the Party condemned the earlier legal writings containing relatively liberal views, which were branded "poisonous weeds" in the flower garden.

Although China is one of the largest nations in the world, the number of legal titles published yearly seems small indeed [6] — even in the mid-1950's, which Western scholars consider the golden years in legal publishing. In comparison with Chinese publication figures for other fields, legal output is very modest. Table 1.2 presents publication figures for all broad subject classes for 1956 (the year in which the figure for legal publications is highest) and for 1958 (the year after Hundred Flowers and one in which legal publication figures are third highest).[7]

Significant Monographs Briefly Noted

The following are brief notes to introduce a few Communist Chinese legal titles which are of research value. It is beyond the dimensions of this paper to include an annotated bibliography of all important legal monographs; therefore, only a small number of legal titles are described below. They have been selected because they are relatively rare (except for three or four items which were generally available to foreign researchers at the time of publication) and because they are not well known to Western students of Chinese law.

1. Kuo-wu-yüan fa-chih-chü fa-chih-shih yen-chiu-shih (Legal His-

6. Japan published more than 450 legal monographs (excluding government publications) in 1966. See *Shuppan nenkan* (Publication yearbook), Tokyo, 1967. The output of Japanese legal monographs for 1966 (including government publications) is estimated to be very close to the figure for all legal monographs published in Communist China since 1949.

7. The subject classification used in the table is that adopted in the *Ch'üan-kuo tsung shu-mu* in its editions covering publication for the years 1956 and 1958. The figures for all subject classes other than law (the State and Law and Legal Science) are taken from the bibliographies without recounting. The figures for law are based on our own counting of the legal items listed in the bibliographies. Our figures for law vary slightly from those given in the *Ch'üan-kuo tsung shu-mu*, due to different methods of counting.

Table 1.2. Number of Chinese Communist Publications
by Subject, 1956 and 1958.

Subject	1956	1958
Works and biographies of Marx, Engels, Lenin, and Stalin	38	74
Works and biographies of Mao Tse-tung	11	54
Philosophy	138	198
Religion and atheism	26	21
Social science and political science	603	950
Economy, political economy, and economic policy	1677	1933
National defense and military affairs	44	85
State and law and legal science	122	83
Culture and education	1129	1380
Fine arts	718	811
Linguistics and philology	186	389
Literature	3129	4916
History	400	337
Geography and economic geography	225	168
Natural science	612	1014
Medicine and hygiene	533	923
Engineering and technology	2173	5564
Agriculture, animal husbandry, and fishery	1224	2279
Comprehensive reference works	47	64

tory Research Office, Bureau of Codification, State Council), *Chung-kuo fa-chih-shih ts'an-k'ao shu-mu chien-chieh* (Brief introductory bibliography of reference works on Chinese legal history), Peking, Legal Press, 1957, 228 pages, 2,500 copies printed.

This legal history bibliography, compiled during the Hundred Flowers period, is probably the most comprehensive work of its kind produced in Communist China. Its publication indicated that the government at that time agreed with the view of some jurists that there exists at least some continuity of law, and that it is therefore important to study the legal history of China.

This bibliography was compiled by Li Tsu-yin, Yang Ch'ing-yüan, and Wang Kuo-t'ang, members of the Legal History Research Office of the Bureau of Codification. It lists 932 titles, totaling 10,607 volumes. The books listed are grouped into ten categories: (1) works of legalists, (2) materials on legislative history, (3) laws and decrees,

(4) regulations and other norms, (5) materials on social and administrative institutions, (6) forensic medicine, (7) trials and decisions, (8) prisons, (9) official correspondence regarding judicial matters, and (10) miscellaneous. Under each entry there is a brief annotation consisting of the number of volumes, year of printing, type of printing, and brief description of content.

Tung Pi-wu, President of the Supreme People's Court at the time the bibliography was published, wrote the following foreword: "The compilation of this brief introductory bibliography is only the beginning of a systematic study of research materials on the legal history of our country. It is hoped that those who are interested in this field will continue to expand and develop research work on legal history."

While this statement represented the government's desire, during the Hundred Flowers period at least, to make a serious study of China's legal history, there has been no conscientious follow-through on the study of that subject since the end of the Hundred Flowers.

2. Chang Jo-yü, Fa-hsüeh chi-pen chih-shih chiang-hua (Talks on the basic knowledge of legal science), Peking, Chinese Youth Press, 1963, 172 pages.

This book, written in popular style, is probably the most important law book published in China during the 1960's. Meant especially for young laymen readers, the author discusses Marxist-Leninist general theories of law and the nature and function of Communist Chinese law. He also dwells upon enactment, application, and observance of law.

The first of five chapters discusses the nature, origin, and development of law in China. The author claims that Communist Chinese law has a severely strong class nature, is the product of irreconcilable class contradictions, is a manifestation of the will of the ruling class, and finally, is an instrument of the dictatorship of the ruling class. Law, according to Chang Jo-yü, "is a behavior norm existing solely in a society where there are classes. It is a manifestation of the will of the ruling class. It is enacted or recognized by the state. It is a behavior norm which relies on the state's compulsory force to guarantee its implementation in order to consolidate the dictatorship of the ruling class" (p. 16).

Chapter two discusses the nature of law in the People's Republic of China as well as the relationship between law and Communist

Party policy. The author concludes that the policy of the Party is the soul of law, and that law is the crystallization of the Party's policy as well as an instrument to implement Party policy.

Chapter three discusses the function of socialist law in Communist China as well as the causes of crime in a socialist society. "Fundamentally, crime," according to Chang Jo-yü, "is the product of the exploitation system whose basis is private ownership of the means of production." The socialist system of society and state does not produce crime, he says, but is susceptible to it because of the pernicious influences left over from the old society on which the new socialist one is built. In Communist China, Chang reports, ". . . the remnants of reactionary influence [inside China] have not been completely wiped out; in addition, the eradication of the influence of the thought of the exploiting class necessarily takes a relatively long period of time. Therefore, in our country during the transitional period, crime cannot be extinguished" (p. 92).

This chapter also deals with various kinds of punishment: death, life imprisonment, imprisonment for fixed terms, control, detention, confiscation of property, and deprivation of political rights.

Chapter four discusses the enactment and application of law and states three principles for making laws: (1) start from practice and carry out the mass-line; (2) embody relative stability and also relative adaptability in order that law may incessantly serve the revolution; and (3) be easily comprehensible to the masses. This chapter also includes a statement about the function, nature, and organization of various political-legal organs — courts, procuracies, and the police — as well as a discussion of the features of judicial procedures.

The last chapter asserts that the masses, and especially the Communist cadres, must understand the importance of observing laws since the existence of law aids in the process of distinguishing enemies from the people. If laws are ignored, they cannot serve as an instrument for uniting the people, isolating enemies, consolidating the people's democratic dictatorship and developing the socialist revolution and construction.

This work, although advertised in Communist Chinese newspapers and described in detail in *Cheng-fa yen-chiu*,[8] cannot be purchased directly from Mainland China, Hong Kong, or Japan. The book is

8. Lu Tun, "Introducing *Talks on the Basic Knowledge of Legal Science*," CFYC, no. 4 (1963), pp. 51–53. The preceding comments are based on information from this article.

mentioned in a recently published Japanese bibliography and is probably in the possession of a Japanese legal scholar or institution.

3. Pei-ching shih jen-min fa-yüan pi-shu-ch'u (Secretariat of the Peking Municipal People's Court), *Jen-min ssu-fa kung-tso chü-yü* (Some aspects of the people's judicial work), Peking, 1950, 84 pages, 20,000 copies.

This is probably the most informative work on a people's court produced during the early years of the People's Republic. To my knowledge, no other book containing such detailed information on the administration of justice has been published and made available to the public. This work is indispensable for the study of legal development during the initial stages of the People's Republic.

The book is a series of articles, each devoted to one aspect of the court's work. The first deals with the founding of the Peking Municipal People's Court, its organization, the number of cases adjudicated, general and specific principles governing the handling of criminal and civil cases, the work of the detention house, conciliation work, mobile trials, legal propaganda work, and the reform of "old" judicial personnel. Another article is a report submitted by the President of the Court in which he discusses trial work and the achievements and defects of the Court.

Additional sections of the book contain a discussion of the reform work administered by the detention house; a rather detailed description of the organization of the Court; a list of regulations governing the organization of the detention houses of the Municipal People's Court (with illustrative chart); an extract of the remarks made by the President of the Court in which he discusses various aspects of the official field study of conciliation activities in seven districts in the municipality of Peking; and a brief description of several judicial work methods — collective trials and trials conducted outside the Court (mobile trial, judge stationed in a district, and on-the-spot trials). Finally, the book provides eleven very informative statistical tables concerning conciliation, civil, and criminal cases.

4. Chung-kuo jen-min ta-hsüeh min-fa chiao-yen-shih (Teaching and research office of civil law of the Chinese People's University), *Chung-hua jen-min kung-ho-kuo min-fa tzu-liao hui-pien* (Collection of materials on the civil law of the People's Republic of China), Peking, vol. I, 1954, 642 pages, 611 copies printed; vol. II, 1954, 422 pages, 593 copies printed.

Compiled primarily for the use of students at the Chinese People's University in their study of civil law, *Collection* contains decrees, resolutions, and directives relating to civil law, which were issued by both the central and local governments. Both volumes are available in Europe (they were probably acquired by a European diplomat while he was stationed in China), and Xeroxed copies of these are available in the United States.

The documents in volume I are grouped under the following categories: (1) general; (2) subject of rights; (3) object of rights; (4) rights over things — ownership rights of housing and land; *tien*,[9] pledges, and mortgages; (5) debts; (6) contract; (7) sale and supply; (8) hire of work for capital construction, orders of processing; (9) lease; and (10) commission agency, deposit, and warehousing.

Volume II contains documents on: (11) carriage — railway, sea, and automobile; (12) loan and final settlement of accounts; (13) insurance; (14) invention; (15) marriage law — general; marriage; divorce; parent-children relationships; the question of marriages of revolutionary soldiers; the question of marriages of minority nationalities and aliens; and (16) succession.

This work is indispensable to students of Communist Chinese civil law, for it includes many important legal documents selected from such publications as *Ch'uan-pei ch'ü ssu-fa kung-tso shou-ts'e* (Handbook of judicial work in North Szechwan District), *Yün-nan sheng jen-min fa-yüan ssu-fa kung-tso shou-ts'e* (Handbook of judicial work in Yunnan Provincial People's Court), and *Huan-nan cheng-pao* (Political gazette of South Anhwei), which are not available outside of Communist China.

5. Chung-kuo jen-min ta-hsüeh min-fa chiao-yen-shih (Teaching and research office of civil law of the Chinese People's University), *Chung-hua jen-min kung-ho-kuo min-fa ts'an-k'ao tzu-liao* (Reference materials on civil law of the People's Republic of China), Peking, Chinese People's University, part I, 1956, 1,434 copies,

---

9. The following definition of the term *tien* appears in Chapter VIII, Article 911, of the Nationalist Chinese Civil Code:

> *Tien* is the right to use an immovable of another person and to collect fruits therefrom by paying a price and taking possession of the immovable.

The entire chapter sets forth the provisions governing *tien*. Since the Communist legal documents on *tien* included in the work cited deal primarily with the *tien* problems that took place before 1949, the Nationalist definition of *tien* might serve to explain the term.

pp. 1–196; part II, 1956, 1,835 copies, pp. 197–532; part III, 1957, 1,835 copies, pp. 533–636.

Another indispensable source for students of civil law, *Reference materials* contains many legal documents which are not included in the two major statutory series, *Chung-yang jen-min cheng-fu fa-ling hui-pien* (Collection of laws and decrees of the Central People's Government), and *Chung-hua jen-min kung-ho-kuo fa-kuei hui-pien* (Collection of laws and regulations of the People's Republic of China).

Part I includes the texts of 43 legal documents under the heading "general provisions." Part II contains legal documents grouped under the following headings: (1) debt and contract; (2) sale; (3) supply; (4) hire of work; (5) lease; (6) warehousing; (7) carriage; (8) loan and final settlement of accounts; and (9) insurance. Part III deals with: (1) writing for publication; (2) invention; (3) marriage and family; and (4) succession.

Presumably published for internal use only, the book thus far is unobtainable outside of China.

6. Chou Chia-ch'ing, *Hun-yin-fa chiang-hua* (Talks on the marriage law), Peking, Chinese Youth Press, 1964, 107 pages, two printings, 26,000 copies.

Written in popular prose for mass consumption, the book consists of seven talks, each on a different aspect of the marriage law. In addition to explaining the law and stressing the importance of observing it, *Talks* discourages early marriage; advocates planned parenthood; and discusses divorce.

Publication of *Talks* was advertised in the *People's Daily* but bookstores in Hong Kong and Japan have been unable to obtain it from the publisher. Some American universities, however, have succeeded in obtaining it from Mainland China through exchange.

7. Legal Press, *Kung-an kung-tso yüeh-chin chi* (Collection of writings on the leap forward of public security work), Peking, 1958, 275 pages, 20,000 copies.

This book contains articles, editorials, and special reports selected from various provincial newspapers. Topics range from various aspects of public security work, conciliation and handling committees, and patriotic pacts, to cooperation among the three branches of political-legal organs — courts, procuracies, and the police. Vivid descriptions of criminal cases are included. This title was designed to be used both as a reference work for public security cadres and other political-legal cadres and students and as reading material for the masses during the campaign to educate people in the observance of law.

8. Kuo-wu-yüan fa-chih-chü fa-chih-shih yen-chiu-shih (Legal History Research Office, Bureau of Codification, State Council), *Ch'ing-shih-kao hsing-fa-chih chu-chieh* (The treatise on criminal law in the draft history of Ch'ing, annotated), Peking, Legal Press, 1957, 122 pages, 2,800 copies.

The original text of *The Treatise on Criminal Law in the Draft History of Ch'ing* is one of the most important materials on the history of criminal law of the Ch'ing dynasty. It was compiled by the Bureau of Ch'ing History (which was set up in 1914), under the general editorship of Chao Erh-sun, and published in 1927. This succinct legal history consists of three parts. Part I summarizes the evolution of the Chinese legal system and describes the codification history of the Ch'ing dynasty. Part II gives a historical survey of crime and punishment in China. Part III discusses the institutional innovations regarding trial, prison, and amnesty in the Ch'ing dynasty.

The text was written in archaic classical style, lavished with abbreviated and esoteric expressions and intricate allusions, and is extremely difficult to understand. However, it was extensively annotated in the mid-1950's by a group of four prominent mainland Chinese legal scholars: Li Tsu-yin, Ts'ai Shu-heng, Lu Wei-ch'ien, and Yang Ch'ing-yüan. They were assigned by the Bureau of Codification of the State Council to make a study of the above work as one of a series of legal history research projects, which included the compilation of a bibliography of Chinese legal history (see the first item in this section), and the annotation of the T'ang Code. The publication of this annotated text in 1957 was another indication that the government during the Hundred Flowers period recognized the importance of legal history. This fact is, in turn, reflected in the official statement of the Codification Bureau: ". . . the use of the concrete history of our country to interpret the general Marxist-Leninist principles on the state and law has great significance in our present scientific legal research and judicial establishments" (p. 1).

An annotated English translation of the text is being prepared by legal scholars[10] in the U.S. This projected work will include commentaries by the Bureau of Codification and ancillary data drawn from other sources of Chinese legal and historical literature.

The following are minor statutory compendia of laws relating to a single topic; they often include legal documents which cannot be found in the two major Communist Chinese statutory series.

9. *Nung-ts'un shih-yung fa-kuei shou-ts'e* (Handbook of laws and regulations applicable to villages), Peking, Legal Press, 1958, 420 pages, 200,000 copies.

This book contains selected policy documents of the party and state organs, and the laws and regulations which are applicable to rural areas. It also includes reports on economic and cultural activities in the rural areas. The documents are grouped under the following headings: (1) agricultural production; (2) agricultural water conservation; (3) forestation and protection of forests; (4) agricultural taxes and loans; (5) controlled purchase and sales; (6) land; (7) culture, education, and public health; (8) marriage, military service, and public security; and (9) appendices.

10. *Shang-yeh shih-yung fa-kuei shou-ts'e* (Handbook of laws and regulations applicable to commerce), Peking, Legal Press, 1958, 524 pages, two printings, 30,000 copies.

The texts of 80 documents on commerce, including Party directives; laws and regulations; and articles by government officials on trade problems, are found in this handbook.

11. *Lao-tung pao-hu fa-kuei hsüan-pien* (Collection of selected laws and regulations for the protection of workers), Peking, Legal Press, 1961, 227 pages, 5,500 copies.

This book contains regulations and other legal documents concerning safety measures for workers.

12. *Chung-hua jen-min kung-ho-kuo yu-kuan kung-an kung-tso fa-kuei hui-pien* (Collection of laws and regulations relating to public security work of the People's Republic of China), Peking, Masses' Press, 1957, 150 pages, four printings, 98,000 copies.

This book, compiled for the use of police personnel, contains laws and regulations relating to public security work. Suppression

10. Professor Kenneth Wang of St. John's University Law School in New York, who conducted a Chinese law course during the years 1962–1963 at the University of Michigan Law School, and I are collaborating. Miss Kathryn Haun is assisting me with my part of this joint effort.

of counter-revolutionary activities, administrative control of security, organization of public security agencies, control of foreign nationals, and border security and examination are treated. Texts of legal documents issued between October, 1949, and June, 1957, are included.

13. *Min-tsu kung-tso shih-yung fa-kuei shou-ts'e* (Handbook of laws and regulations applicable to nationalities work), Peking, Legal Press, 1958, 570 pages, 8,000 copies.

The laws and regulations concerning Chinese ethnic minorities are grouped under the following categories: (1) state organs; (2) nationalities' affairs; (3) productive construction; (4) culture, education, public health and marriage; and (5) appendices containing newspaper editorials, speeches, and articles by party leaders and important government officials.

14. *Ch'ang-k'uang ch'i-yeh shih-yung fa-kuei shou-ts'e* (Handbook of laws and regulations applicable to industrial and mining enterprises), Peking, Legal Press, 1958, 469 pages, 60,000 copies printed.

Legal documents dealing with protection of workers (safety precautions), wages, welfare, marriage, public security, and illiteracy reduction, are included in this handbook.

Periodical Legal Literature

Important periodical sources of data on legal developments in China are government gazettes and law journals. Other journals dealing with more general social science topics often contain information useful to the student of Chinese law.

Three Government Gazettes

1. *Chung-yang cheng-fa kung-pao.* Probably the richest source materials on the administration of justice in the early years of the People's Republic are the 1950–1952 issues of *Chung-yang cheng-fa kung-pao* (Central political-legal gazette,[11] hereafter cited as CYCFKP). The CYCFKP was founded in January, 1950 and the

11. Mr. Christopher Howe of the London School of Oriental and African Studies has a full set (1950–1954) of *Chung-yang cheng-fa kung-pao* (Central political-legal gazette; hereafter, *CYCFKP*). The Committee on East Asian Libraries of the Association for Asian Studies obtained permission from Mr. Howe in 1966 to have the gazette photoduplicated. As a result, a Xerox or microfilm copy of this hitherto rare serial is now held by most major academic centers in this country.

last issue bearing this title appeared in September, 1954. Presumably, *Chung-hua jen-min kung-ho-kuo kuo-wu-yüan kung-pao* (Gazette of the State Council of the People's Republic of China) became the successor to the CYCFKP in October, 1954, subsequent to the promulgation of the Constitution.

The first issue of CYCFKP appeared on January 15, 1950. According to the foreword in this issue, the gazette included summarized reports of political-legal work and various kinds of materials for the study and reference of government cadres at all levels; in addition, there were important laws and decrees, regulations, directives, and resolutions of the Central People's Government and the Government Administration Council (pre-Constitution predecessor of the present State Council). Since there is considerable overlapping of the statutory material in this title and in the *Chung-yang jen-min cheng-fu fa-ling hui-pien* (Collection of laws and decrees of the Central People's Government),[12] it is chiefly these informative summarized reports and other reference materials which make this gazette valuable.

According to the "Brief Rules Governing the Organization of the Editorial Committee of CYCFKP," [13] this committee was appointed by the Committee of Political and Legal Affairs of the Government Administration Council, which was listed in the gazette as its publisher. The editorial committee appointed for the first two issues of the gazette consisted of eleven members.[14] For issue number 3 and subsequent issues, two representatives, one each from the Supreme People's Procuracy[15] and the Supreme People's Court,[16] were added to the editorial committee, and at the same time the scope of the gazette was expanded to include statutes, summation reports,

---

12. Each publication contains many statutes that are not found, but should have been included, in the other. Judging from the fact that numerous similar or closely related materials are listed in both publications, it would seem that their absence was due to considerations of expediency rather than to a deliberate editorial policy. Up to the end of 1952, CYCFKP did not contain statutes pertaining to finance and economics. For bibliographic information on the *Collection of Laws and Decrees of the Central People's Government*, see Tao-tai Hsia, *Guide to Selected Legal Sources of Mainland China* (Washington: Library of Congress, 1967), pp. 75–128, and the translated titles of the laws and other legal documents contained therein.

13. CYCFKP, no. 1 (1950), back cover.

14. P'eng Tse-min (chairman), T'ao Hsi-chin (vice-chairman), Chou Ch'ing-wen, Yeh Tu-i, Wu Hsin-yü, Chang Shu-shih, Yang Ch'i-ch'ing, Liu Ko-p'ing, Wang Huai-an, Yeh Lan, Ch'iu O-lun.

15. Chou Hsin-min.

16. Chu Ho-fang.

and other material relating to these two judicial organs. As a result, the research value was further increased.

The importance of the 1950–1952 issues of the gazette as a source for research on legal development in China during that period is indicated by the stipulation of the editorial committee of the gazette that all government agencies must designate the gazette as required reading for all political-legal cadres.[17]

From 1950 to 1952 the gazette published forty-two issues and was a "certificated" publication — available to authorized personnel only. With issue number 1 of 1953, the gazette became an "open" (*kung-k'ai*) item and certificates were no longer required to obtain it. From that point on, however, its research value decreased drastically for it no longer contained special authoritative articles, summation reports, and such; its contents were confined chiefly to statutory materials, a large proportion of which were also published in the *Collection of Laws and Decrees of the Central People's Government*.

Also in 1953, the gazette became a monthly publication, published by the Codification Committee of the Central People's Government. All together, eighteen issues were published from January, 1953, to September, 1954, under the new format.[18]

CYCFKP published three indexes. The first appeared in issue number 22, pages 68–76 of the gazette, and covered the first twenty-one issues; the second in issue number 42, pages 37–51 (issues 22 through 42); and the third index appeared in the issue for November–December, 1953, pages 65–68 and covered all 1953 issues. There is no index available for the eight issues published in 1954.

2. *Chung-hua jen-min kung-ho-kuo kuo-wu-yüan kung-pao*. The probable successor to *CYCFKP* for the post-Constitutional period was *Chung-hua jen-min kung-ho-kuo kuo-wu-yüan kung-pao* (Gazette of the State Council of the People's Republic of China, hereafter cited as *KWYKP*), which was founded in 1954. This gazette contained many decisions, directives, and other documents — issued by the State Council and its subordinate bodies — which were not included in the *Chung-hua jen-min kung-ho-kuo fa-kuei hui-pien* (Col-

---

17. *CYCFKP*, no. 22 (1950), p. 77.
18. Although from January, 1953, to September, 1954, the gazette was advertised as a monthly publication, three issues were published bimonthly (May–June, 1953; November–December, 1953; and February–March, 1954) during this period.

lection of laws and regulations of the People's Republic of China).[19] The latest issue of the *KWYKP* currently held by the Library of Congress is number 30, published on December 31, 1959. From 1954 to 1959, a total of 194 issues was published. The *KWYKP* published a yearly index.

3. *Chung-hua jen-min kung-ho-kuo ch'üan-kuo jen-min tai-piao ta-hui ch'ang-wu wei-yüan-hui kung-pao* (Gazette of the Standing Committee of the National People's Congress of the People's Republic of China) was founded in 1957. The latest issue held by the Library of Congress is number 4, published in September, 1965. An examination of the available early issues of this title shows that practically all of the documents contained therein were also included in the *Collection of Laws and Regulations of the People's Republic of China*. This gazette also published an annual index.

Law Journals

1. *Cheng-fa yen-chiu* (Political-legal research, hereafter cited as *CFYC*), founded in May, 1954, is China's best known and most important law journal. From the time of its first publication on May 1, 1954, until 1960, *CFYC* was a bimonthly publication and was more readily available in its original form outside China during this period. It became a quarterly in early 1961 and, to my knowledge, was thereafter only available to foreign institutions through exchange channels. The last known issue published was number 2 in 1966.[20]

From 1954 to 1961, the journal was an official organ of Chung-kuo cheng-chih fa-lü hsüeh-hui (Chinese Political-Legal Association, hereafter referred to as CPLA). According to the March, 1956, work report of this association, most of the contributors to *CFYC* were CPLA members. It was also reported at this time that seventeen countries in Asia, Europe, Africa, and America, received this journal through gift and exchange.[21]

Beginning in 1962, the journal became a joint publication of CPLA and the Institute of Law of the Chinese Academy of Sciences

19. For the bibliographic information concerning the *Collection of Laws and Regulations of the People's Republic of China* and the English translated titles of the laws and other legal documents contained therein, see Tao-tai Hsia, pp. 75–76, 129–249.
20. The Daian Co., Ltd. has reprinted the whole set of *CFYC*. Copies of this set are available at the Library of Congress and other major academic libraries.
21. "Work Report of the CPLA," no. 2 (1956), p. 2.

and was described in the first issue of that year as a "political-legal theoretical publication" of the two institutions. Its multi-faceted editorial policy was declared to be:

To propagandize and elucidate the theory of state and law in Marxism-Leninism and in the works of Mao Tse-tung;

To propagandize and explain the general and specific policies of the Party and the state concerning domestic and foreign important political events;

To propagandize and explain the revolutionary legal system of China, especially the basic experience concerning the work of the revolutionary legal system since the founding of the People's Republic;

To implement the policy of "letting a hundred schools contend" and to launch academic discussions on legal science;

To criticize the political and legal thought of modern revisionism and the bourgeoisie; and when necessary, to publish selected foreign materials related to the above; and

To report legal research activities.

The journal also stated that it was published for the use of the personnel connected with legal research organizations and political-legal organs, and for the teachers, students, and researchers of the political-legal institutions of higher learning.[22]

The articles published between 1954 and 1965 generally followed the Chinese political climate of the time. Hence, articles with more scholarly content appeared during a politically less rigid period between 1954 and mid-1957, while the articles published immediately after the Hundred Flowers period were generally "anti-rightist" polemics.

According to the "Brief Regulations Governing the Soliciting of Manuscripts," published in all 1954 and in some 1955 issues, the journal welcomed the following categories of articles:

1. Theoretical and historical research on the state and law in Marxism and Leninism

2. Problems on the various specific branches of legal science

3. Essays elucidating the system of people's democracy and the revolutionary legal system; and articles which briefly describe the experience of political and legal work

22. *CFYC*, no. 1 (1962), p. 49.

4. Criticism of "old" countries, "old" theories on the state, the "old" legal system, and the "old" legal science

5. Informative articles on the theory and practice of Soviet political-legal activities

6. Reviews of and notes on political-legal books and periodicals

7. Other scholarly works on politics and law, and reports on academic political-legal activities, both in China and abroad.[23]

Table 1.3. Number and Subject Distribution of Articles Published in Cheng-fa yen-chiu.

I. General theories		309
A. Mass line	50	
B. Anti-rightists struggle	66	
C. Theory of state and law	187	
D. Struggle against revisionism	6	
II. Constitutional law		31
III. Criminal law		61
IV. Civil law		47
V. Judicial system (including judicial procedure, lawyers, and notaries)		106
VI. International law (including international relations)		65
VII. Miscellany		161
A. Legal history	13	
B. Legal science	148	
1. Legal science in general	19	
2. Translations	40	
3. Criticisms	55	
4. Political-legal education	34	
	Total	780

Table 1.3 shows the subject categories among which the journal's articles were distributed, and the number of articles published within each category. In general, party and state documents which contain policy announcements and resolutions are excluded from this table, as are all articles in issue number 4 and subsequent issues of 1960, if published, and in issues number 1 and number 2 of 1966, none of which were available to me at the time of writing. The subject headings used in the chart were taken from the Japanese monograph, *Nihon ni okeru Ajia-Afurika kenkyū no genjō to kaidai — bunken*

23. CFYC, no. 1 (1954,) inside of back cover.

mokuroku kaidai Chūgoku: hōritsu (Present conditions and problems of Asian-African studies in Japan. Bibliography and bibliographic introduction. China: Law).[24]

In 1954, the year in which the journal was founded, the only available information lists six men — Ho Ssu-ching, Fei Ch'ing, Ch'en Ch'uan-kang, Ch'en Shou-i, Yeh Tu-i, and Sun Ya-ming — as standing members of the CFYC editorial committee.[25]

One year after its founding, the committee was reorganized. The membership list for 1955 included two categories — standing members and regular members. Standing members of the editorial committee were Wang Ju-ch'i, Fei Ch'ing, Ch'en Shou-i, Yeh Tu-i, Kuo Lun, Lei Chieh-ch'iung, Yang Yü-ch'ing, and Liu Shih. The chairman of the editorial committee was Wang I-fu of the Ministry of Internal Affairs and Kuo Lun of the Chinese Political-Legal Association was vice-chairman. The regular committee members and their affiliations were: Wang Ju-ch'i, Ministry of Justice; Wang Kuei-wu, Supreme People's Procuracy; Yin Chao-chih, Ministry of Public Security; Jen Chung-chieh, Supreme People's Procuracy; Li Wen, Codification Bureau, State Council; Ho Ssu-ching, Chinese People's University; Chou Keng-sheng, Ministry of Foreign Affairs; Hsü P'ing, Central Political-Legal Cadre School; Sun Ya-ming, Standing Committee of the National People's Congress; Mei Ju-ao, Ministry of Foreign Affairs; Ch'en Shou-i, Peking University; Ch'en Yü-t'ung, Legal Press; Ch'en T'i-ch'iang, Chinese People's Institute of Foreign Affairs; Fei Ch'ing, Peking Political-Legal Institute; Yeh Tu-i, National Committee of the Chinese People's Political Consultative Conference; Lei Chieh-ch'iung, Peking Political-Legal Institute; Yang Hua-nan, Chinese People's University; Ts'ai Yün-ling, Central Political-Legal Cadre School; Yang Yü-ch'ing, Chinese Political-Legal Association; Liu Shih, the First Office of the State Council; Ch'i I-fei, Codification Bureau, State Council; Lou Pang-yen, Peking Political-Legal Institute; Lu Ming-chien, Supreme People's Court; Wei Tse-t'ung, Ministry of Internal Affairs. One member, Kuo Lun, was listed separately from the standing members under the title of convener.[26] A number of these members — for example, Mei Ju-ao, Ch'en T'i-ch'iang, Lou Pang-yen, Lu Ming-chien, Yeh Tu-i, and

24. Ajia-Afurika sōgō kenkyū soshiki (Asian-African comprehensive studies group), Tokyo, 1966, 130 pages.
25. CFYC, no. 1 (1954), inside of back cover.
26. CFYC, no. 1 (1955), p. 66.

Yang Yü-ch'ing — were condemned as rightists after the Hundred Flowers came to an end.

In 1958, another reorganization of the editorial committee took place. At this time a group consisting of Wang Kuei-wu, Lu Shih, Chang Tzu-p'ei, Yang Hua-nan, Sun Ya-ming, Chou Hsin-min, Kuo Lun, Ts'ai Yün-ling, Li Meng, Chin Mo-sheng, and Hsiao Yung-ch'ing was referred to simply as the editorial committee members. Two officers were also listed separately: editor-in-chief, Kuo Lun, and deputy editor-in-chief, Chin Mo-sheng.[27]

To my knowledge, the last reorganization of the editorial committee occurred in 1964. The membership list for this year again included two categories: (1) standing members — Wang Min, Kuo Lun, Liu Shih, Hsiao Yung-ch'ing, and Sun Ya-ming; and (2) regular members — Ma Chün, Liu Shih, Li Yüan, Hsü P'ing, Han Ming-li, Wang Min, Sun Ya-ming, Chang Chien, Kuo Lun, Wang Shen-chih, Lu Shih, Chang Tzu-p'ei, and Hsiao Yung-ch'ing.[28] According to the Japanese jurists who visited China in August, 1965, Kuo Lun was then still the editor-in-chief of the journal, in addition to his regular post as a vice-president of the Peking Political-Legal Institute.[29]

2. *Fa-hsüeh.* The second most important law journal in Communist China was *Fa-hsüeh* (Legal studies), which was published between June, 1956, and September, 1958. Founded as a quarterly journal of the East China Political-Legal Institute, it was originally called *Hua-tung cheng-fa hsüeh-pao* (East China political-legal journal), and it published three issues in 1956. The title was changed to *Fa-hsüeh* in early 1957, when it became a bimonthly published jointly by the East China Political-Legal Institute and the Shanghai Association of Legal Science.[30] At that time it was advertised as "a journal to publicize the Marxist-Leninist theory of law and to explore and discuss concrete problems concerning the socialist legal system,"[31] and as "professional reading material for legal workers."[32] It was further described in another law journal as "an academic pub-

27. *CFYC*, no. 3 (1958), p. 69.
28. *CFYC*, no. 4 (1964), p. 11.
29. The Third Group of Japanese Judicial Delegates Visiting China, *Kakumei no naka no Chūgoku 1965* (China in revolution), Tokyo: Rōdō jumpō sha, 1966, p. 318.
30. The Shanghai Association of Legal Science was scheduled to be established in December, 1956. Noted in *Hua-tung cheng-fa hsüeh-pao* (East China political-legal journal), no. 3 (1956), p. 4. Hereafter, *Hua-tung.*
31. *FH*, no. 6 (1957), inside of back cover.
32. *Hua-tung*, no. 3 (1956), inside of back cover.

lication that combines political-legal theory and political-legal practice" and is "closely affiliated with the legal researches of the Preparatory Committee of the Shanghai Association of Philosophy and Social Sciences." [33] Most of the contributors to the journal were jurists affiliated with judicial organs and law schools in Shanghai.

A number of articles published in the journal during the Hundred Flowers period are of academic value. The article which attracted most attention in China at that time was probably Yang Chao-lung's "The Class Nature and the Inheritable Nature of Law." [34] Since the majority of these writers received their legal education in the pre-Communist era and some had American or European legal training, their writings often reflect Nationalist and Western legal concepts. As a result, they bore the brunt of the Communist attack subsequent to the brief relaxation period, and after the Hundred Flowers period ended in mid-1957, the articles became more "*hung*" (red) and less "*chuan*" (professional; "expert").

In 1958, the journal became monthly. Although we lack documentary proof, it is generally believed that publication ceased with issue number 9 in 1958. As far as I can establish, *Fa-hsüeh* published a total of eighteen issues.

In 1957 in the sixth issue of the journal, a text of brief regulations governing the soliciting of manuscripts was published (p. 61). It stated that "since *Fa-hsüeh* is a journal which propagandizes the Marxist-Leninist theories of law and explores the concrete problems concerning the Socialist legal system, it especially welcomes articles concerning theoretical research based on practice."

The manuscripts should take one of the following forms:

1. Comments and brief comments
2. Essays, special essays, and research reports
3. Criticisms, discussions, and colloquia proceedings
4. Book and periodical reviews and notes; articles introducing academic thoughts and works
5. Lectures (discourses); explanations of and replies to questions; study guidance
6. Investigation reports; compendia of research materials, statistics, and historical materials
7. Academic activities
8. Miscellaneous

33. *CFYC*, no. 3 (1956), p. 31.
34. *Hua-tung*, no. 3 (1956), pp. 26–34.

Table 1.4. Number and Subject Distribution
of Articles Published in *Fa-hsüeh*.

I. General theories		
A. Mass line		14
B. Anti-rightists struggle		56
C. Theory of state and law		41
	Subtotal	111
II. Constitutional law		12
III. Criminal law		56
IV. Civil law		28
V. Judicial system (including judicial procedure, lawyers, and notaries)		75
VI. International law and international relations		20
VII. Miscellaneous		
A. Legal history		3
B. Legal science		14
C. Activities of professional institutions		7
D. Other		11
	Subtotal	35
	Total	146

Table 1.4 shows the number of articles on various subject categories published in the journal. The subject headings used in this listing were taken from the Japanese publication *Present Conditions and Problems of Asian-African Studies in Japan*.[35]

3. *Cheng-fa i-ts'ung* (Collected political-legal translations), published bimonthly by the Chinese Political-Legal Association (CPLA) from January 1956 to the end of 1958, contained mainly translations of legal writings of the Soviet Union and other Communist countries. It was described as "a sister publication of *Cheng-fa yen-chiu*" and was designed to relieve the space devoted to such translations in that journal.

The journal was jointly published by the CPLA and the Institute of Law of the Academy of Sciences beginning in 1959, and its title was changed to *Cheng-fa yen-chiu tzu-liao hsüan-i* (Selected translations of political-legal research materials). It became at this time an irregularly published journal of approximately 120 pages per

35. See footnote 24.

issue. In January, 1959, it was announced that the journal planned to publish two or three ordinary issues and occasional special issues.[36] Three numbers were tentatively scheduled (April, July, and October) in 1959. In addition to legal translations of materials from Soviet and other Communist sources, the journal was to include "political-legal materials of bourgeois nations that merit China's study and criticism." Generally, the articles were either digests or translations of excerpts from foreign legal literature. Some "technical essays" on China's own legal research were included. The journal thereafter became a "certificated" publication and its availability was limited to authorized readers only.[37]

4. *Other Journals.* In addition to the three which have been described in detail there are a number of other journals which deserve the attention of students of Chinese law. *Chiao-hsüeh yü yen-chiu* (Teaching and research) is a pedagogic journal of the Chinese People's University which occasionally carries articles on courses given in the University's law department, including reviews and commentaries on the teaching materials used. University academic journals such as *Chi-lin ta-hsüeh jen-wen k'o-hsüeh hsüeh-pao* (Kirin University journal of humanistic sciences) and *Pei-ching ta-hsüeh hsüeh-pao* (*Jen-wen k'o-hsüeh*) (Academic journal of Peking University [Humanistic sciences]), sometimes contain scholarly legal articles of considerable length which, in most cases, are the fruits of research of law professors in these academic institutions. The Peking Political-Legal Institute also puts out a legal publication entitled *Chiao-hsüeh chien-pao* (Bulletin on teaching).[38] There are two additional law journals worth mentioning: *Cheng-fa chiao-hsüeh* (Political-legal teaching) and *Cheng-fa hsüeh-hsi* (Political-legal study). It is uncertain whether these law journals have ceased publication; none of the issues of these titles are held by the major libraries in the United States.

My Guide to Selected Legal Sources of Mainland China lists (on pages 253–255) a number of journals of a general nature which only occasionally contain legal articles. However, in view of the paucity of research sources and of the relevance of law to a wide range of topics, students of Chinese law might give these their attention.

36. CFYC, no. 1 (1959), p. 38.
37. *Ibid.*
38. CFYC, no. 6 (1955), p. 53.

Newspaper Legal Literature

Chinese newspapers are without question an indispensable research source for specialists in Chinese law. Legal literature in newspapers[39] is of two types: (1) news items on legal development, and (2) articles similar in quality to those published in law journals. For future publication, the Far Eastern Law Division of the Library of Congress has begun to compile a list of articles belonging to the latter category, and it has thus far amassed one thousand titles.

However, because the task of locating and recording news items on legal development from Chinese newspapers is time-consuming, researchers are referred to the newspaper clipping files which have been gathered by various institutions in Hong Kong and Taiwan which specialize in "China watching." The Union Research Institute newspaper clipping file is held by several academic libraries in this country, one of which is the Center for Research Libraries, Chicago. I have also examined the newspaper clipping files on law which were gathered by the *China News Analysis* in Hong Kong and by various China-watching institutions in Taiwan. Most of these files are not yet available in this country. In general these files are a bit difficult to use because the articles are not as systematically arranged as they might be, and the subject categorization for certain items is sometimes determined arbitrarily.

Newspaper source material on legal matters at the local level has not been well tapped. For instance, the Library of Congress has about 800 provincial and other local-level newspapers published in various parts of China. (Of this collection, mostly noncurrent and with gaps, about 375 have been sorted, examined, and their holdings recorded by the Library.) A careful screening of these local news-

39. Many of the principal Communist Chinese newspapers are indexed in the *Ch'üan-kuo chu-yao pao-k'an tzu-liao so-yin* (Index to the materials in the important Chinese newspapers and periodicals), a monthly compiled and published by the Shanghai Library of Newspapers and Periodicals until 1959, and thereafter, by the Shanghai Library. As of issue no. 39 (January 1959), the index adopted a new format and has been published in two parts: Philosophy and the Social Sciences, and the Natural and Technological Sciences. The latest issue of the Philosophy and the Social Sciences section of the index which is available at the Library of Congress is July, 1960. A few national newspapers such as *Jen-min jih-pao* and *Kuang-ming jih-pao* also have published their own monthly indexes. However, the serious gaps existing in the indexes which are held by research libraries in this country have reduced their usefulness.

papers would probably yield a considerable amount of data regarding the administration of justice at the provincial, *hsien,* and village or commune levels.

As in the case of legal literature in periodicals, most newspaper articles of academic value were published around the time of the Hundred Flowers. One rich source of scholarly newspaper articles on law during the Hundred Flowers period is the *Cheng-fa shuang-chou-k'an* (Political-legal biweekly), compiled by the Research Department of the CPLA and published in Peking's *Kuang-ming jih-pao* (Kuang-ming daily) during the months, January–May, 1957. This newspaper, devoting a full page to the biweekly, published fifty-four legal articles of considerable scholarly substance. Since this minor but relatively concentrated source of legal literature from a Chinese newspaper often eludes the notice of Western students of Chinese law, a list of these articles is given in Appendix II.

Since most of the informative news items and scholarly essays on legal development were published around the Hundred Flowers era, the following description of the major national Chinese newspapers taken from an official Chinese handbook[40] published during that period should be of interest to students of Chinese law in gleaning research data from such sources:

1. *Jen-min jih-pao* (People's daily), organ of the Central Committee of the Communist Party of China, featuring general news and special articles dealing with domestic and international life.

2. *Kuang-ming jih-pao* (Kuang-ming daily), published by the other political parties, featuring mainly cultural and educational news.

3. *Ta kung pao* [Impartial daily], a daily, featuring mainly economic and international news.

4. *Wen-hui pao* (Wen-hui daily), a daily whose readers are mostly intellectuals.

40. This description of the leading national newspapers was taken verbatim, with one omission, from the *Handbook on People's China* (Peking, 1957), pp. 157–158. I have supplied the translated titles for *Ta kung pao* and *Wen-hui pao*. The translation of the title *Ta kung pao* was purposely omitted in the *Handbook* due to ideological considerations because the word "impartial" as viewed by the Communist Chinese contradicts their theory of class struggle in which impartiality is not permitted. Hence, *Ta kung pao* (Peking) was renamed *Ch'ien-chin pao* (March forward news) in September, 1966, and was thereafter published every three days. According to *Shin Chūgoku nenkan* (New China yearbook) of 1967 (special issue on the Cultural Revolution), p. 226, *Kung-jen jih-pao* has been renamed *Chung-kuo kung-jen pao* (Chinese workers' news) since the Cultural Revolution.

5. *Kung-jen jih-pao* (Daily worker), organ of the All-China Federation of Trade Unions, featuring activities of the Chinese workers.

6. *Chung-kuo ch'ing-nien pao* (China youth news), a daily, organ of the Central Committee of the New Democratic Youth League of China.

All the newspapers listed above are published in Peking except *Wen-hui pao* which, with a Peking edition, is published in Shanghai.

A list of other national and regional newspapers[41] follows: *Pei-ching jih-pao* (Peking daily), *Chin-jih hsin-wen* (Today's news), *Chung-kuo shao-nien pao* (Chinese youth news), *Hsin-shao-nien pao* (New youths' news), *K'o-hsüeh hsiao-pao* (Science news), *T'ieh-tao chien-she* (Railroad construction), *Chien-k'ang pao* (Health news), *Tien-yeh kung-jen pao* (Electric workers' news), *Chung-kuo yu-tien kung-jen pao* (Chinese post and telecommunication workers' news), *Kuang-po chieh-mu pao* (Broadcast news), *T'uan-chieh pao* (Unity news), *Shang-yeh kung-tso* (Commercial work), *Liang-shih chou-pao* (Foodstuffs weekly), *Chiao-shih pao* ('Teachers' news), *T'ien-chin jih-pao* (Tientsin daily), *Hsin-wan pao* (New evening news), *Ho-pei jih-pao* (Hopei daily), *Pao-ting jih-pao* (Paoting daily), *Shan-hsi jih-pao* (Shansi daily), *Nei-meng-ku jih-pao* (Inner Mongolia daily), *Hu-lun-pei-erh pao* (Hulunpeierh news), *Liao-ning jih-pao* (Liao-ning daily), *Shen-yang jih-pao* (Mukden daily), *Lü-ta jih-pao* (Port Arthur-Darien daily), *Chi-lin jih-pao* (Kirin daily), *Yen-pien jih-pao* (Yenpien daily), *Hei-lung-chiang jih-pao* (Heilungkiang daily), *Ha-erh-pin jih-pao* (Harbin daily), *Chieh-fang jih-pao* (Liberation daily), *Hsin-wen jih-pao* (Daily news, or News daily), *Hsin-min pao* (New people's news), *Ta-chung jih-pao* (Masses' daily), *Ch'ing-tao jih-pao* (Tsingtao daily), *Chi-nan jih-pao* (Tsinan daily), *Hsin-hua jih-pao* (New China daily), *Nan-ching jih-pao* (Nanking daily), *An-hui jih-pao* (Anhwei daily), *Che-chiang jih-pao* (Chekiang daily), *Hang-chou jih-pao* (Hangchow daily), *Fu-chien jih-pao* (Fukien daily), *Hsia-men jih-pao* (Amoy daily), *Hu-pei jih-pao* (Hupeh daily), *Ch'ang-chiang jih-pao* (The Yangtze River daily), *Hsin Hu-nan pao* (New Hunan news), *Ch'ang-sha jih-pao* (Changsha daily), *Nan-fang jih-pao* (Southern daily), *Kuang-chou jih-pao* (Canton daily), *Kuang-hsi jih-pao* (Kwangsi daily), *Ho-nan jih-pao* (Honan daily), *Cheng-*

41. This list is taken, with the exception of those newspapers already mentioned in the previous list, from *Jen-min shou-ts'e* (People's handbook), Peking, 1958, p. 623.

chou jih-pao (Chengchow daily), *Chiang-hsi jih-pao* (Kiangsi daily), *Shen-hsi jih-pao* (Shensi daily), *Hsi-an jih-pao* (Sian daily), *Kan-su jih-pao* (Kansu daily), *Ch'ing-hai jih-pao* (Tsinghai daily), *Hsin-chiang jih-pao* (Sinkiang daily), *Ssu-ch'uan jih-pao* (Szechwan daily), *Yün-nan jih-pao* (Yunnan daily), *Kuei-chou jih-pao* (Kweichow daily), *Hsi-tsang jih-pao* (Tibet daily).

Legal Education and Research Institutions in China

A large percentage of scholarly legal publications originated from what is commonly referred to in China as *cheng-fa yüan-hsiao* (political-legal institutions of higher learning), and from the Institute of Law of the Chinese Academy of Sciences. It is pertinent at this point to examine briefly these legal educational and research institutions.

Institute of Law of Chinese Academy of Sciences[42]

The Institute of Law of the Chinese Academy of Sciences (*Chung-kuo k'o-hsüeh-yüan fa-hsüeh-yen-chiu-so*) was established in Peking in October, 1958. Chang Yu-yü, a veteran Communist, and Chou Hsin-min, a non-Communist Party member, were appointed to the posts of director and deputy director, respectively. According to a recently published study on Communist China, [43] two additional deputy directors were appointed later. They are Han Yu-t'ung, the wife of director Chang Yu-yü and a prominent jurist in her own right as well as a former departmental deputy chief justice of the Supreme People's Court,[44] and Wang Shen-chih, a council member and a secretary of the CPLA[45] (Japanese jurists on a visit to China in 1965 reported that they had met a third deputy director: Chieh T'ieh-kuang).[46] The Institute was officially described as a research organ of the new people's legal science, guided by Marxism-Leninism and the thought of Mao Tse-tung.[47] While conducting and advanc-

42. The information on the CAS Institute of Law in the following pages was chiefly drawn from Chou Hsin-min, "The Preparatory Work for the Founding of the Institute of Law and Its Research Programs Henceforth," CFYC, no. 5 (1958), pp. 73–75.

43. Fei-ch'ing yen-chiu tsa-chih-she (The institute for the study of Chinese Communist problems), *I-chiu-liu-ch'i fei-ch'ing nien-pao* (1967 yearbook on Chinese Communism), Taipei, 1967, p. 1437.

44. *Jen-min shou-ts'e*, 1958, p. 330.

45. CFYC, no. 4 (1964), p. 33.

46. See Appendix I in *Kakumei no naka no Chūgoku 1965*, pp. 317–24.

47. CFYC, no. 5 (1958), p. 31.

ing legal research, the Institute was to cooperate with the political-legal institutions of higher learning, political-legal government agencies, and other research institutions and groups related to law. Administratively, the Institute comes under the Academy's Department of Philosophy and Social Sciences.

According to Chou Hsin-min, "The Preparatory Work for the Founding of the Institute of Law," all legal research must be conducted in accordance with the following principles: (1) observe the mass line, (2) closely link theory with practice, (3) value the present and belittle the past, and (4) destroy the old and create the new. Chou stated:

> We must first engage in research regarding the fundamental problems of legal theories and practice which need to be urgently resolved. Next we must study the basic principles of important legislation and their theoretical basis. In the process of conducting such research, we must at the same time thoroughly criticize bourgeois legal science in order to eradicate its remaining influence in the political-legal work of our country.

What are those urgent and fundamental problems of legal theory and practice referred to above? Chou enumerated the following projects as examples:

(1) The Marxist-Leninist legal theories and the works of Chairman Mao Tse-tung;

(2) The history of legal development during the period of new democracy (including the time of Soviet areas and liberated areas) and subsequent to the founding of the People's Republic of China;

(3) The system of society and state in China;

(4) The two kinds of contradictions;

(5) The people's communes;

(6) The policies of reform-through-labor and education-and-rehabilitation-through-labor (*lao-tung chiao-yang*);

(7) The problems of civil legislation in China;

(8) Marriage law and labor law;

(9) The judicial system (tentatively including the procuratorial system) and various judicial procedures;

(10) The legal system of various Socialist countries; and

(11) Criticism of the legal systems of capitalist countries.

Most of the research projects of the Institute are joint ventures during which the Institute may conduct its research with either the political-legal government agencies or political-legal institutions of higher learning, whose key personnel are to serve as the Institute's part-time research associates.

The original plan for its organization called for the founding of three research units — state law, criminal law, and civil law — within the first year of the Institute's establishment in 1958. Within five years the Institute would set up research units or divisions dealing with theories of state and law; history of state and law (including the three stages of the historical development of law: the legal history of old China; the history of the development of law during the period of new democracy; and the legal history of the People's Republic of China); state law (including administrative law and financial law); criminal law (including criminal procedure); civil law (including civil procedure); administration of justice; labor law; regulations governing agricultural producers' cooperatives; and international law.

However, the above organization schedule was devised before the establishment of the people's communes. Because of the social changes caused by the development of the communes, the Institute decided that new standards for the study of legal science were necessary to deal with those changes. Instead of the units previously planned, then, the Institute eventually set up three temporary research divisions which would be subdivided into sections by subject after the actual demands of the legal projects were ascertained. The Institute also established units for the training of a research staff, library service, and editing, translating, and publication service.

The Institute planned to have a research staff of 120 people within three years after its founding (1958–1960) of whom 30 were to be senior researchers, 45 intermediate, and 45 junior.

During its first five years (1958–1962), the Institute planned to expand its staff to 200 scholars (50 senior researchers and 75 each of the intermediate and junior levels).

When Japanese jurists visited the Institute in 1965, there were within the Institute four research divisions dealing with: (1) theory of state and law, which includes state law (constitutional law) and marriage, civil, and labor law; (2) legal history (primarily contemporary and revolutionary legal history); (3) criminal law, including civil and criminal procedure; and (4) international law, a newly-established division.[48]

Under the management of the Institute director were two staff offices (for administrative affairs and for academic research activities) and a library. The Institute had sixty-six members. There were fifty-six *kan-pu* (cadre), forty-one of whom (including the director and deputy directors) were engaged in research. One of the problems faced by the Institute upon its establishment was a shortage of upper and middle class research workers who were both "red and expert." At that time, the forty-one researchers were divided into three classes: six senior researchers, fifteen intermediate, and twenty junior, the levels equivalent to the position of professor, assistant professor, and teaching assistant, respectively. Less than one-third of the researchers were women; although the average age was forty — the six senior researchers were considerably older — nearly all the researchers were young people.

Upon graduation from the university, students came to the Institute as researchers. Few had had any practical experience, and consequently, some were sent abroad for study, chiefly to the Soviet Union and Bulgaria. The basic course of study for research students included the following subjects: Marxist-Leninist legal theory, especially the thought of Mao Tse-tung; legislative problems in China, including the history of legal development; the study of legal systems in the Socialist countries; criticism of the legal systems of capitalist countries; the study of the social system and state system of China, especially the study of experience and legislation in the revolutionary legal system, and the study of strengthening the dictatorship of the proletariat based on the mass line; and the study of the legal theories of modern revisionism and criticism of the (Yugoslav) legal theories of the total people's state, party, and law.

One characteristic of legal study in China is the emphasis on combining theory with practice. Application of this principle could be seen in the Institute's research projects, during which researchers were required to live with the masses while conducting field investigations; and in the researchers' practice of participating in trial activities when not exercising judicial functions themselves. Group re-

48. See remarks made by deputy director Han Yu-t'ung, which Fujita Isamu repeats in *Kakumei no naka no Chūgoku 1965*, p. 75.

search was heavily stressed, and whether investigations were conducted individually or collectively, all completed research had to be discussed by a group. This group method was to assure the linking of theory with practice and the mass line approach in research.

Legal scholars in the West might be curious to know how research projects linking theory with practice are conducted. The following brief account of the Institute of Law's research project on communes, which is drawn from an article by a deputy director of the Institute, may throw some light on the question.[49]

In June, 1957, while still in its formative stage, the Institute decided to carry out its investigations through field research rather than through research in the office. Researchers were asked to leave their offices and to go to the lower levels of society, thereby combining research with practice.

The main motives behind this decision were to acquire an understanding of the actual conditions of political-legal work as well as to make a full investigation of the following relationships: social class, economic, labor, and civil affairs. The research teams went to the basic level courts, street affairs offices, and agricultural cooperatives to engage in a type of research which emphasized the practical aspects of the people's lives.

There was some question as to whether the researcher should go to the basic level merely to collect materials or whether he should participate in labor while he conducted his investigations. Because the researchers assigned to conduct these investigations were young intellectuals who had no experience in the hardships of physical labor, the Institute authorities decided that they must participate in productive activities whenever possible. They must eat, live, and work with the masses.[50] Wang Shen-chih, deputy director of the Institute, claimed that participation in physical labor by the researchers enabled them to establish close relationships with the masses, which facilitated the implementation of their investigative work and strengthened their viewpoints on labor and their sentiments toward

49. Wang Shen-chih, "A Brief Account of the Activities of the Institute of Law," *CFYC*, no. 1 (1959), pp. 54–55.

50. The work style of the "four with's" (*ssu-t'ung*) — eating, living, working, and consulting with the masses — has been declared as the correct way for judicial cadres to administer justice. See the excerpt of the "Report on the Work of the Supreme People's Procuracy" delivered by the Chief Procurator, Chang Ting-ch'eng, on December 26, 1964, at the National People's Congress in *Jen-min shou-ts'e* (1965), p. 18.

the masses. Thus, through this process, the researchers became both red and expert.

Not long after the investigation units went to the basic levels, the nationwide people's commune movement was launched, and the Institute immediately made this campaign its new research project. In order to acquire a more complete understanding of the development of the people's communes in various areas, the investigation team was enlarged and divided into four sections. One section was sent to the urban people's communes of Peking; two sections were sent to the suburban people's communes of Peking (one to agricultural communes and the other to a commune centered around large factories); the remaining section was sent to people's communes in other cities.

During the investigation period, the Institute adopted the "disperse, assemble, redisperse, and reassemble" method. The research was begun in September, 1958, and by early October of the same year, various sections returned to the Institute to hold the first Symposium on the People's Communes. They considered the following topics:

1. Nature, tasks, forms of organization, and scope of communes
2. The political-legal work after the introduction of communes
3. The effect of the commune movement on the state, legal, and social systems of China
4. The nature of the ownership and distribution systems of the people's communes

Following this symposium, sections were sent out for a second time to people's communes to conduct further research on the above topics, and in early November these sections held another symposium at the Institute. At both symposia, the leading members of the Party Committee and the leaders of political-legal organs were invited to make reports on the movement. These reports not only described the development of the people's commune movement, but also raised many theoretical questions. Such questions led to the formulation of topics for reports, each of which was assigned research personnel.

By the end of November, these reports were completed, and research personnel rushed to complete their individual projects for the second half of 1958. At the same time, several additional symposia were held at the Institute to discuss the question of the remnant legal power of the bourgeoisie.

At the end of 1958, the researchers of the Institute were asked to study the Resolution of the Central Committee of the Chinese Communist Party on the Establishment of People's Communes in the Rural Areas and to examine the articles written on communes in the light of that document in order to rectify weaknesses and errors contained in their writings. The Institute also summarized the research work conducted during the past year and drafted programs for 1959. Investigation sections of the Institute were reorganized. Two sections which had been assigned to urban people's communes continued to study these communes in depth. Two others were assigned to prepare the projected book "Basic Knowledge of Legal Science."

In May 1960, the People's Commune Research Unit of the Institute of Law (Chung-kuo k'o-hsüeh-yüan fa-hsüeh-yen-chiu-so jenmin kung-she yen-chiu hsiao-tsu) compiled a collection of documents and other materials on the people's communes. This collection, *Kaochü jen-min kung-she ti hung-ch'i sheng-li ch'ien-chin* (Raise high the red banner of the people's communes and march on victoriously), was published in two volumes. Volume I covers the period from the beginning of the communization campaign to August, 1959, and volume II, from August to December, 1959. However, some of the essays contained in principal newspapers and periodicals published in January–February, 1960, were also included in this collection. Although it was announced that additional volumes would be compiled, no further information concerning their publication is available.

The work comprises the important policy directives of the Party and state since the communization campaign; important directives issued by the Communist leaders at the central, provincial, and municipal levels; and essays and field investigations. In addition, it includes reports published in principal newspapers and periodicals.

Political-Legal Institutions of Higher Learning

In 1949, shortly after its seizure of power, the Communist government established the Political-Legal University (Cheng-fa ta-hsüeh)[51]

51. For the by-laws governing admission to this short-lived institution, see *JMJP*, August 11 and 22, 1949. The university was to provide ideological and legal training

and the Chinese Research Academy of New Legal Science (Chung-kuo hsin-fa-hsüeh yen-chiu-yüan),[52] both in Peking, for the purpose of training judicial personnel. The former was merged into the Department of Law of the Chinese People's University (Chung-kuo jen-min ta-hsüeh)[53] in Peking, which was established in 1950. The Department of Law of the Northeast People's University (Tung-pei jen-min ta-hsüeh)[54] in Changchun was also founded in 1950.

The objectives of these post-1949 law schools, according to a Chinese jurist, were "to create a set of new teaching systems, course outlines, and teaching methods which are to be used as samples of teaching reform." [55] In 1951 the Central Political-Legal Cadre School (Chung-yang cheng-fa kan-pu hsüeh-hsiao)[56] was founded in Peking; and the Chinese Research Academy of New Legal Science was merged with it for the purpose of training incumbent political-legal cadres, and "to train some of the political-legal teachers in order to

---

to "in service" judicial cadres. See "Outline of the Plan for the Training Class in Rotation of the Judicial Cadres of the Ministry of Justice of the Central People's Government," CYCFKP, no. 9 (1950), pp. 19–20.

52. The Academy was described as a research organ of the new legal science, "the general policy of which was to study the theoretical knowledge of Marxism-Leninism, and especially the thought of Mao Tse-tung; to study the knowledge on the policies of the New Democracy; to study New China's knowledge of law and judicial work. The educational objectives of the Academy were to firmly establish the new philosophy of life in which the researchers are to serve the people, and the new legal philosophy in which the researchers are to serve the people's democratic dictatorship." See "Outline of the Plan for Teaching of the Research Academy of New Legal Science," Chung-kuo hsin-fa-hsüeh yen-chiu-yüan yüan-k'an (The journal of the Chinese research academy of new legal science), no. 1, p. 15, quoted in Chou Hsin-min, "Review of the Development of Legal Science in New China in the Past Ten Years," CFYC, no. 5 (1959), p. 44. The task of the Academy, according to Shen Chün-ju, the President of the Academy and the President of the Supreme People's Court during the pre-Constitution era, is "to reform 'old' judicial personnel, lawyers, and law professors." See Tung Pi-wu, "The Question of Reforming 'Old' Judicial Personnel," a speech delivered at the inauguration ceremony of the Chinese Research Academy of New Legal Science on January 4, 1950, CYCFKP, no. 3 (1950), p. 44. Chung-kuo hsin-fa-hsüeh yen-Chiu-yüan yüan-k'an is probably the first post-1949 Communist Chinese law journal. To my knowledge, no issue of this journal is available in the United States at the present time.

53. Hsü P'ing, "The Revolutionary Significance of Political-Legal Educational Reforms Must Be Affirmed," CFYC, no. 5 (1957), p. 19. For a detailed description of the Department of Law of the Chinese People's University, see CFYC, no. 2 (1954), pp. 74–76.

54. For a detailed description of the Department of Law of the Northeast People's University, see CFYC, no. 3 (1954), pp. 65–66.

55. Hsü P'ing, "Revolutionary Significance," p. 19.

56. For a detailed description of the Central Political-Legal Cadre School, see CFYC, no. 2 (1954), pp. 73–74.

obtain experience in using new teaching materials and methods." [57]

The departments of law of the People's University and the Central Political-Legal Cadre School seem to have been, at least in the past, under more strict Communist Party control than other political-legal educational institutions. They have been described by a jurist as "the machine tool for establishing Socialist political-legal education" and were said to be "the target of rightists' concentrated attack in the rectification campaign." [58]

From 1952 to 1953, due to the Judicial Reform Campaign, the law departments in all universities and other political-legal educational institutions were twice reorganized by the government.[59] Subsequently, four new political-legal institutes — East China Political-Legal Institute (Hua-tung cheng-fa hsüeh-yüan) in Shanghai,[60] Peking Political-Legal Institute (Pei-ching cheng-fa hsüeh-yüan),[61] Central-South Political-Legal Institute (Chung-nan cheng-fa hsüeh-yüan) in Wuhan,[62] and the Southwest Political-Legal Institute (Hsinan cheng-fa hsüeh-yüan) in Chungking[63] — were established. In addition, the teaching program of the Department of Law of Wuhan University (Wu-han ta-hsüeh)[64] was overhauled. In 1954 the Department of Law was re-established at three universities — Peking University (Pei-ching ta-hsüeh), Fu-tan University (Fu-tan ta-hsüeh) in Shanghai, and Northwest University (Hsi-pei ta-hsüeh) in Sian.[65]

However, a Japanese legal scholar who visited China in 1959 [66]

57. "Plan of the Political and Legal Committee of the Government Administration Council Regarding Propositions for the Establishment of the Central Political-Legal Cadre School," *Chung-yang jen-min cheng-fu fa-ling hui-pien* (Collection of laws and decrees of the Central People's Government), Peking, 1953, pp. 33–34.

58. Hsü P'ing, "Revolutionary Significance," p. 19.

59. Chou Hsin-min, "Review of the Development of Legal Science," p. 44.

60. For a detailed description, see CFYC, no. 2, 1955, pp. 61, 65.

61. CFYC, no. 2 (1954), pp. 22, 76.

62. CFYC, no. 2 (1955), pp. 64–65.

63. CFYC, no. 3 (1954), pp. 66–67.

64. CFYC, no. 4 (1954), pp. 50–52.

65. For a detailed description of the departments of law of these universities, see CFYC, no. 3 (1955), pp. 50–52.

66. Masao Fukushima, "Legal Research and Education," in the Japanese Delegation of Jurists Visiting China, *Chūgoku no hō to shakai* (Chinese law and society), Tokyo, Shin dokusho sha, 1960, pp. 87–88. Fukushima also reported that the Law Department of the Sun Yat-sen University (Chung-shan ta-hsüeh) in Canton was merged with the Law Department of Hupeh University. However, a department of law is not found among the departments listed under Sun Yat-sen University in Leo A. Orleans, *Professional Manpower and Education in Communist China* (Washington, 1961), p. 177. According to Orleans, his "list of institutions of higher education, their departments, and fields of specialization" was taken from *Current Background,*

reported that the Law Department of Wuhan University had been absorbed by the newly created Law Department of Hupeh University (Hu-pei ta-hsüeh) in Wuhan. He also learned that the East China Political-Legal Institute and the Department of Law of Fu-tan University were merged into the Shanghai Academy of Social Sciences (Shang-hai she-hui k'o-hsüeh-yüan).[67] In early 1958, the Northeast People's University was renamed Kirin University.[68]

In addition to the law schools mentioned above, China has another type of legal education institution. For instance, the Szechwan Political-Legal and Public Security Institute (Ssu-ch'uan cheng-fa kung-an hsüeh-yüan), obviously both a law school and a police academy, was mentioned in a 1959 issue of *Cheng-fa yen-chiu*.[69]

Law, although recognized by the People's Government as a *chuan yeh* (professional discipline) on a par with medicine, science, and technology, is not considered a desirable field of specialization by university students.[70] In China today formal legal education can be

---

no. 462 (Hong Kong: U.S. Consulate General, July 1, 1957) which translates a brochure issued by the Ministry of Higher Education entitled, "Guide to Institutions of Higher Education."

67. The Political-Legal Research Institute of the Shanghai Academy of Social Sciences was mentioned in an informative article entitled, "The Colloquies of the Legal Science Circles of Shanghai and Sian on 'Questions on the Nature and Functions of the Law in the Stage of Socialism of Our Country,'" CFYC, no. 4 (1962), p. 39. This article also mentioned the law department of Sian Political-Legal Institute, whose history is not noted in the Mainland Chinese periodicals and newspapers available to this writer.

68. The Law Department of Kirin University is noted in CFYC, no. 4 (1959), p. 22, and no. 2 (1963), p. 42. It is also included in the list of institutions of higher education in Leo A. Orleans, *Professional Manpower*.

69. No. 6 (1959), p. 21.

70. There are many reasons for the Chinese students' attitude toward specializing in law, prominent among which is the fact that students majoring in the natural sciences and engineering usually are given more consideration in job assignments than are students of the humanities, social sciences, and law. The treatment which the Communists accorded those trained in law during the Nationalist period doubtless also discouraged interest in the study of law. Official evidence of the unpopularity of legal training among students appears in the following passages from the *I-chiu-wu-ssu nien shu-ch'i kao-teng hsüeh-hsiao chao-sheng sheng-hsüeh chih-tao*: ". . . presently part of the young students still do not have a sufficient understanding of the function of political-legal work during the period of national construction and of its weighty significance. They feel that after the country enters the period of construction, the significance of political-legal work must decline. Some of them look down upon political-legal work. Part of the middle school students even retain the views that "boys should study engineering, and girls should study medicine" and "only mediocre students study politics and law." [Those having such attitudes] are not willing to take the entrance examination for colleges of politics and law. These views are incorrect. Our country's socialist construction is an organic whole, and the work of its various units is interrelated and indivisible. Of course, in order to emphasize the development of heavy

obtained at either the department of law of a university or a political-legal institute. The 1958 issues of a government-compiled guide to schools of higher education contained the following description:

> The educational objective of law as a field of specialization is as follows: The primary task of the political-legal institutes is to train practical political-legal workers for the courts, procuracies, lawyers' organizations, public notary offices, other state organs, and enterprise units. The primary task of the departments of law at the comprehensive universities is basically the same as that of the political-legal institutes. In addition, they are also to train a small number of teachers.[71]

The university law departments generally require five years of study[72] beyond high school while political-legal institutes demand only four years.[73] The required courses usually include thoughts of Mao Tse-tung, fundamentals of Marxism-Leninism, political economics, dialectical and historical materialism, history of the Chinese revolution, logic, theory of the state and law, history of the state and law, state law, civil law, criminal law, civil procedure, criminal procedure, organization of people's courts and people's procuracies, administrative law, labor law, land law and the law concerning communes, legal medicine, international law, foreign languages, and

industry to hasten the realization of socialist industrialization, we need large numbers of industrial construction personnel and to attract relatively more young students to study industrial technology. This is not to say, however, that politics and law are not important, that there is no need for students, or that [the field] is not worthy of study . . . There is a certain definite reason for some young students slighting political-legal work and feeling that those who study law are the worthless and the lackluster. In the old society politics and law were instruments for suppressing the people; the old colleges of politics and law were [institutions] to nurture a group of the children of landlords, bureaucrats, and bourgeoisie, to prepare them to become the vassals of the reactionary ruler in order to cheat and suppress the people and to maintain the reactionary political power whose aim was exploitation" (*I-chiu-wu-ssu nien shu-ch'i kao-teng hsüeh-hsiao chao-sheng sheng-hsüeh chih-tao* [Guide to admissions to schools of higher education for the summer of 1954], Peking, 1954, pp. 143–144).

71. Ministry of Higher Education of the People's Republic of China, *Kao-teng hsüeh-hsiao chao-sheng sheng-hsüeh chih-tao (chuan-yeh chieh-shao pu-fen) 1958* (Guide to schools of higher education [part on the introduction to fields of specialization] of 1958), Peking, 1958, p. 178. Hereafter cited as *Guide 1958.*

72. Shang Shih, "The Schools of Higher Education on the Present-day Mainland, Part I," *Tsu kuo* (Fatherland; also carries title China Monthly), no. 11 (1965), pp. 23–24.

73. *Guide 1958,* p. 178. It is interesting to note that there is a discrepancy in the *Guide 1958* about the number of political-legal institutes in existence in that year. Page 5 of the *Guide* states that there are five such institutes, but page 178 mentions only four.

Chinese. In addition, a number of supplementary courses and more advanced courses may be elected.[74]

Details on Recent Activities of Two Legal Education Institutes

The following information on the Peking Political-Legal Institute and the Law Department of Peking University was taken from a description written by one of the group of Japanese jurists who visited China in 1965.[75] It is probably the latest published information on Chinese legal education immediately prior to the Cultural Revolution.

1. *Peking Political-Legal Institute.* Professor Hsiao Yung-ch'ing, Chairman of the Department of Law of Peking University, told the visiting Japanese jurists that the Peking Political-Legal Institute had two major tasks — to conduct a short training course for the in-service cadres and to conduct a regular course to prepare young people to become political-legal cadres. It admitted approximately four hundred students annually and required a four-year course of study. This course was one year shorter than that of the law department of Peking University, and the Institute's curriculum was not necessarily identical to that of the university's law department.

2. *Law Department of Peking University.* Hsiao gave a much more detailed description of his own institution. According to him, the law department of Peking University was administered by four men, a chairman and three vice-chairmen,[76] who served concurrently as administrators and as professors of law. Each of the three vice-chairmen had a separate duty: one assisted the chairman, one was in charge of teaching, and one was in charge of research and training personnel. These four men constituted the nucleus of what was known as the administrative office of the department of law.

74. *Ibid.*, pp. 178–179, and Masao Fukushima, "Legal Research and Education," pp. 87–88.

75. *Kakumei no naka no Chūgoku 1965.*

76. *Kakumei no naka no Chūgoku 1965*, p. 320. Jui Mu was identified here as a vice-chairman of the Department of Law of Peking University. Jui, a specialist in civil law, has published a large number of legal articles and has also been criticized mildly for his rightist thinking. For a list of Jui's articles, see my *Guide to Selected Legal Sources of Mainland China* (Washington: Library of Congress, 1967), p. 345. Another prolific legal writer, Wu Lei, was here described as a vice-chairman of the Department of Law of the Chinese People's University. Wu, a professor of criminal law and criminal procedure, was also criticized after the Hundred Flowers period for advocating that lawyers be allowed to keep professional secrets. Wu later made a self-denunciation stating that his previous view was "extremely wrong and absurd." For a discussion of this episode, see Hsia, *Guide to Selected Legal Sources of Mainland China*, pp. 57–58.

There were five teaching and research offices within the department which were concerned with the following subjects: theory of state and law; criminal law and procedure; civil law; history of state and law; and international law. Each office consisted of a chairman and several faculty members who were specialists in the particular field. These teaching and research offices played an important role in organizing and executing individual and collective research. The department as a whole had fifty-one teachers at that time, of which there were seven professors (*chiao-shou*), seven assistant professors (*fu-chiao-shou*), ten lecturers (*chiang-shih*), and twenty-seven teaching assistants (*chu-chiao*).[77]

There were 160 regular students and 15 research (graduate) students. At that time, 60 percent of the students came from the families of peasants and laborers, and in the previous year, 65 percent of the students were from this background. The student body was divided into five classes, and the study of law was a five-year course (as are all courses of study at the university, with two exceptions: the four-year library science course and the six-year natural science course which was scheduled to be shortened to five years in 1966). Graduate students had a three-year course of study, of which the first one and a half to two years were spent in research and the remainder in preparing the thesis. The admission of research students to the university was determined by each teaching and research office, the proposed research project being one of the considerations.

All students were required to take a basic course of study which included political theory, philosophy, history of the Communist Party, two foreign languages (to be chosen from English, German, French, or Russian), and militia training. In addition to these basics, law students were required to take political economy, logic, introduction to law, constitutional law, criminal law,[78] civil law, criminal procedure, civil procedure, law governing the organization of courts and procuracies, international law, private international law, criminology, history of the state and law of China and of foreign countries, history

77. Similar to the Nationalist Chinese system, both lectureships and teaching assistantships constitute part of the normal academic hierarchy, and these positions are generally filled by full-time faculty members. The position of assistant professor in China is roughly equivalent to an associate professor in the United States, while a Chinese lecturer is equivalent to an American assistant professor, and a Chinese teaching assistant is similar in position to an American instructor or teaching assistant.

78. See Appendix I for an example of a criminal law course outline.

of political thought of China and of foreign countries, and political institutions of capitalist countries. There was no separate course for police law but the "Regulations for Punishment in Connection with the Violation of the Security Control of the People's Republic of China" [79] was included in the criminal law course. Nor was there a separate course for labor law because labor disputes are not adjudicated by law courts but rather by labor administrative organs. The school year was divided into two semesters which included a six-week summer vacation and a three-week winter vacation. During the five-year course of study, each student had to spend one month in productive labor and ten weeks in practical training. Each student was also required to write a thesis.

For the faculty (professors, assistant professors, lecturers, and teaching assistants), promotion from teaching assistant to lecturer generally involved four to five years of teaching experience, while the rise to assistant professor involved achievement in research by the lecturer as well as his approval by the Ministry of Higher Education.

Tuition at the university was free, and 70 percent of the students received "people's scholarships." The amount of the scholarship varied but could not exceed Jen-min-pi (JMP)[80] 17.50 per month. Research students received an average monthly payment of JMP 45.00. These stipends were used by the students primarily for meals and other expenses, as the costs of room and books were paid out of state funds. Faculty members lived on campus in rent-free residences supplied by the university, which also provided a medical insurance program. According to Professor Hsiao Yung-ch'ing, faculty monthly salaries were as follows: professors — JMP 280; assistant professors — JMP 200; lecturers — JMP 114; and teaching assistants — JMP 70. In comparison, the average monthly wage of the worker was JMP 50 (a grade 8 laborer in a machine factory in Mukden made JMP 104 per month, while a grade 1 worker in the same factory made only JMP 33 per month).

Nationalist Chinese Writings on Communist Chinese Law

Another light on Chinese Communist law is that cast from Taiwan, although the majority of judges, lawyers, and law professors in

79. For the text, see FKHP, 6:245–261.
80. According to the official exchange rate, the value of one Jen-min-pi (JMP) is equivalent to about U.S. $.42.

Taiwan are either ignorant of or oblivious to legal developments in Mainland China. This is largely due to the antisubversion statute[81] and other Nationalist preventive measures against Communist infiltration which discourage researchers from conducting serious, objective, and scholarly legal studies of the Peking regime in the academic institutions in Taiwan. Therefore, Nationalist Chinese studies of Communist Chinese law are not made by prestigious legal scholars, but rather by the intelligence community .The intelligence agencies which prepare these studies also become the exclusive possessors of the studies because books on Communist Chinese law are generally excluded from the literary collections of Nationalist Chinese universities with law departments. Ordinarily, these legal studies are not made available to the public, nor are they sold in bookstores.

The following is a nearly exhaustive list of post-1949 Nationalist Chinese writings on Communist Chinese law. Some of the bibliographic information is incomplete because I gathered it during a trip to Taiwan in the winter of 1967, and it was not feasible to examine each item carefully during my brief visit there. The list is arranged chronologically.

Chien-fei ssu-fa chih-tu (Judicial system of the wicked bandits), compiled and published by the Bureau of Investigation, Ministry of Interior, 1950.

Wei hun-yin-fa chi fei-ch'ü hun-yin chiu-fen (The bogus marriage law and marital disputes in bandit-occupied territory), compiled and published by the Bureau of Investigation, Ministry of Interior, 1950.

Kung-fei ssu-fa kai-ko chih yen-chiu (Research on the judicial reform of the Communist bandits), compiled by the Second Department, Ministry of National Defense, published in 1953.

San-nien fei-ch'ing (*Ssu-fa pu-fen*) (Condition of the bandits in the past three years [Part pertaining to administration of justice]), compiled and published by the Bureau of Investigation, Ministry of Justice, 1953.

Fei-wei "Hsien-fa ts'ao-an" ti p'ou-shih (Dissection of the bogus

81. Regulations Governing the Searching and Cleansing of Bandit Spies During the Insurrection-Suppression Period were promulgated by Order of the President on June 13, 1950, and came into force on the same date. Article 14 of the regulations was revised by Order of the President on December 28, 1954. The Chinese text of the statute can be found in Liu Ling-yü, *Liu-fa ch'üan-shu t'ung-shih* (Complete book of six laws generally annotated), Taipei, 1965, pp. 1107–1108.

"Draft Constitution" of the bandits), compiled and published by the Planning Board, Executive Yüan, 1954.

Fei-wei ti-fang ssu-fa chih p'ou-shih (Dissection of the local administration of justice by the bandits), compiled and published by the She-k'ao-hui, 1954.

Kung-fei ti ssu-fa kung-tso (The judicial work of the Communist bandits), compiled by the Bureau of Investigation, Ministry of Justice, 1956.

Kung-fei i-nien lai ssu-fa kung-tso ti ch'ing-k'uang fen-hsi (Analysis of the condition of judicial work by the Communist bandits in the past year), compiled by the Bureau of Investigation, Ministry of Interior, 1957.

Kung-fei ssu-fa chih yen-chiu (Research on administration of justice by the Communist bandits), by Ch'en Shan, Yang-ming-shan chuang, 1957.

Fei-ch'ü ssu-fa chih-tu N 1 (The judicial system of the bandit-occupied territory N 1), compiled by the Sixth Section, Central Committee, Nationalist Party of China, 1958.

Kung-fei ssu-fa chih-tu chih yen-chiu (Research on the judicial system of the Communist bandits), compiled and published by the Bureau of Investigation, Ministry of Justice, 1958.

Kung-fei fa-chih wen-t'i ti fen-hsi (Analysis of the question of the Communist bandits' legal system), compiled and published by the Bureau of Investigation, Ministry of Justice, 1959.

Kung-fei ssu-fa hsien-k'uang (The present condition of judicial work of the Communist bandits), compiled and published by the National Security Bureau.

A number of Communist Chinese legal documents have been reprinted by various intelligence agencies in Taiwan. These are:

Wai-Meng wei "Meng-ku jen-min kung-ho-kuo" hsien-fa (Constitution of the bogus "Mongolian People's Republic" of Outer Mongolia), compiled by the Office of Investigation, Mongolian and Tibetan Affairs Commission, 1954.

Wei cheng-wu-yüan kung-pu pao-chang fa-ming-ch'üan yü chuan-li-ch'üan chan-hsing t'iao-li (Provisional regulations for the protection of the right to invent and the patent right, promulgated by the bogus Government Administration Council), compiled by the Bureau of Investigation, Ministry of Interior, 1950.

Wei "Chung-hua-jen-min-kung-ho-kuo hsien-fa ts'ao-an" chi fu-chien (The bogus "Draft Constitution of the People's Republic of China" and its annexes), compiled and published by Yang-ming-shan chuang, 1954.

Fei-wei fa-kuei chi-yao (Collection of important bandit and bogus laws and regulations), compiled and published by the Bureau of Investigation, Ministry of Justice, vols. I and II, 1961; vol. III, 1962.

Kung-fei fa-ling kuei-chang hui-pien (Collection of laws and regulations of the Communist bandits), compiled by the Bureau of Investigation and Statistics, Central Headquarters, Nationalist Party of China.

Wei cheng-wu-yüan fa-pu fei-chih li-yung pan-fa (Measures for the utilization of waste paper, issued by the bogus Government Administration Council), compiled by the Bureau of Investigation, Ministry of Interior, hand-written copy.

Chien-wei Su-Huan pien-ch'ü jen-min ts'ai-ch'an-ch'üan pao-chang t'iao-li (The bogus regulations governing the protection of people's property rights in the Kiangsu-Anhwei border area), compiled by the Bureau of Investigation and Statistics, Central Headquarters, Nationalist Party of China, hand-written copy.

Researchers would be wise to examine more general Nationalist Chinese journals in addition to those monographs mentioned above (which are primarily concerned with a study of Communist Chinese legal development) as these general publications occasionally contain articles on Communist Chinese law. The following eight Nationalist Chinese serial publications are devoted to the study of current events in Communist China.

Chung-kung wen-t'i chuan-k'an (Chinese Communist affairs), published by the Institute of Political Research, bi-monthly, in English, title also in Chinese.

Fei-ch'ing yüeh-pao (Chinese Communist affairs monthly), compiled and published by the Institute of International Relations, in Chinese, title also in English.

Fei-ch'ing chien-pao (Brief accounts of the condition of the bandits), compiled and published irregularly by the Bureau of Investigation, Ministry of Justice.

Fei-ch'ing shu-p'ing (Narrations and comments on the condition of the bandits), compiled and published by the Bureau of Investigation, Ministry of Justice, monthly.

Fei-ch'ü hsien-k'uang (The present condition in the bandit-occupied territory), compiled and published by the National Security Bureau, biweekly.

Kung-fei pao-cheng shih-lu (Factual accounts of the despotic rule of the Communist bandits), compiled and published irregularly by the Bureau of Investigation, Ministry of Justice.

Fei-ch'ing yen-chiu (Studies on Chinese Communism), compiled by the Editorial Board of Studies on Chinese Communist Problems, monthly, in Chinese, title also in English.

Ti-ch'ing yen-chiu (Studies on the condition of the enemies), compiled and published by the Office for the Study of the Condition of the Enemies, Executive Yüan, weekly.

These journals occasionally contain articles on Communist Chinese law. For example, two articles written by Ts'ai Hsüan entitled, "The Chinese Communist Court and Judicial System" and "The Supreme People's Procuracy and Its System," are in *Fei-ch'ing yen-chiu*, vol. I, no. 2 (February 1967), pp. 85–92, and *Fei-ch'ing yen-chiu*, vol. I, no. 3 (March 1967), pp. 71–76, respectively. Another example is Hsüeh Cho-chiang's article, "The Judicial System of the Peiping Regime" in *Chung-kung wen-t'i chuan-k'an*, vol. II, no. 2 (April 1965), pp. 21–25.

Finally, a number of studies of the Communist Chinese legal system reportedly have been prepared by military-run educational and research institutions in Taiwan. These studies are usually in mimeographed form and designated for internal use only; therefore, they are not available to foreign researchers. Some of them contain important legal documents such as people's courts decisions on criminal cases, correspondence from the people's reception offices of the people's courts, and conciliation documents issued by the local people's courts and the people's government at the village level. A number of these documents dated 1963 were reportedly taken from Communist China by Nationalist guerrillas during their raids in the coastal area of Fukien province.

Nationalist Chinese writings on Communist Chinese law often are not well documented, and as a result, their value to scholars is somewhat limited. Nationalist Chinese writings also tend to be polemical and therefore require readers with a certain degree of sophistication to wade through the arguments and sort out what is pertinent. It is unavoidable that Nationalist studies and evaluations of Communist legal development are slanted and over-critical; in spite of these shortcomings, however, Nationalist Chinese studies should not be ignored by researchers. They contain many valid and astute observations, and reflect expert knowledge of Chinese Communism frequently acquired by Nationalist Chinese analysts through personal experience. In addition, even studies of lesser research value may lead the researcher to an original source which he will find informative.

In conclusion, a reference work on Communist China compiled in Taiwan is worth special attention by students of Communist Chinese law—*I-chiu-liu-ch'i fei-ch'ing nien-pao* (1967 Yearbook on Chinese Communism), a summary of the Chinese Communist situation, 1949–1967, Fei-ch'ing yen-chiu tsa-chih-she (The institute for the study of Chinese Communist problems), 1967, 1437 pages.[82] This is the most comprehensive general reference work on Communist China ever published by the Nationalists. In Chapter 5, "Political Affairs of the Chinese Communist Regime," there is a section on Communist Chinese political-legal work (pp. 444–475). Five sub-sections deal with people's courts; people's procuracies; system of the Ministry of Public Security; reform through labor; and suppression and liquidation of counterrevolutionaries.

Conclusion

Tung Pi-wu, former President of the Supreme People's Court and present Vice-Chairman of the People's Republic of China, in a speech delivered at the Eighth National Congress of the Communist Party of China in 1956, stated, "It must be pointed out that our jurists have not yet produced a single fairly good book explaining the legal system of our country — a book written with knowledge of the theories of jurisprudence and in accordance with the Marxist-Leninist point of view. Up to the present all we have is a few pamphlets!" [83] To this day, after more than a decade, Tung's assessment of legal monographs in China is still generally valid. China has experienced a gradual but steady deterioration of legal publications, both in quantity and in quality, since the end of the Hundred Flowers period. The amount of periodical and newspaper legal literature has also

82. A 1968 edition has also been published.
83. "Speech by Comrade Tung Pi-wu," *Eighth National Congress of the Communist Party of China*, 3 vols. (Peking, 1956), 2:90.

diminished. The most important national law journal, *Cheng-fa yen-chiu*, suspended publication in 1966 and all available mainland newspapers have remained mute on the subject of China's recent legal development,[84] except for a few scattered reports on demonstration trials.[85] With the advent of Mao Tse-tung's Great Proletarian Cultural Revolution, the activities of the Red Guards suggested, for a time, that China had entered a state approaching total lawlessness. But Red Guard excessive behavior had, in the main, been curbed by the end of 1968.

Even Yang Hsiu-feng, the President of the Supreme People's Court, the highest judicial official in China, has fallen victim to the Red Guards. According to a Red Guard publication, Yang has committed suicide.[86] Previously, there had been a report that he had been publicly paraded through the streets, and his name had been omitted from the list of dignitaries at important state occasions.[87] Although he apparently had not been legally removed from office prior to his reported suicide, there had been indications that he had been purged. Two of the Vice-Presidents of the Supreme People's Court, Wu Te-feng and Wang Wei-kang, also appeared to be in political trouble.[88]

The key slogan used in the Cultural Revolution — Chairman Mao's dictum, *"tsao-fan yu-li"* (to rebel is justified) — is antithetical to the

84. Chinese newspaper articles reporting the activities of political-legal institutions, including law schools, during the Cultural Revolution are very rare. The few published pieces dealt exclusively with ideological matters of little scholarly interest. For instance, a recent article described how the students of the Peking Political-Legal Institute (Pei-ching cheng-fa hsüeh-yüan), under the guidance of the Preparatory Unit of the Revolutionary Committee — a Red Guard organization — constructed a stage with their own hands utilizing makeshift materials, thereby saving money for the state. The author states that this episode illustrates that since the students of the Institute are able to create something by relying solely on themselves, they also possess the power to change the world through their proletarian world outlook which is based on self-reliance. See Ch'un-lei of the Political-Legal Commune of the Peking Political-Legal Institute, "It Should Not Be Slighted," *JMJP*, July 24, 1967.

85. For instance, the *JMJP* of June 14, 1966, devoted almost a page to the demonstration trial of Yang Kuo-ch'ing, a youth accused of slashing two foreigners in Peking. For a discussion of this case, see Tao-tai Hsia, "Justice in Peking: China's Legal System on Show," *Current Scene*, vol. 1, no. 1 (January 16, 1967), pp. 1–12. For a more recent report on demonstration trials, see *JMJP*, Nov. 13, 1967.

86. Canton [?] *Hung-tien-hsün* (Red telegraphic dispatch), no. 3 (March 27, 1968). An English translation appears in *SCMP*, no. 4157 (April 11, 1968), pp. 5–6.

87. See Reuter's news report by Vergil Berger, Peking, September 15, 1966, published in the *Washington Post*, September 16, 1966. For instance, Yang Hsiu-feng's name was not listed among the dignitaries who attended Peking's May Day celebrations on May 1, 1967, and National Day celebrations on October 1, 1967. See *JMJP*, May 2, 1967, and October 2, 1967.

88. Canton [?] *Hung-tien hsün*.

principle of legality to which adherence is declared in the Constitution of the People's Republic.[89] Such a hostile attitude toward the rule of law does not suggest any change in the regime's lack of interest in developing a sound judicial system in the near future.

The Red Guards' espousal of defiance of authority and order is hardly conducive to serious legal research. Early in 1966, all institutions of higher learning, including law schools, suspended classes and academic activities for eighteen months and did not reopen until October, 1967.[90] Whether or not classes are being successfully convened as of late 1968 is questionable. All publishing houses have been concentrating on printing the works and quotations of Mao Tse-tung and other ideological literature. No scholarly legal publication can be expected to appear until the dust settles.

As of late 1968, however, there are signs that the Revolution is going through its last phase and that urban order rather than unrest is again becoming the norm. Not every Chinese official approved the extent to which Red Guard lawlessness went. As early as October 1966 — when the Red Guard movement was just beginning and its worst excesses were still to come — Premier Chou En-lai had already begun to try to restrain the more destructive surges of the Revolution. In a speech delivered to representatives of the Red Guards, Chou tried to delimit the young people's power. Obviously unhappy about the arrests and imprisonments made by the Red Guards, he reminded them that ". . . judicial powers belong to the law courts." [91]

As the Red Guard movement subsides, the functions of the political-legal organs — courts, procuracies, and the police — will be gradually restored, although probably with innovations.[92] As a conse-

---

89. Article 100 of the Constitution promulgated in September, 1954, reads, "Citizens of the People's Republic of China must abide by the Constitution and the law, uphold discipline at work, keep public order, and respect social ethics." For the text of the Constitution, see *FKHP*, 1:4–31.

90. News dispatch from Peking by David Oancia of the *Toronto Globe and Mail*, published in the *New York Times*, October 24, 1967.

91. Speech by Premier Chou at Reception of Red Guard Representatives at Chung-nan-hai on October 3, 1967, in *Current Background*, compiled by the American Consulate in Hong Kong, no. 819 (March 10, 1967). This issue contains translations of eleven speeches alleged to have been made by Chinese Communist leaders in the heat of the Cultural Revolution from July through October, 1966.

92. An innovation adopted during another cataclysmic period in post-1949 China, the Great Leap in 1958, is the system of *san-chang lien-ho pan-kung* (one joint office for three chiefs — court president, chief procurator, and police chief); *san-yüan t'ao-lun* (case to be discussed by the three members — judge, procurator, and pre-trial ex-

quence, foreign researchers can expect legal information to begin trickling from China again. It is unlikely, however, that there will be any significant progress in more orderly development of China's legal system for some time to come.

In view of the fact that data on current legal developments in Communist China is virtually unobtainable, students of Chinese law in the West must be satisfied with aging source materials. But the task of studying the law of Communist China has barely begun in this country. Although published Chinese legal materials have always been far from abundant, academic studies of Communist Chinese law should not be too much impeded by the paucity of research data since only a small portion of these existing sources have yet been explored by legal scholars in the West. Contrary to the claims of some Communist Chinese jurists,[93] there is always some continuity in the development of law. What is past is prologue. Therefore, the study of contemporary Chinese law should not be ignored or delayed despite the lack of accessible information on its present stage of development.

aminer); *san-chang ting-an* (decision on a case to be made by the three chiefs); and *tang-wei p'i-chun* (all decisions to be approved by the Party Committee). For the discussion of this new approach, see Chung-kuo jen-min ta-hsüeh fa-lü-hsi kuo-chia yü fa-ch'üan li-lun chiao-yen-shih (Office of Teaching and Research on the State and Law, Department of Law, Chinese People's University), *Lun jen-min min-chu chuan-cheng ho jen-min min-chu fa-chih* (On the people's democratic dictatorship and the people's democratic legal system), Peking, 1958, pp. 205–206.

93. Yang Chao-lung, an American-educated jurist, during the Hundred Flowers period discussed the subject of continuity of law in his article, "The Class Nature and Inheritable Nature of Law," *Hua-tung*, no. 3 (December 1956), pp. 26–34. Yang was later denounced as a rightist for his espousal of the continuity of law theory.

Appendix I

First Draft Outline for a Course in Criminal Law*

General Provisions

Topic A: *Chairman Mao's principles regarding two types of contradictions and the people's democratic dictatorship are the theoretical basis of criminal law in our country.*

1. The guiding significance of Chairman Mao's principles on criminal law regarding the two types of contradictions and the people's democratic dictatorship.

2. The contradictory nature of crimes.

3. The standard and method for differentiating crimes resulting from different types of contradictions.

4. Different ways of handling different types of contradictions.

Topic B: *Criminal law is the instrument of the dictatorship of the proletariat in our country.*

1. Suppressing enemies, punishing crimes, protecting the people, consolidating the proletarian dictatorship, and safeguarding Socialist construction are the basic tasks of criminal law in our country.

2. Criminal law in our country must serve the political tasks of the state in accordance with the situation of class struggle.

3. Criminal law in our country must be guided by the general and specific policy of the Party.

4. Criticize the reactionary criminal laws of the imperialists and the Kuomintang. Expose and criticize the plot of bourgeois rightists to alter by usurpation the nature of criminal law in our country.

Topic C: *Crime and its causes.*

1. What is crime? The line of demarcation between crime and non-crime. Criticize the absurd utterance of the bourgeois rightists that "guilt is determined inconsistently by expediency."

2. Constituent elements of crime.

    (a) Acts that are gravely injurious to society (including the consequences of the acts, the cause-effect relationship of the acts and their consequences, and the time and place of committing the acts).

    (b) The one who commits a crime must reach a given age of responsibility and must be capable of assuming responsibility.

    (c) The act of committing a crime must be due to either intention or negligence (including the motive in committing a crime and the intent to commit a crime).

3. Causes of crime. Crime is a product of the system of exploitation. Criticize the reactionary substance of the bourgeois theory on the causes of crime. Reasons for the continued existence of crime in our country; the relationship between changeable patterns of crime and the class struggle.

---

* *Chiao-hsüeh yü yen-chiu* (Teaching and research), no. 4 (1958), pp. 55–56.

Criticize the absurd utterance of the bourgeois rightists that the Socialist system creates crimes.

Topic D: *Several defensive lines for the prevention of crime.*
1. The patriotic pact is a positive and effective measure for organizing and mobilizing the masses in crime prevention.
2. Punishment in connection with the violation of security control is an important measure in the struggle against minor offenses and in the prevention of crime.
3. Education-and-rehabilitation-through-labor is a creative method of preventing crime in that it resorts to compulsory education to reform and affords employment to the offenders.
4. Punishment is an important means of penalizing and reforming criminals and of preventing crime.

Topic E: *Our country's punishments are a powerful weapon in the struggle against crime.*
1. The basic difference between the nature of punishments in our country and that in the bourgeois nations.
2. The kinds of punishments in our country — the death penalty and suspension of death penalty; imprisonment for life; imprisonment for a definite period; suspension of the punishment of imprisonment for a definite period; control; expulsion from the country; deprivation of political rights; confiscation of property; fines.
3. Meting out of punishment. "Facts are the basis; law is the criterion" is the guiding thought for meting out punishment. Punishment must be determined by the nature, circumstances, and degree of seriousness of the crime. It must take into consideration the condition of each individual criminal, and must be done in accordance with the provisions of pertinent policies and laws. It must reflect the situation of class struggle and the condition which has prevailed at the time and place of the crime. Criticize the absurd utterance and the false, degrading accusation of the bourgeois rightists that there is "no standard for meting out punishment" in our country.

Topic F: *Our country's reformation of criminals through labor.*
1. The nature and tasks of our country's organs in charge of reform-through-labor.
2. The specific and general policies pertaining to reform-through-labor.
   (a) Combining class struggle and humanitarianism.
   (b) Combining control-punishment and thought reform.
   (c) Combining productive labor and political education.
3. Several basic systems pertaining to the reformation of criminals through labor.
4. Criminals who have undergone reform-through-labor — their release, rehabilitation, and employment.
5. Criticize the false, degrading accusation of the imperialists and bourgeois rightists on the reform-through-labor policy of our country.

Specific Provisions

Topic A: *Crime of counterrevolution.*

1. Resolute suppression of counterrevolutionaries is a gravely important political task in our country. The necessity of suppressing counterrevolutionaries viewed from the standpoint of the rule of class struggle. The great achievements and principal experiences derived from campaigns for the suppression of counterrevolutionaries. The present situation of class struggle and the task of continuing the struggle against counterrevolutionaries. Criticize the various absurd utterances of the bourgeois rightists intended to defile the suppression of counterrevolutionaries.

2. "Combining punishment and leniency" is the basic policy of the Party and the state on criminal matters in the struggle against counterrevolutionaries. The policy of "combining punishment and leniency" — the basis of its adoption and its main contents. The employment of this policy under different situations of class struggle.

3. The characteristics of counterrevolutionary crime.

4. Types of counterrevolutionary crime.

Topic B: *Crime against the personal rights of others.*

1. The significance of struggling for suppression of crime against the personal rights of others.

2. Crime of homicide.

3. Crime of rape.

4. Crime of having carnal knowledge of female minors.

Topic C: *Crime against property of others.*

1. The significance of struggling for suppression of crime against the property of others.

2. Crime of robbery.

3. Crime of larceny.

4. Crime of fraud.

5. Crime of corruption.

Topic D: *Several other criminal offenses.*

1. Crime of arson.

2. Crime of hooliganism.

3. Crime of smuggling.

4. Crime of speculation.

Appendix II

List of Articles from *Cheng-fa shuang-chou-k'an*

All the titles listed below are *Cheng-fa shuang-chou-k'an* (Political-legal biweekly) articles which made up one page of a given edition of *Kuang-ming jih-pao* (Kuangming daily). Therefore, the names of the biweekly and the daily will be omitted from each entry, and only the issue number of *Cheng-fa shuang-chou-k'an* and the date of *Kuang-ming jih-pao* will be given.

Administration of Justice

1. Ch'ing-yün and Cho Ch'ang. "A Brief Discussion on 'Notification of Juridical Suggestion.' " No. 7 (March 26, 1957), p. 3.
2. Ho Te-kuei. "It Is Hoped that the Leading Political-Legal Departments [will] Strengthen Their Assistance to Subordinate Cadres in Their Learning." No. 3 (January 2, 1957), p. 3.
3. Hsiung Hsien-chüeh. " 'Facts Are the Basis and the Law Is the Criterion' Is the Basic Guiding Principle in Trial Work." No. 5 (February 26, 1957), p. 3.
4. Li Pang-ning. "On the System of People's Assessors." No. 11 (May 13, 1957), p. 3.
5. Tai Ching-ch'un. "The Three Organs — Public Security, Procuracy, and Court — Should Further Implement the System of Divided Responsibility and Mutual Restraint." No. 4 (February 12, 1957), p. 3.
6. Wang Hsiang. "The Problem of Increasing Complication of Cases During the Course of Adjudication." No. 12 (May 27, 1957), p. 3.
7. Yü Chi-sheng. "How to Carry Out Pre-trial Preparatory Work." No. 2 (January 15, 1957), p. 3.

Civil Law and Civil Procedure

8. Chang Ch'iu-chen. "The Difference Between Examination of Contracts by Legal Departments of Enterprises and Notarization by the Notarial Organs of the State." No. 3 (January 29, 1957), p. 3.
9. Hsi. " 'Handling Matters According to Law' Discussed in the Light of a Problem Pertaining to the Real Property Tax." No. 4 (February 12, 1957), p. 3.
10. Li Ju-t'ao. "Opinions on Withholding Parts of the Wages of Employees and Workers, Whose Obligations Resulting from Civil Actions Are Being Fulfilled, for the Sustenance of Their Children." No. 7 (March 26, 1957), p. 3.

Criminal Law and Criminal Procedure

11. Ch'ien P'ing. "Citizens Have an Obligation to Serve as Witnesses." No. 6 (March 12, 1957), p. 3.
12. Hsü Li-sheng. "On the Question of Employment and Wages of Persons Who Have Been Granted Conditional Release." No. 12 (May 27, 1957), p. 3.

13. I-kuang. "Conquer the Thinking of Subjectivism; Raise the Quality of Investigation of Cases." No. 9 (April 15, 1957), p. 3.

14. Kao I-han. "How Should the Confessions of Defendants Be Evaluated Correctly?" No. 6 (March 12, 1957), p. 3.

15. Shih K'o. "A Discussion on the Question of Reforming Vagabonds." No. 9 (April 15, 1957), p. 3.

16. Wei-te. "A Discussion Starting with a Mishandled Case." No. 3 (January 29, 1957), p. 3.

17. Yang Shih-hua. "Opinions on the Question of 'Service Review' in Connection with Persons Who Have Been Given a Suspended Sentence of Imprisonment for a Specific Term." No. 5 (February 26, 1957), p. 3.

Inheritability of Law

18. Chang Ching-hua. "Discusses the Inheritability of Law." No. 5 (February 26, 1957), p. 3.

19. Chang Ching-ming. "My Views on the Inheritability of Law." No. 4 (February 12, 1957), p. 3.

20. Chang Hsin. "Can We Simply Regard Law as a Cultural Phenomenon and Discuss Its Inheritability Thereby?" No. 12 (May 27, 1957), p. 3.

21. Ch'eng Hsiao-ho. "Two Questions Pertaining to the Inheritability of Law." No. 11 (May 13, 1957), p. 3.

22. Chu Ch'i-wu. "The Class Nature of Law and the Inheritability of Law Viewed from the Standpoint of International Law." No. 11 (May 13, 1957), p. 3.

23. Li Hao-p'ei. "A Discussion on the Inheritability of Law and on the Science of Law." No. 10 (April 29, 1957), p. 3.

24. Ni Jen-hai. "A Way of Looking at the Inheritability of Law." No. 8 (April 1, 1957), p. 3.

25. Shen Tsung-ling. "Some Differing and Supplementary Views." No. 10 (April 29, 1957), p. 3.

26. Shen Tsung-ling. "What Is the Class Nature of Law?" No. 4 (February 12, 1957), p. 3.

27. Wu Ch'uan-i. "On the Question of the Inheritability of Law." No. 10 (April 29, 1957), p. 3.

28. Wu Ch'uan-i. "Can Law Have Inheritability on the One Hand and Be Free from It on the Other?" No. 12 (May 27, 1957), p. 3.

29. Yang Po-yu. "Are There Contradictions Between the Inheritability of Law and the Class Nature of Law?" No. 8 (April 1, 1957), p. 3.

30. An editor of the biweekly. "A Discussion on the Question of Class Nature and Inheritability of Law and of the Science of Law." No. 10 (April 29, 1957), p. 3.

Lawyers

31. Chang Ju. "The Right of the Accused to Defense Is Conferred by Law." No. 3 (January 29, 1957), p. 3.

32. Huang P'ao. "Correctly Expand the Work of Advocacy." No. 8 (April 1, 1957), p. 3.

33. Kuo K'o-hung. "The Question of Prescribed Rights of Agency Arising from the Role of Lawyers in Civil Actions." No. 2 (January 15, 1957), p. 3.

Legal Research

34. Chang Chih-jang. "The Important Role of Judicial Cadres in Their March Toward Science." No. 1 (January 1, 1957), p. 3.

35. Chin Mo-sheng. "A Discussion Starting with the 250 Theses on Legal Science." No. 1 (January 1, 1957), p. 3.

36. Fan P'u-chai. "A Brief Discussion on the Clerical Staff in the Government of the Ch'ing Dynasty: An Introduction to 'Shao-hsing Secretaries' and 'Clerks in Law Courts.' " No. 1 (January 1, 1957), p. 3.

37. Ho Chin-yü. "A Discussion on How to March Toward Science by Civil-Administration Cadres." No. 7 (March 26, 1957), p. 3.

38. Kung Shih. "It Is Hoped that an Institute for Legal Research Will Be Established at an Early Date." No. 2 (January 15, 1957), p. 3.

39. Li Ku. "Pay Attention to the Consolidation of Historical Records on Law." No. 7 (March 26, 1957), p. 3.

Marriage Law

40. Liu Cheng-wen. "What Are the Outstanding Problems in Today's Divorce Cases?" No. 6 (March 12, 1957), p. 3.

41. Wu Te-chin. "A Brief Discussion on the Spirit of Legislation of the Socialist Countries in Regard to Support of the Parents by Sons and Daughters." No. 6 (March 12, 1957), p. 3.

People's Congress

42. Ku Hui-wen. "Conscientiously Implement the System of People's Congresses." No. 9 (April 15, 1957), p. 3.

43. Sun T'ien-fu. "A Discussion on Several Questions Pertaining to the Work of Inspection." No. 8 (April 1, 1957), p. 3.

44. Wang Fang-ming. "A Discussion on the Question of Bills Introduced by Local People's Congresses at Various Levels." No. 9 (April 15, 1957), p. 3.

Procuracy

45. Chang Fu-hai. "How the People's Procuracies of Our Country Conduct Trial Supervision." No. 2 (January 15, 1957), p. 3.

46. Wang Li-chung. "What Is the Significance of Doing General Supervision Work Well?" No. 3 (January 29, 1957), p. 3.

47. Yü-ku. "Why Arrest Cases Must Be Reviewed By and Have the Approval of People's Procuracies." No. 1 (January 1, 1957), p. 3.

Miscellaneous

48. Ao-yü. "A Discussion on the Question of Relocating People for Land Reclamation." No. 2 (January 15, 1957), p. 3.

49. Kan Chung-tou. "A Discussion on the Masses' Viewpoint in the Work of Civil Administration." No. 3 (January 29, 1957), p. 3.

50. Li Chung-hai. "The New System of Preferential Treatment and Assistance in Rural Communities." No. 7 (March 26, 1957), p. 3.

51. Liao Kao-ying. "How to Treat Citizens' Complaints." No. 8 (April 1, 1957), p. 3.

52. Miu Hung-ch'ang. "The 'Five-Guarantee' System of Higher Agricultural Producers' Cooperatives." No. 12 (May 27, 1957), p. 3.

53. Pan-jo. "Relying on the Masses in Carrying Out Supervisory Work." No. 5 (February 26, 1957), p. 3.

54. Wu Tse-han. "A Tentative Discussion on Plagiarism." No. 5 (February 26, 1957), p. 3.

Appendix III

Communist Chinese Legal Publications in Collections in Nationalist China

Most of the present-day Communist Chinese legal institutions germinated in the red-controlled areas before the founding of the People's Republic of China in 1949. Many of the important statutes promulgated in China during the past eighteen years are actually revised versions of legal norms dating back to those issued in pre-1949 red-controlled areas during various periods of the "revolutionary civil wars." For example, the Counterrevolutionary Act and the Marriage Law, both issued in 1950, have their earlier, pre-People's Republic versions. In addition, such characteristics of the present-day Chinese legal system as the parental approach to dispensing justice,* the absence of or disregard for judicial procedure, and the educative role of law, were clearly discernible during the initial stages of Chinese Communism. Therefore, in order to understand today's legal system, researchers should have a firm grasp of the concepts behind the pre-1949 Communist Chinese judicial system and the legislation it produced.

The various intelligence libraries in Taiwan have a significant number of valuable original materials on pre-1949 Communist Chinese law. Because some of these works were seized by Nationalist forces during various periods of civil war, it is possible that even mainland collections lack the originals. The intelligence agencies in Taiwan have made some of these original materials available to libraries outside. For example, one of the most valuable bodies of materials on justice and the law in pre-1949 China, *Ssu-fa-hsing-cheng-pu tiao-ch'a-chü so ts'ang Chung-kung fa-lü wen-chien* (Communist Chinese legal documents held by the Bureau of Investigation, Ministry of Justice), which consists of hand-copied documents bound in twenty-eight volumes which I brought back from the Far East in 1962, is part of the collections of the Far Eastern Law Division of the Library of Congress and the University of Michigan Law School. In addition, a microfilm copy of the private collection of Communist Chinese materials of Ch'en Ch'eng, the late Vice-President of Nationalist China, has been acquired by many libraries in this country. It contains many pertinent items relating to Communist Chinese law, a listing of which may be found below.

However, it has been the policy of Taiwan authorities to deny outsiders permission to make microfilm copies of most pre-1949 legal materials. Therefore, the only way to acquire copies of these documents is to make arrangements to have them hand-copied; and in most cases, permission to have them hand-copied is granted only on the condition that microfilm copies of the handwritten ones will not be made by the foreign libraries which have acquired them.

Except for a very small number of legal documents of recent vintage reportedly captured by Nationalists during their raids in the Fukien coastal

---

* It is interesting to note that this parental manner of dispensing justice was also a characteristic of the traditional Chinese legal system. In Imperial China, the local magistrates were referred to as *fu-mu-kuan* (parental officials).

areas, post-1949 Communist Chinese legal materials held by the Nationalist Chinese are not very impressive. Practically all of their holdings can be found in the collections of the Far Eastern Law Division of the Library of Congress and in other academic libraries in this country.

Legal Items in the Ch'en Ch'eng Collection

Ch'en Ch'eng Collection: Shih-sou tzu-liao shih kung-fei tzu-liao (Materials on Communist bandits held by the Materials Office of Old Man Stone), 1931–1934.

The following is a list of the legal items in the Ch'en Ch'eng collection, which consists of documents and publications issued by the Chinese Communists during the period when they were in the province of Kiangsi. It consists of twenty-one reels.

1. Decision concerning the present work of suppression of counterrevolutionaries, and the elimination of A-B Corps bandits, local bandits, and Big-Knife-Society bandits. Central Kuang-ch'ang Nuclear District Council (Chung-yang Kuang-ch'ang chung-hsin hsien-wei), April 10, 1934, mimeographed, reel 4.

2. Letter from the Central Bureau to the party organs at various levels concerning the struggle against the A-B Corps and against other counterrevolutionary cliques. Reprinted by the Political Department, 2nd Division, 3rd Group, Chinese Workers' and Peasants' Red Army, January 4, 1932, mimeographed, reel 4.

3. Directive issued by Lo-k'ou *hsien* Government to soviets at various levels (under its jurisdiction) concerning the suppression of counterrevolutionaries. Lo-k'ou *hsien* Soviet, August 15, no year given, mimeographed, reel 4.

4. Regulations of the Chinese Soviet Republic concerning punishment of counterrevolutionaries. Central Executive Committee, March 7, 1934, mimeographed, reel 6.

5. Regulations concerning marriage. Proclaimed by the Central Government of the Chinese Soviet Republic, December, 1931, printed from movable type, reel 6.

6. Judgment issued by the Adjudication Department Tribunal of the I-huang *hsien* Soviet, Kiangsi Province (Nos. 5 and 7), 1933, mimeographed, reel 6.

7. Directive concerning the work of adjudication organs. Order No. 14 issued by the Department of People's Deputies on Judicial Administration (Ssu-fa jen-min wei-yüan-pu), Provisional Central Government, Chinese Soviet Republic, June 1, 1933, printed from movable type, reel 6.

8. Work program of the Adjudication Department of Hsing-kuo *hsien* Soviet, after it conducted a training-practice session for the clerks of various adjudication departments under its jurisdiction, December 31, 1933, mimeographed, reel 6.

9. *Administration of Justice* (Issues No. 1 and 2), compiled by the Adjudi-

cation Department of Kiangsi Provincial Soviet, June 6, 1933, lithographed, reel 6.

10. The *Kiangsi Provincial Adjudication Department Semi-Monthly* (Issue No. 7), November 11, 1933, mimeographed, reel 6.

11. On the question of setting up an investigative network and on the procedure for confiscating properties of convicts. Orders "Chung" No. 4 and No. 10 issued by the Department of People's Deputies on Judicial Administration (Ssu-fa jen-min wei-yüan-pu), Chinese Soviet Republic, 1934, mimeographed, reel 6.

12. On the question of depriving the right to compensation for death or injury and of setting up an investigative network. Orders "Chung" No. 3 and No. 4 issued by the Department of People's Deputies on Judicial Administration (Ssu-fa jen-min wei-yüan-pu), Chinese Soviet Republic, April, 1934, mimeographed, reel 6.

13. On announcing the offenses committed by Liu Yü-kung. Proclamation No. 6 issued by the Lower Military Adjudication Department of the Red Army, Chinese Soviet Republic, August 24, 1934, handwritten, reel 6.

14. Circular order of arrest. Headquarters, Chien-Li-T'ai Branch Military District, Chinese Workers' and Peasants' Red Army, May 20, 1933, mimeographed, reel 6.

15. Circular order of arrest No. 6 issued by the Kiangsi Soviet Government. Kiangsi Provincial Soviet, April 16, 1933, mimeographed, reel 6.

16. Judgment No. 31, issued by the Adjudication Department Tribunal of the Wan-t'ai *hsien* Soviet, Kiangsi Province, September 1, 1933, mimeographed, reel 6.

17. Laws and decrees pertaining to emergency mobilization. Mao Tse-tung, Hsiang Ying, and Chang Kuo-t'ao, November, 1932, printed from movable type, p. 72, reel 6.

18. Regulations governing contests on revolution, mimeographed.

19. Provisional organic regulations governing the military adjudication department of the Chinese Soviet Republic, Central Executive Committee, Chinese Soviet Republic, February, 1933, printed from movable type, reel 7.

20. Selected important provisional laws and regulations governing the Red Army. The 2nd Division Cadre-training Corps, February 1, 1932, mimeographed, reel 7.

21. Regulations governing contests on revolution among designated groups in the various *hsien* of Kiangsi Province. Kiangsi Provincial People's Council, 1932, mimeographed, reel 7.

22. On guarding military secrets. Compiled by the Army Corps Political Department, October 30, 1933, mimeographed, reel 8.

23. Counterrevolutionary acts committed by Huang Chung-yüeh and others. Army Corps Political Department, 1932, printed from movable type, reel 8.

24. Directive concerning delivering convicts under guard. Instruction No. 7 issued by the General Base of the Chinese Workers' and Peasants' Red Army, November 13, 1933, mimeographed, reel 9.

25. Organic regulations governing the workers'-peasants' procuratorial department. Provisional Central Government of the Chinese Soviet Republic, November, 1931, printed from movable type, reel 10.

26. Provisional law governing elections in the soviet area. Central Executive Committee, August 9, 1933, printed from movable type, 25 pages, reel 10.

27. Detailed rules governing elections in the Chinese Soviet Republic. Central Executive Committee, Chinese Soviet Republic, December, 1931, printed from movable type, reel 10.

28. Ten principles of government of the Chinese Soviet Republic. November, 1931, printed from movable type, reel 10.

29. Provisional law governing elections in the soviets (with explanation of the provisions). Central Department of People's Deputies on Internal Affairs (Chung-yang nei-wu jen-min wei-yüan-pu), October 29, 1933, mimeographed, reel 10.

30. On Cheng Hui-wen's dismissal from office as Minister of People's Economy of Kuang-ch'ang *hsien*, and the investigation and possible prosecution he faces. Order No. 4 issued by the Department of National Economy, Kiangsi Provincial Soviet, February 22, 1934, mimeographed, reel 10.

31. Directive issued by the Political Department of the 3rd Army Corps of the Red Army concerning punishment of local bullies, bad gentry, and landlords. Mimeographed, 1932, reel 10.

32. Report issued by the Political Department of the 7th Division of the 1st Army of the Red Army on penalizing Wang Ping-nan. January 13, 1933, mimeographed, reel 10.

33. The question of registering former bad elements who voluntarily surrendered to the authorities and reformed of their own accord. Proclamation No. 1 issued by the Adjudication Department of the Kiangsi Provincial Soviet, October 1, 1933, mimeographed, reel 10.

34. On the scope of procurator's responsibilities. March 28, 1934, lithographed, reel 10.

35. Index to regulations, resolutions, orders, and proclamations pertaining to labor matters; index to orders and proclamations pertaining to public health matters. Documents issued between 1931 and 1934, inclusive, reel 10.

36. Confiscating properties of landlords. Order of the People's Council, Chinese Soviet Republic, January 12, 1933, reel 11.

37. Collective contracts and labor contracts. Central Executive Bureau of the Soviet Area, All-China Federation of Trade Unions, January 18, 1933, mimeographed, reel 11.

38. Resolution concerning suppression of counterrevolutionaries in the Soviet Area. Central Bureau of the Soviet Area, January 29, 1932, printed from movable type, reel 14.

39. Step up the suppression of counterrevolutionaries in order to win a complete victory in the second revolutionary war. Proclamation No. 2 issued by the Wan-t'ai Ho-tung Committee of the Communist Party of China, April 24, 1931, mimeographed, reel 14.

40. Resolution of the Central Bureau on reviewing the work of suppression

of counterrevolutionaries. Central Bureau, December 20, 1932, mimeographed, reel 14.

41. The main aspects of the question of suppressing counterrevolutionaries. Compiled by the State Bureau of Political Security, August, 1933, mimeographed, reel 14.

42. The question of suppressing counterrevolutionaries. Central Military-Political Institute, December 12, 1931, mimeographed, reel 14.

43. Implementing the policy of winning over the masses in order to further step up the struggle against the A-B Corps and all the other counterrevolutionary cliques. Proclamation No. 6 issued by the Central Bureau of the Soviet Area, Communist Party of China, January 27, 1931, mimeographed, reel 14.

44. Classes and the class struggle. Compiled by the General Political Department, Chinese Workers' and Peasants' Red Army, March 12, 1932, mimeographed, reel 16.

45. Provisional principles governing the organization of the Internal Affairs Department of the Provisional Central Government of the Chinese Soviet Republic. Passed by the 16th Standing Session of the People's Council, June 20, 1932, mimeographed, reel 16.

46. Provisional organic law governing local soviets of the Chinese Soviet Republic (a draft). Central Executive Committee, December 12, 1933, mimeographed, 22 pp., reel 16.

47. While stepping up the campaign to investigate rice-field holdings and to purge the countryside, it is necessary to severely suppress the counterrevolutionaries. Order No. 9 issued by the Fukien-Kiangsi Provincial Soviet, Chinese Soviet Republic, reel 18.

48. Land law of the Chinese Soviet Republic. Passed by the 1st National People's Congress of the Chinese Workers', Peasants', and Soldiers' Soviet, December 1, 1931, lithographed, reel 18.

2 Interviewing Chinese Refugees: Indispensable Aid to Legal Research on China

Jerome Alan Cohen

In the summer of 1966 Mainland China's only existing law review, *Political-Legal Research*, fell casualty to the "Great Proletarian Cultural Revolution." A number of social science journals that have discussed legal problems also discontinued publication. Is this the *coup de grace* to research on the legal system of the People's Republic of China?

Surely the study of Chinese Communist law had already been difficult enough, both for scholars in China and for those on the outside. The research efforts of Chinese lawyers had been severely hampered by officialdom, even during the short-lived political liberalization of 1956–1957. In 1957, for example, the Dean of the Law Department of Wuhan University complained that

> under the present circumstances, data concerning the actual trials taking place in different grades of court up and down the country are barely accessible to people like us engaged in legal education. . . . The result is, theories inevitably become divorced from reality in teaching. It is the same with research.[1]

It has been much harder, of course, for foreign scholars to grasp the realities of Chinese justice. During the decade that followed the founding of the People's Republic in 1949 some Soviet and East European scholars enjoyed unique access to Chinese legal documentation and personnel. More recently, certain Japanese have been favored. By and large, however, relatively few foreign lawyers have been able to visit the mainland, and those who have done so have generally been given an opportunity to make only superficial observa-

Note: Reprinted from the *Journal of Legal Education*, 20 (1967), 33–62.

1. "We Must Create Conditions to [Let a Hundred Schools] Contend in Legal Studies," *KMJP*, June 12, 1957, p. 3, translated in Roderick MacFarquhar, ed., *The Hundred Flowers Campaign and the Chinese Intellectuals* (London: Stevens and Sons, 1960).

tions. Moreover, the bulk of China's operative legal norms is not published. Those legislative and administrative prescriptions that are published are obtainable outside of China, but they offer only an incomplete, idealized, and often dated image of the legal system. One cannot look to the decisions of courts or administrative agencies for clarification, because these are not made public in any systematic fashion. A number of books and pamphlets on law have appeared, most of them in the mid-1950's, but there are serious questions about the extent to which they are currently authoritative. Many Chinese newspapers that until 1959 were excellent sources of information about law in action are now both hard to obtain and largely uninformative. The scholarly quality and informational content of the two available legal journals sharply declined in the late 1950's, and by 1959 one of them, *Legal Studies*, had ceased publication.

Those of us who have spent years preparing to undertake research on the Chinese Communist system may well ask whether, having barely acquired our training, we are already on the verge of obsolescence. Recent events thus make it particularly appropriate to consider the potential contribution of refugee interviewing to understanding contemporary Chinese law.

I would like to be able to present the comforting message that life can be beautiful — that by resort to refugee interviewing we can surmount all obstacles to research on Chinese law. Yet obviously no such claim can be made. This does not mean, of course, that interviewing can safely be ignored. Indeed, the principal question before us concerns the extent to which research in various aspects of Chinese law can purport to be comprehensive and balanced unless it includes interview data as well as more conventional sources.

This last statement implies that interviewing is an unconventional source; and so it is, especially for that conservative breed, the legal scholar. Only in recent years have lawyers who study the American legal process begun to engage in interviewing on a significant scale, and one still must characterize as "pioneering" such research as Macaulay's on the settlement of business disputes[2] and Carlin's on individual practitioners.[3] If lawyers have been reluctant to undertake interviewing on native soil, can they be expected to embrace it, or

2. S. Macaulay, "Non-contractual Relations in Business: A Preliminary Study," *American Sociological Review*, 28 (1963), 55.
3. Jerome E. Carlin, *Lawyers on Their Own* (New Brunswick, N.J.: Rutgers University Press, 1962).

even to accept its results, in exotic, extremely difficult, and highly political circumstances?

In 1957, after two trips to Moscow, where he talked with judges, procurators, advocates, Ministry of Justice officials, and law professors, Harold Berman published an article on the legal implications of de-Stalinization. Although Berman's interviewing differed in nature from that under discussion here, what is interesting for our purposes is that, at the outset, he felt compelled to note:

> Though not yet generally recognized as an important technique of legal scholarship, interviewing would seem to be an almost essential method of learning about changes in a legal system which are taking place but which have not yet been completed. Further, with respect to Soviet law, it is an indispensable method of discovering certain important developments which are not mentioned in Soviet textbooks, treatises, journals or published legislation received abroad.[4]

By the same token, in introducing a recent study that drew upon refugee interview material as well as Chinese publications, I mentioned some of the problems associated with interviewing and stated that "material of this nature is not the ordinary stuff of legal research and must be treated with proper caution." [5]

Because they have greater experience and sophistication in conducting empirical research than we do, our colleagues in the social sciences can perhaps afford to be less apologetic. Yet few of them appear to believe that problems of interviewing can be lightly dismissed. Inkeles and Bauer devoted their first three chapters to explaining and justifying the Harvard project's methodology in carrying out an extensive program of depth and survey interviews among Soviet refugees.[6] And in 1962 the Subcommittee on Research on Chinese Society of the ACLS-SSRC Joint Committee on Contemporary China held a spirited two-day conference on the merits and methods of interviewing displaced persons from China. Plainly enough, the challenge of interviewing is as great as the need for it.

4. Harold J. Berman, "Soviet Law Reform — Dateline Moscow 1957," *Yale Law Journal*, 66 (1957), 1191 n2.
5. Jerome A. Cohen, "The Criminal Process in the People's Republic of China: An Introduction," *Harvard Law Review*, 79 (1966), 469, 476.
6. Alex J. Inkeles and Raymond A. Bauer, *The Soviet Citizen* (Cambridge, Mass.: Harvard University Press, 1959), pp. 3–64.

In order to provide a basis for evaluating both the contribution that refugee interviewing can make to research on Chinese law and the problems involved, I will summarize my experiences during a year's stay in Hong Kong. When in August 1963 I arrived in the "fragrant harbor," I had few preconceptions and was eager to try my luck. To be sure, I had gleaned from social scientists who had spent time in Hong Kong maxims such as "beware of Nationalist Chinese refugee agencies" and "it's better to do without an interpreter." Moreover, before leaving the United States I had conducted experimental interviews with four recent arrivals from China and had learned a few basic principles, such as the futility of using Chinese legal terms when talking to laymen. Yet essentially I was, as Chairman Mao would put it, "poor and blank."

Before confronting the initial and persisting difficulty of how to meet qualified informants, I had, of course, to decide upon the qualifications that I sought. Because no lawyers had yet done interviewing and because relatively little had been published in the West on the Chinese Communist legal system, I did not begin by limiting inquiry to a particular subject but simply tried to locate people who could be helpful on any aspect of post-1949 legal developments. What I hoped to get from interviewing was a clearer understanding of the structure of China's legal institutions, how these institutions actually functioned and meshed, and how they related to the political, social, and economic systems.

I could not anticipate whether I would find reliable, intelligent, and articulate people whose experiences warranted extensive investigation, or whether I would have to be content with attempting to cull data from a large number of persons, none of whom was especially informative. I did not intend, however, to undertake survey research in an effort to generalize about the Communist legal system by extrapolating from data obtained by questioning a sample of refugees. The difficulties of finding among Hong Kong's refugees a "representative sample" of Mainland China's population seemed too great, particularly for a neophyte, and given the state of our knowledge of the Chinese legal system, such a scientific statistical project seemed premature. Had my primary aim been to ascertain popular values and attitudes relating to law, such as contemporary conceptions of justice or the extent to which traditional antilegal prejudices still flourish, the survey technique would have been essential, whatever the difficulties.

But it did not seem to be the appropriate way to begin a search for descriptive data concerning operation of the legal process.[7]

Finding Informants

A television reporter who had hoped to do a program on "China watching" in Hong Kong was very disappointed when I told him of the relatively mundane ways of finding qualified informants. He had visions of cameras grinding as I aided terrified creatures across a barbed wire border amid a hail of gunfire. I actually spent most of the first month becoming acquainted with our neighbors and with members of Hong Kong's various communities — bureaucratic, diplomatic, legal, business, intellectual, journalistic, and welfare — and sought to enlist their assistance in meeting knowledgeable Chinese emigrants. This network of personal associations gradually began to produce introductions to a variety of people. A private research organization came up with a few good prospects: a very bright girl who had just finished college in Lanchow, a Peking University student whose education had been "broadened" by a term of reform through labor, and an engineer from a factory in Canton. A local official knew of a former police officer from Fukien province. A friend at one of the consulates introduced me to three men with long experience as Communist Party officials. The staff member of a relief agency sent me a Chengtu landlord's son who had been jailed as a counterrevolutionary. A university teacher introduced a close friend who had been expelled from his government post, had undergone "socialist transformation" of his business, and had been sentenced to "control," a sanction that resembles closely supervised probation. An American sociologist arranged a meeting with a Canton man who had worked his way from patrolman to a responsible job in the police force. And informants occasionally knew of someone else who proved helpful.

I met some of the most valuable informants by chance. A widely-traveled former bureaucrat who had held a number of economic posts struck up a conversation when he saw me reading the *People's Daily* on a bus. The sister of a housewife who had just come from northwest China for a visit brought her to our tennis club one afternoon. An experience in Macao provides a classic illustration of the role of

7. See Victor Hao Li, "The Use of Survey Interviewing in Research on Communist Chinese Law," chapter 3 in this volume.

chance. By November it had become apparent that Hong Kong had large numbers of intelligent emigrants who could explain where law fits into contemporary Chinese society and who could describe the organization and operation of the urban and rural authority structure. There was also no lack of people who could relate their own case histories of involvement as, in the Chinese vernacular, "targets" of either the informal or the formal legal process. Understandably, however, the potentially most valuable category of emigrants — those who had professionally administered the legal system as judges, procurators, lawyers, police, and Party officials — proved to be the most inaccessible. Thus, when a Canadian journalist offered to introduce me to a former Communist judge who had left the mainland for Macao in 1962, I decided to spend a few days in that nearby Portuguese enclave, whose placid appearance conceals the fact that it is perhaps the last of the authentic Sydney Greenstreet-Peter Lorre movie locations.

As I had feared, the judge turned out to be a holdover from the previous regime who had continued to serve for only six months in the earliest days of Communist rule. He had some interesting things to say about the Nationalist era and the transition to Communism. Nevertheless, I was keenly disappointed and began to explore other sources in Macao. Through the good offices of a local relief organization, I managed to talk with a number of people who had recently arrived from the mainland. One of them, a man named Liu, was a Vietnamese of Chinese origin. He had gone to China to study at Nanking University but had been deported by the police as a hoodlum because of his penchant for women, good food, and travel and for the black market speculation he found necessary to support these activities. At the end of an afternoon session in which he described his extended detention and interrogation by the police, I proffered an envelope containing a modest "honorarium" as a tangible expression of my thanks. While shyly looking away and protesting that he had no interest in money he took the envelope and disappeared. A moment later he returned and, without a trace of embarrassment, complained about the excessive modesty of my thanks. I explained that as a scholar I had not the funds available to government agencies and journalists and that I had to husband my limited resources to sustain the necessarily lengthy interviews that I hoped to have with some as yet unfound former judicial officials. I implied that, if he found such a person, I might be able to express my appreciation in a more substantial way.

Hardly mollified, Liu sulked off. But within an hour he was back full of smiles and proudly presented another recent arrival named Tao, whom he guaranteed to be a law school graduate and a recent Shanghai judge. Although the circumstances hardly inspired confidence in Tao's authenticity, I had tea with both Liu and Tao. Tao, who was in his late twenties, spoke with the assurance of a Shanghai man. It was evident that he had spent some time in local government affairs, but the more we talked, the more transparent his lack of legal credentials became. He emphatically denied, for example, that any law review was published in China, and when asked to name his law school courses, he gave preposterous titles bearing no resemblance to published information on legal education.

During our conversation Tao, who did not realize that I was returning to Hong Kong that evening, mentioned that a law school classmate named Leng, also a Shanghainese, was employed on a Hong Kong newspaper. As I could not afford to overlook any prospect, the next day I asked a friend to inquire about Leng. The editor of the newspaper in question reported that no such person was employed there, but, he volunteered, there was a Chinese from Singapore on the staff who had actually gone to law school in Peking and who until 1957 had served as law clerk of a court in northeastern China. To my relief, this gentleman easily rattled off the answers to questions that Tao had muffed. My research moved into a new stage.

As the Macao experience demonstrated, not all of those who offered to provide introductions acted as friends or good samaritans. Liu, after all, hoped to earn a substantial broker's fee. Others had more complex aspirations. I spent many a delicious lunch attempting to size up the motives of the would-be middleman across the table. Not infrequently, he would ask, "Have you friends at the Consulate?" This was not an easy question to cope with. Like most American scholars in Hong Kong, within a few weeks after arrival I met and became friendly with several of our government's local China experts. Yet the middleman's question usually probed for something more than my social connections. On some occasions it reflected fear of involvement with a possible CIA agent. At other times it was asked out of hope rather than fear, in order to discover whether a visa to the United States might be a reward for services rendered. I had to deny any affiliation with the intelligence community, since I had none. I also had to make clear my inability to influence the award of visas. The art, however, was to surmise the nature of the particular middleman's concern and to present the facts in a way that would not deprive him of all incentive to cooperate. I once denied any Consulate connections so vigorously that a Shanghai businessman lost interest in producing a promised judge. On the other hand, by admitting that certain Consulate officials were social friends, I probably lost one or two other opportunities.

Middlemen also hoped for other rewards. One enterprising citizen asked me to speak at the annual Christmas pageant sponsored by an orphanage that was under his supervision. He also wanted letters of introduction that would ease his way on a proposed tour to show movies on China at American universities. When my suspicions were aroused, I discovered that his desire to tour America was largely stimulated by the fact that irregularities in the financial affairs of his orphanage had come to the attention of the local Attorney General's office. Another businessman simply wanted me to enlist support for his application to the American Club, a principal social center for Hong Kong's commercial elite.

Even the most cooperative intermediary could not always produce the scarce legal professionals whom I sought. As in fishing, the saddest tales are of the ones that got away. There are many reasons why former mainland legal personnel would not want to discuss their experiences. I have already mentioned fear of involvement with intelligence organizations. People who emerge from the political pressure cooker that is Communist China into the relatively free but politically complex Hong Kong environment often strive to be wholly apolitical and to concentrate on earning a livelihood. Some worry that imparting official information to an American — an activity that is deemed traitorous in China — might bring retaliation against themselves or their families, either in Hong Kong or on the mainland. Moreover, although they were sufficiently unhappy to leave China, some retain a great sense of pride in their country's progress and refuse to provide material for those who may be seeking to damn the regime. Some simply wish to forget an unpleasant past, especially if they played an unattractive role, as is the case with former policemen and judges who dispensed harsh punishments. Some have concealed their past from the Hong Kong government and even from present family, friends, and business associates. The principal of a group of profitable private schools, for example, was reliably reported to have served as a judge in Canton for seven years; he rebuffed the efforts of a variety of intermediaries, and when in desperation I called to introduce myself, he furiously denied any judicial experience, claimed that he had only been a teacher, refused to see me, and demanded the names of his "accusers." According to people who had known him in Canton, the principal feared that exposure might put an end to his lucrative new career. A Chinese from Bangkok who had recently completed law school in Peking would not talk to me because, although barred from returning to Thailand, he was preparing to return illegally and wanted to minimize his contacts.

Perhaps the most frustrating cases of lost opportunity were those in which, after learning that the Hong Kong government knew of a highly informed person, I failed to persuade the responsible officials to reveal his identity and whereabouts. Although the Colonial authorities, who were sensitive to possible reactions from Peking, never raised an objection to my unobtrusive questioning of a relatively small number of residents, toleration of my activities, I was told, did not imply cooperation.

Informants' Characteristics

What kinds of people did all these efforts yield? I will describe only the thirty-eight Chinese emigrants whom I systematically interviewed. For purposes of convenience, I include in this group the four persons whom I met in the United States before leaving for Hong Kong and another whom I saw upon my return. The group is also composed of four people to whom I talked at length in Macao. It does not consist of those who, on preliminary scrutiny, appeared to be uninteresting or, as in the case of "Judge" Tao, unreliable. I also will not deal with a variety of special persons who were kind enough to see me. These included Chang Kuo-t'ao, one of the founders of the Chinese Communist Party, who left the mainland after breaking with Mao in 1938; two former American soldiers who had defected during the Korean War and who left China in mid-1963 after a decade of life among the urban masses; some White Russians headed for resettlement in Australia after a lifetime in China; a few Western businessmen and diplomats who had just given up residence in China; and a larger number of Westerners, including tourists and journalists, who had recently traveled there.

Only five of my thirty-eight were women. Only four of the group had reached forty years of age by the time I met them, and these were all in their early forties. Most were in their twenties and early thirties. Because I sought people who were intelligent and articulate as well as knowledgeable, the group was overwhelmingly composed of what the Chinese Communists call "intellectuals," in the sense that twenty-nine had been educated at universities or technical colleges. Most of the former police officials had not received higher education, but, of those who had not, several had attended police academies for a few months. Three of the thirty-eight came from wealthy peasant families, two from poor peasant stock, and several each from the proletariat and the very rich. Most, however, were from comfortable bourgeois, intellectual, or official backgrounds.

Although many of those interviewed had held various jobs, they can be listed according to their principal work experience. Six had been police officials. Three had served as judicial personnel, two of these having also at one time acted as "people's lawyers." Eight had worked in factories in some responsible capacity. Five had been principally students, and there were three doctors, two staff members of rural commune organizations, one small entrepreneur, three employees of government agencies in Peking, two schoolteachers, one librarian, one peasant, two housewives, and one man who had simply been unemployed most of the time. In the early months, when I was trying to understand the legal system's relation to other institutions, I was happy to talk with all kinds of people. As the year wore on, however, time pressures required me to become more selective. Because I began to focus on a study of the criminal process, I gave preference to people with relevant experience, although I continued to be interested in persons who knew about other areas of law. I never succeeded, unfortunately, in meeting someone with long tenure as a procurator. Nor did I find anyone who had been graduated from a Chinese law school in the 1960's.

If we break the group down according to each member's principal place of residence on the mainland since the advent of Communism, we find rather broad geographic distribution. Thirteen lived in southeastern China, six in Shanghai, twelve in the area between Shanghai and Peking, two in the northeastern provinces, and five in north-western China. The three judicial personnel were from different areas, but all of the police officials were from the southeast.

More significant perhaps than geographic distribution is the heavy concentration of urban dwellers in the group. Only two of the police officials had broad rural experience, and apart from the two commune staff members and the single peasant, a commune doctor was the only other person who had been permanently assigned to the countryside. A number of others, however, had spent time in rural areas, because they had been "sent down" (hsia-fang) there for a time under the regime's policy of requiring urban residents periodically to work in the countryside, or because they had received administrative or criminal sanctions that imposed rural labor.

Five of the six police officials and one of the factory staff had been among the elite of China — members of the Communist Party. Ten of the thirty-eight, on the other hand, had been detained as criminal suspects. Most of these had been convicted and sentenced either to reform through labor or, as in the case of two overseas Chinese, to deportation. A few had not been convicted but had been released only after long investigation. At least seven others, including several of the police officials, had been "targets" of struggle meetings and had been subjected to administrative sanctions including re-habilitation-through-labor (lao-tung chiao-yang.) One policeman said that he left, hurriedly, to escape arrest for having wounded his wife's lover with a pistol. It is probable that several other persons had also been in trouble with the regime before their departure but were reluctant to admit this to me. During our early meetings two police officials maintained that they "chose freedom" — one even claimed he had been influenced by the Voice of America. Later sessions re-vealed, however, that blemishes on their records had halted their upward mobility and had furnished a major stimulus to their de-parture. Although almost half of the thirty-eight appeared to have suffered no significant formal or informal sanctions, most of them had left China because of dissatisfaction. Frequently emphasized factors were poor economic conditions, unrewarding job assignments, and excessive regimentation. One man reported that he had been barred from membership in the Chinese Young Communist League because he was an overseas Chinese and that therefore his career in the bureaucracy looked unpromising. Several people from bourgeois backgrounds could not adjust to their humble status under Communist rule. Yet some of the group left the mainland largely to rejoin families living in Hong Kong or abroad, without any significant feeling of dissatisfaction.

Most of the thirty-eight emigrants had left China during the two-year period preceding our meeting. Some had been among the many thousands who crossed the border into Hong Kong when barriers suddenly dropped for a few weeks in the spring of 1962. Others had arrived very recently. Since refugees sailed or even swam to Macao virtually every day, there, of course, it was possible to meet people fresh out of the water. Given my research needs, however, in selecting informants, immediacy of arrival was not as important a factor as others. A few of the very best informants had left China as early as 1960.

Almost half of the group had come out with exit permits; the others had "escaped." But it is not easy, or perhaps even meaningful, to specify whether certain informants had left with or without the regime's legal permission. When in 1962 border guards looked the other way, had those who crossed into Hong Kong without permits left illegally? Had a police official who issued himself an exit permit left legally? Or a family man who bribed his way to a permit? What of the student who, as in past vacations, obtained a permit to visit her family in Hong Kong for the summer but this time decided to stay? In evaluating the kinds of people interviewed, the mode of their departure does not seem to be a major factor.

Of much greater importance is the informant's post-arrival situation. Half of those interviewed were employed at the time we met, although roughly half of this group were hoping to find better jobs. Of the unemployed, some had just arrived and were being supported by welfare organizations. Others were living off relatives or trying to make ends meet by a variety of means while waiting, like Mr. Micawber, for something to turn up. Several had sold articles to the newspapers and were hoping to become journalists or China experts, and a few had been compensated for providing material to local government and diplomatic agencies, private research institutions, and visiting scholars. Although employment was generally available in Hong Kong, at least for those willing to take menial jobs (in Macao conditions were worse), the people who were of greatest interest to me — intellectuals and former officials — had difficulty in adjusting to

Hong Kong's occupational demands. Many lacked commercial in-
stincts and experience and were handicapped by their inability to
speak either of Hong Kong's major languages, Cantonese and English.

I have already mentioned the variety of motivations that stimulated
middlemen. Informants' motivations were equally diverse. Unlike
some East European refugees I have known, none of my informants
seethed with the desire to expose the horrors of Communism to an
innocent world. One did, however, want help with a manuscript he
thought would be the Chinese *Doctor Zhivago*. Some agreed to see
me merely as a matter of courtesy or curiosity because I had sought
them out. Several felt flattered that a scholar was eager to learn something from them, and a few seemed to appreciate the opportunity to
tell their story in confidence to someone. Others were doing a favor
for a middleman friend. Most who thought they possessed useful information undoubtedly anticipated some form of *quid pro quo* for
their cooperation. They often hoped for an introduction to a prospective employer. The most optimistic, convinced that a visa to the
United States would solve all their problems, aspired to an invitation
to an American university. Some informants, of course, were mainly
interested in earning money to tide them over the difficult period of
transition to a new life.

Whether and how to pay an informant was always a delicate problem. There were serious drawbacks to deciding, as a matter of principle, not to pay compensation. I had to take into account that even
those who earned a respectable livelihood might welcome enhancing
their income, and some people obviously needed money desperately.
Moreover, particularly in view of the informants' indoctrination in
Chinese Communist ideology, any attempt to extract information of
significance without paying for it might be resented as the latest
illustration of the Westerner's habit of exploiting Chinese. Conversely, it was also reasonable to believe that the commercial individualism of the Hong Kong environment might influence the expectations of some. (Fortunately, however, none of my informants
had the temerity of the ex-judge who in 1961 attempted to sell me
four slender volumes of what purported to be his judicial decisions for
a mere U.S. $12,000.) On the other hand, educated Chinese are often
reluctant to become involved in face to face financial dealings.
Furthermore, an offer to pay for information might be resented as

typical Western arrogance and an insult to the informant's status. It might also magnify the risks of the informant's unreliability by making him too willing to say what he might think I want to hear and to hold forth on topics that lie beyond his personal knowledge. Finally, compensating informants presented a problem of expense, and incredible though it seems to some, there are limits to the resources of even foundation-backed American academics. (In view of the widespread suspicion that our government uses foundations as intelligence gathering instruments, it was ironic that my sponsor, the Rockefeller Foundation — faithful to the spirit of its founder, who liked to give away dimes — had actually rejected my request for funds for interviewing.)

I resolved the compensation dilemma in the light of each individual's contribution and situation. I offered no compensation to ten informants. I talked to them from three to ten hours each. Since my usual standard of compensation for informants was H.K. $8 (U.S. $1.40) per hour, had I paid them, none of these persons would have earned a large amount. In view of the fact that all of them were in relatively comfortable economic circumstances and were well-educated, after consulting with Chinese friends or intermediaries I decided that it would be insulting, or at least embarrassing, to offer what to them would have been an insignificant sum. It seemed more appropriate to express my appreciation through social courtesies such as inviting them to lunch, dinner, or tea, sending a modest gift, or trying to get them a better job. However, I did pay seventeen others to whom I talked for similar brief periods, as they were in dire straits and obviously would welcome even a small "honorarium." I interviewed the eleven remaining informants for twelve to one hundred fifty hours per person, seeing five of them for more than eighty hours each. This constituted a considerable imposition upon their time and deserved tangible recognition. Moreover, even for those with decent jobs, the sums involved became significant. Only one of these eleven, whom I called my "tutors," refused to accept compensation on a businesslike basis. After weeks of meeting with me, this lone holdout — a former Shanghai businessman and intellectual — asked me for a large "loan" to ease him over an "emergency situation." We eventually compromised on my "lending" him an amount equal to that which he had earned according to my calculations.

Where to Interview

I met and screened prospective informants in a variety of places. I tried to hold the initial meeting in a "neutral," social setting, often a restaurant. This helped to create a cordial atmosphere for establishing rapport; at the same time it avoided bringing to my office or apartment people whom I might not want to see again. If, however, the person seemed to be sufficiently interesting to warrant another session, I generally arranged an appointment at my office or apartment. Restaurants proved to be an unsatisfactory location for systematic interviewing. If they were crowded, the noise often hindered my hearing. If they were empty, I stood out like a sore thumb. In either event, it was awkward to take notes in public.

In the early months I had no office and saw people at home. This had its drawbacks. Since we lived at Kowloon's border with the New Territories, it was very inconvenient for informants from Victoria island to reach us. Furthermore, the relative opulence of an upper middle class apartment distracted a few of the recent arrivals and may have exaggerated their expectations of compensation. More distracting to me, if not to my informants, were the occasional interventions of my very young children. Also, as we became more aware of local health problems, contacts between certain visitors and the children became a matter of parental apprehension. I especially recall the first home session with a student who had recently arrived from Peking. He was accompanied by his aunt, a Hong Kong resident, who during our conversation coughed repeatedly into a handkerchief. Whenever she coughed, the student would mumble something to her that I could not at first make out. On about the fifth occasion it dawned on me that after each spasm he would say, "Any blood?" At that point I determined to find an office.

Fortunately, the Universities Service Centre, a private organization sponsored by an American foundation named Education and World Affairs, had just established itself in temporary quarters in a downtown hotel. When the Centre, which was created to facilitate the work of visiting scholars, agreed to give me an office, I was delighted. However, hotel interviewing also had certain disadvantages. Again, the connotations of a well-appointed environment were undesirable. In addition, several of my regular visitors worried about being identified by hotel employees who might be Communist agents. Nevertheless, I found the hotel a distinct improvement and subsequently interviewed at home only when an informant refused to come to the hotel. Things further improved when the Centre leased a quiet building for its own quarters.

The problem of finding a suitable place to interview was greater in Macao, which is much smaller and less bustling than Hong Kong. The few non-Portuguese Westerners who live in Macao are well known. Newcomers are conspicuous, especially if they spend their time speaking Chinese to refugees. Moreover, from the center of Macao China is plainly in view just across the water, Chinese gunboats patrol offshore, Chinese Communists are said to control many of the hotels, restaurants, and other businesses, and stories circulate of Communist retaliation in Macao against those who have betrayed their country. In these circumstances, the reluctance of some recent arrivals to be interviewed in a hotel room or restaurant or in the semi-public atmosphere of the backroom of a relief agency was hardly surprising. On two occasions I was able to hold lengthy conversations in a private house, but in other cases I simply muddled through in less satisfactory places.

The Interview Process

Although conditions in Hong Kong were less tense than those in Macao, upon meeting each potential informant I found it very important to assure him that I was a *bona fide* academic and that in using interview material I would protect his anonymity. Despite the fact that the intermediary had usually made similar representations, often informants were understandably skeptical about my identity. If I was a teacher, why wasn't I teaching? Why did I have no affiliation with any of Hong Kong's universities or colleges? Were there really charitable foundations that for disinterested reasons provided funds for research on China? What was the Universities Service Centre? My extremely detailed questioning about legal processes and my demonstrated lack of interest in political, military, and economic data gradually persuaded most people whom I saw at length that I probably was a law professor and not an intelligence agent or a journalist. A few, however, remained dubious, or hopeful, to the end. A former police official whom I interviewed longer than anyone else never did understand why I ignored his repeated offers to discuss the locations of Chinese air bases.

My assurances that I would maintain the informant's anonymity gained credibility from the fact that I did not use an interpreter and generally no one else was present. Before leaving for Hong Kong, when my spoken Mandarin was very shaky, I once experimented with use of an interpreter but found it hard to establish rapport with my informant. I lost control of the conversation as the interpreter and informant chattered away at a speed beyond my comprehension. Moreover, recalling the admonition of Brandeis that responsibility is the developer of men, I decided that the best way to improve my Chinese was to do it myself, however slow the pace. My only other experience with an interpreter came in Macao when I talked with the Nationalist judge who had briefly remained in the Communist judiciary. Although he understood Mandarin, he spoke only Cantonese, and since I understood no Cantonese, I recruited an interpreter. As our Cantonese-English conversation proceeded, even though my interpreter spoke English well, I became increasingly uneasy. A number of the judge's answers seemed confused and inconsistent with his previous statements. I finally decided to go over much of the same ground again, asking questions and receiving answers in Mandarin. This allowed the judge to hear what I wanted to know directly from me and to monitor the interpreter's translation of his answers. It soon developed that the interpreter, being unfamiliar with the subject matter and too confident of his competence, had misconstrued the situation in several respects. At that point I determined to confine myself to Mandarin-speaking informants. In pre-Communist days this might have been a major limitation upon my work. Because the Communists have effectively enforced Mandarin as "the national language," however, the people whom I principally sought — intellectuals and officials — all spoke Mandarin, even though it often was not their native tongue. The accents of people from certain provinces were staggering at first, but with the aid of pencil and paper, after several hours I would become accustomed to the fact that in the case of a man from Fukien, for example, every *fu* meant *hu* and every *hu* meant *fu*.

After trying to assure a potential informant of my scholarly seriousness, I usually asked him to tell me his life history. In all but a few instances the standard response of refugees to whom I was introduced was, "I don't know anything about law." (Fortunately no one went on to say, "But I know what I like.") Hearing their life history gave me an opportunity to make my own determination about the relevance of their knowledge to my concerns. It also enabled me to judge their qualities as observers and reporters and to express an interest in them as human beings, a gesture which would be important to the success of any further meetings I might want to schedule. If, from their life history and their manner in telling it, other meetings seemed promising, I would try to persuade them to cooperate. I emphasized the value of their knowledge, thereby enhancing their self-respect, and indicated, in a fairly general way, my willingness to help them within the modest limits of my capabilities.

At our next meeting I would begin to explore aspects of the informant's experience in systematic and detailed fashion. This required a certain amount of skill and patience. If, as Frankfurter liked to define them, lawyers are experts in relevance, the same cannot be said of all refugees. Some informants, of course, were much less responsive to my inquiries than others. Indeed, during preliminary screening a few answered in such disjointed and bewildering fashion that to interview them seemed futile; especially pathetic were two intellectuals who had studied at Western schools during pre-Communist days, who had undergone thought reform under the Communist regime, and who had found it very difficult to make the further readjustment to Hong Kong life.

To some extent, of course, informants were culturally unprepared for the phenomenon of interviewing, a matter that over-polled Americans can easily forget. Even British businessmen from whom I sought information about legal problems of trade with China often appeared uncomfortable. As one of them put it: "I say, this is rather irregular. You American professors come in off the street and expect us to tell you how we run our affairs. I know your American businessmen put up with this, but we're simply not used to it." The problems were more substantial in interviewing Chinese, who are accustomed to establishing a personal relationship before communicating anything of significance and who, in answering a question, often resort to man-t'an — talking around a subject for a time before gradually coming to the point. The informants who seemed most comfortable and most responsive were former Party members and government personnel, a fact that probably reflects their role as modernizers of Chinese society.

The responsiveness of informants obviously depended to a large extent upon the way in which they were questioned. Experience soon demonstrated that the more successful I was in repressing my inclinations to subject the witness to drumfire questioning, the more likely he was to talk freely. It was essential to create an atmosphere of discussion rather than one of interrogation, especially because the latter had unfortunate connotations for many of my informants. It was also vital to phrase questions in objective language. Having taken pains to assure informants of my objectivity, it would have been absurd to use terms like "Red bandits" to refer to the Communist Party. I tried to speak in the jargon of the mainland, including contemporary idioms and colloquialisms whenever possible. The form in which questions were posed was as important as the language in which they were couched. However obvious the answer appeared, I tried to resist the temptation to use leading questions. I also tried to be on guard against putting questions in ways that would entice an informant to fit the data into my terms rather than his own. I usually asked simple, neutral questions such as, "Have you ever heard of mediation committees?" "What is a comrade's court?" and "How is a public security station organized?" And I found myself saying, almost *ad nauseum*, "Then what happened?"

It was unwise, of course, to attempt to preclude all digressions, for through them one occasionally stumbled onto new information or an explanation not previously perceived. They also provided many fascinating insights into Chinese society. Moreover, every informant had some things that he simply had to get off his chest. After talking for awhile, he usually understood the need to bring the conversation back to the point of departure.

I recorded the substance of every interview in detail by taking copious notes throughout each session. This required me to pause frequently and thus slowed down the pace of the discussion. But the advantages of contemporaneous recording, with an opportunity immediately to clarify matters that seemed murky when put on paper, seemed to outweigh the disadvantages of delay. I had considered other alternatives but had rejected them for reasons of convenience and expense. Having a secretary record the discussion would have destroyed the confidential, informal relationship that I tried to create. Furthermore, my efforts to find an able stenographer-typist who was fluent in Mandarin and English and familiar with Communist jargon, legal terminology, and recent history were unsuccessful, and in any event it would have exceeded my budget to hire a person of such competence. I did not want to have to train a secretary and correct the large number of errors that one could reasonably expect in these circumstances. It would have been even more difficult for a secretary to transcribe interviews from a tape recorder. (I was fresh from the frustrations of having corrected the transcript of my remarks at an American conference that had been conducted exclusively in English; each time I had mentioned the "Hundred Flowers" campaign, for example, it had been taken off the tape as the "hundred dollars" campaign.) In addition, the use of a tape recorder might also have made some of my informants uneasy, or so at least I rationalized my anti-electronic predilections.

After each session I would jot down a list of questions to be pursued at the next session. It was often necessary to review both published materials and other interviews relating to scheduled topics in order to assure comprehensive coverage and to prepare my vocabulary for the session to come. Despite the apparent reasonableness of giving an informant advance notice of the subject of our next meeting, an early experience with a former factory official led me to be wary of this practice. After a few meetings made it clear to both of us that in the near future we would exhaust his relevant knowledge, this informant, who was unemployed and in need, began to show anxiety about the prospect of terminating our relationship. At the end of one session he asked me what our next topic would be, so that he might get his thoughts in order and perhaps prepare one or two organizational charts. Although I at first thought this might be attributable to commendable scholarly conscientiousness, close questioning the following day indicated that my informant did not have personal knowledge of some aspects of the topic and had prepared for the meeting by gathering the experiences of some knowledgeable friends. When I explained that I was only interested in his personal experiences, he replied that he thought he was being helpful by studying the topic for me much as a research assistant might.

Problems of "Bias"

The failure of an informant to distinguish between what he knew from personal experience and what he assimilated from others or supposed to be true was one of the major hazards of interviewing. The ex-factory official's desire to be helpful and to maintain his usefulness was widely shared. Many informants enjoyed the role of playing China expert for a naive foreign scholar, and those who were most prone to overstate their knowledge frequently warned me about the tendency of "the others" to exaggerate.

Not surprisingly, I found that informants varied considerably in memory. Happily for my purposes, one police official had an amazingly retentive mind. Of course, a given individual could accurately recall certain events and be hazy or wrong about others; for example, the Peking University student who had been to reform through labor gave an account of labor camp life that corresponded to that of many other persons, but he insisted, contrary to all published data and other interviews, that the anti-rightist campaign had swept through the university in the fall of 1958 rather than a year earlier. By and large, people who had been in trouble with the law remembered their own cases in detail. Administrators of the legal system, on the other hand, had no difficulty in describing legal processes but could recall relatively few concrete cases without the stimulus of my putting detailed questions or hypothetical situations involving various kinds of legal problems.

Few would-be informants were motivated by bad faith, and as I have indicated earlier, these could be screened out rather easily. Certain informants did, however, display progressive degrees of candor about personal matters such as why and how they left China. Some of the former legal officials were understandably shy about discussing their responsibilities for meting out severe punishments, and it is probable that others put the best face on their own past conduct. It even took several weeks before one man was willing to confide that he was actually Fukienese, not Cantonese, an admission that I managed to receive with equanimity.

Whenever refugee interviewing is discussed, everyone is quick to point out the dangers of informants' hostility toward the regime. Most of my group had left China because of dissatisfaction with Communist rule, and because my research had come to focus on the criminal process, I interviewed many who had suffered some type of informal or formal coercive sanction before their departure. In this situation I obviously had to be aware of the likelihood that selective perception of events and related thought processes would result in biased responses. Other researchers' discussions of interviewing prob-lems had also cautioned me that the need for social acceptance and self-justification led refugees to conform to the anti-Communist ex-pectations of their new environment, that this inevitably produced further distortions in the recollection and articulation of experiences in China, and that the risks of distortion were gravely magnified when the interviewer was an American.

Yet in practice, at least so it seemed to this sociological neophyte, political bias presented relatively little difficulty. A variety of factors may account for this, including the emphasis with which I explained, at the outset of every interview, that I was not engaged in an opinion survey, would not go into political attitudes, and was only interested in detailed, objective information about the operation of the legal system. This did not deter all those who clearly disliked the regime from giving vent to their animus. I had to listen patiently, for ex-ample, to the disillusionment of a former policeman who had twice been disciplined by his superiors. Yet after our "speak bitterness" session ended and he relaxed, I reminded him of my interests, and he proved to be a mine of detailed information on the day to day functioning of the basic level police apparatus. Those who conjure the spectre of political bias invalidating all interviews might consider what biased answers could be given or would go undetected in re-sponse to questions such as: "Can you describe the organization of a public security station?" and "Was anything ever stolen from you or your family? If so, what did you do about it?"

A biased informant could, of course, paint a lurid picture of some aspects of criminal justice, and I had to be cautious in evaluating ac-counts of abuses. I found a number of verifying devices helpful. If intensive questioning at the time the story was related still left me in doubt, I would often arrange to see the informant several weeks or months later and would casually raise the matter again. Or if I had introduced him to another scholar, I would compare my version of the story with that given to my colleague. I occasionally asked an ex-perienced Chinese friend to talk to the informant about the story. I would also evaluate it in the light of other interviews and, without disclosing identifying details, would ask other informants for their reactions to it. Data from documentary sources often provided corroboration of a general, if not specific, nature. The army's secret "Bulletin of Activities" [8] and the captured Fukien Party documents,[9] for example, assured me that recurring refugee accounts of recent abuses in the criminal process were unlikely to be fabrications.

Especially satisfying to me was the vindication that published sources gave to the police official who had a phenomenal memory. Despite the fact that his ability to spout off the substance of organizational charts, secret regulations, and case histories inspired my admiration, I was never wholly confident of his reliability. He was something of a Chinese James Bond. He liked to wear dark glasses, meet in dingy restaurants, and say that he was being urged by the Party to return to the mainland. He made frequent trips to Macao and, during a six-weeks' interruption in interviewing, even claimed to have sneaked into Shanghai as a member of the crew of a Hong Kong ship. Yet despite this penchant for mystery, his information passed repeated tests of its credibility. There was, however, one fascinating account that remained unverified at the time of my departure from Hong Kong. This was his highly detailed report about how in 1958 in his rural area of Fukien province there was actually a secret merger of the police, the procuracy, and the courts. Although I realized that virtually none of my other informants had been in a position to have inside knowledge of rural law enforcement procedures, I felt very uneasy about my inability to obtain any corroboration of what appeared to be an interesting and significant institutional experiment. In checking law review articles and official speeches of the period, I found general statements that the three law enforcement departments "have become one fist, attacking the enemy with even more strength," [10] but this hardly provided satisfactory confirmation. I was troubled because I could not rely on this report without further support. What worried me more, however, especially against the background of the

8. See J. Chester Cheng, *The Politics of the Chinese Red Army* (Stanford: Hoover Institution on War, Revolution and Peace, 1966), pp. 204–205, 281, 502.

9. See *Fan-kung yu-chi-tui t'u-chi fu-chien lien-chiang lu-huo fei-fang wen-chien hui-pien* (Collection of bandit documents seized by anti-Communist commandoes in a surprise attack upon Lien-chiang [County], Fukien [Province]), edited by the Ministry of National Defense, Intelligence Bureau, Republic of China (Taipei, May 1964), pp. 232–234.

10. Chang Wu-yün, "Smash Permanent Rules, Go 1,000 Li in a Single Day," CFYC, no. 5 (1958), pp. 58–61.

informant's eccentricities, was that, if he were unreliable on a matter of such importance, he might be unreliable in many other respects as well. Fortunately, over a year after my return, in an obscure non-legal journal, I found explicit corroboration that such an experiment had taken place in certain areas.[11]

I should emphasize that many informants appeared less biased against the Communist regime than would be expected on the basis of their experience and situation. Ambivalence was a more common attitude than outright hostility. Pride in their nation's accomplishments seemed to mix with resentment and disillusionment. The realities of their Hong Kong existence also may have made them view their unhappiness on the mainland with some perspective. A few told me that they would never have left had they been able to foresee the misery that lay ahead.

Terminating the Interview Relationship

Interviewing, especially in a foreign tongue, is tiring. As Stanley Lubman put it in a recent letter from Hong Kong:

> Uninterrupted interviewing can be most wearing, I find. There comes a moment, sitting in a little room with some fellow for the tenth time, when there is a stark realization that he thinks you may be crazy, if not a spy, and you wonder how you will ever understand anything about him and the forces that shaped him into the person across the desk; at this point, it is wise to retire from interviewing for a while.

Interviewing is also extremely time-consuming. Much as I enjoyed talking with many informants, it became increasingly clear that a year was a very brief period for research in Hong Kong and that I could not afford to spend much time with even the most interesting people once their knowledge of legal affairs had been explored. Yet it was a delicate problem to terminate the interview relationship with people whom I had seen for a length of time. In certain situations, of course, there was no difficulty, because it had been an imposition for the informant to see me. In most cases, however, informants were reluctant to sever our ties. Understandably, those who were being

11. Jen Chen-to and Ho En-t'ao, "How to Establish China's New System of Criminal Litigation," *Chi-lin ta-hsüeh jen-wen k'o-hsüeh hsüeh-po* (Kirin University journal of humanistic sciences), 2 (1959), 121, 123.

paid worried about the impact upon their income. The loss of psychic income seemed more of a factor in some cases. A few of the most sensitive informants had to be assured that my decision to terminate our talks in no way reflected a judgment that they were unreliable. One or two informants felt that we had genuinely become friends and wanted to know whether, having extracted their information, I no longer had any interest in them. Although my interviewing was not concerned with psychological exploration, given the plight of the refugees, it is not surprising that a few whom I saw several hours a day for a number of weeks came to depend upon this opportunity to discuss their problems with a sympathetic outsider.

Some informants had no objection to ending our talks but wanted to know what I would do to assist them in a permanent way. They quite properly feared that once out of sight they would be out of mind. Fortunately, in many cases I was able to meet this request by introducing the informant to a friend on the staff of a local refugee agency, which would support a recent arrival for four months, help him to adjust to Hong Kong by sending him to school to learn a trade or rudimentary English, and find him a low level job. This agency was not available, however, to aid people who had been in Hong Kong for a time or who already had some kind of job. In those cases I tried to provide informants with a direct introduction to a prospective employer. This was not an easy task, because I knew few businessmen, and those whom I did know had little satisfactory work to offer. I was seldom successful in finding better employment for informants, and this inevitably created disappointment and suspicion, especially because many believed that in Hong Kong a Westerner who really wanted to help them could certainly do so. Even former officials, who have been educated to universalistic values, seemed culturally unprepared for an employment market in which the best available man gets the job. After twice trying to explain this principle to a disbelieving former police official who was over-optimistic about being hired by a friend of mine, I finally told him what was also true — that other applicants were sponsored by people who were closer friends of the employer than I. At that point the informant began to take me seriously. In the case of the most valuable informants, such as former Party members or police officials, if they were willing, I was usually able to devise some interim solution to their problem by introducing them to another scholar eager to interview them.

If a number of efforts to aid an informant failed, I usually resorted to the "don't call me, I'll call you" technique. This often worked. But certain people would reappear months after I thought we had parted. One man, whom I had interviewed in October and only once, turned up shortly before the Chinese new year, the traditional time for repaying one's debts. He told me a heartrending tale about how desperately his mother, who was on the mainland, needed money for stomach surgery. Clutching his middle with filial empathy, he pleaded for a loan amid a flood of tears. When I checked this story with his employer, I was told that he had recently been fired for loafing and that he had run up a series of debts to sustain his taste for the fast life of a motorcycle cowboy. Another man whom I had seen briefly would stop by my apartment from time to time in an attempt to persuade me to invite him to the United States. As the number of informants grew and as they became aware that my year was drawing to a close, the pressures upon me became rather oppressive. This problem was the only thing in Hong Kong that I did not regret leaving. I still receive mail from three informants who are determined to get visas to this country.

The Fruits of Interviewing

What, aside from a fund of anecdotes, did all these efforts produce? I think it fair to say that they vindicated the promise that led me to Hong Kong. I had hoped to obtain a clearer understanding of the structure and functioning of China's legal institutions, and interviewing contributed to this goal in a variety of ways.

It often induced skepticism or caution about the existence or vitality of certain highly publicized institutions. Between 1958 and 1964, for instance, there were many articles written about the nationwide significance of adjustment (*t'iao-ch'u*) committees, which were supposed to be a more powerful and improved version of the neighborhood mediation committees that had reportedly been organized throughout China in the mid-'50's. Yet, while all informants knew about mediation committees, few had ever heard of adjustment committees, and those who had gave the impression that in most places they had never become operationally effective.

The function of people's assessors in criminal trials provides another illustration. Chinese law (following Soviet law) prescribes that, except in minor cases, two laymen are to serve as judges together with a single professional judge and that each is to have an equal vote. The regime's propaganda has proclaimed this to be a major vehicle for the participation of the masses in the administration of justice. Yet interviews indicated that assessors rarely played an independent role in criminal trials, even in the period during the mid-1950's when a serious attempt was made to institute a Soviet-style legal system.

Of course, interviewing often confirmed published data. When, for example, informants from various cities unanimously testified to the existence of urban residents' committees, published reports of the nationwide establishment of those mass organizations seemed amply verified. And the fact that virtually the only people who knew about comrades' courts were a few who had worked in large factories in northern China tended to corroborate newspaper accounts of how experiments with this imported Soviet institution had been conducted on a limited basis and only in northern industrial enterprises.

Interviewing was also valuable in tracing the history of certain institutions. Although Chinese publications clearly reveal major shifts in the Party line, they do not always describe the impact of such shifts upon particular institutions. This is especially true with respect to the demise of an institution, which, unlike its birth, often goes unannounced. In 1956–1957, for example, publications afforded extensive evidence of the gradual establishment of offices for legal advice that were staffed by newly-created people's lawyers. However, since the anti-rightist movement of 1957–1958, little mention has been made of these offices. Moreover, although Chinese pronouncements during the anti-rightist movement indicated that the role of lawyers had been circumscribed to some extent, details were lacking. Thus, in the early 1960's it was still possible for a conscientious scholar who confined himself to published Chinese sources to describe the 1956–1957 system of people's lawyers in the present tense. Interviewing, on the other hand, plainly revealed that the offices for legal advice have continued to function only in token form, if at all, and that, except for occasional show trials, lawyers have virtually ceased to function.

Interviewing provided much detailed information about processes whose operation was previously known only in a general way. In recent years Chinese publications have ceaselessly preached the necessity of control by the local Party committee over the police, procuracy, and courts, but until the opportunity to question former police officials presented itself the mechanics of how this control was actually exercised remained opaque. Similarly, documentary sources offered only limited insight into Chinese interrogation techniques, while interviewing brought home the diversity, subtlety, and efficacy of those techniques and the fact that law enforcement officers are carefully trained in their use.

Interviewing contributed a considerable amount of information not only about the components of the administration of justice but also about their interrelationships. For example, published sources suggested that the Chinese employed three major categories of sanctions: criminal sanctions; informal sanctions such as group criticism and struggle; and administrative sanctions including supervised labor (which allows an individual to remain in society but under a strict and stigmatizing regimen) and rehabilitation-through-labor (which isolates him in a labor camp). What remained fuzzy, however, were the criteria for determining in a given case the appropriate category of sanctions and the appropriate sanction within that category. Obviously, Chinese law enforcement officials enjoyed a large degree of discretion. Nevertheless, my informants made it clear that that discretion was not unbounded, and they did much to clarify the factors that influenced its exercise. By way of illustration, several former police officials reported that whether supervised labor or rehabilitation-through-labor was meted out to a "bad element" was ordinarily a matter of administrative convenience determined by factors such as whether he was a family man or a floater and whether the need for his labor was greater locally or at a rehabilitation camp.

Similarly, it was not enough to know that mediation committees continued to operate on the scale described in the press during the mid-'50's. One naturally wanted to know what their relation was to other extrajudicial neighborhood agencies that, according to published sources, also settled disputes and dispensed minor sanctions. Did members of the mediation committee actually play as important a role as leaders of the local residents' committee, security defense committee, or Party or Young Communist League unit, or the neighborhood patrolman and his superiors at the station house? Was there a functional division of labor among these local elite? Although interviewing could not furnish statistical answers to such questions, it did cast a good deal of light upon the interrelations of the local sanctioning agencies. There was, for example, a high degree of consensus among the informants that the patrolman and his station house superiors were the most authoritative persons in city neighborhoods and that altercations of any importance usually gravitated toward them and away from mediation committee members.

Documentary sources also indicated that adultery was a crime, but how vigorously was it prosecuted? Even in totalitarian China, one had to expect that law enforcement resources were not infinite and that priorities had to be accorded to the suppression of certain types of antisocial conduct. Interviewing was helpful on this problem also. As one former police official put it: "Sure, adultery is a crime. But if we had prosecuted everyone who committed adultery we would never have had time to handle the counterrevolutionaries."

Interviewing made more general contributions as well. One of the most important of these was that it heightened my sensitivity to the implications of published data. For foreigners to learn to read even the simplified jargon of Chinese Communism is difficult enough. Yet the more enduring challenge is to remain alert while wading through mountains of repetitious clichés that induce a tedium akin to cruel and unusual punishment. It was all too easy, for example, to overlook the significance of statements such as those that, in better days, the recently purged Lo Jui-ch'ing often made, instructing the police to give absolute obedience to the local Party committee. One could dismiss them as merely a leader's lip-service to the current Party line when discussing his particular area of responsibility. The importance of such statements did not become apparent until interviews revealed that, at least in certain times and places, tensions existed between police officials who, although Party members, strove to do their job as skilled law enforcement experts and professional Party administrators who often intruded into the sanctioning process.

An informant's offhand remark would frequently incapsulate aspects of the relation between the criminal process and Chinese society. Once, when inquiring about the consequences of being convicted of a crime, I asked an ex-bureaucrat what would happen if a convicted counterrevolutionary and his intended spouse applied for a marriage license. He replied: "No one would ever want to marry a counterrevolutionary. People are afraid to have any contact at all with them, even after their release." Others supported this view. And on several occasions I asked a layman-informant why, if it was suspected that someone's home concealed evidence of a crime, the police simply did not break in and search the place. To my surprise, I was told: "Policemen can't do that. They need to get a search warrant." Inasmuch as it is not difficult to obtain a search warrant, such remarks, when taken in isolation, may mislead the uninitiated to exaggerate the degree of privacy enjoyed by Chinese citizens before the advent of the Red Guards. Nevertheless, former public security officers confirmed that in practice the statutory requirement of a search warrant was often taken seriously, and the laymen-informants' perception of the situation suggests that, at least in calmer periods, the apolitical citizen may feel a modicum of personal security vis-à-vis the state, a hypothesis that survey interviewing might some day seek to test.

Finally, in addition to illuminating my research in many ways,[12] interviewing made a very important intangible contribution to one who came to Chinese studies long after the mainland was closed to American scholars — it lent vividness to the subject of this research. Here, instead of stacks of newspapers and magazines, were real people whose lives had only recently been caught up in what to me had previously been a fascinating but abstract academic puzzle. The goal of reconstructing "reality" may well be unattainable. Yet a year in Hong Kong gave me the flavor of events, a feel for the stuff of Chinese life, that enhanced my zest for the quest.

It is a truism to note that in every country the law in action differs from that on the books. The slowly accelerating interest in empirical research in the United States and elsewhere reflects the desire of scholars to deal with a closer approximation of reality than that obtainable from legislation and judicial and administrative decisions alone. One may regard it as an attempt to turn a vice into a virtue, but it does seem that the paucity of such conventional published sources in mainland China may not be entirely disadvantageous to students of contemporary Chinese law, because it gives us an added impetus to experiment with modes of research that seek, in the words of Chairman Mao, to link theory with practice. In view of the difficulties of conducting empirical research on the mainland and in view of the large numbers of Chinese who have left their country

12. For more extensive evidence of the contribution that interviewing can make, see Jerome A. Cohen, *The Criminal Process in the People's Republic of China, 1949–1963: An Introduction* (Cambridge, Mass.: Harvard University Press, 1968), pt. 2.

since the Communist takeover in 1949, it requires little imagination to recognize that the interviewing of Chinese emigrants may offer important research possibilities.

My experience with depth interviewing suggests that, to the extent qualified informants are available, it is an indispensable tool for the understanding of contemporary Chinese legal processes. Several years before I went to Hong Kong to conduct this experiment, a man who had served as a trial judge in mainland China from 1950 to 1954 wrote me:

> For your reference the following are some of my suggestions on the correct study of Communist Chinese law: . . .
>
> Of course, you should collect the legal documents promulgated by the Communist Party as the main source of your research. However, I am convinced that this method will never enable you completely to understand the nature of Chinese Communist law. In addition, it will have a seriously dangerous influence on the thought of your students.
>
> I recall that before the fall of the Chinese mainland young students with curiosity tried to understand the nature of the Communist Party from its documents. As a result, many young people went over to the Communist side. In the early period of the Communist occupation of the mainland, capitalists, former political officials, landlords and many other people of various strata were taken in by the Communist policies and decrees, such as New Democracy, the Common Program, the Land Reform Law, the Counterrevolutionary Act, and so forth. They returned to the mainland from various places where they had sought refuge, only to lose their property and their lives. Even to date, many young overseas Chinese are attracted by the brilliant documents published by the Communist Party. They do not realize that the published document is one thing, and practice is another.
>
> This is especially true for those legal scholars who live under social systems that are different from Communist China's and whose methods of research are entirely different. In free countries the judiciary is independent, and everyone is required strictly to observe the express rules of law. This, however, is not the case in Communist China. When I was receiving my special judicial training, I was repeatedly told that in the execution of law, the interest of the various political movements is imperative. Law is flexible. Any mechanical application of legal provisions will result in the

error of dogmatism. After all, law is an instrument of political class struggle. Therefore, during each political movement secret instructions constantly came down from superiors. These instructions were the criteria on which court decisions were based, and they were by no means open to the public. Thus, in doing your research work, you should never accept at face value the published policies and statutory documents. Instead, you ought to try to understand the essence of Communist law from living examples while studying the statutes and decrees published in each period. If you depart from this, it will not be possible to achieve anything.

There was, of course, the danger that this was written merely in an effort to demonstrate the writer's value to the academic world, and I remained skeptical about whether the benefits of interviewing would outweigh its drawbacks. Today, however, I believe that he was fundamentally correct.

This is not to make light of the serious problems of perception, recollection, and articulation that one confronts when probing the experiences of even the most conscientious informant. The account of my own interviewing plainly reflects a concern with these problems and should lead others to suggest refinements designed to enhance reliability. Nevertheless, despite elaborate precautions, some distortion will undoubtedly creep into the responses of those who seek to recall the past, and neither interviewer nor informant can ever be certain that personal experience has always been separated from second hand knowledge. But we should not judge interviewing by standards higher than those applied to other methods of inquiry. Few members of the scholarly community would maintain that the *People's Daily* presents an unbiased view of Chinese affairs. Nor would it be reasonable to assume that the rare visitor who is permitted to conduct interviews in China receives an unvarnished image. Yet we do not exclude those sources from our research base.[13] Instead, we evaluate them for what they are worth in the light of all other relevant data. As Inkeles and Bauer have written:

> The entire doctrine of social science interviewing and questioning is based on the explicit premise that the response which a person

13. Jan Myrdal, *Report from a Chinese Village* (New York: Pantheon Books, 1965) illustrates both the value and the limitations of interviews conducted in contemporary China. The author's interesting introduction discusses his research methods and some of the problems they raise.

makes to a question *may* be consciously or unconsciously biased by virtue of the relationship of the person answering the question to the situation in which the question is asked. And, in making this assumption, the social scientist is adopting the same attitude toward his source of information that the historian does in evaluating a document, or the economist in his assessment of the statistics he uses. All this is no more than to say that the problems of acquiring information by interviewing emigrés may be somewhat distinctive and acute, but they are continuous with the problems of all interviewing, and in fact with all problems of data gathering and evaluation.[14]

The major question, it seems to me, is not whether refugee interviewing produces distorted data, but whether we can afford to shun such interviewing and to confine our research to the distorted picture of Chinese law that emerges from other sources of information. The principal value of refugee interviewing is that it enhances the dimensions of our image of Chinese justice by presenting a large body of otherwise unavailable data about the experiences of both ordinary citizens and working level administrators. This information and these perspectives do not merely supplement other sources but they also provide an essential corrective to the distortions inherent in those sources. Thus, although refugee interviewing would leave much to be desired as the sole basis of our knowledge, it is an important tool for coping with the "Rashomon" problem — the elusive task of reconstructing reality. It provides further support for the proposition that "fruitful legal research can be conducted in sources which the Uniform System of Citation has yet to recognize." [15]

Unfortunately, those who agree with this view still cannot feel confident about the prospects for legal research on China. The number of new informants appears to be dwindling almost as rapidly as the volume of published sources. The past few years have witnessed nothing comparable to the great influx of refugees that took place in the spring of 1962, and newcomers who have had a professional concern with the legal system have been both few and difficult to locate. Consequently, people who were first interviewed in 1963–1964 have continued to be in demand by scholars who have subse-

14. Inkeles and Bauer, *The Soviet Citizen*, p. 42.
15. David F. Cavers, *Report of the President*, Walter E. Meyer Research Institute of Law, 1964–1966, p. 7.

quently arrived in Hong Kong. This raises the spectre of increasing resort to picked-over professional informants, with all the hazards that that implies for interviewing's reliability and importance. Moreover, the situation has very recently become even less promising. As part of the price of settling its dispute with China, Portugal had to agree to abandon its traditional policy of freely allowing Chinese emigrants to enter Macao, and the fact that refugees have actually been turned back suggests that this agreement was not mere window-dressing.[16] To make matters worse, the new order in Macao appears to preclude interviewing, at least in the immediate future. Because Macao has not been as satisfactory a place for interviewing as Hong Kong, loss of access to it might not be a grievous blow to those of us who study contemporary China. But loss of Macao as a refugee way station on the route to Hong Kong could significantly reduce the existing trickle of informants and make historians of us all.

16. See *New York Times*, February 23, 1967, p. 6.

3 The Use of Survey Interviewing in Research on Communist Chinese Law

Victor Hao Li

The quantity of documentary material on Communist Chinese law, though minute when compared with the huge volume of material on Western law, is, nevertheless, substantial. A number of collections of laws and regulations, several textbooks on civil and criminal law, two legal journals, and innumerable pamphlets and newspaper articles discuss matters ranging from the Constitution to traffic regulations. Yet, to construct from this material a complete and accurate picture of the legal system in China is virtually impossible because the documentary material does not provide information on all aspects of law. Much is published on family law and labor insurance, but torts and common crimes are hardly discussed at all. Other areas are discussed, but not in sufficient detail. For example, we know that various neighborhood bodies are active in settling minor disputes, but we do not know the precise manner in which such work is carried out. Even where the documentary sources are relatively complete and specific, we cannot be certain of their accuracy. Thus, a thorough study of the available documentary material still leaves many gaps in our understanding of law and legal administration in China.

I undertook my interviewing project in Hong Kong in 1965–66 to attempt to fill some of these gaps. I was interested in learning how "civil law" problems are handled in China. The documentary sources made it appear that, at least in the 1950's, the legal profession and institutions such as the courts and mediation committees were extremely active and effective. I wanted to check whether this was in fact so and to find out whether there were other means of handling these problems which were not discussed in the documentary sources. My intention was to interview a large cross section of refugees in Hong Kong and Macao about their experiences of a legal nature and about their knowledge of and attitude toward law. Thus, I hoped to determine the extent and types of legal problems they encountered and the processes by which these problems were resolved.

Other scholars have had considerable success interviewing refugees with expertise on particular matters. I was uncertain, however, whether interviewing the "average" refugee about legal matters would yield any significant results, or even whether I would be able to find more than a handful of people willing to talk with me. In addition, although I had conducted several trial interviews with Chinese refugees now living in New York and had read about sampling and interview techniques, I had no formal training in this method of social research. This lack of experience gave rise to many problems which, were I to conduct another survey in Hong Kong, I would solve differently.

In this article, I will describe the methods used and the problems encountered in my initial attempt to interview on a relatively large scale. I will also discuss several issues related to the validity and limitations of interviewing, and to the feasibility of using systematic surveys as a method for studying China.

Finding Subjects

Finding informative subjects who were willing to be interviewed was difficult. Many refugees were afraid to speak with outsiders about China. Most were unfamiliar with the concept of academic research and thought that anyone studying China must be working for an intelligence agency. Even when they were satisfied that a particular interviewer was not an "agent," they could not be certain that the Communists felt the same way. Rightly or wrongly, many refugees believed that giving information to an American interviewer jeopardized the safety of relatives and friends still in China or even their own safety in Hong Kong. In balancing the meager benefits they derived from being interviewed against the possible troubles they courted, some decided that they would rather not be interviewed.

Still others were willing to be interviewed but could not be used. They knew too little (for example, those who were too young or who seemed to have poor memories) or were inarticulate. Others, especially people from rural areas, were not relevant to my study. I preferred, in this first attempt at large-scale interviewing, to concentrate on urban area legal experiences, since towns and cities are more compact than rural areas and are the center of government activities. Further, at that point in my work, I did not want to get involved in the vagaries of agricultural production problems.

Two other groups were willing but unusable subjects. The first included those who had already been interviewed by other scholars. I was concerned that a few refugees might have been interviewed by many scholars and thus might have a greater impact on Chinese studies than their knowledge warranted. I therefore wanted to limit my survey as much as possible to "new" refugees. In the second group were the over-anxious — those who appeared to have political motives in wanting to be interviewed or who believed there was easy money to be made. These people fabricated stories in order to make themselves appear more knowledgeable, and hence more valuable to the interviewer.

Despite these exceptions, there still remained a large number of refugees who were not adverse to being interviewed and who could be used in the survey sample. The problem, of course, was finding them.

Before I arrived in Hong Kong, I had hoped to be able to set up adequate sampling procedures so that the final correlations would have a more general significance than merely the sum of several hundred interviews. In the early stage, however, careful sample selection was impossible. Finding refugees was so time-consuming a task that I usually had to interview anyone willing to talk to me, as long as he had lived in an urban area for a reasonable length of time and had left China within the last three or four years.

Locating and contacting refugees was both difficult and delicate. The local authorities discouraged large-scale, overt soliciting for subjects such as newspaper advertisements. There were, however, a number of other, more discreet means by which refugees could be found.

The various research organizations in Hong Kong usually had on hand a few "resident refugees" who could be interviewed. Many of these people, however, had already been interviewed by other scholars. While "experienced interviewees" were quite useful in helping me formulate the questionnaire and learn about the problems of interviewing, they were usually involved in other aspects of research on China and, when interviewed, tended not only to relate their personal experiences but also to present "experiences" synthesized from their work.

Some of the welfare and refugee relief organizations were willing to help recruit refugees. I went through the files of these organizations selecting likely candidates for interviews. The organization then sent a note to each person asking him to come to the organization's office, where I would meet him and attempt to set up an interview. Trying to contact these persons directly was impractical; almost none had telephones, and personal visits required too much time. I tried writing letters to some of them, but never received any replies.

I had hoped that the entire sample could be filled in this manner, but unfortunately this method proved to be ineffective. In one typical case I spent a day going through the files of a refugee relief organization and found about forty persons whom I wanted to interview. Letters were sent to each person and appointments were set at ten minute intervals for a day a week later at the office of this organization. Of the forty, sixteen showed up for their appointments. Of these, six refused to be interviewed and one turned out to be too young. Times for interviews were arranged with the other nine, but only three actually kept the appointment. The other six either did not want to refuse when asked, though they had no intention of coming, or had changed their minds after having had time to think about it. In any case, two days of work plus many hours of waiting resulted in only three interviews. After a number of such experiences, I discontinued this method of finding refugees.

During the first six months private contacts, especially reporters for Chinese newspapers, were the best sources of refugees. At every opportunity I would tell people that I was trying to study urban life in China and would like to be put in touch with refugees who had lived in urban areas. About half of the first hundred refugees interviewed were found in this manner. After each interview I also asked the refugee to introduce other refugees to me. He was often willing to do so, since he had already been interviewed and had found it relatively simple and harmless. An additional twenty or thirty refugees were found in this manner.

While a certain number of subjects could be obtained through personal contacts, this method had some serious drawbacks. The supply was uncertain and unsteady. It was also extremely time-consuming to maintain these contacts. Each contact had to be repeatedly phoned or visited and reminded of my continued interest in this matter. This could be handled conveniently when the number of contacts was small, but it became burdensome once the number grew.

About six months after I started work in Hong Kong, I began using a new system for finding refugees. In the course of my interviews, I had found several seemingly intelligent and honest refugees who had many contacts with others. I hired a few such persons on a part-time basis, usually to copy interview records or to help organize an indexing system for my documentary material. Part of their job, however, was to act as "introducers" and keep me supplied with refugees. In addition, two or three other such persons were paid H.K. $3 (about U.S. $.50) for each refugee they brought to be interviewed. I had four principal introducers, two formerly from Canton, and one each from Shanghai and Peking. About 100 of the last 150 refugees were obtained through their introductions, the rest coming from private contacts.

The maintenance of a steady and controlled supply of refugees with a minimum of effort from me was not the only advantage of this new system. The introducer was personally known to the refugee, and thus the refugee would believe to a considerable extent the introducer's assurances that I was reliable, discreet, and not involved in intelligence work. In addition, the introducer would also specify the amount of compensation, and thus the subject would not have any false expectations.

Many problems, however, were inherent in using paid introducers. One was that the introducer might bring in "fake" refugees in order to earn his fee. This was avoided by careful selection of introducers and by constant examination of the results of the interviews. With the type of questions asked, especially those concerning neighborhood organizations, "fake" refugees could usually be recognized without difficulty. Another problem was that the introducer might brief the refugee beforehand so that I would get a "better" interview. To deal with this, I continually stressed to the introducer that I was trying to measure the extent of a refugee's knowledge, and therefore was as interested in what he did not know as in what he did know. Thus, the refugee who knew comparatively little was just as acceptable and useful as one whose knowledge was very extensive.

A more serious problem was that each introducer brought in refugees from his own circle of friends and acquaintances. The refugees introduced by the same person often tended to have similar backgrounds, experiences, and attitudes; the information they gave also tended to be similar, and some patterns which appear might be traced to this fact. I am not sure how to deal with this problem other than to warn the reader that it exists. Perhaps the use of a large number of introducers of vastly different backgrounds would lessen the dangers of this situation.

When I first started work, I had considered conducting a part of my interviews in Macao where refugees were easier to find. Even though the Macao government was less cooperative than the Hong Kong government and the distance between Hong Kong and Macao made it difficult to supervise interviewing projects in both places, I was afraid I would be unable to find enough refugees in Hong Kong alone. Finding the proper assistant to conduct interviews in Macao presented some special difficulties. Many people were unwilling to do this kind of work in the tense political atmosphere there. A Hong Kong research organization employee stationed in Macao was recommended to me, but his political activities made him a distinct liability. I tried using a Macao correspondent for a Hong Kong newspaper, but his habit of submitting an exciting and edited "story" rather than merely recording the refugee's answers to the questionnaire limited his usefulness. Fortunately, at this time the system of paid introducers began to function properly, and it was no longer necessary to work in Macao. Table 3.1 describes the make-up of my sample.

The Questionnaire

In interviewing refugees with extensive knowledge of particular matters, the use of a fixed set of questions was sometimes not advisable. I found that while the interviewer should direct the discussion toward the problems he is studying, the form of the interview should be extremely flexible and tailored to the knowledge and personality of the refugee. Rather than being bound by the preconceived framework of the interviewer, the "specialist" refugee should be encouraged to make use of his expertise and expand on or digress from the prepared topics.

In a survey of people with less specialized knowledge, however, a fixed set of questions was necessary. If a free form of interview rather than a fixed-question form had been used, the study might have

Table 3.1. Refugees Interviewed.

Total	250
Sex	
male	218
female	32
Age	
under 18	7
18–35	194
over 35	38
unknown	11
Class background	
landlord or capitalist	74
small capitalist or professional	60
overseas Chinese	52
rich peasant	9
middle peasant	19
poor peasant	14
unknown	22
Educational level	
primary school	64
junior or senior high school	142
college	27
unknown	17
Party or Young Communist League Members	71

yielded little more than several hundred unrelated life histories. However, by asking each person the same questions, I was able to correlate the data and ascertain patterns of legal experience, knowledge, and attitudes. In addition, I intended to use an assistant to conduct some of the interviews. A fixed set of questions was a means of providing sufficient guidance for the assistant, as well as insuring that all the necessary questions were asked.

Over a period of about two months, a questionnaire was gradually developed. It was tested in about thirty interviews and extensively revised through four drafts. The questionnaire was designed to be as flexible as possible while still maintaining control of the interview. Questions were worded to allow maximum initiative and variation in the responses. If a response raised an interesting point not covered by the questionnaire, this point was pursued to its conclusion. Whenever necessary, a second interview was conducted to explore a particularly interesting matter or to study further a refugee who appeared to be especially knowledgeable in legal affairs. To achieve the greatest degree of effectiveness, and to avoid the possibility of unduly upsetting the local authorities (who seem to tolerate refugee interviewing if it is done quietly and on a modest scale), the questionnaire was orally administered rather than distributed to be filled in by the refugee himself.

The questionnaire consisted of four sections. The first section dealt with the life history and personal background of the refugee. He was asked about his family and education, whether he was ever a member of the Communist Party, Young Communist League, or Young Pioneers, and whether he was ever declared a counterrevolutionary, a rightist, or a bad element. The principal purpose of this section was to obtain a chronological list of all jobs (including positions in neighborhood organizations) held by the refugee. This list was used to "categorize" the person, as well as to provide some check on his knowledgeability and veracity. It was also a source from which refugees with particular kinds of backgrounds and experiences could be located.

The second section of the questionnaire attempted to measure the amount of contact the refugee had had with the formal legal organs and to determine the processes by which these organs handled legal matters. After some preliminary inquiries, the refugee was asked whether he himself had ever been to a particular organ, such as the court. If so, a separate series of questions were asked concerning the substance of the matter that brought him to court and the positions of the various parties. Further questions were asked about the steps taken, privately or officially, to deal with the matter before bringing it to court, the process by which the court handled the case, and the final result of the case, including appeals to other organs. The refugee was also asked whether he knew of others who had gone to court. If he did, this series of questions was put to him again regarding his friend's experience.

The same pattern of questioning was repeated to elicit information about experiences with the reception office of the court, the procuracy, the office for legal advice, the notarial office, and the public security organs.

Section three dealt with the neighborhood-level organizations — the public security station, the street office, the mediation committee, the residents' committee, and the residents' small group. This section examined the organizational structure and the functions of each body and the backgrounds and promotion patterns of the persons who held positions in these bodies. In addition, section three inquired into other means of dealing with legal matters, including letters to newspapers and to other organs not previously mentioned, appeals to the Party or Young Communist League, the use of private mediators, and the use of big-character posters.

Section four focussed on several specific problems in civil law. For example, it asked whether the refugee had ever made a will or inherited property and whether he had ever paid or received compensation for tortious acts. Where any of these had occurred, inquiry was made as to the circumstances. This section also experimented with the use of hypothetical cases. Some hypotheticals were directed at the refugee's knowledge of the substantive legal rules. Thus, one case asked him to divide an estate among certain given heirs; another case tested his familiarity with the payment of labor insurance and other welfare benefits. Other hypotheticals tried to elicit the process by which various disputes were resolved and the attitude of the refugee toward appealing to official bodies for assistance. For example, a dispute between a husband and wife or between two neighbors was described, and the refugee was asked what the disputants would do and how they would solve their difficulties.

Much of the work of devising the questionnaire centered around the proper formulation of the questions. On a superficial level this meant that leading questions, technical terms, and legal jargon had to be avoided, and that "realistic" hypotheticals had to be created. On a more subtle level it involved finding equivalent English and Chinese expressions which had precisely the same meaning. It was very difficult, for example, to find the appropriate Chinese term for the word "dispute," vague even in English. The most common translation for "dispute" is *chiu-fen*. While this was usually satisfactory, many refugees, particularly Cantonese-speaking ones, seemed to require a fairly high degree of conflict before a disagreement would be considered a *chiu-fen*. At least, they seemed to require a higher degree of conflict than I had intended. For example, some refugees did not consider bickering among neighbors or arguments between husband and wife to be *chiu-fen*, even when residents' committee and mediation committee officials had to intervene. In order to include these lesser conflicts, I finally resorted to using the formula "dispute, quarrel, or disagreement" (*chiu-fen, ch'ao-chia huo i-chien pu-t'ung*) or simply "dispute or disagreement."

The reverse situation also occurred. In some cases a Chinese term has developed a gloss to its regular meaning such that the usual English translation no longer conveys the entire meaning. For example, the term *t'iao-chieh* is usually translated "to mediate." It is often understood in China, however, to mean mediation by an official. Thus, if a refugee were asked how a particular dispute was "mediated," he might discuss only the work of various residents' committee and mediation committee members and not mention the efforts of relatives and friends to settle the quarrel. A similar problem arose with respect to the term *ch'u-li*. Instead of merely meaning "to handle," many refugees understood it to mean "handling by someone in an official capacity." Therefore, when such terms were used, great care had to be exercised to assure that both the refugee and I were using them in the same sense.

The Interview

It was apparent from the beginning that I had to employ an assistant to conduct some of the interviews. Each interview lasted about three hours, and another two hours were needed to write up the results. Obviously, I could not handle 250 interviews by myself as well as carry on the necessary documentary research. I was fortunate in finding a very intelligent and capable person to assist me. He was a college graduate who had taught school for several years in Shanghai before leaving China in 1962. His familiarity with conditions in China and his knowledge of the Shanghai dialect proved to be extremely useful in interviewing. In addition, he had previously worked for several other scholars and so had some idea of what scholarly research entailed.

In order to familiarize my assistant with interviewing techniques and to pass on to him what I had already learned about interviewing, we conducted about twenty interviews together. At first I would conduct the interview while my assistant listened and observed; later he conducted the interview and I observed. After each session we discussed any problems that had arisen during the interview. Eventually my assistant conducted interviews independently. I checked the results of each interview and discussed with him any matters which were unclear. In the beginning, I chose at random and reinterviewed about ten percent of the refugees to determine the dependability of my assistant's results. Later the number of spot checks was reduced to about one in twenty. No significant deviations were found between the results of his interviews and mine, although he understandably tended to follow the questionnaire much more closely and did not depart from the set form to pursue what I considered interesting legal issues. In addition to the spot checks, I conducted supplementary interviews whenever a refugee seemed to possess extensive knowledge of law or to have had a particularly interesting experience of a legal nature.

The use of assistants was not always satisfactory. Near the end of my stay in Hong Kong, I hired a second interviewer. The same process of training him through jointly conducted interviews was used. This assistant, however, caused me a great deal of difficulty. Despite close supervision, the results of his interviews showed such a remarkable degree of similarity that I was unsure of their reliability. While this merely may have been a reflection of similarity in the persons interviewed, it may also have been a result of carelessness in the manner of asking questions or a result of the use of leading questions.

A number of books and articles have been written about interviewing techniques.[1] Some describe a kind of mystical rapport that develops between the interviewer and the interviewee, while others attempt to provide scientific formulae for eliciting information. In fact, interviewing is neither mystical nor wholly scientific, and not

1. See, for example, W. Bingham, B. Moore, and J. Gustad, *How to Interview* (New York: Harper, 1959); H. Hyman, *Interviewing in Social Research* (Chicago: University of Chicago Press, 1954); R. L. Kahn and C. Cannell, *The Dynamics of Interviewing: Theory, Technique and Cases* (New York: Wiley, 1957); C. Moser, *Survey Methods in Social Investigation* (London: W. Heinemann, 1958); C. Selltiz, M. Jahoda, M. Deutsch, and S. Cook, *Research Methods in Social Relations*, rev. ed. (New York: Holt, Rinehart and Winston, 1959); and P. Young, *Scientific Social Surveys and Research*, 4th ed. (Englewood Cliffs: Prentice-Hall, 1966). See also, E. Maccoby and N. Maccoby, "The Interview: A Tool in Social Science Research," in G. Lindzey, *Handbook of Social Psychology* (Cambridge, Mass.: Addison-Wesley, 1954).

much can be said to describe or explain it. One must actually conduct an interview in order to know what it is like and what must be done. Essentially one must put the subject at ease and then guide the discussion along the intended lines, making sure that leading questions are avoided. Although a prepared list of questions may be used, sufficient flexibility must be retained to accommodate the different experiences, personalities, and ways of thinking of different informants.

In my survey, where generally a refugee was interviewed only once for a few hours, there was little time or opportunity to develop personal relations with him or to cultivate his friendship and confidence. Nevertheless, a minimum amount of trust was necessary if there was to be a free discussion and exchange. Part of this minimal trust was established through the assurances given by the introducer, paid or otherwise; the rest was gained by clearly explaining to the refugee what my study encompassed and what I wanted him to do. In addition, although most urban refugees spoke Mandarin fairly well, the interviews were conducted whenever possible in the informant's native dialect. Not only was he more comfortable speaking his own dialect, but he could also be made to feel a closer relationship with the interviewer. If a refugee was from an area such as Shanghai, whose dialect I cannot speak, the interview was conducted by my assistant.

In the actual process of interviewing, the refugee came to my office, either alone or with his introducer. After the preliminary amenities, I explained that I was a student from the United States who was trying to learn about life and conditions in China. The refugee, having lived in China for many years, undoubtedly had many experiences and insights which could add to my understanding. I stressed the fact that my work had no political ties or overtones of any kind, and that the results of my study would only be used to write a thesis for which I would receive a degree from Harvard University, a name known to many of the refugees. On the whole, the refugees accepted this explanation quite readily. The idea that they were helping a student, especially a student of Chinese descent, seemed to be their most common justification for allowing themselves to be interviewed by me. Most refugees made some nominal protests about their ignorance of legal matters, but once that was done, they spoke quite freely and often at considerable length.

Several other important steps were taken to gain the confidence and cooperation of the refugee and to allay his doubts. Unless the refugee offered to tell me his full name, I usually asked only for his surname. I explained that no names were used, but instead a number was assigned to each person interviewed. Whenever I could find the refugee again through the introducer, I did not ask for his address. Thus, I tried to make the refugee feel as secure as possible; he could not be traced either through my records or through the results of the interview. In addition, I showed him the questionnaire and told him these were the only questions he would be asked, and that he could decline to answer any question at any time. A look through the questionnaire verified for him, often to his surprise, that the questions actually were of a commonplace and non-political nature. At the same time, I stressed to the refugee that I was trying not only to find answers to these questions but also to measure how much people living in China do *not* know. Hence I did not expect him to be able to answer all of the questions and an "I do not know" answer was just as useful to me as an elaborate one. Through this explanation I hoped to reduce the tendency of many refugees to embellish their experiences by means of extrapolations or outright fabrications.

The questionnaire was designed to be administered in about two and a half to three hours. I found that if the session lasted much longer than that, both the interviewer and the refugee would begin to tire and the quality of the data obtained would decline. I paid the refugee H.K. $15 (about U.S. $2.70) for each session. Where a session was particularly lengthy or where the refugee possessed specialized knowledge, I sometimes paid H.K. $20. Every effort was made to prevent the refugee from being embarrassed by the payment and from feeling that he had "sold" information. The continued goodwill and cooperation of persons I had interviewed was essential to my being able to find more persons to interview. If a refugee went away feeling unhappy or that he had lost face, he would not ask his friends to come to see me, and he might even urge them to avoid being interviewed by me. Payment was usually made by slipping an envelope into the refugee's hand as I thanked him for his help at the conclusion of the session. Some quietly put the envelope into their pockets; most made a nominal protest but kept the money quite willingly after I explained that it was merely "carfare money" plus a slight compensation for their time. In cases where I thought the refugee would not accept money, a gift-wrapped Parker pen of equivalent value was presented.

Often the refugee hoped that I could help him find a job in addition to giving him monetary compensation. When a refugee had been especially helpful, I made every effort to secure suitable employment for him. In other cases, I introduced the refugees to several construction companies to work as manual laborers. Some of the refugees did not want menial work. They were not unemployed but merely looking for better employment, and manual labor is the lowest in terms of pay and status. By refusing to take the job that I suggested, however, they could not ask me to find another.

Interviewing as a Tool for Research

The use of interviews, surveys, and polls as research tools is quite common and widely accepted in most fields of social science. Nevertheless, there is some resistance to the acceptance of refugee interviewing as a valid and useful method of studying China. One principal objection is that the average refugee knows so little. After all, it is said, what can be learned from asking a refugee who was formerly a street cleaner about the intricacies of the five-year plan or the nuances of a particular political campaign?

This objection is not an incorrect one — it merely misses the point. It is indisputable that refugee interviewing has definite limitations, and that it cannot fill in all the gaps in our knowledge about China. Refugees cannot provide information on many matters, and can speak meaningfully only about their own attitudes, experiences, or professions. Only a most unusual refugee can shed light on areas such as the nuclear capability of China. Refugee interviewing is limited also by what a refugee is willing to discuss. Many refugees will not talk about political or military matters, or personal matters particularly sensitive to them. In addition, what they will discuss may be vague or fragmentary; these fragments must then be constructed into a coherent picture, a process that is often not possible.

Yet every man is an "expert" on some matters. By having lived in China for many years, most refugees necessarily know a great deal about China, although this knowledge may be limited to certain areas. While the man in the street cannot discuss the five-year plan, he may be able to describe in detail the livelihood of the urban poor.

On a more concrete plane, perhaps a simple test for judging the usefulness of refugee interviewing is to ask whether the information and insights I derived from my interviews significantly altered views formed from studying documentary sources. If so, then clearly the use of refugee interviewing should be accepted and encouraged. This paper is not an appropriate place to discuss the substantive findings of my work; nevertheless, I shall describe in very general terms three examples which illustrate how data from interviews can supplement or modify impressions gained from reading documentary sources. In each case, without the interview data our picture of China would have been quite different and perhaps incorrect.

First, interviews provided a different view of the function and influence of the reception office of the court. Only a few newspaper articles discuss the work of this office, and not much emphasis is placed on its importance. By comparison, many more articles are written about lawyers and the office for legal advice or about the relatively inactive notarial office. In general, the reception office is described as a subdivision of the court where one can submit complaints or make inquiries about legal matters. The cadres in this office also mediate minor disputes and help the masses write legal documents. In addition, many judges have scheduled times when they "receive the masses" at the reception office and discuss legal problems.

According to the refugees, however, the reception office plays a major role in the administration of judicial affairs. The neighborhood organs are useful for minor matters and the court for serious criminal cases, but when other problems of a legal nature arise, the reception office is often the place where these problems are resolved. A number of persons interviewed had brought disputes to the reception office to be settled. This was done not as a prelude to bringing suit, but in order to find a mediator with more official standing than the local mediation committee member. Others went to the reception office for legal advice. In one case, a woman was thinking of bringing suit on a complex property dispute and wanted to know whether she had good cause of action. The reception office thought she did, and a complaint was filed. When asked why she did not go to a lawyer for advice, she replied that the reception office, unlike a lawyer, could give an authoritative answer. In another case, a man felt that the labor reform sentence imposed on his brother was too severe and wanted to file an appeal. After considering the matter for a few days, the reception office cadre said that in his opinion, the sentence was not so severe that a reduction on appeal was likely. The man then dropped the matter.

Second, the interviews revealed that the refugees tended to belittle the work of the mediation committees. Scores of articles have been written about the effectiveness of these committees and the enormous number of cases they handle. Although refugees recounted many instances where the mediation committee or a mediation committee member did resolve disputes, most refugees claimed that the mediation committees were quite ineffective. Virtually all the members of these committees were housewives, often the neighborhood busy-bodies who poked their noses into everyone's affairs. Whenever a dispute arose, they would rush in and scold both sides, but they had neither the stature nor the ability to assist in the actual settlement of the dispute. Where the parties could not resolve their differences by themselves and outside help was needed, it was very often the local patrolman or a cadre from the street office[2] who acted as mediator, rather than the mediation committee member. The published statistics reflect impressive achievements because, as one former mediation committee member explained, every dispute at which a mediation committee member was present was recorded as a "case handled," regardless of the pettiness of the matter or the insignificance of the role played by the committee member. Moreover, a case was regarded as "successfully handled" so long as the disputants were peacefully parted, even though no real solution of the underlying disagreement was achieved.

Third, interviews can also be used to probe problems not discussed in the documentary sources. For example, by studying the documentary sources alone one may not become aware of the strong tendency of people in China to suppress incipient disputes. Most people do not want their affairs to become a public spectacle. Likewise, they do not want to give the officials the impression that they tend to get involved in disputes and hence are troublemakers. This attitude was brought out especially clearly in the hypothetical cases posed in the questionnaire. When asked what the disputants, par-

2. A government organ one level above the residents' committee. The street office handles such matters as distribution of ration coupons, neighborhood welfare work, and health and sanitation work, as well as some mediation of minor disputes.

ticularly the aggrieved party, would do, the refugees very often replied, "*suan-le*" (forget it).

Despite the usefulness of refugee interviewing as a means of gathering information about China, it must be recognized that there are
many methodological problems associated with it. Biases in the response and in the sample introduce distortions in the data obtained.
By analyzing the biases in terms of what conclusions are drawn from
the data, however, it becomes apparent that these problems can often
be surmounted.

It is often claimed that information obtained from interviews is
not reliable. This is sometimes described by the cliché that refugees,
especially ones who are paid for the interview, are trying to please
the interviewer and thus tell the interviewer what he wants to hear.
This description is most unfortunate. In the first place, it is not true.
Except for some very obvious matters and for situations in which the
interviewer has been very heavy-handed in his questioning, the refugee does not know what the interviewer wants to hear. How does the
refugee know the "right" answer to questions such as, "Which members of your residents' committee held outside employment in addition to their residents' committee positions?" In the second place,
there are many reasons for doubting what a refugee says. Thus, a
refugee may have a poor memory, may exaggerate or lie, or may be
terribly biased against the regime. To subsume all these reasons
under a single concept merely confuses the issue. Each should be
examined separately, and perhaps with clearer analysis the problem
of reliability may not be as serious as it might at first appear.

Bad memory is not a serious problem as far as reliability is concerned. Through careful and patient questioning, the interviewer
can often refresh the recollection of the refugee. Even when this
cannot be done, the result is that the refugee says nothing, rather
than that he gives incorrect information. Nor is outright and intentional lying a great difficulty. Unless the interviewer knows very
little about his subject, lies and fabrications can usually be spotted.
This is especially true when several hundred people are asked the
same question. An answer which does not follow the usual pattern
is quickly evident, and one is put on notice to probe further. In addition, it is very hard to lie about some matters. For example, a
refugee might successfully claim his class background is middle
peasant when in fact it is landlord, but it is difficult for him to say

that he has been party to a court case and be able to give the necessary details when in fact he has never been to court. By controlling the type and the form of the questions asked, the opportunities for lying can be reduced.

Many refugees claim, consciously or unconsciously, to know more or to have had more experiences than is in fact true. Often they do this not only for the purpose of being paid more or being interviewed again, but also to gain the respect of the interviewer by appearing more knowledgeable as well as to enhance the subjects' own feelings of importance. This problem is difficult to handle, because the alterations are usually subtle and have some basis in fact. The refugee may have adopted someone else's experiences as his own or may have synthesized "experiences" from what he has read and observed. Giving the refugee a chance to relate both his own experiences and the interesting experiences of others helps to reduce the frequency of this problem. Moreover, careful questioning on the details may reveal whether or not a particular matter was a genuine personal experience.

Occasionally a refugee will change some of the facts to give the interviewer a picture that is "more correct." For example, if residents' committee members are known to be usually women but the ones in a particular refugee's residents' committee are mostly men, he might say that the members are mostly women in order not to convey the "wrong idea." The frequency of such alterations can be minimized by emphasizing to the refugee that his own experiences are the focus of the interview, although he may state where his experiences differ from the norm.

A related problem is that with the passage of time and the change of circumstances, the refugee may have reinterpreted past events. This is especially troublesome where case histories are sought. In every dispute the refugee always describes himself as being in the right and his opponent as being unreasonable and obstinate. If the refugee had lost the dispute, then the mediator or judge clearly had acted in an unfair manner. The telling of one-sided stories is not, of course, unique to refugees talking about China. Most people in relating their personal experiences tend to place themselves in the best possible light, even when this may require shading the facts. By retaining a skeptical yet sympathetic attitude, the interviewer usually can obtain a fairly reliable account of the case.

The problem of antiregime bias is harder to deal with. In most cases a refugee would not have left China unless he was discontented with life there. The dark side of conditions in China may be all he has seen or what he remembers most vividly. In addition, some refugees feel a need to rationalize their leaving China for Hong Kong and thus tend to exaggerate the bad things they experienced.

Bias affects certain matters more than others. It tends to distort statements which involve value judgments and opinions, while having less effect on statements of a purely descriptive or "factual" nature. What, for example, is a "biased" answer to the question "How many persons were elected to your residents' committee, and what were the duties of each?" By phrasing questions in such a way that the refugee must give simple factual replies instead of stating conclusions, the danger of bias can be reduced. Even where attitudes and value judgments are involved, not all results are rendered unusable by this antiregime bias. For example, many of the refugees were members of the "five (or four) elements." One would expect, therefore, that they would have been less inclined to seek assistance from an official or to invoke the official apparatus than the "average" person. Thus when these refugees state that they would ask a residents' committee or street office member rather than a private person to act as mediator for their disputes, one can properly infer that this reflects the general pattern of behavior.

It is impossible to eliminate all inaccuracies and biases from what a refugee says. Indeed, given the great number of factors that enter into perceiving, understanding, remembering, and relating an event, it is questionable whether there is such a thing as "reality" and whether there can be a "true answer" which reflects this "reality." These problems should not, however, invalidate all data obtained through interviews. The same problems arise when using documentary sources. In fact, the process of evaluating the reliability of statements is not unique to refugee interviewing or to Chinese studies. In all dealings, mundane as well as scholarly, matters affected by inaccuracy and bias must be evaluated. In each case, on the basis of one's knowledge and understanding, an informed judgment is made as to what is reliable and useful and what is not, and then the matter is accepted for what it is worth.

One general suggestion can be made which may improve the reliability of interview data obtained from Chinese refugees. Where feasible, subjects should be selected from the same city or *hsien*. This enables the researcher to concentrate his energies and thus collect more information about a particular place. This extra data provides valuable crosschecks whenever several refugees are familiar with the same matter. The problem of local variation is eliminated for each individual study.

Closely related to the problem of bias in the response is the problem of bias in the sample. While the former involves the reliability of an individual refugee's statements, the latter involves the validity of extrapolating generalizations from the statements of many refugees. As with response bias, the manner in which sample bias affects the data must be analyzed in terms of the particular conclusions one is trying to draw from the data.

For most purposes, refugee samples obtainable in Hong Kong are not representative of the parent population of China.[3] (After more work in this area, however, it might turn out that the refugee population in Hong Kong is more representative of the Chinese population, or at least of the Kwangtung population, than is usually believed.) Many aspects of the background of a refugee distinguish him from the "typical" Chinese. At the same time, however, there are areas of a refugee's experience and knowledge which are not affected by his refugee status and are not different from the experience and knowledge of a "typical" Chinese. This is especially true for matters of a "factual" nature such as descriptions of the organizational structures of various bodies or the chronologies of particular events. In these limited areas, it is possible to obtain a sample which fairly closely approximates the parent population, or at least the parent population of specific localities. Thus, for example, to learn about the size of the cloth ration, one can interview a large number of refugees and then select from this number a satisfactory sample based on such objective characteristics as geographical distribution and type of employment.

In the many cases where representative samples cannot be found, data from survey interviews is still extremely useful. After all, the object of such interviewing need not be the obtaining of statistics

3. The Hong Kong refugee population contains too many southerners, too many persons with overseas Chinese connections, and too many persons disgruntled with the Chinese regime. It may also contain an extraordinary number of persons with get-up-and-go, since an unusual amount of gumption seems to be required for a person to abandon everything and take off for Hong Kong.

which are mathematically valid within a certain percentage of error. It can be equally fruitful to combine information and insights derived from interviews with one's own knowledge and construct models which attempt to depict accurately various aspects of Chinese society. This can be done in a number of ways. Case histories can be gathered. While these cannot be converted into statistics, they are concrete examples of how various Chinese institutions operated in fact and of what specific rules were applied. In addition, responses to questions can be examined, and patterns can be identified. As with case histories, these patterns can be the bases of predictions on how Chinese society in fact functions. Comparisons can be made of subgroups within the sample which have counterparts within Chinese society. Thus one might compare the amount and the kind of dealings with judicial and neighborhood organs that persons with "good" class backgrounds have as opposed to persons with "bad" class backgrounds, or compare the types of legal problems that arise in urban areas and in rural areas.

My study may not be a "survey" in the Gallup poll sense — it may be more accurately described as large-scale individual interviewing. Regardless of terminology, the application of concepts and techniques used in sociological and psychological research can greatly increase our knowledge of China by adding the experiences and minds of the refugees to our list of available sources of information about China.

4 The Development of Chinese International Law Terms and the Problem of Their Translation into English

Hungdah Chiu

In 1951, the Chinese delegate to the United Nations proposed [1] to the General Assembly that the Chinese text of the Genocide Convention [2] be revised. The reason for revision, as stated in the Chinese proposal, was that there existed a number of discrepancies between the Chinese text originally prepared by the United Nations Secretariat and the other official texts. The Chinese delegate included in his proposal a new Chinese text for consideration by the General Assembly. [3] Of the proposed changes the most important one related to the Chinese translation of the term "genocide." [4] The term had originally been translated by the Secretariat as *wei-hai chung-tsu* (lit., "to cause harm or to destroy *racial* groups"), while the new Chinese text translated the term as *ts'an-hai jen-ch'ün* (lit., "to cause harm to or to destroy *human* groups *in a ruthless manner*"). The new translation is closer to the meaning of the term "genocide" which, as defined in Article 2 of the Convention, encompasses any act "committed with intent to destroy, in whole or in part, a national, ethnical, racial or religious group." The Chinese proposal was adopted by the General Assembly on December 21, 1952, by Resolution 691 (VII).

More recently, an item in the *New York Times* [5] revealed that the delay in the signing of the Space Treaty [6] adopted by the United Nations General Assembly was due to difficulties encountered in

Note: Reprinted from *Journal of Asian Studies*, 27, no. 3 (May 1968), 485–497. Abbreviations used in this chapter will be found on page 157.
1. See U.N. Doc. A/1880 (1951).
2. Adopted by the General Assembly Resolution 260 (III), December 9, 1949.
3. See U.N. Doc. A/2221 (1952).
4. For a comparison of the new Chinese text and the Chinese text prepared by the Secretariat, see *ibid.*
5. *New York Times*, January 15, 1967.
6. Treaty of Principles Governing the Activities of States in the Exploration and Use of Outer Space, including the Moon and Other Celestial Bodies, adopted on December 19, 1966, by General Assembly Resolution 2222 (XXI).

preparing the Chinese text. It was said that Chinese translators had difficulty in translating into Chinese terms such as "the province of mankind" and "celestial body." [7]

These two incidents make it evident that there are real problems in translating international law terms into Chinese — problems which Chinese scholars have faced since the middle of the nineteenth century. Not so evident, however, are the problems which have only lately begun to trouble scholars engaged in translating Chinese international law terms into English. The purpose of this paper is to examine these problems.

The Origin of Chinese International Law Terms

The first book of Western international law introduced to China was Wheaton's *Elements of International Law*, translated into Chinese by W. A. P. Martin and his Chinese associates and published in 1864.[8] The terms used in Martin's translation can generally be classified into two categories: (1) terms borrowed from traditional Chinese sources such as codes, regulations, and historical material, and (2) terms devised by Martin and his associates.

Martin's translation contains a few terms derived from traditional Chinese law. For example, the term *lü-li* (lit., "laws and regulations") is used to translate the English term "law";[9] and the term *li* (lit., "practice" or "precedent") is used to translate the English term "usage." [10]

More numerous, however, are terms derived from other traditional Chinese sources. The term *kuo-shu* which traditionally referred to a

7. The Chinese translations later adopted by the United Nations of these two terms are *t'ien-t'i* (celestial body) and *jen-lei ch'üan-t'i chih shih* (the province of mankind).

8. For the history of the introduction of international law to China, see generally, Immanuel Hsü, *China's Entrance into the Family of Nations: The Diplomatic Phase, 1858–1880* (Cambridge, Mass.: Harvard University Press, 1960), pp. 121–31. See also W. A. P. Martin, *Cycle of Cathay* (New York: Revell, 1896), p. 221; George G. Wilson, "Henry Wheaton and International Law," in Henry Wheaton, *Elements of International Law*, Text of 1866 with notes (Carnegie Endowment for International Peace: Classics of International Law) (New York: Oxford University Press, 1936), pp. 13a, 16a; Tyler Dennett, *Americans in Eastern Asia* (New York: Macmillan, 1922), pp. 385, 559–561.

9. Martin's Chinese preface. It was stated in the preface that international law "is like the laws and regulations of the various states, hence it is also called *wan-kuo lü-li.*"

10. Martin, 1:4; Wheaton, p. 8.

note sent by one state to another, presumably of equal status,[11] is one example. Martin used this term in translating the term "letter of recall" (a letter the head of one state sends to the head of another when recalling his envoy from the latter state) as *chao-hui kuo-shu*.[12] Since a "letter of recall," like the traditional *kuo-shu*, is in fact a note sent between states of equal status, Martin's term is particularly appropriate.[13] Other examples of terms which owe their origin to traditional Chinese sources are: "pirate" (*hai-tao*),[14] "treaty" (*yüeh* or *meng-yüeh*),[15] "peace treaty" (*ho-yüeh*),[16] and so forth.

There were, to be sure, some traditional Chinese terms, currently used in translating Western international law terms, which Martin did not use. *Chung-li* (lit., "occupying a middle position"), for example, was in common use as early as the period of the Warring Kingdom (475–221 B.C.)[17] and is at present the accepted translation of the term "neutrality." Martin translated this term as *chü-wai*,[18] which literally means "outside the area [of conflict]." "Ambassador" is now translated as *ta-shih*, a term which can be traced back at least to the Northern Sung dynasty (A.D. 960–1127),[19] whereas Martin translated it as *ti-i-teng ch'in-ch'ai* (lit., "imperial envoy of the first

11. See Hsü Shih-tseng, *Wen-t'i ming-pien* (A style of writing), 1580, 21:38. Some letters or messages between the states of Sung and Liao (eleventh-twelfth century) were in the style between equals. Several examples given in *ibid.*, pp. 47–49.

12. Wheaton, p. 315; Martin, 4:13. The Chinese term *chao-hui* is a literal translation of the English term "recall."

13. This translation is in part retained today. The current Chinese (Nationalist and Communist) translation of "letter of recall" is *tz'u-jen kuo-shu*, which literally means "letter of resignation." Kozhevnikov (C), p. 310; Ts'ui Shu-ch'in, *Kuo-chi fa* (International law), Shanghai, Shang-wu yin-shu kuan, 1947, 1:174–75.

14. Martin, 2:49; Wheaton, p. 184. For examples of the use of the term *hai-tao* in Chinese historical materials, see *Dai kanwa jiten* (Great Chinese-Japanese dictionary), 6:1170.

15. Wheaton, p. 317; Martin, 3:14. For examples of the use of the term *yüeh* or *mien* in ancient China, see Ch'en Ku-yüan, *Chung-kuo kuo-chi fa su yüan* (The origin of Chinese international law), Shanghai, Shang-wu yin-shu kuan, 1934, pp. 221–22. In one section of his work, Martin also translated the term "treaty" as *t'iao-yüeh* which is currently the accepted translation of that term. Wheaton, p. 332; Martin, 4:19.

16. Wheaton, p. 610; Martin, 4:69. For examples of the use of the term *ho-yüeh* in Chinese historical materials, see *Dai kanwa jiten*, 2:981.

17. *Chan-kuo ts'e* (Strategies of the warring states), Shanghai, Shang-wu yin-shu kuan, 1935, 7:75. See also *Dai kanwa jiten*, 1:314.

18. Wheaton, p. 480; Martin, 4:38.

19. During the eleventh and twelfth centuries the relationship between the states of Sung and Liao was one between equals. The head of the envoy sent by Sung to Liao during that period was commonly referred to as *ta-shih*. See Nieh Tsung-chi, "Envoys between Sung and Liao," *Yen-ching hsüeh-pao*, 27 (June 1940), 6.

class").[20] "Self-defense" is now translated as *tzu-wei*, which can be traced back at least in the period of Three Kingdoms (A.D. 220–280),[21] whereas Martin translated it as *tzu-hu*.[22] The term "ratification" was translated by Martin as *chun* or *chun-hsing*[23] despite the fact that twenty-two years earlier it had already been translated into Chinese as *p'i-chun*, which is the translation currently in use.[24]

Traditional Chinese sources, however, could only provide a small number of terms for Martin's translation, and as a result many new terms had to be devised. The following are examples of terms devised by Martin:

English	*Chinese Romanization*
sovereignty	*chu-ch'üan*[25]
mediation	*chung-pao*[26]
reprisal	*ch'iang-ch'ang*[27]
contraband	*chin-wu*[28]
blockade	*feng-kang*[29]
negotiation	*shang-i*[30]
privilege	*ch'üan-li*[31]

20. Wheaton, p. 278; Martin, 4:3.
21. See *Dai kanwa jiten*, 9:414.
22. Wheaton, p. 86; Martin, 2:1. Martin also translated the term "self-preservation" as *tzu-hu*, but in Wheaton's treatise, self-preservation is a much broader concept than "self-defense." *Cf.* the following passages quoted from Wheaton: "Of the *absolute* international rights of states, one of the most essential and important, and that which lies at the foundation of all the rest, is the right of self-preservation . . . This right necessarily involves all other incidental rights, which are essential as means to give effect to the principal end. Among these is the right of self-defense" (Wheaton, pp. 85–86).
23. Wheaton, pp. 322, 328; Martin, 3:16.
24. Article 8 of the 1842 Treaty of Nanking and its Chinese text. Imperial and Maritime Customs, *Treaties, Conventions, Etc., between China and Foreign States* (Shanghai: Statistical Department of the Inspectorate General of Customs, 1908), 1:164.
25. Wheaton, p. 29; Martin, 1:17.
26. Wheaton, p. 355; Martin, 3:26. In one section of Martin's translation, he translated the term "good offices or mediation" as *t'iao-ch'u*, Wheaton, p. 106; Martin, 2:12. The current translation of "mediation" is *t'iao-t'ing*, "good offices" is *wo-hsüan*.
27. Wheaton, p. 363; Martin, 4:2.
28. Wheaton, p. 535; Martin, 4:52.
29. Wheaton, p. 575; Martin, 4:55.
30. Wheaton, p. 317; Martin, 3:14.
31. Wheaton, p. 283; Martin, 3:6.

Not all of Martin's terms were accurate; some, in fact, were quite misleading. For instance, he translated "real property" as *chih-wu*,[32] which actually means "trees, flowers and other plants"; and he translated "personal property" as *tung-wu*,[33] which means "animals."

It should be noted that some of Martin's translations of English terms were in the form of explanations rather than equivalents. Thus, the term "intervention" or "interference" was translated as "*yü-wen t'o-kuo cheng-shih*,"[34] which literally means "inquiring about the political affairs of other states."

There were, however, some terms which Martin was unable to translate into Chinese even in the form of explanations. The term "subject" (now translated as *chu-t'i*) is one example. In a passage on subjects of international law, Wheaton wrote: "§1. Subject of international law. The peculiar subjects of international law are Nations, and those political societies of men called States." [35] The corresponding passage in the Chinese version translated by Martin, if literally retranslated into English, would read: "§1. [No translation of the section title] Men in groups establish states and there are affairs in the intercourse among states or nations; this is the concern of the public law." [36]

Several years after Martin finished his translation of Wheaton's work, he translated several other books on international law into Chinese.[37] Many of the Chinese terms used in the later translations were the same as those used in the translation of Wheaton's treatise, though some improvements were made.[38] In addition, Franzer's Chinese translation of Phillimore's *Commentaries upon Interna-*

32. Wheaton, p. 112; Martin, 2:17. Martin explains the term *chih-wu* as including houses, land, and other immovables, not just trees. Martin, *ibid.*
33. Wheaton, p. 112; Martin, 2:17.
34. Wheaton, p. 87; Martin, 2:2.
35. Wheaton, p. 27.
36. Martin, 2:16. The Chinese text is as follows: "*Ti-i chieh. Jen ch'eng-ch'un erh li-kuo, erh pang-kuo chiao-chi yu shih, tz'u kung-fa chih so-lun yeh.*"
37. *Hsing-chao chih-ch'ang* (Charles de Marten, *La Guide diplomatique*), 4 vols. (n.p., 1876); *Kung-fa pien-lan* (Theodore D. Woolsey, *Introduction to the Study of International Law*), 6 vols. (Peking: T'ung wen kuan, 1877); *Kung-fa hui-t'ung* (Johann Kaspar Bluntshcli, *Le Droit international codifié*), 10 vols. (Peking: Pei-yang shu-chü, 1898); *Lu-ti chan-li hsin hsüan* (Les Lois de la guerre sur terre: Manuel publié par l'Institut de droit international), Shanghai, 1883.
38. E.g., "interference" or "intervention" was translated *kan-yü. Kung-fa pien-lan,* 1:10; Theodore D. Woolsey, *Introduction to the Study of International Law*, 3rd ed. (New York: Charles Scribner, 1871), p. 58.

tional Law (2nd edition, 1871)[39] also retained many of Martin's terms and at the same time improved upon some of them.[40]

In the nineteenth century, the major difficulty in translating international law terms into Chinese was the lack of a competent bilingual translator with sufficient knowledge of international law. Martin's proficiency in Chinese was inadequate and his Chinese associates had practically no knowledge of international law. Under such circumstances, it is hardly surprising that many of the Chinese international law terms which they devised proved to be unsatisfactory. These terms were replaced in the early twentieth century by more satisfactory terms which had been devised by Japanese international law scholars.

The Influence of Japan

The first book on international law which the Japanese acquired was Martin's Chinese translation of Wheaton's work, which was introduced to Japan in 1866.[41] As early as 1862, however, Japan had begun to send students to study international law in Europe.[42] (China, in comparison, did not begin to send students abroad until 1872.) As a result, Japan soon had some scholars who were proficient in Western languages and who also possessed a basic understanding of the concepts and terminology of international law. Naturally, these scholars were in a better position than persons like Martin to translate international law terms into Japanese, and by the early twentieth century, a number of international law books had already been published in Japan. In 1902 the Japanese Association of International Law was established and in the same year began to publish *Kokusaihō zasshi* (Revue de droit international).[43]

During the early decades of the twentieth century, the Chinese,

39. *Ko-kuo chiao-she kung-fa lun*, 16 vols. (Shanghai: Hsiao ts'ang shan-fan, 1896).

40. E.g., the term "prescription" was translated by Martin as *lao-ku*, but Franzer translated it as *nien-chiu shou-yung*. Martin, 2:66; *Ko-kuo chiao-she kung-fa lun*, 1:293.

41. See Ōhira Zengo, "The Reception of International Law by Japan," *Shōgaku tōkyū* (The economic review), 4 (December 1953), 299–314.

42. See Shinobu Jumpei, "Vicissitudes of International Law in the Modern History of Japan" [English], *Kokusaihō gaikō zasshi* (Journal of international law and diplomacy), 50 (May 1951), 14.

43. See Yokota Kisaburō, *Kokusai hōgaku* (Science of international law), Tokyo, 1955, 1:140–144. In 1912 *Kokusaihō zasshi* was renamed *Kokusaihō gaikō zasshi* (Journal of international law and diplomacy).

recognizing the advantages of Japan's geographical proximity and linguistic similarity, began to send students to Japan to study international law.[44] These students often found it convenient to borrow Japanese international law terminology for the replacement of unsatisfactory Chinese terms and for the translation of hitherto untranslated international law terms. For example, while Martin had been unable to devise a Chinese term to translate "subject," [45] the Japanese devised the term which the Chinese pronounce *chu-t'i*. The Chinese borrowed this term from Japan[46] and still use it today. For another example, the Chinese also borrowed the Japanese translation of the term "extradition." Martin had originally translated it as *chiao-huan*[47] which literally means "return." The Japanese devised the term which the Chinese pronounce *yin-tu*. Since the meaning of this latter compound cannot be deduced from its component characters, the Chinese continued to look for a more satisfactory term. Thus, one scholar used the term *chiao-ch'u*, which literally means "turning over." [48] Apparently, this term was also considered inadequate, and later Chinese scholars abandoned their efforts to find a new translation. The Japanese translation is in common use in China today.[49]

44. For a study of the history of Chinese students in Japan, see Sanetō Keishū, *Chūgokujin Nihon ryūgakushi* (History of Chinese students in Japan), Tokyo, 1960. For a list of Japanese books on international law translated into Chinese, see Sanetō Keishū, *Chung-i jih-wen shu mu-lu* (List of Chinese translations of Japanese books), Tokyo, 1945, pp. 47–73. Many Japanese international law articles in the late nineteenth century and early twentieth century, particularly those in *Kokusaihō zasshi*, were translated into Chinese in *Wai-chiao pao* (Foreign affairs journal).

45. See notes 35, 36 and accompanying text. Nor was the translator of *Ko-kuo chiao-she kung-fa lun* able to translate this term. Thus, the paragraph in Phillimore on subjects of international law which asserts that "states are the proper, primary, and immediate subjects of International Law," was translated as *chiao-she kung-fa chuan yin kuo erh she*, which if retranslated into English would be: "International law is formulated exclusively for states." Robert Phillimore, *Commentaries upon International Law*, 1:79; *Ko-kuo chiao-she kung-fa lun*, 1:1.

46. E.g., in Ch'en Lü-chieh, *P'ing-shih kuo-chi kung-fa* (International law of the peace), primarily based upon lectures given by the Japanese scholar Yamawaki Sadao and published in 1907, the term *"chu-t'i"* was used as the translation of the English term "subjects." For a study of the influence of Japan on modern Chinese terms, see generally, Kao Ming-k'ai and Liu Cheng-t'an, *Hsien-tai han-yü wai-lai tzu yen-chiu* (Study of contemporary Chinese terms drawn from foreign words), Peking, Wen-tzu kai-ke ch'u pan she, 1958, pp. 79–97.

47. Wheaton, p. 176; Martin, 2:46.

48. E.g., the term *"yin-tu"* in Matsushima Haijime's article was translated into Chinese as *"chiao-ch'u."* See *Kokusaihō zasshi*, 6 (1907), 8–29; *Wai-chiao pao*, 17:211 (June 13, 1908).

49. E.g., in Chou Keng-sheng, *Kuo-chi fa ta-kang* (Outline of international law), Shanghai, Shang-wu yin-shu kuan, 1929, the term "extradition" is translated as *yin-tu. Ibid.*, 152.

For still another example, in 1864 Martin translated "international law" as *wan-kuo kung-fa* or *wan-kuo lü-li*, but a Japanese scholar, Dr. Mitsukuri Rinshō, in 1873 translated it with the characters *kuo-chi fa*.[50] This term was adopted by Chinese scholars at least as early as 1907.[51]

In view of this interaction between the Chinese and Japanese international legal language, it is not surprising to find that today China and Japan still share many international law terms. The terms listed below are some of the many international law terms common to both Chinese and Japanese:

English	*Chinese Romanization*
contraband	*chin-chih-p'in*
blockade	*feng-so*
neutrality	*chung-li*
enemy character	*ti-hsing*
consul	*ling-shih*
territory	*ling-t'u; ling-yü*
international comity	*kuo-chi li-jang*
law-making treaties	*li-fa t'iao-yüeh*
dualism	*erh-yüan lun*
belligerency	*chiao-chan t'uan-t'i*

Beginning with the nineteen twenties, the Japanese influence upon the form and content of Chinese literature in international law began to decline as increasing numbers of Chinese scholars of international law began to study in Europe and in the United States.[52] These scholars were able to translate new Western international law

50. Hozumi Nobushige, *Hōsō yawa* (Nightly discourse on law), Tokyo, 1932, p. 179.

51. The earliest Chinese book which used the title *Kuo-chi fa* seems to be Lin Ch'i's *Kuo-chi fa ching-i* (Essentials of international law), which was primarily based on Japanese books on international law and which was published in 1903 by Min-hsüeh hui (Fukien learning association). The Japanese did not reject all of Martin's Chinese translations of Western international law terms. For example, the use of the term *chu-ch'üan* as the translation of "sovereignty" was accepted by Japanese scholars from the very beginning and is still used in Japan today.

52. E.g., Chou Keng-sheng, one of the most prominent international law scholars in China, did graduate study in international law at the University of Manchester and the University of Paris. Another prominent scholar, Ts'ui Shu-ch'in (1906–1957), did graduate study in international law at Harvard University.

terms into the Chinese language without relying on Japanese works.[53] Thus, very few Western international law terms of recent origin have been translated identically in Chinese and Japanese. The following are some examples:

English	Chinese Romanization	Japanese Romanization
war criminal	chan-fan	sensō hanzai jin
disarmament	ts'ai-chün	gumbi shukushō
collective security	chi-t'i an-ch'üan	shūdan teki anzen hoshō
space law	t'ai-k'ung fa	uchū kūkan hō
exchange of notes	huan-wen	kōkan kōbun
veto power	fou-chüeh-ch'üan	kyohi ken

Moreover, since the nineteen twenties, certain Chinese international law terms previously borrowed from Japan have been rejected and new, presumably more intelligible, Chinese terms have been devised. Thus, the term "prize tribunals" was first translated as *chan-li fa-yüan* by Martin, but this was then replaced by the Japanese translation *pu-huo shen-chien so*, which has since been replaced by *pu-huo fa-yüan*.[54] Inasmuch as the term "*fa-yüan*" is the Chinese equivalent of "court," this recent term is more consistent with Chinese usage.[55]

Comparison of Contemporary Nationalist and Communist International Law Terms

Although the Communist Chinese abolished all Nationalist laws when they took over mainland China in 1949, they did not reject the use of all Nationalist legal terms. The terminology employed in the field of international law was left almost completely unchanged.

53. E.g., in Chou Keng-sheng's *Kuo-chi fa ta-kang*, none of the reference books mentioned is in Japanese.

54. Wheaton, p. 23; Martin, 1:14; Chou, *Kuo-chi fa ta-kang*, p. 296; Ts'ui, *Kuo-chi fa*, 2:221. Wheaton used the term "prize tribunal" or "court of prize," while the current English term is "prize court."

55. In *Hai-shang pu-huo t'iao-li* (Maritime prize statute), promulgated on October 30, 1917, by the Peking government, the term *pu-huo shen-chien t'ing* was used to refer to "prize court." See Wang Fu-yen, *Kuo-chi kung-fa lun* (On the public international law), Shanghai, Fa-hsüeh pien i she, 1933, 2:254, 266. The statute was later replaced by a new statute promulgated by the Nationalist government in 1932. The new statute used the term *pu-huo fa-yüan* to refer to "prize court."

The lack of trained international law experts among loyal Communists made it necessary for the new regime to retain Nationalist Chinese international law experts who remained in Mainland China.[56] This fact naturally contributed to the retention of many Nationalist international law terms in the Communist Chinese language of international law. A comparison of one Nationalist treatise and two Communist treatises[57] on international law reveals that among approximately two hundred terms used in these books, less than 10 percent are different. The following are some of the different terms:

English	Nationalist	Communist
cabotage	yen-an mao-i ch'üan	yen-an hang-yün
capitulation	ling-shih ts'ai-p'an t'iao-k'uan	wai-jen t'e-ch'üan t'iao-k'uan
counsellor	ts'an-shih	ts'an-tsan
vassal state	shu-kuo	fu-yung kuo
privilege	yu-li	t'e-ch'üan
courier	wai-chiao hsin-ch'ai	wai-chiao hsin-shih
exequatur	ling-shih cheng-shu	ling-shih wei-jen-shu
clausula rebus sic stantibus	ch'ing-shih pien-ch'ien t'iao-k'uan	ch'ing-shih pu-pien t'iao-k'uan[58]

56. E.g., Ch'en T'i-ch'iang, Wang T'ieh-yai, Mei Ju-ao, Chou Keng-sheng, etc., were all former Nationalist international law scholars. Ch'en and Wang were purged in 1957. Mei was declared a rightist in 1958 but had returned to private life by 1964. See CFYC, no. 5 (1958), p. 19; JMJP, April 25, 1964, p. 5.

57. These three books are: (1) Ts'ui, Kuo-chi fa; (2) Chinese version of Kozhevnikov's Mezhdunarodnoe pravo; and (3) Hai shang kuo-chi fa, Chinese version of Alexander P. Higgins and C. John Colombos' International Law of the Sea, 2nd ed. (London: Longmans, Green, 1951), translated by Wang Ch'iang-sheng and published in Peking in 1957.

58. The term clausula rebus sic stantibus refers to the doctrine that "a treaty is intended by the parties to be binding only as long as there is no vital change in the circumstances assumed by the parties at the time of conclusion of the treaty." Georg Schwarzenberger, A Manual of International Law, 2nd ed. (London: Stevens & Sons, 1950), p. xxxix. The Nationalist translation, if retranslated into English, would be "clause of changed circumstances"; while the Communist translation would be "clause of unchanged circumstances." Despite the difference in the literal meaning of the two translations, both refer to the doctrine of clausula rebus sic stantibus. See Ts'ui, p. 240; Kozhevnikov (C), p. 282. It may be noted that one prominent Communist writer, Chou Keng-sheng, also used a translation which is similar to the Nationalist translation. He used the term ch'ing-shih pien-ch'ien in his article entitled "Looking at the West Berlin Question from the Angle of International Law," Kuo-chi wen-t'i yen-chiu (Studies in international problems; hereafter KCWTYC), no. 1 (1959), pp. 40, 44.

English	Nationalist	Communist
right of angary	*fei-ch'ang cheng-yung ch'üan*	*chan-yung chung-li ts'ai-ch'an ch'üan*
doctrine of continuous voyage	*chi-hsü hang-hai chu-i*	*chi-hsü hang-ch'eng chu-i*
insurgency	*p'an-luan t'uan-t'i*	*wu-chuang pao-tung t'uan-t'i*

Recently, however, new international law terms have tended to be translated differently. For instance, the term "peaceful coexistence" is translated by the Communist Chinese as *ho-p'ing kung-ch'u* (lit., "to stay together peacefully") while the Nationalist Chinese translate it as *ho-p'ing kung-ts'un*, which is a more literal translation. Another example is the translation of the term "outer space," which the Communist Chinese translate as *wai-ts'eng k'ung-chien*,[59] while the Nationalist Chinese translate it as *t'ai-k'ung*.[60] The following are further examples of the different ways in which certain new terms have been translated:

English	Nationalist	Communist
consultation	*tzu-shang*	*hsieh-shang*
genocide	*ts'an-hai jen-ch'ün tsui*	*mieh-chung tsui*[61]
continental shelf	*ta-lu p'eng*	*ta-lu chia*
contiguous zone	*lin-chieh ch'ü*	*p'i-lien ti-tai*
residual sovereignty	*sheng-yü chu-ch'üan*	*ts'an-chüeh ti chu-ch'üan*

59. E.g., see *JMJP*, December 23, 1966, p. 5.
60. E.g., see *Chung-yang jih-pao* (Central daily news), international ed., editorial, January 30, 1967, p. 2. But in the late nineteen fifties Communist Chinese also used the term *t'ai-k'ung* to translate "outer space." E.g., see *JMJP*, December 8, 1957, p. 5. The translation of "outer space" recently used by the official New China News Agency is either *wai-ts'eng k'ung-chien* or *yü-chou k'ung-chien* (lit., "cosmic space"). See New China News Agency foreign language cadre school, ed., *Han-ying shih-shih yung-yü tz'u-hui* (Dictionary of Chinese-English terms of current affairs), preliminary ed., Peking, Shang-wu yin-shu kuan, 1964, pp. 387, 475.
61. The translations used by Nationalist international law scholars are not consistent. Some translate the term "genocide" as *mieh-chüeh chung-tsu* which is very close to the translation used by Communist Chinese scholars. See Lei Sung-sheng, *Kuo-chi fa yüan-li* (Principles of international law), Taipei, Cheng chung shu-chü, 1960, 1:222; Shen K'o-ch'in, *Kuo-chi fa* (International law), Taipei, Hsüeh-sheng shu-chü, 1964, p. 282.

A few Communist Chinese international law terms have been translated from Russian terms found in Soviet literature on international law. For instance, the term *wu-ch'an chieh-chi kuo-chi chu-i* (proletarian internationalism), *t'i-hsi* (system), and *she-hui chu-i kuo-chi fa* (socialist international law) were translated from the Russian terms *proletarskii internatsionalizm, sistema,* and *sotsialisticheskoe mezhdunarodnoe pravo,* respectively. Such terms are, as might be expected, not used in Nationalist literature on international law.

Certain Problems Relating to the Translation of Communist Chinese International Law Terms into English

It should be obvious from the above discussion that almost all Chinese international law terms are translations of "Western" international law terms.[62] Thus, in the process of translating the Chinese into English, it is important to find the English sources from which the Chinese terms were originally derived, rather than simply translating the meaning of those terms without reference to their sources. The necessity for translating Chinese international law terms in this manner can best be illustrated by the following example.

The Chinese term *ch'iang-chih chieh-chüeh* is used in a 1960 article published in *Kuo-chi wen-t'i yen-chiu* (Studies in international problems).[63] Since *ch'iang-chih* may be translated as "coercive" and *chieh-chüeh* as "settlement," the likely translation of the term would be "coercive settlement." But the term "coercive settlement" does not appear in most widely used English international law treatises. The only exception is Starke's *Introduction to International Law,* where the term "coercive means of settlement" is used.[64] However, inasmuch as no evidence can be found in Communist Chinese legal literature that Starke's book is used in mainland China, it is doubt-

---

62. Even the term *pu-p'ing-teng t'iao-yüeh* (unequal treaty) can be found in classical Western treatises on international law. E.g., see Samuel Pufendorf, *De jure natural et gentium* (On the law of nature and nations), trans. from 1688 ed. by C. H. Oldfather and W. A. Oldfather (Washington, D.C.: Carnegie Endowment for International Peace, 1934), 2:1331–1336.

63. Ying T'ao, "Recognize the True Face of Bourgeois International Law from a Few Basic Concepts," *KCWTYC,* no. 1 (1960), pp. 42, 43.

64. Joseph Starke, *Introduction to International Law,* 1st ed. (London: Butterworth, 1947), p. 253.

ful that the Chinese term *ch'iang-chih chieh-chüeh* is a translation (or an abbreviated translation) of the term "coercive means of settlement."

A survey of Western international law treatises, however, reveals that the term "compulsive settlement" is used in volume two of Oppenheim's *International Law*.[65] Since Oppenheim's treatise has for more than thirty years been the most widely used English international law treatise in China and since Oppenheim's treastise was translated into Chinese in 1955 by the Chinese People's Institute of Foreign Affairs in Peking,[66] it seems probable that the Chinese term *ch'iang-chih chieh-chüeh* owes its origin to Oppenheim's treatise. This conclusion is further strengthened by the fact that the article containing the term *ch'iang-chih chieh-chüeh* makes several references to the Chinese version of Oppenheim's treatise.

The difference between "coercive settlement" and "compulsive settlement" is not insignificant. In Oppenheim's treatise, it is stated that there are four different kinds of "compulsive settlement" of disputes, namely, retorsion, reprisal (including embargo), pacific blockade, and intervention. War is explicitly excluded.[67] In Starke's treatise, however, war is included, together with retorsion, reprisal, pacific blockade, and intervention, as one of the five coercive means of settlement.[68] In other words, if *ch'iang-chih chieh-chüeh* is translated as "coercive settlement," the reader may get the wrong impression that *ch'iang-chih chieh-chüeh* includes "war." Obviously, then, the Chinese term must be translated with reference to the English source from which it was originally derived.

To be sure, the choice of possible translations does not always have such serious implications. But there is still good reason for using the original English terms in translating the Chinese international law terms, namely, the desirability of maintaining a consistent and unified vocabulary in order to facilitate communication in international relations.

There is a risk, of course, that by so doing we may overlook con-

65. Lassa F. L. Oppenheim, *International Law*, 6th ed. (London: Longmans, Green, 1940), 2:106; 7th ed. (London: Longmans, Green, 1952), p. 132.

66. The Chinese version of Oppenheim was not available. It is not clear whether the Chinese translation of volume 2 of Oppenheim's treatise was based upon the 6th edition (1940) or 7th edition (1952). I believe that the Chinese version was based upon the 7th edition.

67. Oppenheim, *International Law*, 6th ed., 2:106–07; 7th ed., pp. 132–33.

68. Starke, *Introduction to International Law*, p. 253.

ceptual distortions which may have entered when the Chinese first devised their translations. The term "recognition of belligerency," for example, is translated into Chinese as *chiao-chan t'uan-t'i ti ch'eng-jen*[69] which, if literally retranslated into English means "recognition of a belligerent group." However, such distortions seem to be relatively insignificant and in fact rarely occur.[70]

In some cases, one Chinese term has been used in the translation of several English international law terms. For example, the compound *wai-chiao* is used in the Chinese translation of such terms as "diplomacy," "ministry of foreign affairs" (*wai-chiao pu*), "diplomatic relations" (*wai-chiao kuan-hsi*) and "foreign policy" (*wai-chiao cheng-ts'e*). In translating these terms back into English, it is necessary to select the most appropriate English translation from the context in which they appear.

The translation into English of those Chinese international law terms which were originally derived from European or Russian sources presents even more difficulties than the translation of terms which were derived from English sources. For example, in a 1960 *Kuo-chi wen-t'i yen-chiu* article, one writer states that in the "science of bourgeois international law" there are three theories about the juridical nature of state territory, namely: *k'o-t'i shuo* (lit., "object theory"), *k'ung-chien shuo* (lit., "space theory") and *kuan-hsia shuo* (lit., "jurisdiction theory").[71] Inasmuch as no recent English treatise on general international law mentions these theories, it seems likely that the writer is referring to theories advocated by European "bourgeois writers." But since the study of international law in Communist China is still at a relatively primitive stage of development,[72] it is not likely that the writer had direct access to European sources. Rather,

69. The Japanese translation of this term is the same.
70. The Chinese and Japanese translations of "recognition of belligerency" do not suggest any conceptual distortion in the Chinese or Japanese treatises on international law. For instance, in Ts'ui's treatise, his explanation of the term is similar to that of Wilson. See Ts'ui, *Kuo-chi fa*, 1:51; George G. Wilson, *International Law*, 9th ed. (New York: Silver, Burdett, 1935), p. 69. The Japanese scholar Tabata Shigejirō gave an explanation of the term which is similar to that of Oppenheim. See Tabata, *Kokusai hō I* (International law I), Tokyo, Yūhikaku, 1957, p. 212; Oppenheim, 7th ed., 2:249.
71. Hsin Wu, "A Criticism of the Bourgeois International Law on the Question of State Territory," KCWTYC, no. 7 (1960), pp. 42–43.
72. See Hungdah Chiu, "Communist China's Attitude toward International Law," *American Journal of International Law*, 60 (1966), 263–267.

there is evidence that he obtained his information through a secondary source, a translated Soviet article[73] discussing in the same Chinese terms these very theories.[74]

Having identified the foreign source of these Chinese terms, a further problem is how to translate them into conventional English international law terms. In the English version of Kozhevnikov's *Mezhdunarodnoe pravo*, they are translated, respectively, as "object theory," "space theory," and "theory of competence" (not "jurisdiction theory," the literal translation).[75] These translations are all consistent with the conventional English international law terms and are thus acceptable.[76]

However, when a Chinese term is derived from a Russian international law term which cannot be literally translated into a conventional English international law term, the translation of the Chinese term into English becomes more difficult. For example, in an article entitled *"P'i-p'an tzu-ch'an chieh-chi kuo-chi fa tsai chü-min wen-t'i shang ti chu-chang"* (lit., "A criticism of the views of bourgeois international law on the question of residents"),[77] we find the term *chü-min*, which literally translated into English means "residents." But this translation makes little sense in the context and, furthermore, "residents" is not a term of art used in English treatises on international law.

In the Chinese version of Kozhevnikov's *Mezhdunarodnoe pravo*, the Russian term *naselenie* (population or inhabitants), which in the English version of Kozhevnikov's treatise is translated as "population," is translated into Chinese as "*chü-min*."[78] Thus, it might be assumed that *chü-min* should be translated as "population." But this

73. S. V. Molodtsov, "Nekotor'ie Vopros'i terroitorli v Mezhdunarodnom prave," *SGP*, no. 8 (1954), p. 63. Translated into Chinese in *Hsien-tai kuo-chi fa shang ti chi-pen yüan-tse ho wen-t'i* (Fundamental principles and problems in modern international law), Peking, Fa-lü ch'u pan she, 1956, p. 149.

74. In the Chinese version of Kozhevnikov's *Mezhdunarodnoe pravo* published in 1959, these theories were translated respectively as *tui-hsiang shuo, k'ung-chien shuo*, and *ch'üan-hsien shuo* (lit., "competence theory"). Kozhevnikov (C), pp. 179–80. The first and third terms are different from those used in KCWTYC.

75. Kozhevnikov (E), pp. 177–79.

76. Lauterpacht used the terms "object theory," "space theory," and "competence theory" respectively, in his *Private Law Sources and Analogies of International Law* (London: Longmans, Green, 1927). *Ibid.*, pp. 91–93.

77. KCWTYC, no. 5 (1960), p. 40.

78. Kozhevnikov (R), p. 131; (C), p. 135; (E), p. 136.

translation makes little sense in the context and "population" also is not a term of art in English treatises on general international law.

A glance at Kozhevnikov's chapter on *naselenie* and the Chinese article on *chü-min* reveals that the problems under discussion are those which are generally dealt with in English international law treatises under the heading of "individuals." [79] In other words, *chü-min* as well as *naselenie*, when used in this international law context, correspond to the English international law term "individuals." [80]

Another example is *yüan-shih chan-yu*, a term which appears in the Chinese version of Kozhevnikov's *Mezhdunarodnoe pravo. Yüan-shih chan-yu* is a translation of the Russian term *pervonachal'noe zavladenie*.[81] In the English version of Kozhevnikov's treatise, the Russian term is translated as "prior possession," which is explained as follows:

> In International Law under capitalism and in the bourgeois science of International Law, the discovery of "vacant" land and the establishment over such land, even nominally, of the authority of any State became known as "prior possession," which was considered as legal grounds for the absorption of such territory.[82]

But we cannot find any English treatise on international law referring to the so-called method of acquiring territory by "prior possession." However, in the context of the passage quoted above, it is apparent that the term "prior possession" refers to the method of acquiring territory by way of "occupation," a principle discussed in most English treatises on international law.[83] In view of this, the Chinese term *yüan-shih chan-yu* should be translated into English as "occupation" rather than "prior possession."

79. Cf. pt. 2, chap. 4, of vol. 1 of Oppenheim's *International Law* on "individuals," 8th ed. (1955) and chap. 4, "Population in International Law," in Kozhevnikov, *International Law* (Moscow, 1961).

80. The Chinese equivalent for "individuals" is *ko-jen* and the Russian is *individuum*.

81. Kozhevnikov (C), p. 183; (R), p. 179.

82. Kozhevnikov (E), p. 182.

83. Cf. the following passage is quoted from Oppenheim: "Occupation is the act of appropriation by a State through which it intentionally acquires sovereignty over such territory as is at the time not under the sovereignty of another State." *International Law*, 8th ed. (London: Longmans, Green, 1955), 1:555.

A problem closely related to the problem of translating international law terms into English is the discrepancy between Chinese international law terms used in the Chinese text of diplomatic documents and the English translations provided by the Chinese Communist government. For example, in some treaties, the Chinese text
refers to the term *kuo-chi kuan-li* which should be translated as "international custom." However, the corresponding official English text
translates the term *kuo-chi kuan-li* as "international practice." [84] Since
the term "custom" in international law refers to that practice which
has become legally binding, while the term "practice" refers to usage
which is not legally binding,[85] this discrepancy is not insignificant.
Similar discrepancies in translation also exist in many Communist
Chinese friendship treaties[86] containing provisions relating to the
principle of *hu pu kan-she nei-cheng*. Inasmuch as the term *kan-she*,
as used in Chinese literature on international law, is obviously derived
from the English international law term "intervention," it should be
translated back into English as "intervention." However, the official
English text of those treaties translates the term *kan-she* as "interference." [87] In current English international law terminology, the
word "intervention" generally means the "dictatorial interference by

84. *E.g.*, Article 2 of Friendship Treaty between Communist China and Indonesia,
signed on April 1, 1961, refers to *"kuo-chi kuan-li"* but the English text published
in *Peking Review* translated the term as "international practice." See Ministry of
Foreign Affairs, *Chung-hua jen-min kung-ho-kuo t'iao-yüeh chi* (Compilation of treaties of the People's Republic of China), Peking, Fa-lü ch'u pan she, 1962, 10:7;
Peking Review, no. 24 (June 16, 1961), p. 11. The Nationalist practice is far from
consistent. In Article 6 of the Sino-American Treaty for the Relinquishment of Extraterritorial Rights in China, signed on January 11, 1943, the English text refers to
"international usage," while the Chinese text refers to *kuo-chi kuan-li*; in Article 7,
the English text refers to "international practice" while the Chinese text again refers
to *kuo-chi kuan-li*. But in Article 3 of the Sino-Czechoslovakia Treaty of Amity and
Commerce, signed on February 12, 1930, the English text refers to "international
practice" while the Chinese text refers to *kuo-chi t'ung-li*, which is a more literal
translation of the English term. Ministry of Foreign Affairs, ed., *Treaties Between the
Republic of China and Foreign States (1927–1957)*, (Taipei: Shang-wu yin-shu kuan,
1958), pp. 72, 663, 664.
85. *E.g.*, see Charles G. Fenwick, *International Law*, 4th ed. (New York: Apple-
ton-Century-Crofts, 1965), pp. 88–89.
86. All these treaties concluded from 1950–1965 were published in a single volume
entitled *Chung-hua jen-min kung-ho-kuo yu-hao t'iao-yüeh hui-pien* (Collection of
friendship treaties concluded by the People's Republic of China), Peking, Shih-chieh
chih-shih ch'u pan she, 1965.
87. See Treaty of Friendship between Communist China and Ghana, signed on
August 18, 1961. *Ibid.*, p. 61 (Chinese version); p. 63 (English version), both texts
being equally authentic.

a State in the affairs of another State for the purpose of maintaining or altering the actual condition of things" [88] — a narrower meaning than the word "interference." [89]

Conclusions

The above study permits two conclusions: (1) Insofar as Chinese international law terms are for the most part translations of Western international law terms, they must be translated into English with reference to the sources from which they were originally derived. This method of translation is permissible in view of the fact that the great majority of contemporary Chinese international law terms convey the meaning of Western international law terms without significant conceptual distortions. (2) Except for a few international law terms derived from Russian sources or translations of international law terms of recent origin, the terms used by the Communist Chinese are for the most part identical to those used by the Nationalist Chinese.

88. Oppenheim, *International Law*, 8th ed., 1955, 1:305.
89. Writers in the nineteenth century did not seem to differentiate the term "intervention" from the term "interference." In Wheaton's *Elements of International Law*, the two terms were used interchangeably. *Ibid.*, 87–93. The term "interference" is today not generally used as a technical term in international law. Hence, the best translation of *hu pu kan-she nei-cheng* is "mutual nonintervention in internal affairs."

Abbreviations

In addition to the abbreviations on p. xii, the following abbreviations are used in chapter 4:

Kozhevnikov (R) — F. I. Kozhevnikov, ed., *Mezhdunarodnoe pravo* (International law), Moscow: Gosyurizdat, 1957.

Kozhevnikov (E) — F. I. Kozhevnikov, ed., *International Law* (Moscow: Foreign Language Publishing House, 1961).

Kozhevnikov (C) — Su-lien k'o-hsüh-yüan fa-lü yen-chiu so (Institute of [State and] Law of the Academy of Sciences of the USSR), *Kuo-chi fa* (International law), Peking: Shih-chieh chih-shih ch'u pan she, 1959. [Chinese version of Kozhevnikov's *Mezhdunarodnoe pravo.*]

Wheaton — Henry Wheaton, *Elements of International Law,* 6th ed., ed. W. B. Lawrence (Boston: Little, Brown and Company, 1855).

Martin — W. A. P. Martin (Ting Wei-liang), *Wan-kuo kung-fa* (Public law of ten thousand states), 4 vols. (Peking: T'ung wen kuan, 1864). [Chinese version of Wheaton's *Elements of International Law.*]

5 Japanese Influences on Communist Chinese Legal Language

Dan Fenno Henderson

The Japanese influence on Communist Chinese legal language, though continuing today through the influence of Communist jurists trained in Japanese law, is largely a carry-over from the first four decades of this century. During the period from 1896–1936, the Chinese absorbed and codified their own version of Western-style jurisprudence; an important part of this task was done through the medium of the Japanese legal language and law developed in Japan during the Meiji period (1868–1914). Language conveniences[1] led many Chinese to favor Japanese training over a more direct approach to Western law, and a number of people who subsequently became prominent Chinese jurists went to universities in Japan. Presumably much of the legal terminology which they learned in Japan is still used, because the Communists did not abolish the legal language,[2] though they did abolish the laws of the Republic of China in 1949. Probably little further absorption of Japanese terms has taken place since 1949, because of the meager role for justiciable law in Communist politics generally, and the overriding priority which Communists assign to the unfettered exertion of their power. The following is therefore a survey of the language consequences of the early

1. See Liang Ch'i-ch'ao, "On the Advantages of Studying Japanese Culture," in *Yin-ping-shih wen-chi* (Collected essays of the Ice-Drinker's Studio), vol. 29 (Shanghai: Chung-hua shu-chü, 1926), 19–20: "To speak Japanese [for a Chinese student] takes one year. To write Japanese takes half a year, but to read Japanese only takes a few days."

2. Note that in the USSR there was serious discussion up to 1950 concerning the possibility of abolishing prerevolutionary languages and replacing them with a newly constructed international language. But this was abandoned upon pronouncement of Stalin in 1950, and the Chinese followed. Thus the language inherited from Republican days remains, though rapid language development is of course occurring along with the transformation of Chinese society. See David Finkelstein, "The Language of Communist China's Criminal Law," chapter 6 in this volume; and John DeFrancis, *Nationalism and Language Reform in China* (Princeton: Princeton University Press, 1950), p. 85; P. Kratochvíl, *The Chinese Language Today* (London: Hutchinson, 1968), p. 19.

twentieth century Chinese study of Western-style law through Japanese sources, the Japanese role in the Ch'ing and Republican codification process itself, and finally a statistical comparison of the carry-over from Japanese to Chinese Communist criminal law.

Chinese Absorption of Japanese Legal Language

Extraterritoriality and the Sino-Japanese War

As a result of the Shimonoseki Treaty (1895) and the accompanying Sino-Japanese Treaty of Commerce and Navigation (1896),[3] the Japanese imposed provisions for extraterritorial jurisdiction upon China, similar to those previously imposed upon it by the Western powers. Military defeat in 1895 at the hands of its petty neighbors, the recently westernized Japanese, at last convinced Imperial China of the need to modernize its legal system. In 1896, through an arrangement with Prince Saionji, then serving in the Matsukata Cabinet as both foreign minister and education minister, the first thirteen Chinese students were sent to Japan to study. One of them, T'ang Pao-o, became a prominent lawyer.

The Boxer Rebellion in 1900 further hastened decisions to modernize the laws. The resulting treaties with England and the United States especially encouraged law reform because they pledged those Western powers to forfeit extraterritoriality after satisfactory legal reforms by China. For example, Article 15 of the U.S.-Chinese Treaty of October 8, 1903, provided: "The United States agrees . . . to relinquish extraterritorial rights when satisfied that the state of the Chinese laws, the arrangements for their administration, and other considerations warrant it in doing so." [4]

Still there was considerable debate in China as to how Western law could best be absorbed. Some thought that a direct approach — sending scholars to study in selected Western countries — would have the advantage of authenticity and precise understanding; most preferred an indirect approach through study in Japan, where recently Western law had been shorn of nonessentials and successfully adapted

3. See Articles XX–XXV in *Treaties, Conventions, etc., Between China and Foreign States*, 2 (Shanghai: Statistical Department of the Inspectorate General of Customs, 1908), 1332, 1339.

4. *The Statutes at Large of the United States of America*, 33 (Washington: Government Printing Office, 1905), 2208, 2215.

to justify abolition of extraterritoriality.[5] Most Chinese students were sent to Japan, probably for reasons noted by Chang Chih-tung and Liang Ch'i-ch'ao.[6] Japan was closer, cheaper, and similar in culture, and particularly Japan shared the Chinese written script. Also, Japan had already been through the Westernization process and had absorbed, and could therefore transmit to Chinese, the essentials without confusing refinements.

Chinese Students in Japan (1896–1935)

Of the first thirteen Chinese students to arrive in Tokyo, four returned within three or four weeks, apparently because they were subjected to heckling by Japanese children[7] and also because Japanese food did not agree with them. Such nationalistic antagonisms were occasional irritants in the cultural exchanges between China and Japan throughout the period 1896–1935. For example, some Chinese came to resent the Japanese persistence in calling China "Shina" instead of *Chūgoku* (central country).[8] But these are minor matters, and the fact is that from 1896 until 1906, there was a steady buildup of Chinese students in Japan (1899: 200 students; 1902: 500; 1903: 1,000; 1906: 8,000)[9] to a point where the Kanda district in Tokyo was rather overrun with Chinese students. Although the statistics are conflicting, some estimates claimed that as many as 13,000 students were resident in Tokyo at the peak in 1906.[10] No matter which figure

5. Shimada Masao, "Concerning the Compilation of the Criminal Law Draft at the End of the Ch'ing Dynasty," *Hōritsu ronsō* (Legal review), 34 (1966), 629, 637.
6. See Chang Chih-tung, *Chang Wen-hsiang kung ch'üan chi* (Complete collection of Chang [Chih-tung]), Peking, Ch'u-hsüeh ching-lu, 1937, ch'üan hsüeh p'ien (chapter on encouraging studies), yu hsüeh (study abroad), p. 6; see also Liang Ch'i-ch'ao, "On Translating Books," in *Yin-ping-shih wen-chi, chüan* 2, pp. 35–36.
7. The Japanese children called the Chinese *chan chan bozu*. In the Edo period apparently there were Japanese who walked the streets to sell candy, dressed in Ch'ing-style costumes, with a pigtail hairdo and beating a metal gong. The term *chan chan* came from the sound of the gong. Apparently later the term *chan chan bozu* became a term of derision to refer to Chinese residents in Japan after 1895; see Marius Jansen, "Japanese Views of China During the Meiji Period," in A. Feuerwerker et al., eds., *Approaches to Modern Chinese History* (Berkeley: University of California Press, 1967), pp. 163, 182, noting the change in Japanese attitude toward China from respect to scorn and self-pride.
8. Sanetō Keishū, *Chūgokujin Nihon ryūgakushi* (History of Chinese students in Japan), Tokyo, 1960, p. 217. Unless otherwise indicated the information hereafter concerned with Chinese students in Japan is based on this book, which draws together a wealth of data on twentieth century Chinese students in Japan.
9. Sanetō, *Chūgokujin*, p. 15.
10. Roger Hackett, "Chinese Students in Japan 1900–1910: Three Papers on China," mimeographed (1949), p. 142, quotes the *Japan Weekly Mail* (September 1906) as saying there were 13,000 Chinese students in Japan.

is most nearly correct, the total amounts to a remarkable wave of Chinese students seeking Western learning in Japan. There were so many students that special curricula and schools were provided for them; publishing houses sprang up to publish textbooks catering to Chinese students, and finally a supervisor of students resident in Japan was appointed by the Chinese government.[11] The special schools and curricula, which were set up by several private universities with books especially written to teach the Chinese how to read Japanese, were important to prepare some of the Chinese for integration into the Japanese schools at the level of the higher vocational schools, teachers' colleges, and the universities. For example, Meiji and Waseda[12] Universities (1905) both established special divisions to welcome the Chinese students. Particularly significant in the field of law was the special division set up by Hōsei University, sponsored by Ume Kenjiro, a great comparative lawyer by any standards and one of the three major jurists who had been appointed earlier by the Meiji government to perfect the Japanese civil code in its final form as adopted in 1898. Ume was very sympathetic to the Chinese students in Japan, and in 1908, an enormous total of 1,070 Chinese graduated from the Hōsei special division in law and politics. Meiji University during the six-year period (1902–1908) admitted 2,862 Chinese students and graduated 1,380. Waseda's program was geared more for training of teachers; it took in 762 students in 1905, 850 in 1907, 394 in 1908, and closed in 1910.

Among the graduates from Japanese schools were many persons later prominent in all walks of Chinese life including politics. In 1932, out of forty-five top Chinese governmental positions, eighteen were filled by men who had studied in Japan, thirteen by men who had studied in other countries throughout the world; the rest had not studied abroad. A 1940 tabulation of all Chinese students who graduated from Japanese universities or vocational schools between 1901 and 1939 showed a total figure of 11,966 graduates,[13] or an

11. Ueda Mannen, "Concerning Chinese Students Abroad," *Taiyō* (The sun), 4 (August 1898), 24.

12. Miyasaka Hiroshi, "Compilation of Modern Codes at the End of the Ch'ing and Japanese Scholars: The Criminal Law Draft and Okada Asatarō" in *Senshu daigaku shakai kagaku kenkyū jo geppō* (Monthly report of the Senshu University Social Science Institute), 46/47 (1967), 19.

13. This tabulation excludes Manchurians and several other groups (*e.g.*, 3,810 persons graduated from a school known as *Kobungakuin*, which was defunct by 1909). Sanetō, p. 137.

annual average of about 307. After reaching a peak in 1906 with at least 8,000 students studying in Japan, the number had dropped to 500 by 1909, and in 1911, because of the Chinese revolution, nearly all students returned home. Thereafter the number of graduates from Japanese universities between 1913 and 1931 was roughly three or four hundred a year. For example, in 1931 a Chinese publication showed the following statistics on Chinese students abroad:[14]

Host	Government grant	Private funds	Total
Japan	7	296	303
U.S.	22	124	146
France	4	134	138
Germany	10	57	67
Belgium	0	34	34
England	9	19	28
Italy	0	3	3
Sweden	0	3	3
Denmark	0	2	2
Netherlands	0	1	1
Switzerland	1	0	1
Australia	0	1	1
India	0	1	1
Total	53	675	728

The following figures also show that nearly half of the Chinese students studying abroad were in Japan between 1929 and 1934:[15]

Year	Japan	Other countries	Total
1929	1025	632	1657
1930	590	440	1030
1931	83	367	450
1932	227	349	576
1933	229	402	621
1934	347	512	859

Also, Japanese teachers were hired in large numbers to go to China to teach. A study in 1909 by Nakajima Hanjirō[16] shows that there were

14. Sanetō, *Chūgokujin*, p. 145.
15. *Ibid.*, p. 146.
16. Nakajima Hanjirō, *Nisshin kan no kyōiku kankei* (Ch'ing-Japanese educational relations), Tokyo, 1909.

about six hundred Japanese teachers in China and that many provinces had schools specializing in "law and politics." Professor Yoshino Sakuzo of Tokyo University estimates that about forty-five Japanese law teachers were in China.[17] Some of the famous lawyer-teachers who went to China, besides Yoshino (political science), were Tokyo professor Okada Asatarō (criminal law), Shida Kōtarō, president of Meiji University (commercial law), Kyoto professor Oda Yorozu (administrative law), Ogawa Shigejirō (penologist), and Matsuoka Yoshimasa (Great Court of Cassation and Meiji University); also, Itakura Matsutarō, a public procurator. Okada, Shida, and Matsuoka were most influential in the late Ch'ing codification.[18]

Chinese Translation and Publication Activity in Japan

An invaluable impetus to the development of a modern legal language was the voluminous translation work from Japanese into Chinese done by Chinese students in Japan and later published and exported to China.

By 1900 a translation group called "I-shu Hui-pien She" was established in Tokyo by a number of Chinese students who had learned their Japanese in Tokyo. The leader of the group, Ch'i I-hui, was one of the first thirteen students to come to Japan in 1896. Among this group of translators there were at least four law graduates, and it also included two men who subsequently became ministers of state (Chin Pang-p'ing and Ts'ao Ju-lin) and two others who became ambassadors (Chang Tsung-hsiang and Wang Jung-pao). The I-shu Hui-pien She translating group published many books, including several on law and politics. Also, the publication list included many "double translations" from Western languages into Japanese and then from Japanese into Chinese. In 1904 a Tokyo company, the Hui Wen-hsüeh She (editor, Fan Ti-chi), published in Chinese the *P'u-t'ung*

17. See Yoshino Sakuzo, "Japanese Teachers Employed in Ch'ing China," *Kokka gakkai zasshi* (Journal of the Association of Social and Political Science), 23 (1909), 769.
18. See Marinus Meijer, *The Introduction of Modern Criminal Law in China* (Batavia [Jakarta]: De Unie, 1949; reprinted Hong Kong, 1967), p. 64; Miyasaka Hiroshi, "About Compilation of Codes at the End of the Ch'ing Dynasty," *Hōseishi kenkyū* (*bessatsu*) (Studies in legal history [special issue]), 4 (1963), 187 and note 12; Shimada Masao, "Concerning Compilation of the Criminal Law Draft at the End of the Ch'ing Dynasty — Recalling Okada Asatarō's Contributions," *Hōritsu ronsō* (*bessatsu*) (Legal review [special issue]), 39 (1966), 629; Shimada, "Concerning Compilation of the Civil and Commercial Law Drafts at the End of the Ch'ing Dynasty," *Hōritsu ronsō*, 34 (1961), 119.

pai-k'o ch'üan-shu, a massive encyclopedia in one hundred volumes composed of middle level textbooks for general education on subjects ranging from philosophy, literature, and education to law. This group of translations was pedagogically a very important work for the Chinese, and doubtless a substantial legal vocabulary was adopted or adapted in these translations. The law titles of the Japanese books translated in this encyclopedia include the following:[19]

Iwasaki Shō, *Zeikan oyobi sōkoron* (Treatise on customs houses and warehouses);

Iwasaki Shō and Nakamura Takashi, *Kokuhōgaku* (Science of law and state);

Kajihara Nakaharu, *Minji soshōhō shakugi* (Commentary on the civil procedure code);

Kumagaya Naota, *Hōritsu hanron* (General theory of law);

Kobayashi Ichirō, *Gyōsei saibanhōron* (Treatise on law of administrative adjudication);

Sueta Kei'ichirō, *Shōhō hanron* (General theory of commercial law);

Tanaka Jirō, *Nippon teikoku kempōron* (Treatise on the Japanese Imperial Constitution);

Nakamura Tarō, *Kokusai shihō* (International private law);

Hokujō Motoatsu and Kumagaya Naota, *Kokusai kōhō* (International public law);

Maruo Masao, *Minpō sōsokuhen bukkenhen shakugi* (Commentary on the general provisions book and real-rights book of the civil code);

Maru Masao, *Minpō saikenhen shakugi* (Commentary on the obligations book of the civil code);

Den Yutaka, *Minpō sōsokuhen bukkenhen shakugi* (Commentary on the general provisions book and real-rights book of the civil code); and,

Miura Kikutarō, *Nippon hōseishi* (History of Japanese legal institutions).

From this point onward the translation and publication of Japanese books (and Japanese versions of Western books) into Chinese became a substantial business not only to service the numerous Chinese

19. Sanetō, *Chūgokujin,* pp. 268–9.

students studying in Japan but also for export to China for the rapidly growing market among students of Western learning there. The leading Chinese bookstore in Shanghai for these purposes was the Shang-wu Yin-shu-kuan, which in 1904 advertised a large number of translated Japanese books for sale. Excluding the English language titles, over half of the list of 105 works were clearly translations from Japanese books, and probably it would reach two-thirds if several others, apparently translated from the Japanese version of some Western book, were added.[20] Soon these translating and publishing activities in both China and Japan produced guides and bibliographies for the Chinese students to assist them in selecting their reading. One such list published in 1904 was analyzed by Yang Shou-ch'un into subject-matter categories and by country of origin. His list on law and politics showed the following results:

Japan	35	books
England	5	books
U.S.	2	books
France	2	books
Germany	6	books
Russia	2	books
All others	18	books
Total	70	

Altogether the list shows 321 books translated from Japan out of a total of 533. Sanetō Keishū compiled a list of 2,602 books translated from Japanese into Chinese between 1896 and 1938, of which 372 might be classified as law and politics.[21] This translating and publishing activity to facilitate the transmission of Japanized Western-learning to Chinese students in the early part of this century had an important impact on the publishing business, causing a change to Western style in the physical design, structure, and format of books printed in China — and created important structural and vocabulary changes in the Chinese language.

Law and government courses were the center of most Chinese stu-

20. *Ibid.*, p. 282.
21. Sanetō, *Chung-i jih-wen shu-mu-lu* (Japanese: *Chūyaku nichibunsho mokuroku;* List of Japanese books translated into Chinese), published, but not for sale, by Kokusai bunka shinkokai, 1945. It may be seen at the Hibiya Toshokan, Tokyo.

dents' programs of study in schools throughout Japan.[22] The most popular studies were the "general course" and the course in constitutional government (*kensei*). Both required rather broad backgrounds, and consequently multivolume sets of books were designed and published for Chinese students in law courses in Japan. For example:

Series name	Publisher
Fa-cheng chiang-i (15 vols.)	Ch'un-i Shu-chü
Fa-cheng ts'eng-pien (24 vols.)	Hu-pei Fa-cheng Pien-chi She
Fa-cheng (29 vols.)	Nei-wu She
Cheng-chih lei-tien	Waseda University
Hsin-i Jih-pen fa-kuei ta-ch'üan (Translation of the entire Japanese six codes) 80 vols. (1904)	Shang-wu Yin-shu-kuan

Perhaps the most impressive legal translation was the last one listed above: the Chinese version of the entire Japanese *Roppō zensho* (Six codes). Also, a number of important Japanese-Chinese dictionaries were published specifically for law students in the pre-World War II period. For our inquiry, the fact that entire legal dictionaries were "translated" at these early dates with a direct carry-over of nearly all Japanese legal concepts is highly significant. The more important of these dictionaries with their dates are as follows:[23]

Editor	Title	Publisher	Date
Wang Jung-pao and Yeh Lan	Hsin erh ya	Kuo Hsüeh She	1903
Chang Ch'i-kuang (tr. Hsü Yung-hsi)	Han-i hsin fa-lü tz'u-tien	Ching Shih I-hsüeh-kuan	1905
Ch'ien Hsün and Tung Hung-wei	Jih-pen fa-kuei chien-chu	Shang-wu Yin-shu-kuan	1907
Chang Ch'un-t'ao, Kuo K'ai-wen, Ch'en Chieh	Han-i fa-lü ching-chi tz'u-tien	Keibunkan Shokyoku	1907
Wu Nien-tzu et al.	Hsin shu yü tz'u-tien	Nan-ch'iang Shu-chü	1929

22. See Ariga Nagao, "Following Ch'ing China's Students Abroad," *Gaikō jihō* (Journal of diplomacy), vol. 2, no. 4 (1898); R. Scalapino, "Prelude to Marxism: The Chinese Student Movement in Japan, 1900–1910," in A. Feuerwerker et al., eds., *Approaches to Modern Chinese History*, pp. 191, 209.

23. Sanetō, *Chūgokujin*, p. 349. The Harvard-Yenching Institute has copies of numbers 1, 4, and 5 above, and I have a copy of number 4 in my personal library, filmed from Professor Sanetō's copy now at the Hibiya Library, Tokyo.

Done largely by Chinese students in Japan, many of these major dictionaries and translating projects, including the Japanese six codes (the constitution, civil, civil procedure, criminal, criminal procedure, and commercial codes, as well as many related laws), were completed before the Chinese codes were drafted in 1906–07. They doubtless greatly facilitated the translation of Japanese and Western codes done in 1905 at the Chinese Bureau for the Compilation of Laws (*Fa-lü pien-tsuan kuan*).

Interaction Between Early Japanese and Chinese Efforts to Absorb Western Legal Terms

Even before Japan was opened to the Western world in the 1850's, several foreigners in China had translated English works into Chinese. For lawyers, the most important, perhaps, was W. A. P. Martin's translation of Wheaton's *Elements of International Law*,[24] first published in English in London and Philadelphia in 1836, and in 1864 translated into Chinese in China by Martin, assisted by a commission of scholars appointed by Prince Kung. It was published in 1864 under the Chinese title of *Wan-kuo kung-fa*, and was then adapted for Japanese use and reprinted in Kyoto[25] in 1865.[26] Martin later translated several other international law treatises into Chinese,[27] and Franzer translated Phillimore, *Commentaries upon International Law*, 2nd ed. (1871) into Chinese in 1896 with some innovations in terms but still retaining much of Martin's terminology.[28] In the course of translating Wheaton's book, Martin developed many Chinese equivalent terms for English legal concepts. One of the most famous is his word for "right," pronounced *ch'üan-li* in Chinese and *kenri*

24. See Ting Wei-liang, *Wan-kuo kung-fa* (Public law of ten thousand states), 4 vols. (Peking, 1864); W. A. P. Martin, *Cycle of Cathay* (New York, 1896), p. 221; G. G. Wilson, "Henry Wheaton and International Law," in Henry Wheaton, *Elements of International Law* (text of 1866 with notes), (reprint ed. New York, 1964), p. 13a; T. Dennett, *Americans in Eastern Asia* (1922; reprint ed. New York: Barnes and Noble, 1963), p. 385; Immanuel C. Y. Hsü, *China's Entrance into the Family of Nations: The Diplomatic Phase, 1858–1880* (Cambridge: Harvard University Press, 1960), p. 125. Wheaton lived between 1785 and 1848.
25. Wheaton, *Elements of International Law*, p. 16a.
26. For further information on the Japanese reception of international law, see Ōhira Zengo, "The Reception of International Law by Japan," *Shōgaku tōkyū* (The economic review), 4 (December 1953), 299–314; Shinobu Jumpei, "Vicissitudes of International Law in the Modern History of Japan," *Kokusaihō gaikō zasshi* (Journal of international law and diplomacy), 50 (May 1951), 14.
27. Hungdah Chiu, "The Development of Chinese International Law Terms and the Problem of Their Translation into English," chapter 4 in this volume.
28. *Ibid.*

in Japanese. In 1868, Mitsukuri Rinshō, in searching for a Japanese word for "right," adopted the word *kenri* as used by Martin.[29] The interaction between the Chinese and Japanese, however, often resulted in abandonment of older Chinese equivalents, because they were frequently not suitable for use in conjunction with Japanese equivalents in the overall legal vocabulary borrowed from Japan.

Another point to be borne in mind is that some characters used to represent legal terms had already existed in the traditional Chinese language. But, in their new legal science, the Japanese usually used them with different meanings. An example is the word *kempō*[30] (constitution, *hsien-fa* in Chinese) which had a much broader meaning in the old Chinese (and Japanese) than it does in the new legal system of either country.

In making the new compounds used by both themselves and later the Chinese, Japanese scholars usually followed Chinese rules for constructing polysyllabic words. Examples of such rules are:

1. Combining an adjective with a noun (e.g., *tetsugaku*, philosophy); or combining an adverb with a verb (e.g., *dokusen*, monopoly).

2. Combining two words with the same meaning (e.g., *setsumei*, explanation).

3. Combining a verb and object (e.g., *dōin*, mobilize).

In fact, in the case of number 3 above, where the Japanese attached a verb to an object in making a modern compound, they followed the Chinese rule, even though the purely Japanese rule would be exactly the opposite (e.g., putting the object first as in *monogatari*, tale). But by observing these Chinese rules, the Japanese made mutually compatible compounds which resulted in both languages becoming more precise and, by shortening words, more efficient and reciprocally understandable.

This understanding is possible because Japanese is written in Chinese characters (except for a few new Japanese characters and certain word endings or post-positions which are written in the native Japanese syllabary) and because the Chinese developed a technique for reading Japanese called in Chinese, *ho-wen han-tu fa* and in Japanese, *wabun kandoku hō*. This technique made Japanese under-

29. Osatake Takeshi, "The Compound *kenri* (right)," *Hōritsu jihō* (Legal journal), vol. 2, no. 1 (1929), p. 32.

30. See Sanetō, p. 389, for other old terms instilled with new legal meaning which were then used with the new meaning by Chinese jurists.

standable to a Chinese by enabling him to pick out the subject and then the verb at the end of the sentence, and then back for the object and so on; this process was facilitated by special punctuation to show these differences in syntax.

Doubtless the new translations from the Japanese to the Chinese language produced a difficult "Chinese" for the Chinese students beginning their studies of subjects borrowed from the West, because of the direct carry-over into Chinese of new Japanese compounds, adopted to express Western ideas. But with the passing of time, the Japanese words were absorbed and became in fact modern Chinese by virtue of simply being pronounced in Chinese. In some cases, to assist in digesting Japanese words, the Chinese translators added annotations explaining the new terms when they appeared. For example, the I-shu Hui-pien She, the leading Chinese translation group in Tokyo, in translating the Toriyabe Sentarō work, *Seijigaku teikō* (Summary of the study of politics), put the following note after *chung-ts'ai* (arbitration, or *chūsai* in Japanese): "An arbitrator is a foreign country, which acts as a go-between to make adjustments; it is called the arbitrator country." Then after *shou-hsü* (procedure, *tetsuzuki* in Japanese): "Procedure is a fixed way which must be followed. Thus, in enacting legislation, it is necessary to first publish a draft, and then vote on the legislation and then promulgate it. This method is 'procedure.' " Also, in their own creative writings, some of the Chinese often used Japanese phrasing extensively. Liang Ch'i-ch'ao had a typical Japanized style with textual explanations interspersed. See, for example, his explanation for *hsiang-hsü-jen* (Japanese: *sōzokunin*) and *fa-jen* (Japanese: *hōjin*).[31]

The overall effect of the Japanese language on the Chinese language was indeed enormous in the first twenty or thirty years of this century, but was somewhat obscured until recently, perhaps because of a Chinese disposition to overlook (for political reasons) their indebtedness to Japanese scholarship and Japanese interpretations of Western learning. This situation was well described in 1931 by Jo Hsü, who comments on Chinese translations of Japanese books.

> Japanese use the same script as Chinese. So nouns, etc., can be readily interchanged, and it seems easier to translate Japanese than Western material. But the Chinese from the beginning have looked

31. See Sanetō, *Chūgokujin*, p. 341, for quotations from Liang Ch'i-ch'ao. These terms mean "heir" and "corporation," respectively.

down upon Japan, and therefore looked down upon Japanese scholarship. Thus, generally opportunistic [Chinese] translators all look for Japanese translations of foreign books, render these into Chinese translations, then in their advertisements or on book jackets, they exaggerate to the effect that they were translated from Western originals. However, translations from Japanese are not necessarily bad; nor translations from Western language necessarily good. To the extent there are no mistakes, it matters little that it is a Japanese translation . . . What is a little strange, however, is to speak ill of Japanese works while at the same time stealing the work of the Japanese. Pick up any newly published book, and inspect it, and eight or nine out of ten of them will have come from Japan. Is this not a rather soiled aspect of the new culture.[32]

A Chinese book published in 1958 covered an extensive list of foreign borrowings in current Chinese usage and quite accurately assesses the impact of Japanese on modern Chinese.[33] In a list of 1,270 words broken down by subject matter and country of origin, the sampling of 39[34] law terms all came from Japan, and in all subjects, 84 percent of the commonly used, borrowed terms were of Japanese origin. Mao Tse-tung is quoted as saying in 1942:

We must absorb essential elements from foreign languages and take in foreign words. But we must not use them indiscriminately; we must absorb only those which we can use. The reason is that the old vocabulary is not adequate and we must absorb foreign words into our language. For example, we are now convening this "cadres' meeting" [kan-pu-hui; Japanese, kambukai], but this term "kan-pu" consisting of two characters is, after all, something we have borrowed from abroad.[35]

Word Making and Codification

The process of absorbing Western words into Japanese and then transmitting the Japanese terms to the Chinese language has many variations, some of which are not found in word borrowing between

32. Jo Hsü, Chung-kuo hsin-shu yüeh-pao, no. 2 (1931), p. 45.
33. Kao Ming-k'ai and Liu Cheng-t'an, Hsien-tai han-yü wai-lai tzu yen-chiu (Study of contemporary Chinese terms drawn from foreign words), Peking, 1958.
34. Ibid., p. 131.
35. Mao Tse-tung, Mao Tse-tung hsüan chi (Selected works of Mao Tse-tung), Peking, 1960, pp. 858–59.

Western languages. For example, when a Japanese jurist develops an equivalent for a foreign legal term, he may construct an entirely new Japanese word by combining characters to correspond with the meaning of the foreign word; the sound has no resemblance to the foreign term. This is called "meaning translation" (*iyaku*). Thus, corporation becomes *hōjin* (literally, "law person"). But note that when the Chinese adopt the exact same written characters, they attach their own sounds to them (*fa-jen*); that is, the characters and meaning are the same as the Japanese, but the sound is different from both the Japanese and the Western source.

Or the Japanese jurist could choose characters to approximate the Western sounds, such as when *gasu* is selected for gas. This is a Japanese borrowed word because it takes the Western meaning and sound (but not symbols). This is called "sound translation" (*onyaku*) in Japanese. Another alternative for the Japanese is to choose a combination of characters that existed in the traditional language but had a different meaning.

The following several classes of words have all been borrowed from Japan by the Chinese:[36]

1. Purely Japanese words such as *baai* (occasion), *tetsuzuki* (procedure), *torishimaru* (manage), and *tadashi-gaki* (proviso).

2. Old Chinese words used by the Japanese to designate a European word, which the Chinese then borrowed back *with the new meaning*, such as *kempō* (constitution), *kenri* (right), *keizai* (economy), *bungaku* (literature), and *empitsu* (pencil).

3. Japanese creations new to both China and Japan (e.g., *iyaku*) which serve as equivalents for Western terms. Then the Chinese attach their own pronunciation (e.g., *dempō*, or Chinese *tien-pao* [telegram]).

When the Japanese take a foreign word by the *onyaku* process (e.g., *gasu* for gas) they usually select two Chinese characters which do not show the meaning of the word. However, there are occasional exceptions — compare *bīru* where the Japanese characters mean "wheat beer." Significantly, the characters for *gasu* do not even show an approximated English pronunciation of gas in Chinese; so ordinarily the Chinese would not find such a term useful, though ironically, in this case, they sometimes do use the compound for *gasu* (Japanese) and pronounce it *wa-ssu*.

36. Kao and Liu, *Hsien-tai han-yü*, p. 79.

Some of the most important overall changes in the Chinese language as the result of these borrowings are as follows:

1. The Chinese have adopted a number of Japanese-style word endings such as -ka (-ize) or -shiki (-style) which give the modern language useful flexibility.

2. The combination of two characters with roughly the same meaning facilitates precision of expression, in those cases where one or both of the characters have more than one meaning. For example, yuku (1. to go and 2. to act; Chinese, hsing) can be precisely confined "to act," if it is combined with i (or Chinese, wei) to read "kōi," or "hsing-wei" in Chinese. Thus, the compounds not only multiply the total vocabulary by all of the possible combinations, but also help to distinguish between several meanings of single words.

3. The Chinese have developed certain standard terms as equivalents for standard terms in Japanese. For example, ni motozuite (based on) is rendered chi-yü in Chinese.

4. Some words adopted earlier from Japanese now have been abandoned. An example of this rōdō kumiai (labor union).

5. According to Wang Li:

China has had some polysyllabic words from the beginning, but they have become even more numerous in the modern period. Originally the Chinese did not have as many polysyllabic words as are now found in the Europeanized sentences [of current Chinese]. But to use a rough gauge, the proportion of polysyllabic words found in the ancient period, early period, and the current period is in the ratio of 1–3–9.[37]

In a different book Wang sums up the development: "In the 20 year period from the five-four [May 4, 1919] incident to the present [1944] there have been perhaps more changes in grammar than there were in the period from the Han to the Ch'ing."[38] In addition, Kao Ming-k'ai and Liu Cheng-t'an conclude in a manner refreshingly free from nationalism:

37. Wang Li, *Chung-kuo hsien-tai yü-fa* (Mode of expression in present-day China), Peking, 1943. See also John DeFrancis, *Nationalism and Language Reform in China*, p. 147.

38. Wang Li, *Chung-kuo yü-fa li-lun* (Theory of Chinese expression), Peking, 1944, 2:258.

The influence of Japanese vocabulary on present-day Chinese vocabulary has been very large, and Japanese has been a major source of foreign words. Even more, we can say that it has been the largest source. Much European and American vocabulary have been transmitted into the modern Chinese vocabulary but almost all of it through the medium of Japanese.[39]

The major remaining problem for modern Chinese linguistics is to standardize its borrowings, because there are variations in character combinations used for the same Western idea due to various translators forming combinations independently. A good example of eliminating an unsatisfactory word in the standardization process is the common, almost meaningless, word "democracy." The first Chinese equivalent *te-mo-k'o-la-hsi* has given way to the standard characters, pronounced *minshu* in Japanese, and *min-chu* in Chinese.

Thus, in first translating, then redrafting Western law for their own use, the Japanese were confronted with many Western concepts for which new Japanese terms were needed. By use of the foregoing rules, among others, they created a legal vocabulary which the Chinese could later understand and borrow.

Japanese Assistance in the Chinese Codes

Codification was finally initiated as a part of the reforms sought after the humiliations of the Sino-Japanese War (1894–95) and the Boxer Rebellion (1900).[40] By that time, Japan had already been studying Western law for thirty years and had just completed an intensive codification process culminating in the Meiji Constitution (1889) and five Western-style codes (civil, criminal, civil procedure, criminal procedure, and commercial), all adopted by 1899. These codes were inspired largely by German and French models.[41] As previously noted, two other general factors tended to point to the Chinese use of Japanese legal experts and sources: (1) China and Japan had a shared

39. Kao and Liu, p. 158.
40. The most authoritative English language work on codification of the criminal law is Meijer, *Modern Criminal Law*. See his page 9 for discussion of the Ch'ing memorials and related documents in the decision to import Western law.
41. K. Mukai and N. Toshitani, "The Progress and Problems of Compiling the Civil Code in the Early Meiji Era," trans. D. F. Henderson in *Law in Japan: An Annual,* 1 (Tokyo: Japan-American Society for Legal Studies, 1967).

core of lingual and legal traditions, making it easier for Chinese to communicate with the Japanese; (2) although their traditional sociities had important differences, both China and Japan were striving for a modernization of their respective societies, with Japan but a few paces ahead. For both, the Western codes were not only needed to induce the foreigners to relinquish their extraterritorial rights but were also necessary blueprints for future, radical departures from the past.

It was not a simple translation project which brought Japanese jurists to Peking in 1906 to assist Shen Chia-pen and his Bureau for the Compilation of Laws. This Sino-Japanese exchange was a highly creative process of transmission and reception of legal concepts by codification, raising the most fundamental questions concerning the nature of law, society, and language itself — and the relationship among them. Except for the discussion under "Word Making and Codification" above, we must eschew any expansive consideration of such problems here. Suffice it to say that our technical terms refer, in law at least, to concepts existing only in lawyers' minds, and these legal concepts are highly diverse, partaking of and reflecting, as they do, all the national and individual characteristics derived from the variety of human experience and institutions. Thus, legal concepts abstracted from the strangeness of European society had no conceptual counterparts in the Chinese mind, and there were no terms for them in the Chinese language, because the behavioral patterns from which the European concepts had been abstracted did not then exist, in similar form at least, in China. So, rather than simply translate Western laws into Chinese language, the Chinese codifiers were forced to find Chinese terms for new legal concepts, which had been first devised by Western lawyers to refer to the organizing principles of Western societies and institutions. This was a much more difficult task than assigning language equivalents to physical objects existing alike in Western, Japanese, and Chinese experience (e.g., horse = uma = ma).

A full forty years earlier the Japanese had grappled with this task of legal language making, and we are fortunate to have an extremely candid comment by Fukuzawa Yukichi,[42] founder of Keiō University, upon making a trip to the West in 1860; he commented that, al-

42. Osatake Takeshi, *Ishin zengo ni okeru shisō* (Thought before and after the restoration), Tokyo, 1925, p. 195.

though Western scientific accomplishments were very complicated, he could understand them. But Western law — he could not fathom that law was something that scholars could treat as a subject for scientific studies or that professionals could learn in order to protect the rogues of society in criminal trials. In the traditional (Tokugawa, 1600–1868) society of his time, the "code" (*Osadamegaki*) was strictly for the use of the highest officials; governance was largely an art of power maintenance, and law was an aid thereto to be manipulated by self-interested rulers in a society, which was, as to the private relations of the subjects, largely self-regulated. Law was therefore an instrument to be used by rulers, but it was not for the people nor was it to limit a ruler's actions.[43] This vastly different quality of Western law was noted with great approval by the oriental "discoverer" of the French code, Kurimoto Joun, who had accompanied the shogunal delegation to the 1867 Paris International Exposition. On returning, he wrote about the marvels of the Code Napoleon in his "Memoirs While Gazing from the Window at Dawn" (*Gyōsō tsuiroku*).[44]

The following statement by Mitsukuri Rinshō shows the excruciating labors he underwent in the task of creating Japanese names for theretofore nonexistent concepts derived from a wholly different institutional base:

In 1869 an order came down from the Meiji government to translate the French penal code. (At that time I was serving at the place known as the "Southern College of the University" [*Daigaku Nankō*].) Even though I was ordered to do the translation, I could not understand it at all. However, it was not a matter of complete lack of understanding, though at first I did not understand much of it. But since somehow I thought I would like to translate it, I did get started on the translation all right. However, it was a translation done without commentaries, dictionaries or tutors and I was completely bewildered, but at first I wrote just what I understood, making mistakes as I went. Thereafter, I did successively the civil code, the commercial code, the code of civil procedure, the

43. D. F. Henderson, "Law and Political Modernization in Japan," in R. A. Ward, ed., *Political Development in Modern Japan* (Princeton, 1968), p. 387.

44. In Meiji Bunka Kenkyū Kai, ed., *Meiji bunka zenshū: gaikoku bunkahen* (Complete collection on Meiji culture: part on foreign culture), rev. ed. (Tokyo: Nihon hyōron shin sha, 1955), 7:170.

code of criminal instruction, the constitution, etc., but I really did a hazy translation.[45]

Also, the terminological difficulties springing from vastly different political theories is well shown by the following episode told by Mitsukuri concerning his attempts to translate the term "droit civil" in article 7 of the French civil code:

> Whereupon at that time I translated the words *droit civil* as *minken* ["peoples' powers" or "authority"], there was an argument over what I meant by saying that the people [*min*] have "power" [*ken*]. Even though I tried to justify it as best I could, there was an extremely furious argument. Fortunately, the chairman, Mr. Eto, supported me and finally the matter was resolved.[46]

Mitsukuri began his translation of the French criminal code in 1869 and of the Code Napoleon (civil) in 1870. In 1871 his translation of the civil code was published (in wood block prints), and it went through several revisions and editions as his understanding of comparative institutions ripened. Significantly, by 1886 the Japanese Ministry of Justice had published the *Minpō goi kōhon* (Draft classification of civil law terms) to provide standard legal terminology for its lawyers.[47]

Because of the difficulties mentioned above, it took the Japanese fully three decades to do their initial translations and studies of Western law, after developing an avant-garde core of comparative lawyers by training them under the tutelage of foreign legal experts who served as consultants to the Ministry of Justice or were appointed to chairs in the newly established universities, and also by dispatching talented Japanese scholars abroad. The better known foreign legal consultants included men of various nationalities such as the Frenchmen, Bosquet and Boissanade; the Germans, Roesler, Mosse, Techow, and Rudorf; and the Americans, Verbeck, Wigmore, Terry, and Denison. These foreign experts had left their stamp on Japanese legal circles and on the original Japanese drafts of the proposed codes by 1890. Significantly, it was the new generation of Japanese jurists themselves who in the end redrafted the civil and commercial codes

---

45. Ōtsuki Fumihiko, *Mitsukuri Rinshō kunden* (Biography of Mitsukuri Rinshō), Tokyo, 1907, p. 102.
46. *Ibid.*, p. 102.
47. Mukai and Toshitani, "Progress and Problems."

after the famous "postponement" in the 1890's. Thus, in a two-stage process extending over nearly forty years until 1899, the Japanese developed a corps of comparative lawyers, assimilated Western concepts, translated Western laws, drafted tentative codes of their own with the help of foreign advisers, and at last enacted eclectic codes of their own.

It is little wonder then, given their proximity and similarities of language and cultural background as well as similar problems in achieving modernity, that the Chinese should attempt to utilize the prior experience of the Japanese. It enabled them to reduce considerably the time and labor involved in drafting their own codes.

In looking to the Chinese experience leading up to the decision to establish a Bureau for the Compilation of Laws (*Fa-lü pien-tsuan kuan*), we have noted that it took a military defeat at the hands of the Japanese in 1895 and the rout of the Empress Dowager in 1900 to bring the Manchu dynasty to the realization that extensive reforms were necessary. In response to an edict (*yü*) from the Empress Dowager dated January 29, 1901, requesting suggestions regarding Western type reforms which might be introduced, Liu K'un-i and Chang Chih-tung responded with a memorial (*tsou*) on June 18, 1901, which suggested in its sixth section that extensive legal reform should be made, and explicitly that Japanese and other foreign[48] advisers be used. Finally, on May 11, 1902, Shen Chia-pen and Wu T'ing-fang were appointed in charge of law reforms, and after a lapse of some time they were installed in 1904 in the Fa-lü pien-tsuan kuan as commissioners. They immediately set about translating foreign criminal and criminal procedure codes. Significantly, they had decided to proceed in two ways: first, by a revision of the old Ch'ing code as an interim measure to pave the way for more sweeping reforms; second, to draft an entirely new code along Western lines to replace this revised Ch'ing code at an appropriate date.[49]

In 1902 Liu K'un-i and Chang Chih-tung, charged with recommending commissioners for law reform, had again proposed that Japanese scholars, one for criminal law and another for civil law, be invited to assist with the legal reforms. Actually, however, the Japanese advisers were not invited, or at least did not arrive on the scene, until 1906.[50] Three Japanese were especially active in codifica-

48. Meijer, *Modern Criminal Law*, p. 9.
49. See *ibid.*, pp. 19–37.
50. Miyasaka, "About Compilation of Codes at the End of the Ch'ing Dynasty."

tion efforts at that time, Professor Okada Asatarō (criminal law),[51] Judge Matsuoka Yoshimasa (civil law), and Professor Shida Kōtarō (commercial law).[52] Also, Itakura Matsutarō was active after the fall of the Ch'ing dynasty in 1912.[53] The efforts of Shida on a draft commercial code and Matsuoka on a draft civil code were important, but a new criminal code was the major problem of the Ch'ing government, and it was given priority by Shen Chia-pen and his codification committee. Finally, the new code was enacted by the new Republic as early as 1912, well before complete codes were enacted in the civil and commercial fields.[54] We will therefore focus our attention in this study on the Japanese language influence on the criminal law up to and during the Communist period.

In drafting the criminal code Okada's work was especially important.[55] Apparently he was recommended to the Chinese govern-

51. Shimada, "Concerning the Compilation of the Criminal Law Draft at the End of the Ch'ing Dynasty — Recalling Okada Asatarō's Contributions."

52. Shimada, "Concerning Compilation of the Civil and Commercial Law Drafts at the End of the Ch'ing Dynasty"; Murakami Sadakichi, "History of the Establishment of a Civil Code in the Republic of China," Seigi (Justice), vol. 6, no. 2 (1916), p. 12.

53. "Miscellaneous Report," Hōgaku kyōkai zasshi (Journal of the Jurisprudence Association), 50 (1932), 188; Itakura, "View of China's Legislative Projects," Hōsō kiji (Juristic articles), 29 (1919), 689.

54. The Japanese influences and evaluations of the progress of the Chinese civil and commercial codes can be seen in the following: Shimada, "Concerning Compilation of the Civil and Commercial Law Drafts at the End of the Ch'ing Dynasty"; Murakami Sadakichi, "History of the Establishment of a Civil Code"; Aoki Tetsuji, "Concerning Commercial Law Compilation in Ch'ing China. Request to Dr. Shida," Hōken zasshi (Law magazine), no. 149 (1908); Asai Torao, Shina ni okeru hōten hensan no enkaku (Development of code compilation in China), Tokyo, 1911; compare summary of Murakami Sadakichi's remarks in 1932 in the Hōgaku kyōkai zasshi, 50 (132), 187, 188, where he noted on returning from thirty years of work in China that the Chinese codifiers seemed to feel that their own legal science had progressed to the point where they could learn little from Japan because Japanese legal science was too dependent on the Germans.

55. See his own accounts of his work in China: Okada, "Concerning the Ch'ing Criminal Law Draft," Hōgaku shirin (Hosei University Law Review), 12 (1910); Okada, "Concerning the Completed and the Draft Ch'ing Codes," ibid., 13 (1911), 131–47; Okada, "Legal Institutions of Ch'ing China," Keijihō hyōron (Criminal law review), 3 (1911), 1010–18; Okada, "Shinkoku kaisei keiritsu soan (sōsoku)," Hōgaku kyōkai zasshi, 29 (1911), 371–76. Okada also published several books from 1896 to 1932 on Japanese and comparative criminal law: Okada, Nihon keihō ron (kakuron no bu) (Treatise on Japanese criminal law [special part]), Tokyo, 1896; Okada, Keihō sōron (General treatise on criminal law), 2nd ed. (Tokyo, 1932); Okada, Keihō kakuron (Special treatise on criminal law), Tokyo, 1925; Okada, Hikaku keihō (Comparative criminal law), 2 vols. (Tokyo, 1936). A Chinese edition of Okada, ed., Shin keiritsu (Ch'ing criminal law), Tokyo, 1912 apparently was published in China, but I have not been able to see a copy.

ment by Ume Kenjirō, who was first invited to China, but declined because of his duties in connection with Korean affairs in Japan. Okada (1868–1936) was, it seems, involved somehow[56] in the so-called "seven doctors" (shichi hakushi) incident of May, 1903, wherein seven Tokyo University professors were suspended for their strong views in favor of war with Russia. Complications from that incident may explain Okada's availability for the post in China, for he never rejoined the law faculty of Tokyo University, but taught at Meiji and Waseda Universities after his return from China in 1915. Besides studying in Germany and France (1898–99), Okada had worked as an assistant under Ume in the Japanese codification process. He was therefore well qualified for his position in China, which included teaching at the newly established (1905) law school in Peking and also advising the government on the law reforms and codification.

On arrival in Peking, Okada found that the Chinese had already completed a draft of all of the general provisions (tsung-tse; Japanese, sōsoku) of a criminal code and nine sections of the special provisions. On reading through it, as Okada later noted, the code followed very closely the old (pre-1907) Japanese criminal code of 1882. Therefore, he got permission to start anew on a draft of his own, because Japanese revisions had already been drafted for changes to be enacted in 1907. Okada not only wanted to draw from those Japanese improvements,[57] but we are told that he also had some ideas of his own which he wanted to incorporate into the Chinese draft, though they had not prevailed in the Japanese reform discussions.[58] Indeed Okada did introduce his ideas (for example, concerning the role of the procurator) into drafts of the code of criminal procedure.[59] Later, some of these ideas were embodied in the law of the Republic of China on the advice of Itakura Matsutarō.[60] Thus, the new Chinese

---

56. There is a conflict in the biographical information concerning whether Okada was one of the seven. Heibonsha, Jimmei jiten (Dictionary of personal names) says he was, but Takayanagi et al., eds., Nihon hōseishi jiten (Japanese legal history dictionary), Tokyo, 1967, p. 394, and Asakura et al., eds., Meiji sesō hennen jiten (Chronological dictionary of Meiji events), Tokyo, 1965, p. 464, list seven others (without Okada).
57. Okada, "Concerning the Ch'ing Criminal Law Draft."
58. Okada, "Concerning the Completed and the Draft Ch'ing Codes."
59. Miyasaka, "Compilation of Modern Codes," see note 12, pp. 17–18.
60. Itakura, "View of China's Legislative Projects," see note 53, pp. 689–703.

draft criminal code was at several points different from the new Japanese code (1907), and it also retained several special features of Ch'ing law of continuing importance to late Ch'ing conditions.[61] Compared to the Japanese code of only 264 articles, the new Chinese draft, with 387 articles, was considerably longer.

This draft was presented to the Emperor, who referred it to the Constitution Committee (Hsien-cheng pien-ch'a kuan) for comment in 1907, even before the interim revision of the Ch'ing criminal code was completed (submitted in 1910; enacted in 1911). The new code was too drastic for the conservatives at the top of Ch'ing officialdom. There followed three years of discussion, and, interestingly enough, one of the criticisms was precisely that the new draft criminal code reflected too much reliance on Japanese law and language.[62] In the end, only relatively minor changes were made in the draft as such, but five supplementary provisions were added to the code, which substantially subverted its purposes by reintroducing the old family relations[63] into the new code via the back door. This version with its eviscerating supplements was accepted by the Emperor in 1911 and passed on to the newly established assembly for its deliberation. The draft was approved by the assembly, but the Emperor never promulgated it because by then the Ch'ing dynasty was on the verge of the revolution which swept it from power. Ironically, this same Ch'ing draft, with little change, was enacted the very next year (1912) by the new Republic; but the five supplemental provisions were deleted.

This description of the role of the Japanese language in the Chinese criminal code will suffice for our purposes. No doubt it was during this interaction in the first decade of this century that the major importation of Japanese legal terminology into Chinese jurisprudence occurred, and it is upon this body of terminology that we will concentrate in tracing the continued effect of Japanese legal terms in Communist Chinese usage.

61. Okada, "Concerning the Ch'ing Criminal Law Draft." Later Itakura noted the need to mold and adapt the new legal theory to the peculiar needs of China. "Miscellaneous Report," *Hōgaku kyōkai zasshi*, 50 (1932), 187, 188.
62. Meijer, *Modern Criminal Law*, p. 95.
63. Murakami Sadakichi, *Shina rekidai no keisei enkaku to genkō keihō* (History of the penal system of the Chinese dynasties and present-day effective criminal law), Tokyo, 1932, p. 216.

Statistical Comparison of Legal Terms
in the Criminal Law of Japan and China

As a first step, some sense of the Japanese influence which has carried over into Communist Chinese legal terminology can be obtained by starting with a list of terms selected [64] from the Japanese criminal code (1907), presumably employed by Okada and the Chinese in drafting their criminal code by 1910, and then checking to see how many of these terms can be traced through the several later versions of the Chinese criminal law (codes of 1928 and 1935; and the 1957 Communist Chinese textbook, *Lectures on the General Principles of Criminal Law* [hereafter *Lectures*]).[65] The results of this first step are shown in Table 5.1.

As a second step in measuring the overlap of Japanese and Chinese terminology, I have taken those Chinese terms which occur in the above-mentioned Chinese sources but which are not found in the Japanese code of 1907, and checked to see whether they nonetheless occur in the current Japanese legal literature other than the criminal code itself. The results of this exercise are shown in Table 5.2.

This correlating and counting yields a total of 273 Chinese Communist legal terms selected from the 1957 *Lectures*, about 81 percent (221 terms) of which were also Japanese terms (Table 5.3) and 28 percent (76 terms) were in the Japanese code of 1907 (Table 5.1).

The Non-overlapping Terms (i.e., purely Communist Chinese, Nationalist Chinese or Japanese)

As shown in Table 5.4, a number of terms in each of the sources seem to be exclusively Japanese or Chinese, and some of the Chinese

64. Necessarily some discretion is involved in selecting legal terms from the criminal law codes. I have tended to select all "legal" rather than narrowly "criminal law" terms, and I have also conceived the legal category more broadly. Occasionally, a change in the order of the same two components of two "different" compounds has posed problems which I have resolved usually in favor of distinguishing the terms. Abbreviations in Japanese or Chinese terms I have treated as the same as the complete or original term.

65. Teaching and Research Office for Criminal Law of the Central Political-Legal Cadres' School, ed., *Lectures on the General Principles of Criminal Law of the People's Republic of China* (Chung-hua jen-min kung-ho-kuo hsing-fa tsung-tse chiang-i), Peking, 1957, translated in Joint Publications Research Service no. 13,331 (1962), emphasizes the general (*sōsoku*) over the special principles found in the usual format of both the Japanese and Chinese pre-Communist codes. Consequently, I would surmise that the Communists do use some of these terms in China, though they did not occur in the above treatise.

terms seem to be exclusively Nationalist Chinese. The number of terms which are apparently exclusively Japanese might be reduced by examining a wider sampling of Communist Chinese material, and I feel quite certain that the same would be the case for some of the 110 Nationalist terms found in Japanese law but not found in the rather narrow coverage of the 1957 Communist *Lectures* (Table 5.5). I doubt, however, whether the apparently exclusive Chinese terms counted in Table 5.4 have any substantial use in Japanese.

Table 5.1. Overlap of Criminal Law Terms in the Japanese Criminal Code of 1907 and the Chinese Communist *Lectures* (and also Chinese Nationalist Sources).[a]

Combination of sources in which term occurs	Number of terms
J-1907; C-1928; C-1935; Communist 1957	48
Only in J-1907; C-1928; Communist 1957	9
Only in J-1907; C-1935; Communist 1957	11
Only in J-1907; Communist 1957	8
Total Chinese Communist terms from the Japanese Criminal Code	76

[a] The sources are:

Abbreviation	Title
J–1907	Japanese Criminal Code (1907)
C–1928	Chinese Criminal Code (1928)
C–1935	Chinese Criminal Code (1935)
Communist 1957	*Lectures on the General Principles of Criminal Law*

Note: This chart shows the result of step one in our procedure to measure the overlap of Chinese and Japanese criminal law terms, as described in the text. We have started with two groups of legal terms: those drawn from the Japanese code, and those from successive Chinese criminal law materials up to the present. Then by counting the Japanese terms which run chronologically from the first Chinese code to the later sources we can get an inkling of how some Japanese terminology was transmitted into present Communist Chinese usage.

Two caveats are in order. First, simply the fact that there is a

Table 5.2. Chinese Terms in Japanese Criminal Law Literature (other than the J-1907).

Sources in which term occurs	Number of terms
1. Nationalist only (C-1928)	50
2. Nationalist only (C-1935)	41
3. Communist only (1957)	109
4. Communist terms found also in Nationalist sources (C-1928; C-1935; Communist 1957)	36
5. Nationalist terms found in both sources (C-1928 and C-1935 only)	19
	255

Note: This chart reports the results of the second step in our procedure to measure the overlap of Japanese and Chinese criminal law terms. We took the remaining Chinese terms selected from the same Chinese source but not found in the Japanese code of 1907 and we checked the dictionary to see if they were, nonetheless, Japanese terms.

coincidence of a certain legal term in both the Chinese and the Japanese codes does not mean that it was created in Japan and imported into China, because it could be a traditional Chinese law term which originated in China and was exported to ancient Japan and shared in the usage of both countries up to the present. This is indeed the case with a number of terms, because from the eighth century onward, Japan has shared the tradition of the T'ang codes (for example, the Japanese *Taihō ritsuryō* [702] and *Yōrō ritsuryō*

Table 5.3. Overlap of Communist Chinese Criminal Law Terms with All Japanese Terms.

Total non-J-1907 Communist terms (Table 5.2, lines 3 and 4)	145
Total overlap of J-1907 and Communist terms (Table 5.1)	76
Total overlap of Japanese and Communist terms from *Lectures*	221
Percentage of Communist *Lectures* terms in Japanese (221 ÷ 273)[a]	81%

[a] In addition to the 273 *Lectures* terms, there were 256 J-1907 terms. Of the latter, 76 were counted twice, making a total of 453 terms.

**Table 5.4. Remaining Terms
Which Are Exclusively Japanese or Chinese.**

Sources in which terms occur	Number of terms
Chinese terms not found in Japanese law[a]	
In C-1928 alone	21
In C-1935 alone	13
In Communist 1957 alone	52
In combinations of 1, 2, and 3 above	26
	112
Japanese terms not found in the Chinese sources above	
In J-1907	37

[a] These are the remaining terms from our list; these numbers represent terms not found in either J-1907 or the Japanese Law Dictionary.

[708]), and some of that early terminology was retained in the Japanese criminal law of 1882 and onward. However, it is safe to say that in most cases even an old Chinese word has been given a very different significance in the modern code context, and the Japanese priority in the codification process is proof enough for the purpose of assessing the influences after 1900. Otherwise an exorbitant amount of ink might be spilled arguing the ultimate source and not affect the statistics significantly. For example, Martin's translation into

**Table 5.5. Nationalist Chinese Terms Found
in the Japanese Literature (not in the Communist
Lectures).**

Sources in which term occurs	Number of terms
C-1928	50
C-1935	41
Combinations (both C-1928 and C-1935)	19
	110

Chinese of Wheaton's *Elements of International Law* in the 1850's produced a number of "Chinese" legal terms, and as noted, Mitsukuri Rinshō drew upon the term that Martin had coined in Chinese to represent the Western concept of "right" (*kenri* in Japanese).[66] Hozumi says, however, that a Japanese, M. Tsuda, coined the word, as he had coined the word *minpō* for civil law.[67] Osatake says *kenri* pre-existed in the old Chinese.[68] During their codification processes, the Japanese probably used in a novel legal sense many terms existing before 1900 and available somewhere in both the Japanese and Chinese classical vocabularies. Nonetheless, their use in a new legal science gave them new meaning, and it is this new usage that is significant for our purpose.

The second caveat stems from the insight above. It would surely be an error to assume that the socially operative meanings of identical Chinese and Japanese written symbols remain the same, even though they may have come to China as new legal terms from Japan. Of course, once enacted in China these terms began to live a life of their own in Chinese society and that new life could soon take them far from their Japanese meaning. Indeed, in most cases, it caused some difference in jural meaning.

Also, there are a number of other threads and subsequent legal exchanges between Japan and China in the period of 1912 to date, which in the fullness of time should be explored. For example, surely materials available in Japan would enable us to determine what further use the Chinese made of Japanese consultants and visiting professors between 1912 and 1933. Some continued influence was exerted by Japanese law and lawyers on legal institutions in north China because of the Japanese military occupation of Manchuria and parts of China,[69] for the Japanese authorities in Manchuria did extensive studies on local institutions and comparisons with Japanese law in preparation for codification. Also, the judges in Manchuria were virtually all Japanese-trained.

66. Carmen Blacker, *The Japanese Enlightenment* (Cambridge, Eng.: Cambridge University Press, 1964), p. 105.
67. Hozumi Nobushige, *Lectures on the New Japanese Civil Code* (Tokyo, 1912).
68. Osatake, "The Compound *kenri*."
69. See Paul L-M Serruys, *Survey of the Chinese Language Reform and the Anti-Illiteracy Movement in Communist China*, Studies in Chinese Communist Terminology (Berkeley, California: Center of Chinese Studies, University of California, February 1962), no. 8, p. 137.

Conversely, during the Republican period many Chinese legal scholars, including a number who are now Communist, studied law in Japan, complementing the Japanese legal scholars who studied and taught in China. We know, for example, that Shen Chün-ju, the president of the Supreme People's Court prior to the adoption of the Constitution in 1954, and Tung Pi-wu, who succeeded him during the constitutional period, both studied law in Japan. A number of members of the Codification Committee of the early 1950's also received legal education in Japan. There are also two works which show direct Communist awareness and consultation of Japanese materials:[70]

> *Hsing-fa tsung-tse fen-chieh tzu-liao hui-pien* (Collection of materials by topical comparative arrangement in the general provisions of criminal law), Peking, 1957. Compiled by the Legal Office of the Standing Committee of the National People's Congress in connection with the drafting of the criminal code of the People's Republic of China, this work contains the general provisions of the Japanese criminal code.
> *Jih-pen hsing-fa* (Japanese criminal code), Peking, 1956. From a collection compiled by Hiroshi Suekawa, this book was translated by Chi T'i and published by the Legal Press.

Conclusions

The priority of Japanese experience with Western legal abstractions in the systematic world of modern code law made it efficient for the Chinese to use Japanese advisers and Japanese terminology in codifying their law in the first decades of the twentieth century. The Chinese, in fact, did absorb Japanese legal science (and language) massively through study in Japan, through hired teachers and legal advisers like Okada, and through translation and publication of and subsequent reliance upon Japanese legal dictionaries and encyclopedias, texts, and commentaries. These initial influences created a Japanese-based Chinese legal science and terminology which has

---

70. Tao-tai Hsia, Chief, Far Eastern Law Division, Library of Congress, brought these Communist works to my attention.

retained considerable strength, even in Communist law since 1949, although the terminology is now employed with connotations derived from the changed ideology as well as from the normal changes in meaning that are a consequence of official and social behavior over time.

6 The Language of Communist China's Criminal Law

David Finkelstein

"Chinese is a language more appropriate for the expression of poetic literary fancies than for the conveyance of legal and scientific thought." [1]

It is no wonder that the world is baffled by Communist China's "Cultural Revolution." Not only do the specialists who are skilled in reading between the lines of Chinese Communist utterances disagree about many aspects of the recent upheaval, those whose task it is merely to read the plain lines themselves also seem unable to agree even on the basic meaning of what they are reading. We are informed, for instance, that "eight Red Guards and a member of the Pioneers . . . had been killed by 'class enemies,' according to a Red Guard announcement." [2] Later we are told of "doubts about a report that nine youths were killed last week. Chinese-language experts said the characters on a poster reporting the incident could mean also that the nine young Chinese had been injured." [3] There were more doubts about whether Lo Jui-ch'ing was "taken away" or was "arrested" [4] and still more about whether T'ao Chu was "led" or "dragged" through the streets.[5]

The confusion must seem all the more strange to the Western lawyer, that self-proclaimed priest of precision, who reads these dispatches. How, he must wonder, can there be such uncertainty about simple words like "killing" and "arrest"! Is it simply a problem of translation or are the Chinese themselves plagued with a language which defies precise definition? The question is not a rhetorical one.

Note: Reprinted from the *Journal of Asian Studies*, 27, no. 3 (May 1968), 503–521.

1. Dr. W. W. Yen, quoted in C. K. Ogden, *Debabelization* (London: Kegan Paul, 1931), p. 132.
2. *New York Times*, Aug. 28, 1966, p. 1.
3. *New York Times*, Aug. 31, 1966, p. 8.
4. *New York Times*, Dec. 24, 1966, p. 1.
5. *New York Times*, Jan. 6, 1967, p. 2.

If, in fact, the Chinese language, and particularly the language of Chinese law, is so vague that to understand it really "requires a well-developed sense of guessing," [6] then how can rules be made understandable and how, if we accept Professor Lon Fuller's thesis, can the Chinese Communist legal system be "properly called a legal system at all"?[7] If, on the other hand, we discover that the problem is one of translation, the prognosis for China's legal future may be less gloomy, but our own troubles become no less complex. For then we must deal with the host of problems arising from our efforts to understand and to interpret legal materials belonging to a very different tradition upon which has recently been grafted an ideology alien both to that tradition and to our own.

Professor Harold Berman has pointed out the need for an examination of "the growth of particular legal systems in terms of the growth of the language — the discourse — which is the stuff of which any legal system is made." [8] Regrettably, such a study of Chinese law is at present impossible. Too little is known of the traditional law of China and of the terse classical language which was the medium for its expression, and even less is known of the vernacular language which must have been used to convey its meaning to the illiterate masses whose subservience it was meant to ensure. There is a dearth of scholarly work, also, on the law and legal language of the Republican era and of the Yenan period of Chinese Communism. And finally, the absence in present-day Communist China of both a criminal and civil code which might serve to systematize the law and define its terminology,[9] and the consequent need to scavenge for legal references through a paucity of material of diverse authorship and varying quality,[10] make it hazardous for us to formulate any definitive conclusions about the contemporary Chinese legal language. Obviously, then, any effort to trace the growth of the Chinese legal system in terms of its language must at this stage of our knowl-

6. Bernhard Karlgren, *The Chinese Language* (New York: Ronald Press, 1949), p. 59.
7. Lon Fuller, *The Morality of Law* (New Haven: Yale University Press, 1964), p. 39.
8. Harold Berman, "Law and Language" (unpublished manuscript).
9. Attempts to define current Chinese legal terminology are further impeded by the fact that, to the best of this writer's knowledge, no legal dictionaries have been published by the Chinese Communists.
10. It is clear, for example, that Communist Chinese statutes, though themselves far from exemplifying perfect legal draftsmanship, are, generally speaking, written with somewhat more care than the average article in a Chinese legal journal.

edge be of a most rudimentary nature: the contents must of necessity be "technical" and the conclusions tentative. Having made this apology and armed with this rationale, we shall proceed to examine a few problems related to the language of Communist China's law in general and its criminal law in particular.[11]

"The power of words is the most conservative force in our life." [12]

Upon assuming political power the Chinese Communists purported to abolish the old law;[13] they did not, however, suggest that their language — far older than the law — be likewise discarded. Fantastic though it may seem, the ideal of discarding the pre-revolutionary language had been suggested after the October Revolution in Russia and had gathered such currency in the nineteen thirties and forties that "Marxist linguistics," which maintained that an artificial international language was a prerequisite to the realization of a classless society, became "something like an official doctrine" [14] in the Soviet Union. It was not until June, 1950, that Stalin unequivocally repudiated that doctrine in a series of letters published in *Pravda*.[15] The Chinese lost no time in translating and publishing these letters which, in October of the same year, appeared in pamphlet form and soon became the basis of linguistic study in China.[16]

Stalin ordained that language was not to be considered a part of the superstructure of society. Language does not have a class character; it is simply a tool, created by and in the service of all classes within society. He admitted, however, that "classes do influence

11. The legal language has, of course, not remained static during the years the Chinese Communists have been in power. It would be premature, however, to attempt a periodization study at this time.

12. C. K. Ogden and I. A. Richards, *The Meaning of Meaning* (New York: Harcourt, Brace, 1956), p. 25.

13. Common Program of the Chinese People's Political Consultative Conference, art. 17, Sept. 29, 1949, *FLHP* 1:19.

14. Margaret Schlauch, "The Soviet Linguistic Controversy," *New World Review* (August 1951). Reprinted in Joseph Stalin, *Marxism and Linguistics* (New York: International Publishers, 1951), p. 58.

15. The first letter, published on June 20, was followed by four more on June 29, July 11, July 22 and July 28, respectively. They have all been reprinted in Stalin, *Marxism and Linguistics*.

16. Joseph Stalin, *Ma-k'o-szu chu-i yü yü-yen hsüeh wen-t'i* (Marxism and problems of linguistics), Peking, 1950. The pamphlet actually contains only the first three of Stalin's five letters. A second edition was published in January, 1953. By March, 1957, there had been ten printings.

language, contribute their own specific words and expressions to language, and at times understand one and the same words and expressions differently." [17] As a result, "[t]o a certain extent the vocabulary of the [post-revolutionary] Russian language has changed, in the sense that it has been supplemented by a large number of new words and expressions . . . ; a number of words and expressions have changed their meaning; a number of obsolete words have fallen out of the vocabulary." [18]

One may speculate as to whether, had Hu Shih and others not stimulated in 1917 the so-called "vernacular language" reform, the Chinese Communists could or would have so readily accepted Stalin's pronouncement that language is classless.[19] The least that can be said is that it would have been more difficult for them than it perhaps was for the Russians to argue that their traditional written language was not in large part the product of the elite of a quasi-feudal society.[20] At any rate, in 1950 the Chinese *were* in a position to accept a convenient linguistic doctrine which made it unnecessary for them to ponder the disruptive effect of discarding their national language.[21] And seven years later, when the Chinese finally determined that the "old law" was not to be considered "inheritable," [22] Stalin's doctrine permitted them to make an exception in the case of the language of law; for "if it's the language [of the old Chinese law], then we're not talking about inheritability because language is classless." [23]

There were still, of course, words and expressions related to law

17. Stalin, *Marxism and Linguistics*, p. 37.
18. *Ibid.*, p. 10.
19. Hu Shih was later involved in, though he did not instigate, the so-called "mass language" movement. Although the name might suggest a class view of language, the movement has been described as simply "an extension and refinement of the old . . . 'vernacular language' " movement. John DeFrancis, *Nationalism and Language Reform in China* (Princeton: Princeton University Press, 1950), p. 112.
20. Interestingly enough, the vernacular "national language" had come under attack in the early nineteen thirties for its "bureaucratic taint." DeFrancis, *Nationalism and Language Reform*, p. 231. The few principals involved, however, were not misguided Marxists; they were just opponents of those who advocated subordinating China's dialects to one standard language.
21. It might be argued that if the "latinxua" movement aimed at replacing characters with the Latin alphabet eventually succeeds, the Chinese will have effectively discarded their present language, and not just changed its form. For by cutting off access to the literature of the past, they would be eliminating a major obstacle to arbitrary redefinition of terminology.
22. See Shih Liang (then Minister of Justice), "Thoroughly Break Up the Attack of the Rightists on the Administration of Justice," *KMJP*, Aug. 31, 1957, p. 1.
23. Ni Jen-hai, "A Few Views on the Inheritability of Law," *KMJP*, April 1, 1957, p. 3.

and inherited from previous regimes which had to, and could in accordance with Stalin's doctrine, be discarded. Surprisingly, though, there was only limited discussion in Chinese legal and language periodicals of objectionable legal language. Criticism was levelled at certain offensive terms that belonged to the category which we might call "legalese" or "legal jargon." During the judicial reform movement of 1952–53, for instance, one writer complained:

> The old style written judgment is still used, including such stale terms and excessive phrases as "liang tsao" [the two parties], "sung cheng" [the litigation issue], and "chi-shang lun-chieh" [based on the above discussion]. No regard is paid to whether or not the people understand these terms.[24]

Later, during the anti-rightist movement of 1957–58, it was said that prior to judicial reform "legal jargon was used to intimidate the masses" [25] and that one of the objects of judicial reform had been to eliminate "the intolerably rotten bureaucratic [yamen] habit of . . . playing with words." [26] However, there seemed at times to be less concern about doing away with the "legal jargon" itself than about "vernacularizing" the nonlegal language used in legal documents. The 1954 Draft Constitution was praised, for example, because such terms as *"ju-kuo"* (if), *"i-ching"* (already) and *"tou"* (all) were used instead of the more literary *"ju," "i"* and *"chün."* [27]

There was criticism, also, of language which allegedly embodied "concepts of the Six Codes" of the Kuomintang and was utilized by "the old legal personnel" to "exonerate counterrevolutionaries from guilt." [28] Examples of such language included "not pursuing a person for his actions in the past," "not handling a case in the absence of a complaint," "not handling a case if the party is not qualified to bring the complaint," "criminal matters will not be handled in a

24. "Northwest Carries Out Judicial Reform," *KMJP*, Aug. 24, 1952.
25. Hsiao Hung, "Can We Let the Old Law Revive?," *KMJP*, Oct. 6, 1957, p. 2.
26. T'ao Hsi-chin, "A Discussion of Judicial Reform," *CFYC*, no. 5 (1957), p. 13.
27. See, for example, Lin Han-ta, "Looking at Language Reform from the Point of View of the Draft Constitution," *Chung-kuo yü-wen* (China's language), no. 25 (July 1954), p. 3.
28. See, for example, "Diligently Develop the Judicial Reform Movement," *NFJP*, Sept. 12, 1952; Hsiao Hung, "Can We Let the Old Law Revive?"; and T'ao Hsi-chin, "A Discussion of Judicial Reform." In the T'ao article phrases such as "contractual relationship," "free will" and "private conduct" were also criticized for expressing "concepts of the old civil law which protected the rights and interests of the bourgeoisie."

civil case," "attempted crime," "period of limitations," and "inability to commit a particular crime."

Beyond this there was little overt criticism of the legal language inherited from the preceding regime. Yet other terms, still in use in Nationalist China, are conspicuously absent from the Communist Chinese legal vocabulary. "*Fa-kuan*," for example, a term for "judge" which might be regarded as perpetuating the distasteful distinction between officials and common people that is basic to Confucian thought, is rarely encountered. The rather neutral "*shen-p'an yüan*" is used instead. Equally rare is another term for "judge," "*t'ui-shih*." This term may have been abandoned simply because it is used by the Nationalists and has provided the Communists with material for an abusive pun intended to reproach some of their own judges who, like the "*t'ui-shih*" of the previous regime, allegedly "pushed away their work" (*t'ui-ch'u liao-shih*).[29]

Another example of a term which occurs only occasionally in Communist Chinese legal material is "the suspect" (*hsien-i-fan*). According to one former public security officer, the word has been consciously avoided in order to support the pretense that the investigation organ actually knows a given person is guilty rather than just suspects it.

The Nationalists' term for "reform," *chiao-hua*[30] (literally, "influence through teaching"), has been replaced by *kai-tsao* (literally, "remake"), perhaps because the latter suggests a more thoroughgoing overhaul. The former term for "confession," *tzu-pai*,[31] has for the most part been replaced by *t'an-pai*,[32] an expression which is commonly used in everyday speech to mean "candid." The Nationalists' more literary expression for "deprivation" (of political rights, and so on), *ch'ih-to*,[33] seems to have been replaced by the more col-

29. See, for example, Hsiao Hung, "Can We Let the Old Law Revive?"; and "The Attitude of Pushing Away One's Work" (letter to the editor and reply), *Ch'ang-sha jih-pao* (Changsha daily), Sept. 11, 1956, p. 3.
30. See, for example, the Prison Act, art. 2 (1), *Tsui-hsin liu-fa ch'üan-shu* (Newest book of the complete six codes), Taipei, 1959, p. 220. Hereafter cited as *Six Codes*.
31. See, for example, the Code of Criminal Procedure, art. 100, *Six Codes*, p. 279.
32. At least one mainland writer was still using the term *tzu-pai* in October, 1957. See Liu Ching-lin, "A Discussion of the Evidentiary Value of a Defendant's Confession," FH, 5 (1957), 41. More precisely, the term "*t'an-pai*" means "confession after discovery" as distinguished from "*tzu-shou*," which means "confession before discovery" or "voluntary surrender." See Ning Han-lin, "Voluntary Surrender in the Criminal Law of the People's Republic of China," CFYC, no. 4 (1957), p. 12.
33. See, for example, the Criminal Code, art. 34 (1), *Six Codes*, p. 234.

loquial *po-to;* and *kuan-shu*[34] for "control" has been replaced by the more severe *kuan-chih.* The term *chü-t'i,* used in Nationalist China's Code of Criminal Procedure to mean "seize" (a suspect),[35] has not been encountered in Communist legal writings. It is arguable that the expression *chü-liu,* meaning "detain," is the substitute; but even this, not to mention the reason for the change, is open to question.

In addition to having discarded or revised some legal terminology, the Chinese Communists seem to have introduced "legal jargon" of their own with such phrases as "an offender whose case has already been adjudged" (*i-chüeh-fan*),[36] "an offender whose case has not been adjudged" (*wei-chüeh-fan*),[37] and "believe a coerced statement" (*pi-kung-hsin*).[38] The tortured grammatical construction of this third term renders it incomprehensible to Chinese who have not received their legal education in Communist China, but it apparently derives from the grammatically more orthodox expression *"pi, kung, hsin,"* [39] which loosely interpreted means the practice of "coercing a person, listening to his statement, and then believing it."

Undoubtedly, a more detailed analysis of the language of both Nationalist and Communist law will reveal still other variances and will help to explain the reasons which motivated the changes already noted. But the fact that differences exist should not obscure the fact that the basic language of Chinese criminal law in large part remains.

34. See, for example, the Criminal Code, art. 92, *ibid.,* p. 245.
35. See, for example, the Code of Criminal Procedure, ch. 8, *ibid.,* pp. 278–79. *Chü-t'i* has often been mistranslated as "arrest without a warrant." See, for example, the Code of Criminal Procedure, art. 75, *The Laws of the Republic of China* (Taipei, 1961), p. 1104.
36. See, for example, the Act of the People's Republic of China for Reform Through Labor [hereafter cited as Labor Act], art. 9, Sept. 7, 1954, FLHP, p. 34.
37. See, for example, Labor Act, art. 8, p. 34. It should be recognized that this term prejudges the guilt of a suspect. According to one informant, the logic (or fairness) of this term was the subject of internal debate by legal cadres from 1953 to 1960, at which time a decision was made to discontinue its use. However, the term *fan-jen* (offender) was still being used synonymously with *pei-kao* (the accused) as late as 1962. See, for example, Chang Tzu-p'ei, "Several Problems in the Use of Evidence to Determine the Facts of a Case in Criminal Litigation," CFYC, no. 4 (1962), p. 13.
It should be noted that the terms *i-chüeh* and *wei-chüeh* were used in the Ch'ing Code (*ta-ch'ing lü-li*) to mean, respectively, "already punished" and "not yet punished." See, for example, the 1873 edition of the Code, *Ta-ch'ing lü-li hui-t'ung hsin-tsuan,* reprinted in 1964 in Taipei, 4:2951 (*Hsing-lü su-sung: fa wu kao*).
38. See, for example, T'an Cheng-wen, "Absorb Experience and Teaching, Impel A Great Leap Forward in Procuratorial Work," CFYC, no. 3 (1958), p. 35.
39. See, for example, Liu Ching-lin, "Evidentiary Value," p. 42.

Tou-ou (fight, brawl), *ta-shang* (injure by beating), *t'ung-chien* (adultery), *chui-chi* (pursue and capture), *yüeh-yü t'o-t'ao* (escape from prison), *sheng-shih* (make trouble), and *chiao-so* (incite) are just a few examples of terms which were as much a part of the Ch'ing dynasty's legal vocabulary as they are of contemporary China's.[40]

To be sure, a heavy dose of ideological-revolutionary terminology such as "counterrevolutionaries," "hostile elements," "destructive elements," "reactionaries," "bourgeoisie," "rich peasants," and "rightists" has been introduced, but this has not diminished the stock of ordinary terms describing such ordinary criminals as "petty thieves," "robbers," "embezzlers," "rapists," "arsonists," and "murderers." And although there are now new organizations "of the masses" such as "people's mediation committees" and "security defense committees" and new strange-sounding sanctions such as "speak reason struggle" and "supervised labor," there are still "police bureaus" and "courts" (albeit prefixed by "people's"), "trials," "life imprisonment" and "death penalties." Profiting from the USSR's more than thirty years of trial and error pioneering in the field of Communist law and from Stalin's linguistic doctrine, the Chinese have been able at least to say, as the Soviets had not been able to say until the mid-nineteen thirties,[41] that crime is "crime" and punishment is "punishment."

The existence of some degree of continuity in the language of Chinese criminal law should not, however, be overemphasized. Stalin's statement that "a number of [Russian] words and expressions have changed their meaning" since the Bolshevik revolution should be sufficient warning to students of Chinese law that the Chinese language has undergone, or is undergoing, a similar change. And Chinese legal cadres have themselves explicitly admitted that the old legal terms, so-called "technical terms," are in fact being used with changed "content" or "substance." [42] *Shou-jung* (provide with shel-

---

40. All the terms cited in this paragraph can be found in E-tu Zen Sun, ed., *Ch'ing Administrative Terms* (Cambridge, Mass.: Harvard University Press, 1961).
41. In the RSFSR Criminal Code of 1926, "socially dangerous act" was made the equivalent of "crime" and "measures of social defense" replaced the word "punishment," which was done away with altogether. See Harold J. Berman, *Justice in the USSR* (New York: Vintage, 1963), pp. 34 and 56; and H. J. Berman and J. W. Spindler, *Soviet Criminal Law and Procedure: The RSFSR Codes* (Cambridge, Mass.: Harvard University Press, 1966), pp. 24–26, 40–41.
42. See, for example, Ni Jen-hai and Ch'eng Hsia-ho, "Two Problems Concerning the Inheritability of Law," *KMJP*, May 13, 1957, p. 3.

ter) has thus become a euphemism for what is more nearly a coercive roundup of undesirables.[43] *P'ei-shen-yüan* (one who participates in adjudication), which has been used to translate the Western term "juror," [44] has effortlessly become the word-symbol for the Soviet-inspired "[people's] assessor." [45] *An-chih,* a term which during the Ch'ing referred to the "settlement" or "placement" of banished convicts,[46] has retained its basic meaning but is now used with reference to the placement of "vagrants" and ex-convicts.[47] And *"chien-chü,"* which meant simply "reporting an official's unlawful conduct or dereliction of duty," [48] has become the everfeared, everpresent "denunciation" of any person.

It is perhaps a similar phenomenon in the area of ideological language that has prompted Professor Franz Schurmann to say:

> People who know the Chinese language well are often misled into believing that they "understand" what the Chinese Communists are saying. Such false understanding comes from the fact that the Chinese Communists often use seemingly conventional words with special significance which only someone who has studied the ideology can understand.[49]

Yet, however valid this statement may be with respect to the language of ideology, it does not appear applicable to the language of contemporary Chinese law. For the latter is not always used with "the precision and consistency" that according to Professor Schur-

43. See, for example, the Instructions of the Ministry of Interior Concerning the Work of Placing and Reforming City Vagrants [hereafter cited as Instructions], July 11, 1956, in *FKHP,* 4:212. According to one informant, the meaning of the term *shou-jung* had begun to deteriorate even in pre-Communist China, inasmuch as the places which the Nationalists established for homeless people were not much better than prisons.

44. See, for example, Cheng Ching-i, ed., *Fa-lü ta-tz'u-shu* (Dictionary of legal terms), Shanghai, 1936, 1:1379–80. Hereafter cited as Dictionary.

45. See the Law of the People's Republic of China for the Organization of People's Courts, ch. 3, sec. 2, Sept. 28, 1954, *FKHP,* 1:132. Hereafter cited as Court Law.

46. E-tu Zen Sun, *Ch'ing Administrative Terms,* p. 274.

47. See, for example, Instructions, p. 212, and Provisional Measures for Dealing with the Release of Reform-Through-Labor Criminals at the Expiration of Their Term of Imprisonment and for Placing Them and Getting Them Employment, Sept. 7, 1954, *FLHP,* p. 44.

48. E-tu Zen Sun, *Ch'ing Administrative Terms,* p. 16, and Dictionary, 2:2100. Sun's translation of this term does not appear to be entirely accurate.

49. Franz Schurmann, *Ideology and Organization in Communist China* (Berkeley: University of California Press, 1966), p. 58.

mann characterize the language of ideology, [50] and as a result perhaps the insider as well as the outsider has a "false" or superficial understanding of Chinese legal language. The soundness of this appraisal may have been implicitly acknowledged by one ex-Communist Chinese cadre with whom the subject was discussed who objected to, and cautioned against, a "scientific analysis" of the legal language.

"For the so-called Chinese language is a really froward child, a most recalcitrant thing in the hand of the logical-minded." [51]

Chinese legal material abounds with inconsistent and imprecisely used terminology. Ambiguity is caused, for instance, by indiscriminate use of the term *fa-t'ing*, which, as a term of art in the Communist Chinese legal vocabulary, means "[people's] tribunal," an arm of the "basic level people's court." [52] It is often used, however, even by legal cadres, in the popular and more general sense of "court" or "courtroom." [53] Consequently, it is frequently necessary for the reader to guess at the hierarchical level of the adjudicating body under discussion. In addition to this, he must also attempt to determine from the context whether the term *t'ing-chang* refers to the head of people's tribunal [54] or to the chief judge of a civil or criminal "adjudication division" (*shen-p'an-t'ing*), an organizational unit common to people's courts at every level. [55]

Another term that is used imprecisely is the compound "*ch'i-t'u*," which seems to mean either "plan" or "try," depending on the context. Article 5 of the People's Republic of China (PRC) Arrest and Detention Act, for instance, prescribes that any offender who "is *planning* to escape or is in the act of escaping [emphasis added]" may be immediately detained. [56] "Planning" would seem to be the only meaningful interpretation of the term "*ch'i-t'u*" in this context. But

50. *Ibid.*, pp. 59–60.
51. Achilles Fang, "The Difficulty of Translation," in R. A. Brower, ed., *On Translation* (Cambridge, Mass.: Harvard University Press, 1959), p. 114.
52. See Court Law, art. 17, p. 127.
53. See, for example, Chang Hui, Li Ch'ang-ch'un, and Chang Tzu-p'ei, "These Are Not the Basic Principles of Our Country's Criminal Litigation," *CFYC*, no. 4 (1958), p. 79.
54. See, for example, Liu Tse-chün, "Realizations from My Adjudication Work," *CFYC*, no. 1 (1959), p. 50.
55. See Court Law, arts. 16, 21, 24 and 29, pp. 127, 128, 129 and 130, respectively.
56. *FKHP*, 1:240. This Act was promulgated on Dec. 20, 1954.

in another context, the same term seems best interpreted as "try": "They [revisionists and rightist opportunists] oppose or distort materialism and dialectics; oppose or *try* to weaken the people's democratic dictatorship and the leadership of the Communist Party; and oppose or *try* to weaken socialist reform and socialist construction [emphasis added]." [57] The difficulty of choosing between the two significantly different meanings arises in a context such as the following:

> They [those who "favor the defendant"] do not distinguish cases according to their nature, but emphasize the uniform application of "attempt." For example, after liberation, a counterrevolutionary who owed blood debts habitually sabotaged agricultural cooperativization, gathered together more than ten backward members of the masses, tried [or "planned"?] to make the basic level organizations of the regime collapse and tried [or "planned"?] to murder our cadres. Those who "favor the defendant" believe that this was an "attempt" to "commit a crime" . . .[58]

As another example, the term *sha-jen* can mean simply "kill a person" (homicide) or it can mean "murder." When the authors of the *Lectures on the General Principles of Criminal Law of the PRC* use the term *sha-jen-tsui*[59] (literally, "the crime of killing a person") as an example of an easily distinguished crime the social danger of which is great, and when they discuss the motives for it as being "revenge, greed, jealousy, etc.," [60] they obviously mean "murder." By saying elsewhere that *sha-jen hsing-wei* (literally, "the act of killing a person") "may constitute a crime even though it was a negligent act," [61] they imply — and rightly so — that *"sha-jen"* does not always constitute such a crime. In the absence of a clarifying context, however, the reader is at somewhat of a loss. How, for instance, should he interpret *"sha-jen-an"* — as a "homicide case" or as a "murder case"? [62]

57. T'an Cheng-wen, "Absorb Experience and Teaching," p. 36.
58. *Ibid.*, p. 38.
59. The Teaching and Research Office for Criminal Law of the Central Political-Legal Cadres' School, ed., *Chung-hua jen-min kung-ho-kuo hsing-fa tsung-tse chiang-i* (hereafter cited as *Lectures*), Peking, 1957, p. 114.
60. *Ibid.*, p. 130.
61. *Ibid.*, pp. 63–64.
62. The problem is not imaginary. See, for example, Liu Tse-chün, "Realizations," p. 51. For an interesting discussion of the "kill"-"murder" distinction see Edward Sapir, "Language," in David G. Mandelbaum, ed., *Culture, Language and Personality* (Berkeley: University of California Press, 1958), p. 36.

There are numerous other examples. In Section 2 of the Decision of the State Council Relating to Problems of Rehabilitation through Labor it is prescribed that a part of the salary of those persons receiving rehabilitation through labor "may be deducted in order to provide funds to cover the maintenance expenses of their family members." [63] The problem is that the term which must here be interpreted "funds to cover the maintenance expenses" is *shan-yang-fei*, which Chinese of all political persuasions agree means "alimony" and which is apparently used by the Communists in that sense in the Provisional Measures for Receipt of Fees by Lawyers.[64]

The words "and" and "or" are used in the language of Chinese law as they are in the language of American law — indiscriminately and interchangeably.[65] In a discussion of mental illness, for instance, one author writes: "The person who has the capacity to assume responsibility [for his acts] is a person who has the capacity to understand the nature of *and* to control his own acts [emphasis added]." [66] In other words, for a person to have that "capacity" he must have both elements, understanding and control. Yet the same author then goes on to say that if a person "was unable to understand the nature of *and* control his own act [emphasis added]," [67] he should not be held responsible. Obviously, the latter "and" must be interpreted to mean "or." [68]

Even language which has traditionally embodied clear legal distinctions is no longer being used with its former precision. The term *kao-fa*, for instance, has in the past been understood to mean a "third-party complaint" or "accusation" as opposed to the term *kao-su* (or *k'ung-su*), meaning a complaint by the injured party himself.[69] In

63. FKHP, 6:244. This Decision was promulgated on Aug. 3, 1957.
64. See art. 6 (2) of the Provisional Measures, July 20, 1956, FKHP, 4:236. Although the term *shan-yang* alone means "care for" or "support" and is quite unrelated to divorce, an ex-Communist Chinese cadre confirms that, as in Nationalist China, the term *shan-yang-fei* is commonly used only with reference to the support given to a divorced woman by her ex-husband.
65. David Mellinkoff, in *The Language of the Law* (Boston: Little, Brown, 1963), p. 150, sums up "and-or" usage in Anglo-American law as follows: "*And* could mean *or* when *or* better served the person who had an *and* dropped into his lap."
66. *Lectures*, p. 110.
67. *Ibid.*
68. This interpretation is consistent with art. 27 of the Security Administration Punishment Act of the People's Republic of China, Oct. 22, 1957, FKHP, 4:253: "No punishment shall be given to a mentally ill person who violates security administration at a time when he is unable to understand the nature of *or* control his own acts [emphasis added]."
69. Dictionary, 1:539.

contemporary China not only are laymen confusing these terms, legal cadres are also misusing them. Thus, a reader attempting to preserve whatever precision there is in the traditional legal language sometimes finds himself with this type of contradiction on his hands: "After B [the victim of A's assault] made her third-party complaint, the court sentenced A to several months of imprisonment." [70] Obviously, *kao-fa* no longer necessarily means "third-party complaint."

The situation has not gone unnoticed by the Chinese themselves. The authors of the *Lectures*, for instance, complain that the criminal punishment "reprimand" often goes under the guise of a number of inconsistent names, some of which even blur the distinction between criminal and administrative sanctions;[71] and they also note that the punishment of "control" gives rise to similar confusion.[72] Another author, discussing the language of Soviet law, laments, among other things, the fact that China at present still has no word as satisfactory as a certain Russian expression for "investigation" (*rassledovanie*) and implies that Chinese judicial personnel must be content at least for the time being with the "insufficiently comprehensive" term *chen-ch'a* or its synonym *tiao-ch'a*.[73] Western experts, also, have not been oblivious to the elusiveness of the Communist Chinese legal language.[74]

It would seem, then, that the Chinese Communists can be described in much the same way the early Bolshevik revolutionaries have been characterized:

In addition to caring little for the idea of law, the Bolsheviks were extremely poor legal draftsmen. They lacked the ability to use the same terms consistently even when they wanted to, and they did not always want to. The 1922 and 1926 RSFSR Criminal Codes are

70. Teng P'ing, "Law-Breaking Elements Among the People Definitely May Not All Be Treated as Objects of Dictatorship," *CFYC*, no. 3 (1958), p. 75.
71. *Lectures*, p. 191.
72. *Ibid.*, p. 192. See also Jerome A. Cohen, "The Criminal Process in the People's Republic of China: An Introduction," *Harvard Law Review*, 79 (1966), 492.
73. Wei Chia-chü, "Several Terms Related to Procuratorial Work," *CFYC*, no. 2 (1955), p. 60.
74. See, for example, Cohen, "The Criminal Process," pp. 471–72, 491 n. 45; and Philip Bilancia, "Dictionary of Communist Chinese Legal Terms" (unpublished), p. 162 (discussion of *ch'eng* [punishment] and related compounds states that distinctions are "not always meaningful" and "are sometimes disregarded in usage"). A Nationalist Chinese scholar has written that the definition of crimes in the PRC "is either very broad and imprecise or is not made at all." Lung-sheng Tao, "The Criminal Law of Communist China," *Cornell Law Quarterly*, 52 (1966), 48.

full of unintended inconsistencies and ambiguities. They are also replete with vague, sweeping definitions of crimes in which technical legal terms are used in a popular sense, and popular terms in a technical legal sense.[75]

The only feature which appears to distinguish the Chinese Communists from the Bolsheviks is that the former are as yet codeless.

None of this should be at all surprising. If the Communist Chinese leadership in fact does not want the legal language to be used precisely, it is most likely because too much precision would "tie down the policy makers," [76] for whom law is but another "weapon" in the service of a continuing revolution. The fact that *sha-jen* may or may not mean "murder" or that *ch'i-t'u* may or may not mean "plan" certainly makes it easier for the regime to be harsh with "the enemies" while at the same time lenient with "the people." And the fact that the distinction is blurred between criminal and administrative sanctions tends to facilitate the speedy administration of "justice," unencumbered by procedural niceties prescribed by law.

If, on the other hand, Communist Chinese legal cadres lack the ability to use the legal language consistently, it is simply that a majority of them, being post-revolutionary proletariat-peasant replacements for the "old judicial personnel" removed during the judicial reform movement,[77] have not had much of a legal education. As a matter of fact, they have really not had much of any kind of education. One judge, for instance, entered the "profession" when she was eighteen years old after having received a seventh-grade education.[78] Another, an ex-dockhand, had only two years of schooling.[79] Still another, who had only three years of primary school education, admitted that previously he did "not know what law was" and even that he had "seldom heard the word 'court.' " [80]

But let us not be condescending; there is an occasional Horatio Alger story to be found even in the annals of the American legal profession. If, as the leadership claims,[81] semi-illiterate judicial personnel

75. Berman and Spindler, *Soviet Criminal Law and Procedure*, p. 129.
76. Schurmann, *Ideology and Organization*, p. 60.
77. See Shih Liang, "Thoroughly Break Up the Attack."
78. *Yun-nan jih-pao* (Yunnan daily), Jan. 10, 1953.
79. *Hsin-wen jih-pao* (News daily, Shanghai), Oct. 15, 1952.
80. Cheng Kuang, "A Preliminary Scrutiny of My Old Law Viewpoint," *KMJP*, September 1952.
81. See, for example, Shih Liang.

have proved eminently successful in handling the intricacies of the Chinese language and the technicalities of law, so much the better. There is evidence, though, that the performance of this new "illiterati" has been somewhat less than perfect. Several months prior to the "blooming of the Hundred Flowers," for example, one critic complained that

> the language used in the judgments of the adjudication officers [i.e., judges and people's assessors] of some people's courts has been vague, confusing and void of meaning . . .
>
> [S]ome courts use many wrong characters or simplified characters which they themselves have arbitrarily created, and thus they make their judgments difficult to understand. For instance, "yü" [and] is written as "yü" [at];[82] "mai" [buy] is written as "mai" [sell];[83] and "ch'ü" [to take (a wife)] is written as "ch'ü" [to bring].[84] In one judgment "pei-kao" [defendant] was even written as "yüan-kao" [plaintiff], and as a result, property which should have been awarded to the defendant was awarded to the plaintiff, and everyone concerned had to go through all the procedures again in order to correct the error.
>
> The existence of these problems is, of course, related to the cultural level of some of the adjudication officers . . ." [85]

The fault, however, is not that of the legal cadres alone. As should already be apparent, the Chinese language itself, or to be more precise, the past generations of Chinese people who contributed to the development of the contemporary Chinese language, share much of the blame. The fact, for instance, that *yin-mou* can mean either "secretly plan" or "conspire" [86] and therefore that *yin-mou sha-jen* might mean either a "secretly planned (i.e., premeditated) murder" or a "conspiratorial murder" [87] is an inherited inadequacy of the lan-

82. Both characters are pronounced *yü*, but the former is third tone and the latter is second tone.

83. Both characters are pronounced *mai*, but the former is third tone and the latter is fourth tone.

84. Both characters are third tone.

85. Chin Ts'ao, "Judgments Should Be Written in a Serious Manner," *KMJP*, Jan. 20, 1957.

86. The character *yin* connotes clandestine, not necessarily group, activity. Strictly speaking, the term *kung-mou* (literally, "plan together") should be regarded as the only suitable equivalent for "conspiracy." In fact, however, *yin-mou* is often used to mean *kung-mou*. See, for example, Dictionary, 1:1380, and *Lectures*, p. 21.

87. It seems to mean simply "premeditated murder" in Liu Tse-chün, "Realizations," p. 51.

guage. So is the fact that *mou-sha*, although generally considered to be merely the abbreviated form of *yin-mou sha-jen*, is usually interpreted to mean just "murder" and is not associated with conspiracy at all.[88] This latter phenomenon, the extensive use of ellipsis in the Chinese language, seems to be one of the major reasons why the language of Chinese law is not at present a vehicle for precise expression.

> "However ungracious it may be for the translator to blame his faults upon the ambiguities of the text, he would often be justified in doing so." [89]

Fa-lü yü kuei-tse means "laws and regulations." The same thing can be said more simply — *fa-kuei*.[90] But *fa-kuei* also seems to have a somewhat more narrow meaning than that of the longer form from which it was presumably fashioned. For instance, the Foreword to the PRC's *fa-kuei hui-pien* ("Collection of Laws and Regulations" — here *fa-kuei* is clearly used as a contraction of the longer form) describes the contents as including both *fa-lü* (laws) and *fa-kuei*, which, to avoid redundancy, must be interpreted simply as "regulations." [91] There is, of course, no such thing as a *fa-kuei* (in the narrow sense) to be found in the *fa-kuei hui-pien*; there are only *fa* (laws), *t'iao-li* (acts), *ming-ling* (orders), *kuei-ting* (provisions), *pan-fa* (measures), *kuei-tse* (regulations), *chih-shih* (instructions), and so on.[92] But regardless of this, the term *fa-kuei* is sometimes encountered in a context where it must mean something other than *fa-lü yü kuei-tse*.

The propensity of the Chinese language for ellipsis is of more than mere academic interest; in some contexts the difference in meaning is significant. *Wei-tsao cheng-chü*, for example, seems on its face to mean "fabricating evidence," as when one person, in order to "frame" another, leaves the latter's handkerchief at the scene of a

88. But *cf.* E-tu Zen Sun, *Ch'ing Administrative Terms*, p. 287.
89. Justine O'Brien, "From French to English," in R. A. Brower, *On Translation*, p. 89.
90. The term *fa-ling* presents similar though even more confusing problems. It is perhaps a contraction of *fa-lü yü ming-ling* (laws and orders) but it is often used in series with *fa-lü* and translated as "decree."
91. FKHP, vol. 1.
92. Likewise, there is no such thing as a *fa-ling* to be found in the *Fa-ling hui-pien* (FLHP).

crime.[93] Yet there is reason to believe that *wei-cheng*, though at first glance only an abbreviation of the aforementioned term,[94] may also have the more narrow meaning of "perjury." [95]

Jen-shen ch'üan-li, for another example, refers to the "rights of the person," [96] for instance, the right not to be searched or arrested unlawfully. *Jen-ch'üan*, on the other hand, has the broader meaning of "the rights of people" or "human rights," [97] that is, the right to vote, the right to freedom of religious belief and so forth. But *jen-ch'üan* can also be used simply as a contraction of *jen-shen ch'üan-li*.[98]

The term *t'i-shen* presents another problem which arises from the practice of ellipsis. In Article 12 of the PRC's Law for the Organization of People's Courts *t'i-shen* refers to the power of a higher court, upon discovering an error in an already effective judgment or order of a lower court, to "re-examine" the case itself as opposed to remanding it to the lower court for "readjudication" (*tsai-shen*).[99] The term can apparently be employed when any higher level unit re-examines a case originally handled by a lower level unit within the same organization. Thus, it is also used with respect to a public security bureau's re-examination of a case handled by a subbureau. In this sense, *t'i-shen* is most likely a contraction of *t'i-ch'i shen-ch'a*, which literally means "bring up [a case] for examination." Or perhaps, since we have never encountered the latter phrase in Chinese legal material, it would be more precise to say simply that the longer form can be used to explain the meaning of the shorter.

But *t'i-shen* is used in another sense as well. In one article, for example, a person rather than a case is the object, and the subject is a judge of first instance (not a court of appeal) who, skeptical of the public security bureau's findings and the procuracy's bill of prosecu-

93. See, for example, The Arrest and Detention Act of the People's Republic of China, art. 5, p. 240. The definition of this term apparently does not embrace the act of "making false statements" (perjury) or that of "*using* false evidence." See, for example, *Six Codes*, arts. 168, 169, p. 241; and Chang Tzu-p'ei, "Several Problems," p. 13.

94. See, for example, *Six Codes*, ch. 10 (Title), p. 241.

95. See, for example, Dictionary, 2:1759, and Chang Tzu-p'ei, "Several Problems," p. 14.

96. See, for example, Dictionary, 1:22.

97. See, for example, *ibid.*, p. 27, and Ch'ien Szu, "A Criticism of the Views of Bourgeois International Law on the Question of Population," *Kuo-chi wen-t'i yen-chiu* (Studies in international problems), no. 5 (1960), p. 40.

98. See, for example, "Is It Right for the Public Security Organ to Do This?" *Hsin-hua jih-pao* (New China daily, Nanking), Oct. 28, 1956.

99. FKHP, 1:126.

tion (*ch'i-su-shu*), seems to dispense with public trial and instead personally and privately interviews the accused.[100] In this case *"t'i-shen"* can probably best be explained as *"t'i-ch'i shen-wen,"* "bringing up [an accused] for questioning." [101]

As a final example of the confusion which ellipsis creates, the term *yü-shen* deserves special mention. A 1955 newspaper article explains that the stage at which a case is first handled by the court is called *yü-shen*.[102] At this stage, in theory if not in practice,[103] a judge (called the *yü-shen-yüan*) and two people's assessors preside at a "preparatory" (*yü-pei*) session and "examine" (*shen-ch'a*) the substance of the procuracy's investigation.[104] The inference can be drawn from the article that this preparatory examination[105] takes place only after the procuracy has initiated prosecution, and such an inference is supported by a pre-Communist definition which characterizes *yü-shen* as a post-indictment court "procedure in preparation for public trial." [106]

However, the public security bureau, the organ charged with the initial investigation of cases, like the court also has a *yü-shen* procedure.[107] As described in a 1956 article, the bureau's *yü-shen* precedes the procuracy's investigation[108] and initiation of prosecution and involves the preparation of a *yü-shen* record.[109]

What, then, does *yü-shen* in this latter context mean? Clearly, it is not the court's preparatory examination. But although we can say with certainty what it is not, we cannot say with equal certainty what

100. Yang P'eng and Lin Ch'ih-chung, "Investigate Deeply, Handle Cases Conscientiously," *Fu-chien jih-pao* (Fukien daily), Aug. 14, 1956.
101. In Nationalist China the term *t'i-shen* seems to be the equivalent for "habeas corpus." See *Six Codes*, pp. 310–11. See also Dictionary, 2:1425.
102. "Answering Questions from Readers: On Trial Procedure in Criminal Cases," *KMJP*, March 11, 1955, p. 3.
103. See Cohen, "The Criminal Process," pp. 511–514.
104. Depending on the context, the term *shen-ch'a* can be translated either as "examine" or "investigate." In this instance, where it denotes the scrutinizing of evidence that has already been gathered, "examine" seems to be the more appropriate translation. But where it indicates the actual collection of evidence, "investigate" seems more appropriate. See Cohen, "The Criminal Process," p. 516.
105. The article does not explicitly state that *yü-shen* is a contraction of *yü-pei shen-ch'a* (preparatory examination). Interpreted as "preparatory hearing" or "trial preparation," the term could be an abbreviation for *yü-pei shen-li* or *yü-pei shen-p'an,* respectively. *Yü-shen* has been translated as "preliminary trial" in the *China Law Review*, 3 (January, 1927), table of contents.
106. Dictionary, 2:1748.
107. See Cohen, "The Criminal Process," p. 500.
108. For a description of the procuracy's "investigation," see *ibid.*, pp. 509–511.
109. See Yang P'eng, "Investigate Deeply."

it is. A former public security officer, admitting that neither he nor his erstwhile comrades were particularly concerned with the exact meaning of the term, believes they assumed it meant *yü-pei shen-hsün* or "preparatory interrogation." Yet there is also indication that some legal cadres may interpret it as *yü-pei shen-ch'a* (preparatory investigation),[110] paralleling a Russian (and civil law) term meaning "preliminary investigation," preliminary, that is, to trial and not to any subsequent investigation.[111]

It may be objected that all this does not really matter, that whether the *yü-shen* division of the public security bureau and its activities are designated preparatory (or preliminary) "interrogation" or "investigation," or simply "trial preparation," does not really affect anyone's understanding of what is going on. This is perhaps true, though it should be realized that the different terms seem to suggest different limits to the power exercised by the public security organ. But disregarding this question of the delineation of power, we must agree that, so long as it is clear which organ is doing the "preparatory" work, there is not too much difficulty in determining the basic meaning of *yü-shen*.

It is not always clear, however, which organ is involved. In one 1958 article, for instance, we are told about "cooperation among the 'three families' (the public security and procuratorial organs and the courts)" which resulted in the joint handling of cases by "three officers," a *yü-shen-yüan*, a procurator and a judge, listed in that order.[112] From the context it seems unlikely that the *yü-shen-yüan* refers here to an officer of the court in charge of a judicial preparatory examination. It seems, rather, that it refers to a public security officer who does some kind of pre-indictment preparatory work. The article goes on to say:

After approving arrests, they [the three officers] concentrated all the offenders in an administrative village, conducted a yü-shen and

110. See Wei Chia-chü, "Several Terms," p. 60, and "A Preliminary Understanding of Some Terms in Our Country's Law for the Organization of People's Courts and Law for the Organization of People's Procuracies," CFYC, no. 4 (1954), p. 48.

111. See Berman, *Justice in the USSR*, p. 302. Despite the fact that the Russian term (*predvaritel'noe*) has perhaps inaccurately been translated into English as "preliminary," the Chinese *yü-pei* is best translated as "preparatory." "Preliminary" would be an accurate translation if the term *yü-hsien* were used.

112. Chang Wu-yün, "Smash Permanent Rules, Go 1000 Li in One Day," CFYC, no. 5 (1958), p. 58.

checked the material. After the legal documents of the yü-shen of the case had been completed, the offenders were taken to a place for an on-the-spot hearing [trial].[113]

In this context, then, the term *yü-shen* seems to suggest that the pre-indictment preparatory work involves not a full-scale "preparatory investigation," but simply an examination of previously collected evidence.

The same article reports that in another county the cooperating group consisted only of, in the following order (which may or may not be significant), a procurator, a *yü-shen-yüan*, and a judge. In view of the fact that no mention is made of the public security organ, it may be that this *yü-shen-yüan* is the more orthodox kind, an officer of the court who examines the evidence after the procurator has initiated prosecution. But the group's work procedure, described as consisting of *yü-shen* (which is preceded by an investigation), initiation of prosecution and adjudication, again suggests that *yü-shen* refers to a pre-indictment, as opposed to a judicial, examination. Interestingly, in still another article, we are told of cooperation among four (not three) officers — an investigator, a procurator, a *yü-shen-yüan*, and a judge.[114] In this context, also, the *yü-shen-yüan* appears to be an officer of the court. But as is too frequently the case when dealing with the language of Chinese law, it is not possible to say this with absolute certainty.

Perhaps no language is immune from manipulation by those who, in order to circumvent rules which limit their freedom of action, seek to redefine either the rules or the action. English is no exception: if "blockading" an insubordinate island-neighbor is illegal under international law, the island can simply be "quarantined." But there would seem to be more built-in protection against this sort of artifice where the basic unit of a language is defined less by its relationship to other such units than by its own intrinsic symbolization. The word "quarantine" can be distorted in the interests of creating the illusion of legality; but we have difficulty swallowing it because the "accepted" meanings of the word stick in our throats.

Chinese "words," however, are in this sense more ingestible. The

113. *Ibid.*, p. 59.
114. "Canton's Political-Legal Departments Experiment with Cooperation in Case Handling," *NFJP*, Mar. 30, 1958.

fact that they are defined in large part by the context in which they are used accounts for considerable elasticity of meaning. The term *shen-wen* (questioning), for instance, has been defined as being solely within the province of the court.[115] But use it in a context relating to a public security organ or to the procuracy and it subtly changes to make the accommodation: from an adjudicatory "questioning" it becomes an investigatory "interrogation." In view of the fact that traditional Chinese law, discarded only a few short decades ago after many centuries of use, made no clear distinction between investigation and first-instance adjudication,[116] this result was not unpredictable. Likewise, even had there been no intentional effort by the Communist Chinese to merge areas of authority and to blur jurisdictional boundaries and roles in judicial administration, it still would have been impossible to ensure that *shen-p'an* (adjudication, trial) would remain the sacred preserve of the court. The danger became a reality in the early nineteen fifties when the Soviet-developed institution, the "comrades' court," was adopted by the Chinese in the form of the *t'ung-chih shen-p'an-hui* (literally, "comrades' adjudication committee"). The comrades' adjudication committee explicitly "is not a court"; but despite this fact, it "adjudicates" cases.[117]

The apparent ease with which Chinese terms are stretched to embrace new meanings is not, of course, a phenomenon that has only recently been recognized. Over two thousand years ago a conservative Confucius called for a "rectification of names" in order to make corrupt actualities once again conform to the conventional names which were symbols of propriety.[118] At one point he is said to have exclaimed apropos of this: "A horn-gourd that is neither horn nor gourd. A horn-gourd indeed! A horn-gourd indeed!" [119]

At the end of the nineteenth century, a revolutionary China began to be deluged with "new" actualities in the form of imported Western concepts, among which were legal concepts such as "rights" and

115. Dictionary, 2:1883.

116. See Sybille van der Sprenkel, *Legal Institutions in Manchu China* (London: University of London Athlone Press, 1962), pp. 66–67; and T'ung-tsu Ch'ü, *Local Government in China under the Ch'ing* (Cambridge, Mass.: Harvard University Press, 1962), p. 116.

117. See Wang Ju-ch'i, "How the Enterprise Comrades' Courts Were Established in K'ai-luan Coal Mine," *JMJP*, April 19, 1954, p. 3.

118. See Fung Yu-lan, *A History of Chinese Philosophy*, Derk Bodde, trans. (Princeton: Princeton University Press, 1952), 1:59.

119. Lun Yü, *Confucian Analects*, 6:23. *Cf.* Waley's translation in Arthur Waley, *The Analects of Confucius* (London: Allen and Unwin, 1949), p. 120.

"freedom." As in Confucius' time, the alphabetless Chinese language found it easier in many instances to stretch the old language, rather than create new terminology, to symbolize these new legal concepts.[120] And even when new compounds were created, they could not be entirely satisfactory inasmuch as they were composed of conventional characters with traditional connotations.[121] Twentieth century Chinese law and the language of that law have thus not fully enjoyed the benefits of simultaneous conception and parallel development. As a result, Chinese legal word-symbols are perhaps less readily circumscribed than might otherwise be the case.

Although the Chinese Communists did not create this unfortunate situation, they certainly have not indicated any desire to improve it. We would not be justified in concluding that Communist Chinese criminal law is so incomprehensible that contemporary China cannot properly be said to have a "legal system." But it should be clear from the foregoing discussion that the problems inherent in the Chinese legal language present a serious impediment to the evolution of a system of justice designed to serve the ruled rather than the rulers. If those problems are to be remedied, they must first of course be regarded as detrimental rather than as desirable. When that time comes, years of uniform legal education leading to some sort of legal professionalization will still have to elapse before a standardized and precise legal language can gain acceptance and become engrained in the consciousness of the Chinese elite, not to mention the masses. Until that time, not only outsiders, but the Chinese themselves, will have difficulty "understanding" the language of Communist Chinese criminal law.

120. For an interesting discussion of the problems involved in fitting the Chinese language to Western political and legal concepts, see Victor Purcell, *Problems of Chinese Education* (London: Kegan Paul, 1936), pp. 129–160. See also, A. F. Wright, "The Chinese Language and Foreign Ideas," in A. F. Wright, ed., *Studies in Chinese Thought* (Chicago: University of Chicago Press, 1953), pp. 286–303.

121. Two such compounds are discussed in John K. Fairbank, "How to Deal with the Chinese Revolution," *The New York Review of Books* (Feb. 17, 1966), p. 14.

7 Problems of Translating the Marriage Law

Marinus J. Meijer

The Marriage Law of the People's Republic of China, published on May 1, 1950, was translated into English by the Foreign Languages Institute in Peking and published in English that year by the Foreign Languages Press (FLP). Many official publications of the Chinese government carried it also. Some doubt may be expressed, however, as to whether this translation should be considered an "official" one, because in an official translation one would expect a careful rendering of the Chinese text made by translators well-versed in law. In reality, it seems doubtful that a person with even elementary knowledge of law has ever been employed on this task. Several inaccuracies, which reveal a lack of knowledge of law, occur in the English text.

Article 5 provides an example. The translation reads:

> No man or woman in any of the following instances shall be allowed to marry: a. Where the man and the woman are lineal relatives by blood or where the man and the woman are brother and sister born from the same parents or where the man and the woman are half-brother and half-sister. The question of prohibiting marriage between collateral relatives by blood within the fifth degree of relationship is to be determined by custom.[1]

The error occurs in the last sentence. The translation should be: "As regards the problem of prohibiting marriage between collateral relatives by blood within the five generations, custom shall be followed."

The term five generations (*wu tai*) does not mean "five degrees" in either Roman or Canon law. The term actually includes collaterals as far as the *eighth* Roman degree, that is, five generations of descend-

1. See *The Marriage Law of the People's Republic of China* (Peking: Foreign Languages Press, 1950), p. 3.

ants of each of the four immediate male ascendants (up to the great-great-grandfathers) in the paternal and the maternal lines.[2]

This error is not only a matter of choosing the wrong word, but it reflects unfamiliarity with law on the part of the translators. Such a mistake, however, does not constitute the greatest problem in translating texts concerning the family law of the PRC. The most difficult problems are of another nature.

Translating any law is an arduous task. Every lawyer knows that a law acquires its meaning through application and that for the meaning of the terms and the expressions, the intent of the legislator is usually more important than semantics. The text often conveys only imperfectly the spirit of the law. The divergence between text and spirit increases inordinately when the text is translated into another language.

The Chinese Marriage Law, however, is a comparatively simple document, at least as far as the language is concerned. As an instrument intended to have direct appeal to the layman and all educated masses, the text is terse, and technical legal terms are avoided as much as possible. These qualities stem from the intent of the legislator to make the law a political document. Since it was to play an important role in the transformation of Chinese society, it had to be studied by the population at large. In 1953 three million cadres were mobilized to mount throughout China a massive movement to study the Marriage Law. The dissemination of information on the Marriage Law was much wider than that on the Constitution of 1954. Millions of pamphlets were distributed, and even now little books containing "Questions and Answers on the Marriage Law" are to be found in every bookstore in China. Therefore it would seem that the translation of such a simple and popular text would not entail many difficulties. In practice, however, this has not been the case.

The first clause of Article 6 in the FLP translation reads as follows:

"In order to contract a marriage both the man and woman shall register in person with the people's government of the district or hsiang in which they reside . . ." Instead of "in order to contract a marriage," the first words of Article 6 should have been rendered

2. A diagram of the five generations may be found in the handbook, *Chung-hua jen-min kung-ho-kuo min-fa tzu-liao hui-pien* (Collection of materials on the civil law of the People's Republic of China), Peking, Chinese People's University, 1954, p. 334 (hereafter referred to as *Collection*).

either as "when concluding a marriage" or as "when a marriage is concluded." This, however, is a minor point.

The main problem is to determine what value to attribute to the word "shall" (*ying*) in the passage "the man and woman shall register." Here we come to one of the most important problems of the Marriage Law — the expression of the concept of duty. Of what type is this duty of registration? What does the term *ying* mean in this context? Perhaps this is not a problem of translation in its strictest sense, but the FLP translation, in order to be valuable, should at least have a footnote explaining the meaning of the term in this Article. The nature of the duty expressed by *ying* determines whether the function of registration of marriage is ceremonial or constitutive.

Registration of marriage seems to have been an obligatory procedure in all regulations and laws concerning marriage ever issued in the areas of China ruled by a Communist regime. The temptation to consider registration as a condition for the constitution of marriage therefore is strong. In the text of the first Communist Chinese marriage regulations of 1931, the duty to register is expressed by the word *hsü*, meaning "to be necessary" or "to be required." [3] However, when we look at the Marriage Law of 1934 we find that although in Article 8 the necessity to register (denoted by the use of *hsü*) is maintained, Article 9 states that "all men and women who are living together, whether they have registered their marriage or not, are considered married." [4] From this we can conclude that registration was indeed a duty but that its omission did not result in invalidity of the marriage. The sanction should lie elsewhere.

In Article 7 of the Marriage Regulations for the Shen-Kan-Ning Border Area of 1939,[5] which provides for the parties to request government registration of their marriage, *hsü* is replaced by *te* meaning "can," "may," or "shall." *Te* is also used at several other places in the Regulations. But Article 5, where the free will of the parties to marry is "required," uses *hsü*. Thus Article 7 might be interpreted to mean that the parties, when about to marry "can" or "may" request the

3. The word *ying* is not used. A translation is in Marinus J. Meijer, "Early Communist Marriage Legislation in China," *Contemporary China*, 6 (Hong Kong, 1968), 87–89.

4. *Ibid.*, pp. 89–91.

5. *K'ang-Jih ken-chü ti cheng-ts'e t'iao-li hui-chi, Shen-Kan-Ning chih pu* (Section on Shen-Kan-Ning of the collection of regulations and measures of the anti-Japanese bases), first part, 1942, p. 135. The Shen-Kan-Ning Border Area comprised parts of Shensi, Kansu, and Ninghsia.

municipal or *hsiang* authorities to register their marriage, but that there was no legal obligation to do so. In this way the interpretation of *te* would correspond with its meaning in Article 11, which provides that a man or woman in some circumstances *may* request divorce, but certainly not *shall* request divorce. On the other hand, it is unlikely that the word *te* means "may" or "can" in Article 10, which governs the registration of divorce by mutual consent. It follows that the word *te* has different meanings in the different articles of the Shen-Kan-Ning Marriage Regulations of 1939, and it is probable that it means "shall" in Article 7. The revised Marriage Regulations of this area dating from 1944 maintain the word *te*.

In the Chin-Ch'a-Chi Border Area the Marriage Regulations of 1943 require that marriage be concluded by public ceremony in the presence of two witnesses and that the couple register at the village public office or with the government of the district or the municipality.[6] The duty to hold the ceremony and the duty to comply with registration are governed by the word *ying*, meaning "shall," "should," or "ought to," and generally denoting an obligation of a moral or legal kind. According to Civil Affairs Communication No. 5, of May 27, 1943, of the same border area, both ceremony and registration are obligatory, but a valid marriage may be contracted by performing either of them.[7] The Chin-Ch'a-Chi Border Area was, as far as I have been able to ascertain, the only border area where the public ceremony was introduced by the Marriage Regulations and the passage was literally the same as in the Civil Code of the Republic of China, Article 982, which also used the term *ying*. For divorce, on the contrary, registration was required.[8]

Finally, the Chin-Chi-Lu-Yü Provisional Regulations of the same year revert to the original *hsü*.[9] These Regulations adhered to a stricter attitude toward registration. They required registration of betrothal even on the pain of nullity (Article 6). The expression used

6. *Hsien-hsing fa-ling hui-chi* (Collection of current laws), published by the Chin-Ch'a-Chi Border Area Administrative Committee, 1945, article 5, p. 220. The regulations are translated by M. H. van der Valk in *Conservatism in Modern Chinese Family Law* (Leiden: Brill, 1956), p. 68. Parts of Shansi, Chahar, and Hopei constituted the Chin-Ch'a-Chi Border Area.
7. *Hsien-hsing fa-ling hui-chi*, p. 235.
8. *Ibid.*, p. 221.
9. *Chin-Chi-Lu-Yü pien-ch'ü fa-ling hui-pien* (Collection of laws and decrees of the Chin-Chi-Lu-Yü Border Area), published by the Chin-Chi-Lu-Yü Border Area government, February 1946, article 6. Parts of Shansi, Hopei, Shantung, and Honan were comprised in the Chin-Chi-Lu-Yü Border Area.

is *hsü*, but it is expressly added that only after registration is the betrothal valid. This express provision does not occur in the case of registration of marriage (Article 10), where the expression *hsü* indicates the duty but nothing additional is said.

The Shanghai Court in 1949 distinguished between "relations of living together" (*t'ung-chü kuan-hsi*), described as "unofficial marital relations," and official marriage concluded by public ceremony or registration. The "relationship of living together" was not protected by law.

The Law of 1950 followed, as was shown above, the wording of the Chin-Ch'a-Chi Regulations of 1943 and chose the word *ying*. The use of *ying* throughout the 1950 law is quite consistent, for it is used for any legal duty: registration of marriage (Article 6), registration of divorce (Article 17), support of illegitimate children (Article 15), the duty to provide alimony after divorce (Article 21), the duty of the authorities to issue certificates of marriage and divorce (Articles 6 and 17) and the duty of the violator of the law to shoulder the responsibility for his criminal acts (Article 26). The word occurs eleven times, and seems generally to denote a legal duty, the neglect of which may entail sanctions in different forms; in Article 26 it denotes a duty that can hardly be neglected.

The problem, then, is not whether registration is a duty, but what the sanction is for its omission. On this the text of the law does not enlighten us at all. If the sanction consists of a fine or some other penal measure and the omission of registration does not affect the validity of the marriage, the character of registration cannot be that of a condition without which no marriage exists. If, on the other hand, apart from any penal consequences, omission of registration entails the civil sanction of invalidity of the marriage, registration constitutes the conclusion of marriage, and the marriage system of the PRC would be like the civil marriage system as it has existed in several countries on the European continent and, since 1944, in the Soviet Union. In order to find the answer to this problem of sanctions, we must inquire into the nature of marriage in the PRC and into the reasons why the present regime instituted registration.

De facto marriage in China did not legally exist before the Communists appeared on the scene. Marriage in traditional China was a matter arranged by the respective families of bride and groom. An aspect of public order was involved, inasmuch as a marriage contracted against the law could be dissolved or nullified. Whether or not in traditional China such a union was considered marriage at all is an interesting question. But, in any event, the interference of the state was always *ex post facto* — the magistrate's cooperation or control was not invoked at the conclusion of marriage. In the Civil Code of the Nationalist government no registration of marriage was required — the parties concluded the marriage themselves. They had always to do so by public ceremony, however, in order to establish the new status of the parties; that is, marriage required public recognition. The Nationalist Law of the Register of Families of December 12, 1931, obligated the parties to register their marriage in the civil records but not on pain of nullity.[10] Registration had only the function of conclusive evidence of the existence of the marriage. It is worthy of note that in Nationalist China the state did not interfere in the conclusion of marriage nor even in its dissolution by mutual consent (Civil Code, Article 1049).

The reasons for the Communist imposition of the duty to register are explained at length by Ch'en Shao-yü (Wang Ming) in his introduction of the draft Marriage Law to the Government Administration Council (GAC) in April 1950.[11] He said:

In Chinese history under the imperial dynasties, the Peiyang war lords, and the Kuomintang government, it was not required that people register their marriages with the government organs, but under the governments of the Chinese Soviet Areas, the Border Areas, and the present People's Republic such registration is required. This fact itself already reflects the difference in attitude of the two categories of government toward their relationship with the people. From the slave-owning imperial dynasties to the Kuomintang government there was an antipeople government; the government was the people's public enemy. These governments arbitrarily encroached upon the people, kept aloof from them, and therefore they considered the problems of marriage, to which the people themselves attached so much importance, as entirely

10. M. H. van der Valk, *Outline of Modern Chinese Family Law* (Peking: Vetch, 1939), p. 83. The law on registration of families may be found in Liu Ling-yü, *Liu-fa ch'üan-shu t'ung-shih* (Complete book of six laws generally annotated), Taipei, 1965, p. 1515. The article containing the duty to register marriage is Article 18.

11. *Collection*, p. 254.

private matters, which were of no concern to them. They did not care at all about these matters and adopted an attitude of noninterference. From the time of the government of the Soviet Areas until the present government of the People's Republic, there has been a government of the people themselves. The only duty of the people's government is to serve the people; it has no other interests but those of the people; and it does not interfere in matters in which the people do not want it to interfere. Therefore the people's government cannot keep aloof from that great event of marriage in the life of a man and a woman which also affects the health of the whole people, the happiness of the family, the health of the whole nation and the reconstruction of the State. And not only can the government not keep aloof, but it must show greater concern in these matters than even the marrying parties themselves and their relatives do, and it has to assume more serious responsibility. The concern and the responsibility of the marrying parties and their relatives, which is tainted by the customs of the marriage system of the old society, are always lacking a definite aim and a definite standard. They are aiming at the small profits of the moment, and do not, in fact cannot take into account the real long-term interests of every man and woman who is about to marry, not to speak of the interests of society and the State. The concern and the responsibility of the people's government and its registration agencies are very different from theirs. On the basis of the definite principles of modern sociology and modern science the people's government earnestly takes into account the general interest of the people who marry, and carefully considers the fundamental interests of society and the State. The people's government does not regard the problem of the people's marriage as a private affair that does not concern the public interest of society and the State. Therefore it demands that when concluding marriage the man and the woman are obliged to proceed in person to the local ch'ü or hsiang people's government to register. This is done in order that these agencies may examine concretely in every case whether the marriage indeed is based on the free will of both parties, whether the marriageable age has been reached, whether the marriage is not concluded in contravention of the provision forbidding marriage between [certain] relatives, whether one or both parties have physical defects of the sexual organs or are suffering from a disease on account of which they are unable to marry, whether the rule that one man can only marry one woman and one woman only one man is observed, whether the parties are already married or not, or whether concubinage or bigamy are committed, and finally whether no such illegal acts as marriage by purchase and sale are committed. When these matters have been clearly examined, registration in accordance with the provisions of the law is allowed, and a certificate of marriage is issued. This also means that the marriage is concluded in the interest of the parties and of society and that all legal rights accruing from this marriage are protected by law.

Although the regime obviously intends that everyone register and that marriage be in accordance with the new system, free from "feudal" and bourgeois traces, based on love, common labor, "and struggle for the happiness of the family and the building of the new society" (Article 8), the legislators carefully refrained from saying what the consequences would be if registration were omitted, and even Ch'en Shao-yü's commentary does not inform us in this respect.

In the Chin-Ch'a-Chi Border Area, either registration or a public ceremony was required to make a marriage valid in the eyes of the government. The Shanghai Court in 1949 seemed to adhere to the same views though it definitely preferred registration. In the period after 1950, however, we find conflicting statements. The requirement of a public ceremony and witnesses having been dropped completely from the PRC Marriage Law (1950), registration would seem to be the only formal requirement. But in 1951 the People's Court of Southern Anhwei ruled as follows: "When a man and a woman have in fact concluded marriage but failed to register in accordance with Article 6, if there are no legal impediments as mentioned in Articles 3–5, we can only order them to register *post facto*. To deny marital relations on the ground of this failure in procedure would mean the denial of the fact of marriage, which is not satisfactory [*pu t'uo-tang*]. *In general the relation between husband and wife cannot be determined in accordance with the rigid standard of having registered and received a marriage certificate*." [Emphasis added] [12] The court held that, even though a woman had "married" after the promulgation of the Marriage Law and had failed to register her marriage, it was proper to handle the divorce application according to the provisions of the Marriage Law concerning divorce.

This was not just the opinion of a local court, since it was con-

12. *Ibid.*, p. 342.

firmed by the Supreme Court's branch court for eastern China. The latter, however, did not commit itself so completely as the lower court had, but stated that since at the time in question the work of registration, propaganda, and education of the masses had not yet been carried out thoroughly and everywhere, marital relations stemming from unregistered marriages should be considered legally valid.[13]

The next year, in quite a different context, the question of a *de facto* marriage was brought to the attention of the branch court of the Supreme Court for southwestern China. This time the case concerned a concubine taken before the promulgation of the Marriage Law. The court's pronouncement was couched in very general terms, saying: "A man and a woman who have the intention of living together forever must be regarded as having marital relations, regardless of whether they have performed marriage rites or not."[14] Although the question of registration is not raised here, the recognition of *de facto* marriage in such cases seems quite clear.

Wang Nai-ts'ung, in his booklet *Collection of Interpretative Answers to Problems Concerning the New Marriage Law,* quotes a question and reply which appeared in the *New China Daily* of Chungking immediately after the promulgation of the Marriage Law.[15] The question was: "What procedure must be followed when dissolving the relationship of living together, how should children born from such a relationship be considered, and if the woman at the time of the dissolution of the relationship got into economic difficulties, could she demand part of her living expenses from the man?" The paper replied that such relations had been caused by the fact that formerly there was no freedom of marriage but that since the new Marriage Law, such relations should no longer continue to exist. "Living together without being married is an improper illegal relationship. If the parties wish to separate there is no need for any procedure — they can do so whenever they please." Regarding the children, the newspaper said that they enjoyed the protection accorded by Article 15 of the Marriage Law to illegitimate children, but since the relationship was not protected by law, the provisions concerning property arrangements after divorce could not be applied to the woman. Nevertheless, if she got into economic difficulties

13. *Ibid.,* p. 341.
14. *Ibid.,* p. 351.
15. Wang Nai-ts'ung, *Hsin hun-yin-fa wen-t'i chieh-ta hui-pien* (Collection of interpretative answers to problems concerning the new marriage law), Peking, 1951, p. 98.

after the separation, an understanding with the man should be reached.

Wang's book was published in December 1951, and this view, among others, was severely criticized in the *People's Daily*[16] immediately after publication of the book. The paper wrote:

> The relationship of living together only lacks the legal formality of registration; in all other aspects it completely constitutes [*chü-pei*] the relationship of husband and wife, like working together and rearing the children. If no protection were offered to the property of the woman, this would necessarily be disadvantageous for her.

The *People's Daily* had also asked the Ministry of Justice for its opinion in this matter; the Ministry admitted that "living together in common production by labor" actually constituted *de facto* marriage and that "a distinction should be made between relationships that had commenced before the promulgation of the Marriage Law and those that had commenced afterward."

Several more instances occurred where fairly authoritative Chinese agencies gave different views. One example is found in the report of the Second Investigation Team of the Supreme Court[17] which was sent out to inquire about the implementation of the Marriage Law in 1951. It contains the following passage:

> Registration is not a mere formality but a necessary procedure for the government to examine and approve marriage. The meaning of this examination is primarily to oppose the continued existence of the feudal system of marriage by arrangement. Marriage without registration cannot be recognized in principle.

Yet perhaps the most authoritative government agency except for the Supreme Court, the Legal Committee of the GAC, stated in 1953:

> The fact that, after the promulgation of the Marriage Law and after agencies for registration have been established, people still do not go and register their marriage, is not as it ought to be [*shih pu-ying-kai ti*]. As regards those who have *de facto* married and

16. *JMJP*, January 17, 1952.
17. *JMJP*, May 29, 1952.

have omitted only the procedure of registration, we still recognize that there is a relationship of husband and wife, and they should not necessarily register *post facto*. If they request registration of their own volition, they shall be allowed to do so and a certificate of marriage shall be issued to them. After the Movement for the Implementation of the Marriage Law of March 1953, both the man and the woman at the time of marriage shall observe the system of marriage registration and proceed with registration.[18]

This brings the recognition of *de facto* marriage at least up to March 1953; if after that time registration is omitted, it is not "as it should be." But the Committee still does not say what the consequences of failure to register are after March 1953.

Scholars generally seem to hold that *de facto* marriage is legally valid. Ma Ch'i, according to Niida Noboru,[19] was of the opinion that marrying without registration was unlawful; registration was a legal duty, but *de facto* marriage had to be recognized if the parties living together fulfilled the legal conditions of Articles 3–5 of the Marriage Law and also fulfilled the following three conditions:

1. The man and the woman must firmly believe that they are living in a marital relationship.

2. There must in fact be marital life.

3. The relationship must be publicly recognized by the masses.

If these conditions were not fulfilled there existed a private relationship (*p'ing-tu*) and not a relationship of husband and wife. Besides this, according to Ma, registration provided the effective means to prove the existence of marriage. Probably he meant that otherwise *de facto* marriage had to be proved by the parties.

Seven Chinese writers in a joint article on bigamy and adultery published in 1957 held that "a valid marriage means any marriage registered according to the Law, any marriage concluded before the promulgation of the Marriage Law, and *de facto* marriage if not concluded in contravention of the provisions of the Marriage Law but where only the procedure of registration has not been complied with." [20]

18. *Collection*, p. 311.
19. Niida Noboru, *Chūka jinmin kyōwakoku konyinhō* (Marriage law of the People's Republic of China), in K. Miyazaki, ed., *Shin hikaku konyinhō* (New comparative marriage law), Tokyo, 1960, 1:30.
20. Tung Ch'ing-chih et al. "On Bigamy and Adultery," *Fa-hsueh* (Legal studies), no. 4 (1957), p. 36.

Among Japanese scholars, opinions are divided. Kuroki Saburo, quoted by Niida, considered registration in China different from the civil marriage license:

> It is the conscious spontaneous act of the liberated person to have his marriage confirmed by the government. By the issuance of the certificate the marriage is legally established. Marrying without registering would be in contravention of Article 6. However, persons who are married *de facto* may apply for registration subsequently. One cannot say that when the factual conditions of marriage exist and only the registration is omitted the marriage does not exist before the law.[21]

In Kuroki's opinion, a man who has a spouse in a formally registered marriage commits bigamy when he marries another woman *de facto* (without registration), and will be prosecuted on that account. Registration is not a formality but a necessary procedure by which the government investigates and approves. Unlike the system established by the Russian Code of 1926, registration in China, he felt, is a condition without which the marriage cannot be legally proved. By the examination of the registration agency the marriage is legally confirmed. A couple who provisionally enter into marital relations would be forced by the neighborhood to register.

Another scholar, Asai Atsushi, assumed that registration in China resolves the contradiction between legal marriage and *de facto* marriage and establishes a third type of marriage.[22] According to him there seems to be a dualistic attitude which recognizes registration as well as the social fact of marriage. Registration is not a condition for marriage, but it opens the way for the government to resist feudalism. On the other hand, the government does not simply condone *de facto* marriage but devotes extraordinary effort to the implementation of registration. Asai's view was based on the pronouncement of the Legal Committee in 1953; that is, the possibility of subsequent registration in case of *de facto* marriage.

Some other Japanese scholars who visited China quoted Professor Lei Chieh-ch'iung of the Peking Political-Legal Institute. Mr. Lei's opinion was as follows:

21. Niida, *Chūka jinmin kyōwakoku konyinhō*, p. 35.
22. *Ibid.*, p. 36.

Marriage of course is established when the marriage certificate is provided at the registration, according to Article 6. The government, by means of education and propaganda, definitely causes people to register at the time of their marriage. But even if this procedure is not followed, and a couple is living together, leading a life of husband and wife and fulfilling the conditions of *de facto* marriage, the law recognizes this as marriage and attaches legal consequences to this . . . Since registration is a device for the safeguarding of the freedom of marriage, it certainly has to be complied with. Therefore, although registration is not urged for marriages concluded before the promulgation of the Marriage Law, for those concluded after promulgation, if no registration has been effected, registration is urged and through this the spirit of the Marriage Law is being inculcated.[23]

Niida's own view was as follows: Registration at present (1961) is a means to prevent "feudally" arranged marriage, and it is a measure of control against child marriage, bigamy, concubinage, and so forth. Therefore, the registration agency has been endowed with the power of investigation and has the right to demand to be shown certain documents in proof of the allegations of the parties. On the other hand, it is a means to establish beyond doubt the legal position of the woman and the children at the time of divorce, for the purpose of succession, to establish the duties of the father and the husband, and so on. Without obligatory registration the provisions of the Marriage Law would have no backbone and the ideals of the Law could not be realized. Simple recognition of *de facto* marriage would probably entail all sorts of judicial snags, even assuming that there were a basis for *de facto* marriage in China.

Yet the regime does not want to judge marriage by external legal form only, nor does it adhere to the way of thinking that by simply promulgating a law, the situation could be changed. It wants the law to become a reality and to avoid the mistake made by the Nationalist government of promulgating laws which are not accepted by the people. Therefore, the Communist regime concentrates on education and persuasion. However, as it wishes to view marriage also as a social fact, the attitude of the government is dualistic. On the one hand registration is insisted upon; on the other, *de facto*

23. *Ibid.*, p. 36.

marriage is recognized. This situation Niida explains as a legal phenomenon of the time of transition when the old society changes into a new one. At this stage, registration fulfills the function mainly of opposing the "feudal" marriage system; when the necessity for this struggle no longer exists, it will perform another function "in the establishment of a higher society." [24] Apparently, Niida expected that registration would be permanent though its purpose might change. It seems that Niida considered the present Marriage Law as a transitory one; perhaps for that reason he was hesitant about accepting Asai's opinion that the final stage has been reached in the resolution of the contradiction between legal marriage and *de facto* marriage and their replacement by a third type. Niida prefers a more cautious attitude.

In this connection it is instructive to review briefly the evolution of the institution of registration in the USSR. In the Law of the RSFSR of 1918, registration was obligatory but in subsequent judicial practice unregistered marriages were considered legally valid.[25] Registration was instituted as a means to oppose the influence of the church, not as an effort to replace the church by the state. Marriage at that time was an affair between a man and a woman sanctioned by the state, but the sanction could be given tacitly. The justification for the Law was the principle of protection of the weaker partner in marriage, to end the exploitation of woman by man. Marriage had no connection with the founding of a family; family relations came about by descent only. Marriage as a legal institution would disappear together with the abolition of private property. The interference of the state was strictly provisional and transitional. Marriage was ultimately to repose on ethical principles.

These ideas about marriage were emphasized further in the Code of 1926, where registration was effected "in the interest of the State and society"; as a means of evidence, it constituted an irrefutable presumption of the existence of marriage. The government, according to Bilinsky, did not dare to do away with registration altogether because it feared that the church would reassert its authority in this

---

24. *Ibid.*, pp. 18–20, 39–41; see also Niida Noboru, *Chūgoku hōseishi kenkyū, kazokuhō* (A study of Chinese legal history, family law), Tokyo, Tokyo daigaku shuppan kai, 1962, pp. 552–553.
25. Andreas Bilinsky, *Das Sovietische Eherecht* (Herrenalb/Schwarzwald, 1961), chap. 2, pp. 14–15.

field.[26] In the Code of 1926 *de facto* marriage was recognized, though by implication.

Registration in the RSFSR in this period, therefore, was a weapon against the church. The intention of the regime was not dualistic but to divest marriage of formal legal requirements. One could marry without any formality at all, but if formality was desired, it must be a formality before the state officials and not before the clergy.

The Chinese Communists were not unduly worried over the role of the church in their country but the Chinese family in some ways fulfilled a similar function to that of the church in Russia. The traditional ancestor worship knitted the family members together almost like the members of a religious community. The Chinese family was its own "church" as well as its own economic and cultural unit. Once the subject of marriage was pried loose from the Chinese family, the old family would be weakened. If parental arrangement of marriage was effectively impeded, then family ties would be loosened and finally the whole structure of ancestral worship and family authority would collapse. The effective counteraction of parental authority in matters of marriage together with the destruction of family property which gave this authority certain coercive power had to be among the first measures used by the Communists to rebuild Chinese society.

Therefore the requirement of registration was a necessity from the Communist point of view if a form for marriage were to exist to replace the authority of the family head with the authority of the state. However, a marriage without parental arrangement, without ritual, dowry, or presents, and without presentation of the bride to the ancestors — a purely *de facto* marriage — could also perfectly well perform the function of breaking down the traditional family or the "feudal marriage system" even without the safeguard of registration. In the Marriage Law of the Chinese Soviet Republic of 1934, registration had no constitutive function, only a control function. The correct way was to register, but without registration marriage was still validly constituted. In this respect the Chinese went even a step further than the Russians — they included the validity of *de facto* marriage *expressis verbis* in their Law of 1934. To a certain extent there was, of course, a risk, since marriage could be concluded

26. *Ibid.*

by parental arrangement under cover of *de facto* marriage, but in the regime's view at that time the risk was worth taking. The recognition of *de facto* marriage had the effect of making it clear that marriage was not a sacred thing but a matter that concerned only the parties themselves. Recognition of *de facto* marriage expressed, as in the USSR, the expectation and intent that the family would vanish. The family, as long as necessary, was replaced by a number of obligations between individuals based on consent. The Chinese Communists in 1934 did not seem to want any form of family at all, and the word "family" (*chia-t'ing*) does not occur in that law.

The wording of Article 9 of the 1934 Law[27] seems to preclude the possibility that the article had been incorporated only for the reason of protecting women married *de facto* before the promulgation of the law. It is very clear that the essence of marriage is "living together" and all who do so, now and in the future, are considered married.

In the thirties the disadvantages of the Russian system were already quite apparent, and it was not long before countermeasures were taken there. But either the Russian dangers were thought to be nonexistent in China or they were taken as unavoidable, or the regime considered itself capable of coping with them in other ways. The animosity toward the family, any form of family, among the Chinese Communists at that time was even stronger than it was in Russia, since the family was a formidable enemy, even though its time-honored concepts were already beginning to change.

Since Stalin, developments in the USSR have made a complete turnabout. Marriage, instead of a relationship between two individuals, has become the act of founding a family. The state, for various and complex reasons, became interested in the establishment of a firm, healthy, and stable marriage.[28] Marriage was manipulated in the service of the state, registration became once more obligatory, but this time it acquired the character of an act of loyalty to the regime. The state officiated over marriage as a sacrament, and registration became constitutive of marriage, except for those *de facto* marriages which took place after 1944. These were allowed to be

27. See text at note 4 above.
28. Swerdlov, as quoted in John N. Hazard and Isaac Shapiro, *The Soviet Legal System* (Dobbs Ferry, New York: Oceana, 1962), Part III, pp. 105–106.

registered with retroactive effect. Marriage was regarded as the foundation of the Soviet family. The married couple themselves formed a family, and though most of the old provisions of the Code of 1926 were retained, their spirit was drastically changed. In practice they now served to build the Soviet family. This process took place between 1936 and 1944 and coincided with the abandonment of the idea of the withering away of the state and the law.

Considering the different political development of China, it is hard to say how far the Russian ideas have been influential or applicable in that country. The Border Area period (1934–1945) was one of experimentation and preparation. In the Chin-Ch'a-Chi area a system was found which could be called dualistic. Registration was a legal duty, but a marriage concluded by public ceremony was valid. *De facto* marriage without ceremony, however, was decidedly not valid and was considered a "chaotic situation." The Communist Party program at that time had been frustrated, land reform had been stalled, the economic position of the family was thus left intact, and the attack on the family could only be pursued by rather indirect and inefficient means. Education in the Communist sense could be pursued vigorously, but the undermining of the family was attempted mostly by the means indicated by the 1931 Civil Code of the Republic of China,[29] and the Communist regime was at least temporarily content to handle "semi-bourgeois, semi-feudal" tools for the benefit of the United Front.

Nevertheless, some of the echoes of the USSR were heard in the Border Areas. In the Shen-Kan-Ning area a decree was issued forbidding abortion except for medical reasons; and there were measures for the establishment of prenatal care and for support of young mothers.[30] To some extent this decree was reminiscent of the Russian one of July 27, 1936 [31] which preceded the change there. Considering that such measures were taken, perhaps the strong denunciation of *de facto* marriage in the Chin-Ch'a-Chi area also reflects Russian influence.

29. The means provided by the Civil Code to undermine the traditional family are: voluntariness of the parties to marry, no specific performance of the betrothal contract, a simple public formality at the conclusion of marriage, equality of husband and wife, several systems of matrimonial property regime, possibility of deprivation of parental rights, etc. All these measures limit the authority of parents over their children and that of the husband over the wife.
30. *K'ang-Jih ken-chü ti cheng-ts'e t'iao-li hui-chi,* p. 138.
31. R. Schlesinger, *The Family in the USSR* (London: Routledge, 1949), p. 269.

The total attack against the family was resumed in the years of the civil war (1946–1949) while efforts were made to draft the present Marriage Law to replace the old Border Area regulations. Land reform was executed ruthlessly, and, after victory was won, the new Marriage Law was used to attack the authority of parents and the whole family structure. Indeed, registration, under these circumstances, again functioned as a weapon against parental authority over the conclusion of marriages. The new law no longer contained the article recognizing *de facto* marriage, but while courts and scholars all maintained that *de facto* marriage was valid, only administrative agencies emphasized the importance of registration.

The regime under these circumstances could practically act as a free agent, for no considerations on account of the United Front could any longer be regarded as serious impediments to its movements. One may discard the possibility that Article 9 of the Law of 1934, which maintained that a couple living together was considered married whether or not they registered, would have been deleted out of fear of repercussions from the people. Considerations of principle must be responsible for this conscious omission.

Furthermore, with a very rare exception, the persons, committees, or agencies who so urgently advocated registration, did not threaten any sanctions. The regime seemed determined to press forward with registration, but preferably not by force, and not on the basis of registration as a constitutive element of marriage. This is at variance with the concept of registration in the Soviet Union since 1944.

Still, the regime's views of marriage and the family were not identical in 1950 and in 1934. In the 1950 law there is a definite link between marriage, family, and society. Marriage is the "basis" of the family, and the family is a social cell, as Ch'en Shao-yü stated.[32] Even more clearly, the new third chapter of the law, and especially the important Article 8, indicate that marriage had become more than the mere free union of a man and woman recognized by law but meant the establishment of a family, a group consisting of parents and children dedicated to a common ideal. This is one of the very important articles that distinguish the present law from its predecessors. It recognizes a kind of family, and puts that family in the service of the ideology. Here again one feels strong affiliations with

32. See note 11.

the trend of thought in the USSR, but the systems are not yet completely identical.

The legislators seem to intend to establish through marriage a type of family completely amenable to the political and social ideas of the regime. In this respect the example of the USSR is indeed followed. However, the importance of registration at this stage does not seem any more to be exclusively as a weapon against parental authority, but also as a symbolic expression of allegiance to socialist ideals and therefore something implicitly antifeudal. Registration thus becomes a type of ceremonial.

The education campaign promotes the idea that registration is the "thing to do," and that it is improper not to register. Direct coercion is deliberately avoided. This avoidance is well advised. If not necessary, interference and direct coercion are better replaced by reasoning and persuasion and an appeal to what is sensible and proper. Omission of registration as an act of defiance then loses its meaning, becomes foolish, and can be met with a supercilious smile.

When seen in this way, the attitude of the Communist government does not necessarily seem dualistic. It wishes registration to be an accepted ceremony, natural to the people. This, rather than the stern command of law, is the preferred method of persuasion. The provisions on marriage, except those on bigamy, incest, parental arrangement, and other "feudal" matters, are to serve only as rough structural guidelines. Marriage is publicly living together, governed by ethical principles, which are contained or at least indicated in the Marriage Law. Thus, in a sense, the study of the Marriage Law is not a study of law, but of political ethics, and its prescriptions may be accepted as the old *li*. Judgments are moralizing and even declaratory, handbooks are politically pious, and in adjudication great stress is laid on didactic conciliation. The sense of political and moral duty is preferred to the sense of legal duty, and social censure is preferred to the impersonal compulsion of the law.

Is it necessary to see a resolution of the contradiction between civil marriage and marriage as a social fact in the way registration is regulated in China? As a matter of fact, there has been no civil marriage in China. Marriage has always been a family affair in its preparation and a social fact in its existence, publicized by the celebration. For China there was nothing that had to be resolved. To consider the Chinese Communist attitude toward registration as an abstract way of solving the contradiction between civil marriage and the recognition of marriage as a social fact seems somewhat far-fetched. It is of course attractive to see it in this way: civil marriage with registration as the constitutive element, *de facto* marriage, and (the third form) recognition of *de facto* marriage but with registration as ritual. But the Chinese registrar does not pronounce the parties married, and he may under certain circumstances forbid their marriage. It seems difficult to consider this as such an innovation that one can speak of the resolution of the contradiction. Marriage as a social fact is recognized under certain conditions, and registration is the act of accepting those conditions by those marrying.

One can agree with Niida that registration is in the first instance a means to fight the old traditional institution of marriage, and that later on it may serve some other "higher" purpose.

In summary, registration in China at present has no constitutive force; it is a kind of ceremonial act by which the parties show that they accept the conditions for marriage and the contents of marriage, that is, the rights and duties of husband and wife as expressed in chapter 3 of the Marriage Law, and those between parents and children in chapter 4. Marriage is recognized as a social fact in that *de facto* marriage is basically accepted, but indirect pressure is exerted to obtain registration. From being a device to counteract parental influence and to provide means to exercise and control freedom of marriage, registration has developed into a thought control device. From the point of view of the marrying parties, it is an act of allegiance to the family policy of the regime. Nonobservance of registration means defiance of the regime and is a sign of wrong thought, and as such will entail education at least.

My initial point of departure was the specific problem of translating the term *ying* in the passage "they shall register" in Article 6 of the Marriage Law. Since apparently the sanction for neglect of this duty does not entail nonrecognition of the marriage and does not by itself entail punishment, *ying* must be understood as expressing a duty in the nature of political morality. To describe the nature of this duty in English is difficult: "shall" is too strong and "should" too weak. The correct term lies somewhere in between. The only solution for the FLP translation would be a footnote with reference to the literature.

ethodological Problems in Studying
ninese Communist "Civil Law"

Stanley Lubman

This essay tentatively examines some of the analytical difficulties which Western students encounter in studying Chinese legal and administrative institutions and suggests a functional approach which may help avoid considerable error; it concentrates on some Chinese institutions which seem analogous to Western "civil law" institutions, particularly contract, as they were constituted before the Cultural Revolution began in 1966. This essay is my indirect response to an invitation to write a conference paper on "Some Problems of Translating Chinese Legal Language: Contracts." That topic as thus expressed seemed to reflect a considerable number of questionable assumptions about law in China. One such assumption is that there is a specialized terminology in China — a "legal language" — as there is in the West. The topic implied as well that there is an *institution* of contract, recognizably distinct from other institutions. It seemed to imply that "contract" is a *legal* institution, with an identity within contours of its own, somehow distinct from other arrangements. Unfortunately none of these assumptions can be justified, which dramatizes how careful we in the West must be to restrain ourselves from employing our own notions about the nature of legal institutions, such as contract, in our study of Chinese institutions. We have no other assumptions to begin with, of course, than those formed by our own training and immersion in Western law. Yet if we are to appreciate nuanced differences between institutions in China and elsewhere, we must move from presuppositions rooted in our own systems to others, more neutral. With the limited intention of posing some preliminary questions that may aid our analysis, I have suggested below several adjustments in research perspectives on Chinese law and administration which seem appropriate.

Law as Politics

In the West, legal institutions are generally thought to involve the settlement of specific disputes by officials who act with some regularity in formulating and applying norms to particular circumstances. In one American — and court-centered — view, the "central idea" of law is the "principle of institutional settlement," under which the resolution of social conflict, to be binding, must be reached through constituted procedures.[1] This in turn implies that certain kinds of "legal" decisions, of which adjudication is most prominent, are specialized in terms of the procedures which define the decision-making process and the substantive rules which inform, guide, or compel its outcome. These decisions differ particularly from those made by bodies such as legislatures (and, often but not always, administrative agencies) which possess power and discretion to fashion general prospective arrangements for society and its members. Adjudication implies the use of only *limited* discretion; adjudicators are obligated to engage in the "principled decision" of disputes by the "reasoned elaboration" of pre-existing rules and standards which must serve as the referents for decisions and must be employed as uniformly as possible.[2] Civil law relationships such as contract are formed against a background of rules which define rights and duties and thus indicate the circumstances in which claims arising out of transactions may be vindicated by official, i.e., judicial, action. It is important to recall that in the West the legal rules are only the "background" for contractual relationships, since not only are contractual transactions extraordinarily variable and flexible, but their consequences may also be varied by the parties without much regard for formally vindicating their rights.[3] Regardless of the suppleness of

1. H. M. Hart and A. M. Sacks, *The Legal Process: Basic Problems in the Making and Application of Law* (Cambridge, Mass.: Harvard University Press, 1958), p. 4.
2. See *ibid.*, pp. 155–179.
3. See, e.g., H. J. Berman, "Protection of Rights Arising Out of Economic Contracts under Socialist Legal Systems: A Comparative Approach," *Osteuropa Recht*, no. 4 (December 1968), pp. 217–218: "In the American market economy, most breaches of economic contracts are not the subject of litigation but are settled amicably between the parties. This is partly because a lawsuit, including resort to arbitration, tends to create hostility between the parties and thus to impede their future business relations. Also enterprises which sue for breach of contract acquire the reputation of being litigious, and others will not wish to deal with them. Finally, litigation is apt to be expensive in time and money. It is quite common, therefore, for the parties to seek to 'keep the contract going' despite a breach or, if that is impossible, to accept

contract and the informality of the parties' relationships, however, the formal legal rules provide the contours of these transactions, although lawyers may be too wont to believe implicitly in the direct impact of rules on practice.

Chinese Communist theory, on which it is unnecessary here to dwell at length, begins from altogether different premises. It sees law as the tool of a ruling class placed in the service of politics,[4] and rejects sharp differentiation between judicial, legal, and administrative processes. In the Soviet Union and Eastern Europe, legal theory with common ideological roots has not prevented the development, albeit uneven, of increasingly close-textured doctrine in some areas of social and economic activity, in a context of arrangements regarded in those countries as "legal" and differing in form and function from administrative and political activities. Thus, in the Soviet Union and Eastern Europe, certain relationships are not only defined by normative rules and standards, but are enforced and applied in a relatively principled manner by specialized judicial or quasi-judicial institutions. While to critical Western observers the area of "legal" activity may seem smaller — and the regularity of official acts within that area more variable — in those countries than in the West, their boundaries and internal complexities are perceived. Moreover, other kinds of activity not considered to be "legal" but administrative, such as inter-enterprise contracts, are also characterized by the development of legalistic doctrine and practice.[5]

In China, however, the close intertwining of law with rapidly changing policies has thus far inhibited the development of judicial and quasi-judicial institutions and has interfered with regularized rule-making and dispute settlement by nonjudicial institutions. Policy and practice have varied, however, and ambiguities in the relation of policy to law and administrative practice have been discernible, as has conflict over their closeness. Although, during a brief period of political relaxation in 1957, some Chinese theoretical discussion im-

---

the breach as inevitable and perhaps to share the losses resulting from it." A suggestive case study is Stewart Macaulay, "Non-contractual Relations in Business: A Preliminary Study," *American Sociological Review*, 28 (1963), 55.

4. See, e.g., Chou Hsin-min, "Law Is a Sharp Weapon of Class Struggle," *JMJP*, October 28, 1964, in *SCMP*, no. 3339 (1964), p. 1.

5. See generally D. A. Loeber, "Plan and Contract Performance in Soviet Law," *University of Illinois Law Forum*, 1964 (1964), 128; *Soviet Economic Law: Contracts of Delivery, Soviet Statutes and Decisions*, vol. 2, no. 2 (Winter 1965–66) and no. 3 (Spring 1966).

plied that civil law could have a creative role in adjusting production relationships,[6] no such role has been recognized. However, there is some evidence that in industrial administration the accretion of bureaucratic practice has increased the regularity of decision-making. But the general closeness of Chinese civil law institutions to policy has usually been quite apparent, and as a preliminary to considering the shifts we may have to make in studying Chinese civil law institutions, it is helpful to review some examples of their politicization.

Politicization of Chinese Communist Civil Law: Some Examples

Mediation. A particularly striking instance of the infusion of politics into a legal institution is mediational dispute-settlement, which has been used to implement both general ideological principles and short-term policy decisions. The Chinese Communists have employed mediation committees to settle disputes, particularly in residential units such as urban neighborhoods and rural villages.[7] To a considerable extent, this type of dispute resolution politicized a well-known traditional institution. There may be some "resonances" between traditional and Communist practice;[8] indeed, the use of mediational forms may well reflect the conscious choice of a familiar form by the Chinese leadership because its familiarity to the masses might contribute to their acceptance of it. However, the dynamics of mediation are more complicated than that, since using recognizable and traditional forms is not necessarily inconsistent with endowing those forms with new functions.

Mediation committees have been used, for example, to implement economic policies such as agricultural collectivization by persuading peasants to join or not to leave agricultural cooperatives. Similarly, mediation committees and the "adjustment committees" into which they were sometimes temporarily transformed during the Great Leap Forward were used to aid the establishment of rural people's communes by educating peasants on the virtues of collective living and on the importance of the collective. Quite apart from their links to

6. See, e.g., Chi Meng, "Discussion of the Object of Civil Law Regulation," *JMJP*, January 6, 1957, p. 7.

7. The following discussion of mediation is based on S. Lubman, "Mao and Mediation: Politics and Dispute Resolution in Communist China," *California Law Review*, 55 (1967), 1284.

8. Jerome A. Cohen, "Chinese Mediation on the Eve of Modernization," *California Law Review*, 54 (1966), 1201, 1226.

specific campaigns and policies, mediation committees have generally politicized standards for dispute settlement, so that disputants characterized as "bourgeois" or "feudal" ought to lose to "workers" and "peasants" because of the "laws" of class analysis and the Maoist insistence on class warfare. In addition, mediation has been used to suppress disputes and to aid Party and police control over the populace.

As a result, traditional mediation has been changed: disputes are politicized; the mediators (cadres and activists) are close to or part of the ruling Party-state apparatus; in the Maoist view, unlike in the Confucianist, disputes may be useful social conflict that can teach important political lessons; disputants are now less able to compromise their differences. In the new configuration of institutions, ideology and indoctrination have sometimes been more important than satisfying disputants' claims in terms of the issues involved, such as getting a divorce, quieting noisy neighbors, or obtaining repayment of a loan. Mediation, then, illustrates the use of dispute settlement processes to mobilize, persuade, and control the Chinese populace. It also illustrates the politicization of decision-making in a "civil law" institution.

Notaries. Notarial bureaus also reflect the politicization of civil law institutions. In European civil law countries and the Soviet Union, it should be recalled, notaries are trained legal officials who must verify the legality of certain transactions between individuals.[9] Chinese notarial bureaus, established in the early 1950's and discussed occasionally in the press in the mid-1950's, seem to have been manipulated for other ends.

During the First Five Year Plan (1953–1957), but before the Party completed the "socialist transformation" of industry and commerce in 1956, notarial bureaus were used to supervise and control privately-managed enterprises which entered into contractual relations with state-managed enterprises. An article in the *People's Daily* in early 1955 [10] illustrated the role of notarial bureaus as they were then

9. On Western Europe, see, e.g., R. Schlesinger, *Comparative Law* (Brooklyn: Foundation Press, 1959), pp. 11–12; on the Soviet Union, see, e.g., J. Hazard and I. Shapiro, *The Soviet Legal System*, 3 vols. (Dobbs Ferry, N.Y.: Oceana, 1962), 1:57–58; 3:38–39 (contract of gift notarized in state notarial office).

10. Chang Chia-yung, "Notarial Work Can Effectively Supervise the Performance of Contracts," *JMJP*, March 25, 1955. The balance of this paragraph is based on this article.

defined. Notarial bureaus were charged with ascertaining the legality of contracts and their consistency with policy. Notaries also had to determine, together with the labor union at the private enterprise and with government departments, whether the private enterprise had the productive capacity to fulfill the contract. After making the appropriate determinations, the notarial bureau was to approve the contract and "educate" the parties on their contractual obligations and on the need for performing contracts according to their tenor. In this way, notarial bureaus could help

> increase privately-managed factories and commercial establishments' sense of responsibility before carrying out contracts, and improve [their] style of doing economic work, so that nationally managed enterprises and departments could even better handle their tasks according to the state plan.

To further ensure the close supervision of capitalists, the notarial bureaus were to send copies of contracts to the labor union at the privately-managed factory. Thereafter, both the union and the notarial bureau were charged with investigating the enterprise's performance. This activity of the notarial bureaus was hailed as a form of mass supervision of the bourgeoisie, as an aid in reducing cheating of the state by the bourgeoisie, and as a weapon in "elevating [the bourgeoisie's] law-abiding thoughts."

Later in 1955, more notarial bureaus were established. They were not exclusively charged with supervising the bourgeoisie, as indicated by the temporary regulations on notarial work issued in Canton in June, 1955.[11] These regulations provided for notarization not only of contracts between state and privately-owned enterprises, but also of transactions between private individuals involving powers of attorney, succession, wills, sales, and divisions of jointly-owned property. However, their principal task, as stated in the press during 1955, was still to help maintain contract discipline and thereby help supervise and reform the bourgeoisie.[12]

In 1955–56, the Communist Party launched a drive for the "socialist transformation," i.e., the nationalization, of all industrial and com-

11. "Announcement of the People's Congress of Canton, Kwangtung Province," *NFJP*, June 24, 1955.
12. See, e.g., "Many Cities in the Nation Begin Notarial Work," *KMJP*, June 18, 1955, p. 1.

mercial enterprises which still remained in private hands. As state control was extended, extra-enterprise supervision of the bourgeoisie became less important. The possibility of notarial bureaus discharging other functions, such as supervising performance of contracts between state enterprises, was discussed. By late 1956, articles on notarial work stressed particularly the notaries' role in facilitating remittances to China from abroad. They could help overseas Chinese transfer assets to the People's Republic and all Chinese, regardless of where they resided, dispose of property located abroad by authenticating their identity and their power to dispose of the property. Thus the notarial bureaus could aid the People's Republic in obtaining assets owned abroad by overseas Chinese; in addition they helped further the policy of attracting interest and support among overseas Chinese by allowing them to enjoy property rights within China.[13]

Reflecting these policies, numerous cases were reported in which residents of China signed and notarized powers of attorney or other documents in order to dispose of or gain possession of property situated abroad.[14] Notarial bureaus were also reported to have facilitated the enjoyment by overseas Chinese of property interests within China: by granting a landlord a certificate affirming that an agent was acting for him in collecting rents,[15] authenticating the right of an heir residing abroad to inherit a house situated in China that had been bequeathed to him by his overseas Chinese father,[16] and notarizing the will of another overseas Chinese who had returned to China temporarily.[17]

Notarial work reflected yet another policy in 1956–57, a period in which the new roles of notarial bureaus were significantly mentioned in the press. That period was an interlude of relative relaxation, stabilization, and retrenchment after a succession of intensive political campaigns over the preceding seven years. Reflecting the views

13. On Communist Chinese policies toward overseas Chinese remittances and investment, see, e.g., A. Doak Barnett, *Communist China and Asia* (New York: Harper, 1960), pp. 93–94.
14. See, e.g., "Protect the Rightful Interests of Overseas Chinese," *JMJP*, Oct. 25, 1956, p. 2 (Amoy resident disposing of property in Malaya); "Protect the Legal Interests of Citizens," *Pei-ching jih-pao* (Peking daily), Mar. 31, 1957, p. 2 (son in China unable to succeed to deceased father's property in Indonesia without certificate from notarial bureau sent to Indonesia).
15. "Canton Gradually Develops Notarial Work," *NFJP*, Mar. 9, 1957.
16. "The People's Courts of Various Hsien of Chin-chiang Special Ch'ü Protect the Rights of Overseas Chinese," New China News Agency news release, March 9, 1957.
17. "Protect the Rightful Interests of Overseas Chinese," *JMJP*, Oct. 25, 1955, p. 2.

of at least a significant portion of the Chinese leadership that "the period of revolutionary storm and stress was past," [18] domestic policy briefly emphasized legality and the enjoyment by citizens of rights to own, enjoy, and dispose of property.[19] Several articles published during this brief period stressed how notarial bureaus could prevent litigation arising out of property transactions such as purchase and sale of houses, debts, pledges, and entrusting property to the care of another, by authenticating documents such as wills.[20]

Since June, 1957, when the Hundred Flowers period ended, notarial bureaus have been little mentioned in the press. The political atmosphere, which had briefly encouraged enjoyment of property, has since then generally been explicitly hostile to such antisocialist behavior, and notarial bureaus have apparently had little function in private economic transactions or relations between state-owned enterprises. They continue to exist, evidently; an émigré from China in late 1965 showed me his college diploma, duly authenticated in that year by a Peking notarial bureau.

The extent to which legal and administrative activities have been politicized, as suggested by these examples, is striking. When the leadership wished to tighten control over the bourgeoisie in 1955, such apparently humdrum agencies as the notarial bureaus were enlisted to help implement policy; when nationalization made such activities irrelevant, the energies of the notarial bureaus were directed toward other policy goals. In an underdeveloped country like China, where bureaucratic resources are stretched thin, it should be no surprise that civil law institutions should be enlisted to help implement policies. However, the extent of politicization meant that the notarial bureaus, whatever their resemblances to Western and Soviet institutions with the same names, functioned less to maintain and preserve civil law relationships than to assist in shaping them to fit policy.

Tensions in legal theory. In order to begin to understand the operation of heavily politicized civil law institutions, Western students must be prepared to cease regarding them like the autonomous or

18. Liu Shao-ch'i, "The Political Report of the Central Committee of the Communist Party of China to the Eighth National Congress of the Party," Sept. 15, 1956, in *Eighth National Congress of the Communist Party of China*, 3 vols. (Peking, 1956), 1:81.
19. See, e.g., "Protect the Legal Interests of Citizens," *Pei-ching jih-pao*, March 31, 1957, p. 2.
20. See, e.g., *ibid.*; and "Notarial Work in Canton Develops Gradually," *NFJP*, March 9, 1957, p. 3.

semiautonomous institutions which we are accustomed to thinking about — often artificially — in the West and consider them in their political context, including their relationship to ideology and changing policies. But Chinese Communist ideology contains different strains, and policy and practice have not been constant. Indeed, there has been a considerable amount of intra-Party debate over the function of legal institutions in China. Although the debate has been most clearly articulated with regard to sanctioning institutions such as the formal, adjudicatory criminal process,[21] some of the tensions between different conceptions of legal institutions are evident in Chinese discussions of civil law institutions as well. They can be illustrated here by a minor but suggestive example in the discussion of contracts in the only Chinese Communist civil law textbook which has been obtainable in the West, published in 1958.[22]

Some background is necessary to consider the single aspect of the book which I will discuss below. It seems possible to trace policy discussions about law to conflicts within the Party over major issues, issues no smaller than the aims of the Chinese revolution and the means by which cadres ought to lead China's masses in that revolution. All that I can say here is that an aspect of this ideological conflict with enormous import for legal institutions involves the conflict between "mass line" leadership by mobilizing the masses, and more regularized, bureaucratic means of decision-making and leadership.[23]

The Chinese Communist Party owes a large measure of its success in arousing much of the Chinese populace and vanquishing the Nationalists in 1949 to its mobilizational tactics, centering on the mass line. Mao stated that "correct leadership . . . means: take the ideas of the masses (scattered and unsystematic ideas) and concen-

21. See, e.g., the summaries in Jerome A. Cohen, *The Criminal Process in the People's Republic of China, 1949–1963: An Introduction* (Cambridge, Mass.: Harvard University Press, 1968), pp. 14–16; Shao-chuan Leng, *Justice in Communist China* (Dobbs Ferry, N.Y.: Oceana, 1967), pp. 54–69.

22. Institute of Civil Law, Central Political-Legal Cadres' School, *Chung-hua jen-min kung-ho-kuo min-fa chi-pen wen-t'i* (Basic problems in the civil law of the People's Republic of China), Peking, 1958. Hereafter cited as *1958 Civil Law Textbook*. Richard M. Pfeffer, "The Institution of Contracts in the Chinese People's Republic," pt. 2, *China Quarterly*, no. 15 (1963), p. 115, summarizes well the chapters on contracts, although underestimating the extent to which the contract in China departs from Soviet patterns.

23. The effect of this conflict on the criminal process is discussed in Stanley Lubman, "Form and Function in the Chinese Criminal Process," *Columbia Law Review*, 69 (1969), p. 535.

trate them . . . then go to the masses and propagate and explain these ideas until the masses embrace them as their own, hold fast to them and translate them into action." [24] Mass action assists the Party to carry out policy which it could not implement alone, and thus expresses the Party's dependence on the masses to accomplish desired objectives.[25] It also "directs the cadres' attention to the need for ascertaining, articulating, and aggregating the interests of the masses." [26] The Party uses the mass line to manipulate the populace, of course, because "the Party is guided in its decisions by the conviction that it alone understands the long-run collective interests of the people." [27] The mass line expresses the Maoist insistence on face-to-face leadership by persuasion and on the necessity for the Party to maintain solidarity with the people based on an intimacy forged in hard work and joint struggle. The notions of leadership embodied in the mass line have important implications for the study of any Chinese decision-making process. The mass line aims at mass participation in the execution (but not the formulation) of policy. Furthermore, the mass line often causes blurring and sometimes temporary obscuring of the distinction between governmental and nongovernmental organizations and activities; when the Party employs mass line devices, it uses the state apparatus as only one of a number of simultaneously utilized means for transmitting and implementing policy. Mass organizations such as associations of youth, women, students, intellectuals, workers, and peasants, as well as the media, are also used to elicit the emotional mass response at which the mass line aims.

However, the means used to forge a great revolution are not necessarily appropriate to modernizing a nation; new tasks have called for new talents, and the mass line has conflicted with the bureaucratization of cadres' work. Immediately after Liberation in 1949, cadres found themselves being bureaucratized, because the tasks of reor-

24. Mao Tse-tung, "Some Questions Concerning Methods of Leadership," *Selected Works* (Peking, 1965), 3:117, 119.
25. James R. Townsend, *Political Participation in Communist China* (Berkeley: University of California Press, 1967), p. 72. On the mass line generally, see *ibid.*, pp. 72–74, and John W. Lewis, *Leadership in Communist China* (Ithaca: Cornell University Press, 1963), pp. 72–100.
26. Tang Tsou, "Revolution, Reintegration and Crisis in Communist China" in Ping-ti Ho and Tang Tsou, eds., *China in Crisis: China's Heritage and the Communist Political System* (Chicago: University of Chicago Press, 1968), 2:277, 305.
27. Townsend, *Political Participation*, p. 73.

ganizing and administering Chinese society required greater routini-zation than the tasks of revolutionary mobilization. As one student of these changes has put it, "revolutionaries who had been provoking disorder became functionaries preserving order." [28] Necessarily, the style of a bureaucrat differs from, and may be opposed to, that of a revolutionary cadre who is supposed to mobilize the masses by living and working with them, sharing their hardships, and leading them by persuasion and inspiration in face-to-face encounters. Also, besides differing in style from the mass line, bureaucracy further separates cadres from masses as functional differentiation of cadre roles and functional specialization increase.

Conflict between emphasis on mass line and bureaucratic methods has been constant in China since 1949. During the period when the First Five Year Plan was in force, for instance, the Party fluctuated in its choice of means to implement policy, sometimes using mobili-zational campaigns and sometimes using more regularized modes of leadership. The years before the Plan began in 1953 had seen a suc-cession of turbulent campaigns to promote land reform, suppress counterrevolutionaries, and extend control over the bourgeoisie. But in the first year of the Plan, 1953–54, the leadership stressed disci-pline and order. However, another round of campaigns, to collectivize agriculture, socialize industry and commerce, and "liquidate hidden counterrevolutionaries" in 1955–56 interrupted the administrative stabilization which had begun with the Plan. It was in 1956–57, especially after the Eighth Party Congress signalled a new stabiliza-tion, that civil law institutions most reflected a nascent functional specialization and a new stability. Debates were conducted over whether the mediation committees were needed;[29] the new institution of the people's lawyer was publicized and endorsed, not only as an aid to defendants charged with crime, but also to claimants involved in disputes over family matters and private property;[30] and the notarial bureaus were hailed as protectors of citizens' rights.[31]

Reflecting the new stress on institutions of stability rather than

28. Ezra Vogel, "From Revolutionary to Semi-bureaucrat: The 'Regularization of Cadres,'" *China Quarterly*, no. 29. (1967), pp. 36, 37.
29. See "Should Mediation Committees in the Cities and Countryside Continue to Exist?," *KMJP*, July 16, 1956, p. 2; "Is It Necessary for Us to Retain People's Mediation Committees?," *KMJP*, Sept. 2, 1956, in *SCMP*, no. 1391 (1956), p.7.
30. See, e.g., Fan Cheng, "An Interview with the Tsingtao Legal Office," *JMJP*, Feb. 22, 1957, in *SCMP*, no. 1490 (1957), p. 11.
31. See my discussion of notarial work above.

mobilization, greater interest than before in legal theory was evidently shown in 1956–57. In 1957 textbooks were compiled on both civil and criminal law.[32] The civil law textbook contains extensive discussions of obligations, particularly contracts. The text plainly reflects the politicization of civil law, asserting as it does that civil law, which is "a regularization of politics and policies" is "at the service of the politics of our state." [33] At the same time civil law was recognized as assisting the Party to implement policy by aiding the realization of economic plans.[34] Most of the text is devoted to obligations, which were said to be used "to strengthen the economic relations among socialist organizations and to concretely realize the national economic plan." [35] The book's general arrangement resembles that of the Soviet Civil Code of 1922, superseded in 1960 but still in effect in the Soviet Union when the book was published. Because drafters of the Soviet Code had themselves borrowed heavily from West European codes such as the German Bürgerliches Gesetzbuch, the general plan of the text strongly resembles that of West European civil codes, passing as it does from the general to the specific, discussing first the general concept of "juristic relations" and then proceeding to obligations, to contracts in general, and finally to specific types of contracts.

Nevertheless, the effects of politicization can be seen, for regardless of how familiar the general arrangement of the text might be to comparative lawyers, upon closer look some important concepts are blurred or poorly defined. "Administrative documents" are said to be an important source of civil law obligation although such documents as distribution plans generally do not directly create obligations;[36] mortgages are discussed as administrative conveniences for bank supervision of socialist enterprises but not as legal devices, because state enterprises *never* fail to repay to the state banks obligations secured by the bank,[37] and banks do not foreclose on mortgages which secure loans to handicraft cooperatives.[38] A particularly interesting intrusion

32. The 1958 *Civil Law Textbook* was, according to an editor's note, compiled in the spring of 1957 and revised both later that year and in 1958; the criminal law text was apparently completed in April 1957, although printing and circulation were delayed until August of that year because of a change in policy.
33. *1958 Civil Law Textbook*, p. 16.
34. *Ibid.*, p. 28.
35. *Ibid.*, p. 178.
36. *Ibid.*, p. 180.
37. *Ibid.*, pp. 196–197.
38. *Ibid.*, p. 196.

of political considerations into legal technicalities is the discussion of void and voidable juristic acts.

The text enumerates as the grounds on which voidable juristic acts may be invalidated: fraud, mistake, threat of physical or mental harm, objective unfairness, and defrauding of principals by their agents.[39] These grounds are plainly similar to the grounds used in Western legal systems to declare transactions such as contracts void. However, to these the text adds "all acts made under compulsory order,"[40] which is defined as "the compulsory method employed by a state worker who, in conducting civil law activities to carry out state duties, forces the other party to accept his order."[41] This criterion of voidability is plainly different in kind from the others with which it is included. The other criteria pertain to the relations of the contracting parties *inter sese* regardless of the extent to which they represent the state. The last criterion, however, which flows from "improper use of the means of administrative organization" or "incorrect methods of mobilization,"[42] is linked with the use of coercive state power by cadres in their relationships with individuals or legal entities. The last criterion, then, uses civil law terms to describe essentially political relationships.

This last mentioned criterion of voidability is of interest not only because it reflects the impact of politics on legal theory. More significant here is the fact that the discussion reflects the larger conflict I mentioned above between mass line and bureaucratic conceptions of political leadership. In the Chinese Communist lexicon, "bureaucratism" and "commandism" describe undesirable cadre relations with the masses, "bureaucratism" because it implies aloofness and "commandism" because it implies coercion rather than persuasion.[43] "Commandism" thus represents the negation of the face-to-face contact and solidarity with the masses which the mass line requires. More important than the legal transactions entered into through cadres' efforts is whether they maintain correct modes of leadership; the authors of the text were willing to alter radically the tidiness and

39. *Ibid.*, pp. 85–88.
40. *Ibid.*, p. 86.
41. *Ibid.*
42. *Ibid.*, p. 87.
43. On "bureaucratism," see Franz Schurmann, *Ideology and Organization in Communist China* (Berkeley: University of California Press, 1966), pp. 112, 316–318; on "commandism," see *ibid.*, pp. 113, 246.

consistency of the formal legal criteria of voidability to give expression to a desired political virtue. Thus the law of obligations could reflect not only the impact of ideology, but also some of the ideology's internal tensions. The lesson for Western students is that they must be attentive not merely to the close relations between law and politics, but to the possible effects of ideological conflicts in those relations. These conflicts point up the difficulties which the Chinese have had in adapting civil legal concepts to meet ideological demands and the difficulties which Westerners encounter in their search for civil law relationships or their analogues in Chinese administrative practice.

Law as Administration

The General Problem

Another characteristic of Chinese institutions is the extensive transmutation of legal forms into fluid administrative ones. Law is supposed to serve changing political policies, and decision-making by cadres is denominated as "legal." But it has involved no unique doctrine or decision-making processes, and the cadres themselves have no professional "legal" skills. As a result, "legal" institutions have not differed in style and method of operation from any other administrative activities. They have been fluid and open to change that substantially altered their contours and content.

The lack of differentiation of Chinese "legal" from other administrative activities appeared, for instance, in the criminal process as it evolved during the first ten years of Communist rule. Even when the Chinese Communists expressed interest in adapting Soviet models they refrained from developing an adjudicatory process with real autonomy from police and Party. Relevant here is the competition noted above[44] between mobilizational means of implementing policies associated with the mass line, and more routinized and regularized bureaucratic techniques. The tension between "red" political orthodoxy vs. technical competence in training and evaluating personnel is another basic and related conflict in values which has

44. For one illustration of this conflict, see, e.g., *New York Times*, July 11, 1968, p. 7, reporting a criticism of Lo Jui-ch'ing, former Minister of Public Security, for allegedly urging his cadres to emulate Sherlock Holmes, i.e., to be expert at their work. See generally Lubman, "Form and Function," p. 535.

affected the administration of the criminal process.[45] Also, Party officials, especially those who were simultaneously members of the public security (police) hierarchy, were reluctant to share substantial portions of their control over sanctioning processes. Partly because of these tensions, the history of the criminal process in the 1950's was marked by competition between earlier revolutionary styles of justice and somewhat more routinized Soviet forms. For instance, the Chinese Communists have never really used public trials for any purpose but demonstrating guilt; their long previous use of trials and mass meetings to mobilize the masses and punish "enemies"[46] was too deep-rooted to yield to less dramatic public adjudication.[47] Basically, the activities of courts and procuracy alike were dominated by the police; the formal criminal process, adjudicatory in appearance, has generally constituted a *processing* of suspects in which the most important decisions were made by the police, who could and frequently did intervene at all stages of the disposition of the case.[48] Related to the administrative configuration of the criminal process is the Chinese Communists' lack of concern for adjudication. The notion of vindicating rights, especially individual rights, has little importance. Courts are supposed to resemble as much as possible other agencies which manage and sometimes mobilize people. Thus, criminal adjudication has actually been more like what the Chinese call "the administration of public order."

It is not merely lack of concern for adjudication that characterizes the Chinese criminal process. That process seems to differ further from Western and, increasingly, Soviet sanctioning processes because rule-making and rule-following are frequently disrupted by changing policies. This does not at all mean, however, that sanctioning processes are wholly irrational, and the lack of differentiation of "legal" from other modes of controlling and organizing Chinese

45. On the conflict in cadres generally, see Schurmann, *Ideology and Organization*, pp. 162–167; John Lewis, "Leader, Commissar, and Bureaucrat: The Chinese Political System in the Last Days of the Revolution," in Ho and Tsou, eds., *China in Crisis*, 2:449, 466–467 and sources cited therein.

46. See, e.g., Leng, *Justice in Communist China*, p. 15.

47. Although some efforts were made to regularize trial proceedings, especially during a brief period of political liberalization from mid-1956 to the spring of 1957, émigré interviews suggest that these efforts were unsuccessful. See Jerome A. Cohen, *The Criminal Process in the People's Republic of China*, p. 13.

48. *Ibid.*, pp. 25–46.

society should not lead Western observers to regard Chinese legal institutions as mere shams to cloak arbitrariness. On the contrary, émigré interviews suggest that legal institutions have often (especially between major political campaigns) operated with considerable, although variable, administrative coherence. In short, although Chinese sanctioning institutions may be disorderly, they have also been bureaucratized. Thus, it has been suggested that responsibility and discretion to dispose of many minor cases have been very great at lower levels in the public security hierarchy but that close review has been exercised at middle levels. There is evidence, too, that internal directives gave at least some general guidance which public security cadres could apply in disposing of particular cases.[49]

If volatile sanctioning processes have been bureaucratized, it is hardly surprising to find that, even though the Chinese have not yet developed consistent patterns of rules and institutions which they denominate as "civil law," they have developed administrative patterns, particularly in nationalized industry, which are analogous to more formal Western and Soviet "legal" institutions. The mechanics of economic administration, such as the details of handling relations among enterprises and among enterprises, government, and Party bureaus have hitherto received little close analysis. The balance of this portion of my discussion draws together some information regarding one aspect of this complicated subject, the use of contracts in the Chinese economy, with particular emphasis on resolutions of disputes arising out of such contracts.[50]

The Administrative Uses of Contracts

Industrial contracts. Since the early years of the People's Republic, much promulgated legislation has expressed basic transformations in, and management of, economic relationships, including many with

---

49. *Ibid.*, p. 23.
50. Contracts have been used in different ways as economic policies have changed. For reviews of relevant Chinese Communist economic policies (for instance, on decentralization of industry) see Kang Chao, "Policies and Performance in Industry," in A. Eckstein, W. Galenson, and T. C. Liu, eds., *Economic Trends in Communist China* (Chicago: University of Chicago Press, 1968), p. 549, and Dwight Perkins, "Industrial Planning and Management," in *ibid.*, p. 597. The relation between the use of contracts and major changes in policy is discussed in Richard M. Pfeffer, "The Institution of Contracts in the People's Republic of China," *China Quarterly*, no. 14 (1963), p. 153.

civil law implications. Contracts have not been neglected; in 1950, for instance, legislation was promulgated governing the use of contracts to carry out the annual plans of state-owned enterprises.[51] This legislation, like subsequent legislation and discussion on contracts, emphasized the necessity for clarity of contractual terms, and the duty of the obligor to perform contracts. This early legislation channeled contract disputes primarily, though not exclusively, to an administrative hierarchy: such disputes were to be "handled" (ch'u-li)[52] by financial and economic commissions — either the commissions in the region where both parties were located if they were in the same region, or the central commission, if the parties were located in different regions — but if the "handling" was "ineffective" (wu-hsiao) the parties could theoretically (although they didn't in practice) take the matter to a people's court.[53]

Later legislation and regulations have closely linked plans with some contracts, and these links have been maintained, although the management of industry was centralized during the First Five Year Plan, decentralized during the Great Leap, and then somewhat recentralized thereafter. The contract of delivery of industrial goods and related contracts for delivery of certain essential raw materials have become linked with the distribution plans that govern allocation of important goods and are made pursuant to the plans. As one relatively recent Chinese text puts it:

> Distribution of important products is carried out in a planned manner by the state (central, and relevant local, departments) according to the materials distribution plan. Enterprises may not themselves sell this type of product. Enterprises, in order to acquire means of production whose allocation is planned, must apply to the relevant leading departments, and after the relevant departments have balanced distribution requirements, under unified

---

51. "Temporary Procedures for the Signing of Contracts by Organs, State-managed Enterprises and Cooperatives, promulgated by the Financial and Economic Commission of the Government Administration Council of the Central People's Government," October 3, 1950, in Civil Law Teaching and Research Office, Chinese People's University, ed., *Chung-hua jen-min kung-ho-kuo min-fa tzu-liao hui-pien* (Collection of materials on the civil law of the People's Republic of China), Peking, Chinese People's University, 1954, 1:385.
52. On the translation of this term, see note 94 below.
53. "Temporary procedures . . . ," no. 51, article 10.

leadership the various enterprises sign contracts with each other to organize distribution according to the contracts.[54]

"Temporary basic clauses" issued by the Ministry of Heavy Industry in 1956 provided for the conclusion of delivery contracts by enterprises and other units under the Ministry's supervision, pursuant to the distribution plan drawn up by the Ministry and other departments.[55] It is difficult to state whether they are still in effect or are adhered to, but they are of interest nonetheless, because they reflect Chinese Communist attitudes toward one type of contract during the period of considerable Soviet influence. The "clauses" specified detailed provisions, which the contracts had to include, for such matters as packaging, delivery, transportation, inspection of quantity and quality, and price of goods. They also contained provisions for specific procedures in the event of faulty performance or nonperformance by the supplier, and payment of fines as well.[56] When a supplier was prevented from performing the contract because the supplier's superior unit commanded that the products involved be allocated (*tiao-po*) in a manner at variance with the contract, or because of a "natural disaster that could not have been prevented by human effort," [57] the supplier was required to notify both its superior and its contractual partner immediately; in such cases, it could avoid paying the fines.

The "clauses" provided for payment of compensation and specific performance of duties. In addition, they provided in detail for terms of payment and for computing fines for suppliers' late delivery and failure to meet standards of quality, and for purchasers' delayed payment and rejection of goods in violation of the contract. However,

54. Huang Ta, *Wo kuo she-hui chu-i ching-chi chung ti huo-pi ho huo-pi liu-t'ung* (Currency and currency circulation in our country's socialist economy), Peking, 1964, pp. 90–91. See the summary of procedures for formulating distribution plans and formation of contract relations pursuant thereto in G. Hsiao, "The Role of Economic Contracts in Communist China," *California Law Review*, 53 (1965), 1029, 1044–49.

55. Temporary Basic Clauses on Contracts for the Supply of Products, Ministry of Heavy Industry, People's Republic of China, in Civil Law Teaching and Research Office, Chinese People's University, ed., *Chung-hua jen-min kung-ho-kuo min-fa ts'an-k'ao tzu-liao* (Reference materials on the civil law of the People's Republic of China), Peking, Chinese People's University, 1956, pp. 243–251.

56. *Ibid.*, sections 31–38.

57. *Ibid.*, section 36. A liberal rendering is given here, to avoid translating the term as *force majeure*.

despite the intricacy of these provisions and the use of legalistic terms such as "bear responsibility" (tse-jen) and "reimburse" (ch'ang-fu), and a legalistic approach to drafting,[58] the "clauses" avoided not only third-party adjudication, but avoided clear and unequivocal identification of a third party to settle disputes arising out of the contracts. Thus, the section on fines mentioned only the contracting parties, that is, the section stated only that if one party violates the contract, it must reimburse the other; it did not mention *who* might decide such issues. A supplement (fu-tse) to the "clauses" provided that:

> If in executing the contract, losses that cannot be compensated by fines, or serious disputes occur before state arbitration organs have been established, the parties may report to their superior for arrangement (t'iao-ch'u) and decision (chieh-chüeh).[59]

This section is certainly of historical interest only at the moment, as it expresses a tentative decision to follow the Soviet example and employ an arbitral institution for settling industrial contract disputes — a decision which the Chinese once entertained but soon thereafter rejected.[60] The language of the section indicates that such arbitral organizations did not yet exist in mid-1956, when the "clauses" were promulgated, and that dispute settlement was carried out entirely within ministerial hierarchies. Indeed, a state arbitration organization was apparently still not established by early 1957, as its establishment was urged in an article published in the principal Chinese legal periodical.[61]

By 1958, evidently, the Chinese Communists had decided to retain a wholly administrative mode of settling contract disputes. The *1958 Civil Law Textbook* states:

> At present, our country still has no public arbitration organ. Any dispute between socialist organizations, before conclusion of a contract or during its execution, which the parties themselves cannot

58. E.g., the clause on avoidance of fines in cases in which nonperformance is caused by certain circumstances is phrased to mean: "*If* the contract is not performed, *then* liability follows, *unless* higher orders or unavoidable natural disasters caused the nonperformance."
59. Section 43.
60. See note 62 below.
61. See Jen Chien-hsin, "Strengthen the Work of Economic Contracts and Promote the Smooth Implementation of National Economic Planning," CFYC, no. 1 (1957), p. 31.

solve through negotiation, should be submitted to higher authorities for consultation and settlement and the party who violated the law shall bear pecuniary responsibility or receive administrative punishment.[62]

Evidently, arbitration Soviet-style was considered too rigid and legalistic by the Chinese.[63] Indeed, in this connection Maoist hostility to bureaucracy may be relevant to the decision on dispute resolution in Chinese industry, even though the decision flowed, of course, from more fundamental decisions on industrial organization itself. An attack on Liu Shao-ch'i, the chief target of the Cultural Revolution, condemned Liu, *inter alia*, because of his alleged plans to organize the Chinese economy along "revisionist" Soviet or, worse yet, Yugoslav lines.[64] One charge was that Liu wanted to restrict the role of state organs administering the economy to "the role of an 'arbiter' in disputes arising between industrial enterprises . . ." [65] There is evidence that some progress was made along precisely these lines by expanding the roles of planning and financial institutions.

In 1962 a "Notice of the Central Committee of the Chinese Communist Party and State Council Relating to Strict Adherence to the Procedures for Capital Construction and to the Strict Performance of Economic Contracts" stated:

Disputes which arise in the performance of contracts shall be subject to the arbitration (*chung-ts'ai*) of economic commissions at each level. The People's Bank or the Construction Bank in each area shall be responsible for executing decisions of the economic commission at each level by withholding or paying the price of the goods.[66]

This designation of the economic commissions and the banks as agencies with particular responsibilities for dispute settlement seems to reflect the desire to regularize means of resolving interenterprise

62. *1958 Civil Law Textbook*, p. 212.
63. Two émigrés who graduated from different political-legal schools in 1960 stated independently in interviews in Hong Kong in 1966 that, in 1959, law students were told that in the Soviet Union, industrial contract disputes were settled by *courts*.
64. Ching Hung, "The Plot of the Top Ambitionist to Operate 'Trusts' on a Large Scale Must Be Thoroughly Exposed," KMJP, May 9, 1967, in SCMP, no. 3948 (1967), p. 1.
65. *Ibid.*, p. 4.
66. FKHP, no. 62 (1962–1963), p. 13.

differences. The role of the bank in this regard reflects a post-Great Leap leadership concern for increasing supervision of enterprises' use of their working capital.[67] Such control was intended to foster close supervision of the performance of enterprises in fulfilling their planned targets and was carried out sometimes by means of special investigation by bank personnel at the enterprises. The bank's control was buttressed by its power to sanction poor financial management by disapproving loans needed to enter into transactions.[68] The bank's power with respect to interenterprise disputes has occasionally been discussed, as in a text on banking published in 1964, which indicates that branches of the bank exercise some power to decide interenterprise disputes which may arise when they are notified by dissatisfied customers not to pay suppliers.[69] Thus, the text states that because the bank must have the agreement of the purchaser before it can debit the purchaser's account, the bank can carry out "supervision of performance of the contract." [70] The book adds:

In this way [the bank] can enforce (*tu-ts'u*) the supplying unit's necessary serious observance of the contract in supplying goods according to quantity, quality and time, and protect the proper interests of the purchasing unit.[71]

It appears from highly incomplete evidence, then, that the Chinese rejected third-party adjudication of interenterprise contract disputes and did not decide to establish an independent organ to mediate or arbitrate contract disputes. However, they evidently developed ad-

67. See generally Audrey Donnithorne, *China's Economic System* (New York: Allen and Unwin, 1967), p. 423; *China News Analysis*, no. 391 (1961); *China News Analysis*, no. 448 (1962).

68. Donnithorne, *China's Economic System*, p. 430; *China News Analysis*, no. 448 (1962), pp. 5–6.

69. For an account of a dispute in which two bank branches evidently performed this function and came to opposite conclusions, see *Ta kung pao* (Impartial daily), Peking, Sept. 13, 1965, reporting a disagreement in which a factory which received goods it had ordered from another factory notified its local bank branch not to pay the supplier, the local bank then sided with its depositor in the dispute, and the matter became a conflict between the customer's and the supplier's banks.

70. Li Ch'eng-jui and Tso Ch'un-t'ai, *She-hui chu-i ti yin-hang kung-tso* (Socialist bank work), Peking, 1964, p. 185. A Chinese textbook on commercial finance also refers to the duty of bank personnel to ascertain and decide whether rejection of payment is based on "lawful reason." See *Shang-yeh ts'ai-wu* (Commercial finance), in Joint Publications Research Service translations (hereafter, JPRS), no. 19698 (1962).

71. Li Ch'eng-jui and Tso Ch'un-t'ai, *She-hui chu-i ti yin-hang kung-tso*.

ministrative mechanisms for dealing with contract disputes by increasing the power of economic commissions and banks for those purposes, thereby giving them a function analogous to that of Western courts and arbitration and Soviet arbitration. These efforts must have been necessitated by the continued extensive use of interenterprise contracts, both to implement "general" agreements signed by ministries[72] and to establish direct links between factories.[73] Yet we should not hasten to think that contracts have been thought of as fixing "legal" obligations; the Chinese view seems to be much more flexible. Thus, one discussion on interenterprise agreements states that:

> an economic contract has legal efficacy, and it cannot be cancelled unilaterally. The party which does not fulfill a contract must bear political and economic responsibility . . . [and] must recognize error and compensate the other party's economic losses.[74]

However, this statement is immediately followed by the qualification that the party injured by its partner's contractual breach must handle economic problems arising from the breach "in the spirit of seeking truth from facts," an elliptical statement which seems to imply that enterprises must not rely legalistically on the contract as the exclusive source of the parties' duties to each other and to the state.

Even if contracts are flexible, who can we say is charged with settling disputes arising from them? The superiors of enterprises have been urged to maintain close supervision over them in order to deal with problems which arise or to make "readjustments" in their "cooperation." [75] Interviews in Hong Kong during 1965–1967 with fifteen émigrés who formerly served in managerial or technical capacities in industrial enterprises or state or Party bureaus concerned with transportation or industry suggest that when difficulties in interenterprise relations developed, enterprise managers usually attempted to work out the matters themselves by some compromise solution, such as

72. Sung Chi-shan, "A Brief Discussion of the Nature and Function of Economic Contracts in Industry," *Ching-chi yen-chiu* (Economic research), no. 2 (1965), pp. 33, 34, in *JPRS*, no. 31033 (1965), pp. 59–60.
73. *Ibid.* On direct contracts between enterprises, see also Teng Chan-ming, "On Economic Cooperation Between Industrial Enterprises," *Ching-chi yen-chiu*, no. 3 (1965), p. 19, in *JPRS*, no. 31034 (1965), p. 38; Weng Chan, "Developing Permanent Cooperation and Fixed Supply Sources in Local Industry," *Ching-chi yen-chiu*, no. 4 (1965), p. 1, in *JPRS*, no. 31035 (1965), p. 1.
74. Sung Chi-shan, "A Brief Discussion," p. 65 (translation modified).
75. Teng Chan-ming, "On Economic Cooperation," p. 45.

altering a delivery schedule. If they could not handle the matter in this manner, their superiors probably became involved, as the discussion quoted above suggests. Furthermore, Party bureaus also sometimes became involved. Party bureaus for industry seem to have exercised general supervisory power over enterprises and over enterprises' nominal superiors in the state hierarchy. For instance, some articles on contracts published in 1965 indicate that direct contractual links between enterprises have been stimulated by conferences convened by local Party committees acting jointly with government industrial bureaus.[76] Emigré interviews suggest that enterprise Party secretaries and representatives of Party bureaus participated in conferences aimed at resolving particular disputes, and, further, that they could politicize these meetings by lecturing to enterprise managers, pressing them to "confess errors," and publicizing their "errors" in bulletins circulated to other units. Because of the variety of participants and the frequent criss-crossing of Party and state lines of authority, however, we cannot generalize about when disputes are likely to involve particular participants in the dispute-settlement process, nor is it possible to say when disputes would begin to be considered significant by Party officials.

At the same time, incomplete evidence suggests patterns in interenterprise dispute resolution. If the enterprises could not work out the matter themselves, their superiors in the state industrial hierarchy, economic commissions, and the bank might become involved — singly or together — as might Party industrial bureaus. Little more can be said about the mode of dispute resolution, except that all evidence indicates that it amounts to flexible, highly pragmatic attempts to adjust problems without fixing "legal" blame. Thus contractual dispute resolution in industry suggests that interenterprise contracts have been useful devices of economic administration, without being considered to be sources of legal rights and obligations.

Commercial contracts. The contracts which the Chinese call "commercial contracts" seem to be yet a different blend of civil law concepts and administration. The Chinese employ an assortment of contracts to implement plans for production of commodities, such as

76. The articles by Teng Chan-ming and Weng Chan both acknowledge the leadership of local Party Committees at conferences called by them to promote signing of interenterprise agreements.

grain, which are completely controlled by state plans, and to control production of other commodities whose production is unplanned. The contracts are entered into between commercial departments which purchase the agricultural commodities, such as supply and marketing cooperatives and commercial bureaus, and units of agricultural production which sell the commodities and also purchase manufactures from the state — communes, production brigades, production teams and, sometimes, individual peasant members of these collective units.

The arrangements covered by the commercial contracts vary, and so too does the terminology used to describe them, although not in the nuanced fashion that might be desired by Western students.[77] To some extent, the variations are expressed in terms of whether the contracts involve the entire output of commodities whose production is completely planned ("unified," [t'ung-i] in the Chinese terminology), or only a portion of output. Thus, under a "unified purchase contract," commercial units generally buy all the output of an agricultural commodity from producers, pursuant to the state plan, paying a state-fixed price; producers may retain part of their production for self-consumption, although not for sale. Under a "unified purchase and supply contract" the commercial units also sell to the agricultural producers. When the state purchases a fixed quota, though not all the output of an agricultural commodity and permits the producer to sell some of what it retains the contract may be a "fixed" or "decided" purchase contract (ting-kou, p'ai-kou). When the contract relates to a commodity that is outside the plan, it is called a "negotiated" (i-kou) contract.[78] In any of these contracts, the purchaser may pay to the agricultural seller, when the contract is signed, a sum of money which is used, evidently, not only for expenses incident to the performance of the contract, but for general expenses

77. In this summary of commercial contracts, the English renderings of Chinese terms are those which have been common in the United States Consulate-General (Hong Kong) press translations, similar translations published by the Joint Publications Research Service, and some secondary discussions. See note 94 below for a brief excursus on how changes might be made in the translations to reflect better the function and nature of the contracts to which the terms refer. For a good description of the development of these contracts in changing organizational contexts, see R. Pfeffer, "Contracts in China Revisited, with a Focus on Agriculture," *China Quarterly*, no. 28 (1966), p. 106.

78. See, e.g., "Place Even More Subsidiary Agricultural Products on the Track of Planning," *NFJP*, April 3, 1963.

within communes, brigades, and teams. These contracts, which may be for planned or unplanned products, are called "order contracts" (*i-kou ho-t'ung*).

Some of these contracts are technical expressions of a command directed to the peasants to sell all or most of their production of certain commodities to the state, in quantities and at prices fixed by the state. But when the contracts cover partly or completely unplanned production of a commodity, the producer may have some opportunity to negotiate over the quantity to be delivered and the contract price, although the price may not exceed the rural market price.[79] Indeed, the flexibility inherent in all the commercial contracts other than the "unified purchase" contracts has evidently been used by commune cadres negotiating the contracts to benefit peasant producers by requiring *smaller* deliveries from them than could have been realized.[80]

However, commercial contracts should not be analyzed simply in terms of the parties' latitude for negotiations. The contract cloaks in voluntarism the extraction of agricultural production from the countryside. Therefore, campaigns have been conducted to convince lower-level cadres and the masses that the masses *wanted* contracts,[81] to urge cadres to respect the principle of voluntarism,[82] and to remind all that the performance of contracts is not only an economic but a political duty.[83] State commercial agencies exercise administrative power over their contractual partners, the agricultural producers. Thus, commercial cadres have been urged to "penetrate" into the rural units, in order to investigate local conditions before signing contracts.[84] Plainly this means that commercial cadres must ascertain and decide the amounts that can be extracted from the communes. They must also persuade the peasants of the gravity of contracts and the obligations

79. *Ibid.*
80. "Strengthen the Notion of the State, Concretize the Duty of Purchase," *NFJP*, March 2, 1963.
81. E.g., Meng Ch'ao-ch'eng, "Some Thoughts on the Introduction of the System of Combined Purchasing and Marketing Contracts," *Ta kung pao* (Peking), February 9, 1962, in *SCMP*, no. 2688 (1962), pp. 3–6.
82. *Ibid.*
83. E.g., Kuan Ta-t'ung, "On the System of Contracts for the Exchange of Industrial and Agricultural Products," *JMJP*, March 9, 1962, in *SCMP*, no. 2704 (1962), pp. 11–15.
84. See, e.g., Ch'in Pao-hung, "All-round Application of Commercial Purchasing and Sales Contracts," *Ta kung pao*, Febraury 9, 1962, p. 1. Hsieh Ming, "On the Contract System," *CFYC*, no. 2 (1959), p. 41.

they create.[85] After contracts are signed, commercial departments are urged to supervise performance by the agricultural producers, and to "assist" them.[86] Thus contract supervision is emphasized in commercial contracts even more strongly than in industrial contracts. Occasionally legalistic terminology, which echoes the use of notarial bureaus in industry, has been used in discussions citing the role of commune and other cadres as "supervisory and witnessing organs." [87]

The interweaving of contract with more fundamental issues of controlling the countryside and production of agricultural products is illustrated by occasional failures to harmonize contract and administration. In such cases, there have been failures to enter into contracts at all, *but the obligations they would have expressed were performed anyway*, i.e., delivery of all or part of output.[88] Also, the notion of enforcing commercial contracts in the event of nonperformance seems weak, illustrating the importance of the contracts as precatory and exhortative devices. Years after institution of the commercial "contract system," reports have appeared of the recent "institution" of a system of fines for nonperformance,[89] implying, it would seem, that there were no such sanctions before, and, perhaps, that there were no other legal sanctions for nonperformance.

In short, commercial contracts seem more flexible and less defined than industrial contracts, and they reflect even more clearly than industrial contracts the commands on which they are based.

85. Kuan Ta-t'ung, "On the System of Contracts"; 1958 *Civil Law Textbook*, p. 225.
86. E.g., "Place Even More Subsidiary Agricultural Products on the Track of Planning," *NFJP*, April 3, 1963. This article mentions investigations, loans, "resolution of problems of production" (presumably supplying fertilizer and tools), and sending cadres to "aid" teams in planning tasks.
87. Meng Ch'ao-ch'eng, "Some Thoughts."
88. "Strengthen the Ideological Education of Cadre and Commune Members on the Concept of the State; Cheng-ch'eng Concretizes Purchasing Duties and Promotes the High Tide of Production," *NFJP*, March 2, 1963, criticizing cadres who, instead of signing contracts and educating peasants on their obligations, simply called meetings and assigned production tasks.
89. "Place Even More Subsidiary Agricultural Products on the Track of Planning," *NFJP*, April 3, 1963: "In order to guarantee the performance of contracts and in order to promote the seriousness of contracts, Hsin-hui *hsien* determined a series of workable fines. The peasants also demanded the method of fines. The carrying out of this method of fines is beneficial to the performance of contracts. According to the statistics of the Huang-ch'eng People's Commune, in 1962 the supply and marketing cooperative signed 423 contracts for negotiated purchases with 230 production teams. Three hundred twenty-eight were performed on time and 40 exceeded their quotas. There were only 6 that did not perform of which 3 had been adversely affected by natural disasters, and which after verification, were exempted from the fines."

Some Implications for Research

The Inapplicability of Western Categories

Western lawyers might be tempted to conclude that the flexible administrative arrangements which the Chinese call contracts, but which do not seem to create binding "legal" rights and duties, are not contracts at all. The absence of clearly designated institutions or rules for dispute settlement further complicates analysis. To be sure, we need not employ a Platonic concept of contract to determine the essence of all agreements called "contracts"; contracts do not always have to be ultimately enforceable by a properly attired judge sitting in a proper courtroom. Yet in the West, formation of a valid contract is assumed to have legal consequences, by creating enforceable duties; if such duties are not performed, the aggrieved party may invoke the assistance of an official institution which will determine whether a duty existed, whether it was breached, whether the breach caused any damage, and the *remedial* consequences. Contracts are important, among other reasons, because they anticipate to some extent the remedies which the parties have against each other for failure to perform. Furthermore, it is assumed that the official institution will decide these questions according to articulated rules and standards which have antecedently been recognized as applying to such problems. In China, by contrast, the duties created by contracts are not closely linked to the possibility of remedial action; nor is there evidence of the existence of well-articulated principles conditioning the remedies for violation of a contract. Contracts express duties, to be sure, and, if they are violated, the aggrieved party may invoke the assistance of an official institution — or such an institution may intervene — to bring about remedial consequences. Then again, the aggrieved party may not do anything of the sort, and the breach may lead to no remedial consequences whatsoever. The Western lawyer may object at this point that he knows neither what types of agreements are considered to be contracts in China nor what consequences flow from regarding an agreement as a contract. However, the absence of a notion that agreements create rights, and the absence of adjudicators for dispute resolution should prompt not despair but the formulation of new questions. The ambiguities, to the Western view, of Chinese contracts stem from their administrative and managerial nature. This profound difference from analogous Western arrangements conditions, but ought not deter, further inquiries into the content and operation of agreements.

The Possibilities of a Functional Approach

Study of Chinese contracts takes us far from the conceptual moorings to which Western notions of contract are normally tied, such as declarations of intent, agreement of wills, and creation and enforcement of obligations according to known, universal rules applied in a disciplined fashion according to clearly defined procedures. To some extent, novel problems have been encountered in the study of Soviet contracts, but with reason it has been suggested that, despite their differences, Soviet and Western contractual arrangements share certain characteristics. Among these shared characteristics are the existence of obligations to contract and rules which predetermine essential provisions of contracts, and differences need not prevent fruitful comparative study.[90] Lately, too, it has been suggested that the comparability of Western and Soviet contracts may have increased after the new Soviet economic reform, because contracts may now have come to serve a role in plan-formation as well as in plan-fulfillment.[91] When we study Chinese contracts, however, we must accept more than the restrictions on the freedom of contracting parties that the Soviet plan imposes. We must make an even greater leap — or is it a concession? — to make comparative study possible. We may have to consider as contracts agreements which may — or may not — create what we consider to be duties, and which, in the event of breach may — or may not — be enforced. Yet, standards need not be abandoned. Here, in the face of uncertainty of remedial consequences, begins the search for standards.

Whether or not the Chinese utilize contracts as they are used in the West, whether or not they consider contracts to be "legal" institutions, they obviously fashion arrangements which perform functions similar or analogous to those of Western institutions, contractual or not. In order to understand better the ordering of Chinese society, comparative study is needed. Offered below are some tentative thoughts on guidelines that may be usefully followed in elaborat-

90. A. Tunc, "La Possibilité de comparer le contrat dans des systèmes juridiques à structures economiques differentes," *Rabelszeitschrift für Ausländisches und Internationales Privatrecht*, 27 (1962), 478.
91. D. Loeber, "Contractual Autonomy of State Enterprises Under the Plan," in *Problemes juridiques de l'enterprise d'etat dans les pays socialiste*, p. 17.

ing a method of studying Chinese legal and administrative institutions, as applied to contracts.

It seems preferable to analyze legal and administrative practices and arrangements in terms of the functions they perform, recognizing that several functions may coexist, that apparently similar institutions may have different functions, and that apparently dissimilar institutions may perform similar functions. A functional approach is not new to legal analysis, of course; it was prominent in American legal realism, which used it to identify the social purposes and values served by legal institutions.[92] In comparative law, emphasis on function is not uncommon, but its application in research is not as extensive as it might be. I am seeking here not an intellectual system but different modes of asking questions, sharing Professor Kahn-Freund's view that "one is more inclined to compare methods of fulfilling social objectives than legal doctrine, function rather than structure." [93]

In formulating a tentative functional approach to the study of contracts or any other Chinese legal institutions, it seems advisable to try to clarify them in terms of the purposes which they seem to serve, as an alternative to assuming that they are unitary legal institutions. Thus, Chinese industrial and commercial contracts may not be regarded, either in China or in the West, as creating duties enforceable by remedial action that can be invoked by an aggrieved party. Yet, in China and in the West, contracts plainly share the function of solemnizing duties and obligations. Solemnization is separable from creating the basis for a remedy, and the Chinese separate both from adjudication. To complicate analysis further, apparently similar functions may have underlying differences. So, solemnization in the West is considered important for a variety of ethical and legal reasons, while in China it is more closely related to political mobilization and persuasion. But at least these diverse consequences of contract can be differentiated by functional analysis.

It seems advisable to avoid preconceptions about legal institutions, if by "institutions" in this context we intend to denote established, predictable patterns of decision-making according to clearly iden-

92. See, e.g., Felix S. Cohen, "Transcendental Knowledge and the Functional Approach," Columbia Law Review, 35 (1935), reprinted in L. Cohen, ed., The Legal Conscience: Selected Papers of Felix S. Cohen (New Haven: Yale University Press, 1960), p. 33.

93. O. Kahn-Freund, Comparative Law as an Academic Subject (Oxford: Clarendon Press, 1965), p. 9.

tifiable procedural and substantive rules. Because it is necessary to avoid leaping to generalizations about an institution of contract, it seems necessary to look for specific *types* of contracts. The lengthiest available Chinese discussion of contracts, the discussion of that subject in the 1958 *Civil Law Textbook*, although it employs a highly formal and apparently systematized scheme of organization, nevertheless reveals little interest in a unitary concept of contract. Nothing that has appeared since the textbook was published seems to indicate that the Chinese have since become more interested in legalistically systematizing contractual practices. Because no unifying doctrine exists, and because contracts are used as administrative devices in differing contexts, it seems preferable to distinguish between types of contracts. After beginning by distinguishing between industrial and commercial arrangements, it is necessary to proceed to close factual analysis of every identifiable pattern for the manufacture, processing, distribution and transportation of goods, and the performance of services. Only after such analysis will it be possible to classify and describe, without prejudging[94] these arrangements, and to evaluate their administrative and consensual content and the procedures and criteria for their enforceability.

Until the efforts I have called for here have been made in research using at least a sizable portion of the documentary sources which still

94. Related, of course, to what has been said here, is our need to avoid using Western legalisms in studying Chinese institutions. Otherwise, we shall risk placing fluid Chinese patterns into an overly-rigid mold of Western legal concepts. When the Chinese use an administrative agency, not a mediating or a quasi-adjudicatory agency, to decide contract disputes, they may use the term *ch'u-li* to describe the disposition of the dispute. The term can be rendered into English as, *inter alia*, "decide," "dispose of," or "handle." There is something to be said for using the admittedly vague "handle," which suggests the vagueness of Chinese administrative techniques rather than the precision of Western adjudication.

Also, it may be necessary to infuse functional notions into the translation of Chinese terms. Therefore, while the term denoting the commercial contract for purchase of the entire output of a commodity is translated literally as "unified purchase contract," the more descriptive term "planned purchase contract" would identify its function more clearly. Similarly, the contract for purchase of a commodity not completely covered by the state plan can be translated as "assigned" purchase contract. If literal translation were avoided and the term "planned quota-purchase contract" employed, again the function of the agreement might be more clearly identified.

The argument that translation of Chinese terms could be flexible enough to reflect the functions of institutions need not be belabored here. There is, of course, considerable danger of confusion, since all Western students will not use identical terms; as a result, we may have to fall back on literal translations as the only ones we have in common. Furthermore, the approach suggested here could also lead to the use of barbaric neologisms. However, at least some modest experimentation seems required to aid clear analysis.

remain relatively untouched, it will be impossible to know how profitable the results might be. However, I venture to suggest some of the insights we may anticipate.

For one thing, we may be able to begin generalizing about the relationship between changes in political policies and the operation of legal and administrative institutions. We would thus be able to begin learning about the extent to which such institutions have been thought of and employed by the Chinese leadership (or some part of it) as useful instruments for social change. At the same time, we might also be able to gain insight into the extent to which the institutions have been used to resist changes in policy or to perform functions different from those intended in Peking or in provincial capitals, for example, when commercial contracts are used to decrease rather than maintain or increase the amount of agricultural products extracted from the peasantry.

Further, we should be able to begin to assess tentatively the extent to which administrative practice has become regularized, so that we can distinguish differences in institutions which are often discussed in the West as if they were unitary. I have suggested above that we would learn about contracts — and the administrative contexts in which they are used — if we did this. Similarly, we might learn more about mediational forms of dispute resolution if we distinguished mediation between individuals and mediation of interenterprise disputes. The former, used as an instrument of control, probably possesses less developed standards for resolving disputes than dispute resolution in the industrial context. In industry relatively nonpolitical technical, economic, and financial considerations could influence the solution, and the accretion of bureaucratic practice might be discernible.

Finally, I stress again that I have been concerned here with problems of perspective with which students of China must continuously struggle. Of all the disciplines that can be used in the West to study China, law seems the most difficult to use meaningfully because it is so rooted in Western values. Plainly, we have to learn to adapt our perspectives to the object of our study in order to transcend, without abandoning, our Western context. If we succeed even partially, we will have shaped our views of China so that they will gain both in neutrality and principle.

9 Crime and Punishment: China and the United States

Richard M. Pfeffer

There is broad agreement among Western scholars that under the Communists the criminal process in China[1] is arbitrary, highly politicized, and responsive to class and status differences in its treatment of targets.[2] It is frequently pointed out, quite accurately, that China has no criminal codes and no public-reporter system of judicial decisions and that important substantive laws are often unpublished or, if published, very vague. Theorists of totalitarianism even doubt the existence of legality within such systems.

Laws in China not infrequently are applied retroactively and analogically or, to put it most crudely, on an *ad hoc* basis. Application of what we would classify as criminal law, especially of the law of minor crimes, tends to be by administrative rather than judicial institutions. Even where nominally judicial institutions are employed, as is the case with major crimes, their style is heavily inquisitorial, generally *ex parte*, with little opportunity for the defendant to defend himself either directly or through a lawyer. The proceedings of these institutions are not public. There is no independent judiciary and little separation of powers. The entire criminal process in China today tends to be dominated by the police, under strong Party control.[3]

Note: Adapted from *World Politics*, 21, no. 1 (October 1968), 152–181.

1. This article does not deal with problems of periodization or of holistic analysis. Nor does it deal with what happens to the Chinese criminal process during times of major social disruption, such as the Great Leap of the late 1950's or the more recent Cultural Revolution.

2. Members of the bourgeoisie, for example, tend in like cases to be treated more harshly as suspects and defendants than are members of the peasantry or proletariat.

3. On these points and others, see Lung-sheng Tao, "The Criminal Law of Communist China," *Cornell Law Quarterly*, 52 (fall 1966), 43–68; Fu-shun Lin, "Communist China's Emerging Fundamentals of Criminal Law," *American Journal of Comparative Law*, 13 (winter 1964), 80–93; Henry McAleavy, "The People's Courts in Communist China," *American Journal of Comparative Law*, 11 (winter 1962), 52–65; Franz Michael, "The Role of Law in Traditional, Nationalist and Communist China," *China Quarterly*, 19 (January–March 1962), 124–48; David C. Buxbaum, "Preliminary Trends in the Development of Legal Institutions of Communist China and the Nature of the Criminal Law," *International and Comparative Law Quarterly*, 11 (January

Is this all there is to say? How does a system so characterized function at all? Why would a political system so lacking in regularized procedures be attacked as bureaucratic by Mao Tse-tung in his Great Proletarian Cultural Revolution? What are the standards for implicit comparisons that are found in the above characterization of the Chinese criminal process? And if, as I believe, those standards ultimately have been derived from the Anglo-American criminal law system, has our understanding of that system been accurate or adequate?

I will argue (1) that until recently, at least for comparative purposes, we have accepted as fact a mythology about the American system of criminal justice; (2) that we have not tried very hard to understand the Chinese criminal process; and (3) that sanctioning systems should be compared in their entireties, the comparison ideally involving consideration of how various institutions within each system function and interact at the operating level.

Because most of the writing in the field implicitly or explicitly dwells on the differences between the Chinese and American legal systems, it is hardly necessary for me to belabor these differences. In the light of the argument I offer here, however, the differences, though real and substantial, appear less absolute.

Cultural Biases and Organizational Imperatives

The comparative analysis of criminal law processes has been distorted by a perspective that has emphasized the unique and necessary role of the judiciary as the guardian of legality. This perspective has distorted comparisons on two levels. It implies that the role of the judiciary is uniquely legal, somehow wholly distinctive from administrative processes, which implicitly are less than legal. Second, the perspective assumes that it is accurate to characterize our criminal process as "judicial." Since the Chinese Communist criminal process obviously is not a judicial process, the Chinese must reject the principle of legality. We are back to neat dichotomies.

1962), 1–30; Buxbaum, "Horizontal and Vertical Influences upon the Substantive Criminal Law in China: Some Preliminary Observations," *Osteuropa Recht*, 10 (March 1964), 31–51; and Albert P. Blaustein, ed., *Fundamental Legal Documents of Communist China* (South Hackensack, N.J.: Rothman, 1962), ix–xxix. For an intelligent account of the experiences of two Americans with the Chinese criminal process in the early 1950's, see Allyn and Adele Rickett, *Prisoners of Liberation* (New York: Cameron Associates, 1957).

I take legality to mean rule-following, resulting in the "reduction of arbitrariness by officials." [4] While this definition, like all definitions, is not wholly satisfactory, it seems more useful than more inclusive conceptions of legality that tend to incorporate various elements of Western experience, such as an emphasis on individual rights and the judicial vindication of those rights. The differences between judicial and administrative decision-making, though substantial, are differences of degree.[5] Perhaps one might argue that the

4. Jerome H. Skolnick, *Justice Without Trial* (New York: Wiley, 1966), p. 8. My approaches in this article reflect a substantial intellectual debt to Professor Skolnick's work.

5. Although it is not here appropriate to discuss these differences at great length, the subtlety of the differences can be indicated by a brief comment on Professor Lon L. Fuller's approach, which is set out in his "Collective Bargaining and the Arbitrator," *Wisconsin Law Review*, 1963 (1963), 3–46, especially 18–42.

Fuller argues, in part, that the kinds of questions that can be solved by adjudication are intrinsically limited. Judicial institutions are peculiarly unsuited to deciding questions involving "apportionment," polycentric problems in which, as in a spider web, if one pulls a strand here "a complex pattern of adjustments runs through the whole web." Polycentric problems are typically those before administrative agencies.

The sorts of problems amenable to judicial action are (1) "more-or-less" issues, where "all of the possible decisions may be represented within a single dimension," such as tort cases where an award can range from zero to X dollars; and (2) "yes-or-no" issues "between parties with opposed interests, no other interests being directly affected by the outcome." While Fuller does not say that courts should never try to resolve polycentric problems, he tends to feel that courts should hesitate to do so since, given "the procedural restraints normally surrounding judicial office," the courts should not risk undermining their institutional effectiveness and authority by recklessly venturing to do what they by nature are not well constituted to do.

I have two related reservations to Fuller's approach, which at times seems perilously close to a dichotomous approach to adjudicative and administrative decision-making. First, interests other than those of the parties directly involved are always affected in judicial, as well as in administrative, determinations. Judicial decisions, after all, are not simply relevant to the parties before the court. Using Fuller's approach, one is faced with the bizarre result that appellate decisions, which by their nature have a broader impact than those of courts of first instance, are in some way less judicial than those of courts of first instance. To point out, legalistically, that other parties are not "directly affected by the outcome," while true in a formal sense, may in fact be of little significance.

Second, many, and probably all, issues are more or less polycentric. It is convention, based upon the consensus that provides the foundation for judicial institutions, which allows us to consider particular issues *as if* their ramifications were not infinite. Yet every issue decided in court is like a pebble dropped into a pond — it creates waves that affect, albeit infinitesimally, all waters within the pond's expanse. Again, the implicitly polycentric nature of all issues often is clearest at the appellate level, particularly in important constitutional cases, where the range of considerations is endlessly complex, implicitly if not explicitly involving basic decisions on how society will allocate its resources (e.g., *Brown v. Board of Education* and the whole line of recent cases affecting the rights of criminals).

It is true that the polycentric issues involved are judicially resolved only at a very high level of generality, but it is important to recognize that the most fundamental sort of allocative decisions are made by the judiciary, as well as by the legislature and judicial process incorporates a higher degree of legality, but both processes involve rule-following, and both involve discretion. To put the latter point most bluntly, "Every officer of the law — policeman, President, legislator, attorney, judge, licensing commissioner, draft board member — is in some degree a magistrate. He exercises discretion and thereby affects the rights of citizens." [6]

What does this mean for Communist China? The answer requires a broader understanding of legality in its relation to modern organization. Max Weber saw the close relation between purposive organizational regularity and legality. The legal-rational order for him was characterized by the increasing growth of what we would consider modern organizations.[7] Recently, Franz Schurmann has decisively argued that the very goal of implementing social revolution in a country as large and unwieldy as China requires effective, large-scale organization. In the context of the decline of traditional ethos and social institutions, social control in revolutionary China to a significant extent is a function of ideology and explicit organization.[8]

The importance of organization in the criminal process and its relation to legality is fundamental. As to the first, I would suggest that for comparative purposes every society's criminal process should be taken as a whole and seen as a *community of organizations*.[9] The organizations that make up the criminal law enforcement community will vary somewhat from society to society, but they frequently will

---

administrative agencies. Perhaps Fuller's main point is simply that polycentric issues can be resolved more concretely, more explicitly, and more conveniently by a number of nonjudicial institutions. With that point, I am in fuller agreement.

6. Philip Selznick, "The Sociology of Law," *The International Encyclopedia of the Social Sciences*, vol. 9 (New York: Crowell, Collier, and Macmillan, 1968). The assumptions that have grown up around the basic principle of Anglo-American criminal law that a criminal statute is void if its scope and meaning are vague are confronted in Frank J. Remington and Victor G. Rosenblum, "The Criminal Law and the Legislative Process," *University of Illinois Law Forum*, 1960 (Winter 1960), 481–499. It is there argued that the prevailing condition of criminal law in the United States is one of ambiguity, resulting in the intended or unintended delegation of broad discretion to enforcement agencies to decide what conduct is to be subjected to the criminal process.

7. Max Weber, *On Law in Economy and Society*, ed., Max Rheinstein (Cambridge, Mass.: Harvard University Press, 1954), esp. pp. 334–347.

8. Franz Schurmann, *Ideology and Organization in Communist China* (Berkeley: University of California Press, 1966), esp. pp. 1–16. For contrasting review articles of this important book, see John K. Fairbank, "The State That Mao Built," *World Politics*, 19 (July 1967), 664–77; and Richard M. Pfeffer, "Contradictions and Social Change in Communist China," *Pacific Affairs*, 39 (1966–67), 349–360.

9. I was stimulated to adopt this perspective by Skolnick's *Justice Without Trial*.

include the police, a prosecutorial branch, a hierarchically structured judiciary embodying an appellate system, other supervisory administrative organizations, and, at times, a professional bar.

The purpose of analyzing the criminal process *in terms of a community* is to indicate that the relations between the various component organizations are continuing in nature, based on common interests, characterized by reciprocal influence, and frequently manifested in face-to-face encounters. The purpose of analyzing the process *in terms of separate organizations* is to indicate that within the community there are likely to be antithetical interests and perspectives, in large part based on the differing particular goals of the various organizations (for example, the police and the judiciary).

While no perfect resolution of these differing interests and perspectives is feasible in any society, the societal manner of resolution of conflicts between organizations in a community will set the tone for the entire criminal process. Because of the complexity of the organizational relationships and the apparent irreconcilability of their demands, characterization of various criminal processes as either police systems or judicial systems is regrettably unrefined.

All criminal law enforcement communities can be positioned on a continuum representing differing degrees of concern with the twin goals of legality and efficient enforcement of order. In practice, simultaneous pursuit of these goals by the community may often imply conflicting organizational strategies in concrete cases. The most efficient enforcement of order, for example, often will not be compatible in the concrete case with legality. Still, at another level, at least a minimum degree of legality seems to be required in a criminal process for the efficient enforcement of order.

Professor Lon F. Fuller of the Harvard Law School, it seems to me, would agree with this last point. In his discussion of the "inner morality of law" Fuller argues that certain conditions are essential for the *efficacy* of a system of legal rules.[10] Fulfilling these conditions is a matter of degree, but they must be at least minimally realized as a precondition for creating and maintaining a legal system. The minimal realization of these conditions is equivalent to the minimal degree of legality required to have a legal system at all. Beyond that minimal

10. Lon L. Fuller, *The Morality of Law* (New Haven: Yale University Press, 1964). Fuller's approach, which I here adopt in part, like much of social science may over-rationalize reality by trying to treat it as a "system." I recognize the problem and admit my own complicity in the use of such an approach.

realization, a system achieves higher levels of legality. In short, while all legal systems (and criminal processes) presuppose at least minimal levels of legality, the degree of legality realized may differ from system to system.

Fuller describes these indispensable conditions in a negative manner by writing of eight ways in which a society may fail in "the attempt to create and maintain a system of legal rules . . ." His description also may be taken to indicate eight ways in which a society may fail to create and maintain bureaucratic organization, ways in which each of the component organizations of the criminal law enforcement community may break down to produce disorganization:

> The first and most obvious [way] lies in a failure to achieve rules at all, so that every issue must be decided on an *ad hoc* basis. The other routes [to disaster] are (2) a failure to publicize, or at least to make available to the affected party, the rules he is expected to observe; (3) the abuse of retroactive legislation, which not only cannot itself guide action but undercuts the integrity of rules prospective in effect, since it puts them under the threat of retrospective change; (4) a failure to make rules understandable; (5) the enactment of contradictory rules or (6) rules that require conduct beyond the powers of the affected party; (7) introducing such frequent changes in the rules that the subject cannot orient his action by them; and, finally, (8) a failure of congruence between the rules as announced and their actual administration.[11]

In organizational terms, Fuller's emphasis on rules may be understood in light of the need for organizations to make ultimate organizational goals more specific and concrete and to stimulate and control performance through regularized procedures. The purpose of modern organization, like the purpose Fuller attributes to the institution of law, is "that of subjecting human conduct to the guidance and control of general rules."

It is hard to conceive of a complex organization in which most issues were decided on an *ad hoc* basis, in which the members were not apprised of the organization's specific purposes and of the rules they were expected to observe, in which rules were constantly being changed, and in which rules were intolerably in conflict. Yet, since

11. *Ibid.*, p. 39.

all organizations, like all criminal processes, exist in a state of imperfection and not one of utopia, there always will be a substantial degree of failure to achieve legal-rational ideals. However, a "total failure in any one of these eight directions [that is, a failure to achieve at least the indispensable minimum] does not simply result in a bad system of law [or a bad organization]; it results in something that is not properly called a legal system [or organization] at all." [12]

Large-scale organizations like the Ministry of Public Security in Communist China, then, cannot operate effectively without evolving and enforcing rules and standards. In addition, in order to implement its goals, an organization must combine selective recruitment of its members with varying degrees of intraorganizational socialization to inculcate its values in its members. Without such procedures members will be unable to interpret rules in the light of broader organizational purposes. They will be forced to choose randomly or on the basis of extraorganizational (for example, personal) reasons. Every organization — like the broader legal system itself, of which organizations may be a part — involves a process of shaping men's actions to fit organizational roles. Without such a process there can be no organization. In this sense, at least, there is an inherent tendency toward purposive rule-following, toward legality, in large-scale bureaucratic organizations.

Let me illustrate what the organizational approach to a criminal process implies. It has frequently been pointed out that the Chinese Communists have "not been reluctant to apply proscriptions both analogically and retroactively." [13] This undoubtedly is true, but the degree of its significance largely depends upon the degree to which the Chinese are changing the substantive criminal law. The greater the degree of change, the more latitude for retroactive and analogical applications.[14] However, there is a limit beyond which these prac-

12. *Ibid.*
13. Jerome A. Cohen, "The Criminal Process in the People's Republic of China: An Introduction," *Harvard Law Review*, 79 (January 1966), 528.
14. It should be noted that the issue of analogical application of the criminal law often is treated separately from the more general issue of statutory interpretation. However, statutory interpretation, ideally involving construction of the purpose or spirit of the law, frequently involves analogical reasoning. The problem of adequate warning is at the core in both issues. Our rules of statutory interpretation requiring strict construction of ambiguous provisions in favor of the defendant reflect an awareness of the close relation between statutory interpretation in general and analogy.

tices would cause such disorganization that neither the criminal law enforcement community nor the objects of its attention — the citizens of China — could function.

To apply all new criminal laws retroactively in a context in which laws are changing rapidly obviously would make for such insecurity and frustration of reasonable expectations as to stultify normal societal processes. Not only is it absurd, as Fuller points out, to command "a man today to do something yesterday" [15] and then to punish him for not having done it, but it is also organizationally impossible to do this often or on a large scale. Even if the Chinese criminal law enforcement community had the appallingly great physical resources required to enforce effectively a rapidly changing set of laws retroactively, the members of the community would not understand how to do so. For effective, systematic law enforcement is a process that takes time to understand and that requires at the outset an understanding of reasonable purposive orientations.

This is not to say that one can understand the practice of any organization or community of organizations purely through its formal rules, but this point is as true of organizations in the United States as in China. Formal rules tend to spawn informal practices, which in turn to some degree subvert the regularity of formal procedures, ideally in order to achieve organizational goals more efficiently. Thus, even when members of organizations are wholly committed to the organizational "ideology," [16] they will tend, for example, to violate procedural requirements in order to achieve substantive goals upon which, they accurately judge, the organization places a higher priority. The exercise of police initiative in rooting out criminality in the United States (see below) is a good illustration of this phenomenon. Such deviations from formal procedures, given the fact that the police organization does indeed place a higher priority on the achievement of substantive goals, constitute "positive deviance" from organizational rules. In the case of such positive deviance, the society cannot rely upon the organization itself to restrict such deviance but must depend for that upon other organizations within the community — for example, the judiciary.

Fully successful indoctrination in the organizational ideology, how-

15. Fuller, *The Morality of Law*, p. 59.
16. Schurmann, *Ideology and Organization*, argues that all organizations have their own ideologies (p. 18).

ever, is an organizational ideal. Frequently, if not generally, deviance will not be positive, and when it is not, the organization itself must seek to control deviance. It often tries to exercise this control through incentives, the use of which normally requires standards for measuring the performance of organization members. However, once these standards are set up, to the extent that organizational "indoctrination" has failed, members will attempt to satisfy these standards only nominally, with as little expenditure of effort as possible. There is, then, in all organizations a continuing dialectic between formal rules and standards, on the one hand, and informal practices, on the other.

There is no doubt that some organizations are more effective than others in controlling internal deviance and in approximating the realization of organizational goals. Nevertheless, every organization, if it is to maintain itself, must be at least minimally effective in this respect. No organization can tolerate arbitrary or random action by its members beyond a certain point. There is, then, an inherent need for a substantial degree of regularity in all organizations. At least, an organization must not be characterized by disorganization.

In suggesting the organizational approach to understanding a society's criminal process, I attempt to eliminate distortions common to comparative approaches that are less than rigorous in their investigation of the operational reality of both the familiar component (the American criminal process) of the comparison and the "strange" component (the Chinese criminal process). In the first sort of distortion, the tendency has been to assume the familiar is a known quantity and, since little empirical work had been done on the American criminal process until recently, to treat an ideal image of the familiar, which emphasizes its adversary and due process character, as reality. In the second sort of distortion, both because of the difficulty of obtaining systematic information necessary to fill out the organizational approach and because of the obtrusiveness of spectacular irregularities, such as mass public trials in Communist China, the tendency, particularly in the mass media, has been to characterize the Communist Chinese criminal process as a series of irregularities or barbarities. The comparison of an idealized image with a one-sidedly unfavorable one is obviously not conducive to understanding reality.

In using the organizational approach, I have tried to suggest that our earlier images of the criminal process in Communist China seem to be grossly inadequate as a description of a functioning legal system.

The American Criminal Process: Myth and Reality

Although the idealized due process image of the American criminal process is the one frequently used in comparative analysis, it seems clear that in practice due process considerations, while important, are hardly dominant in the United States. The American criminal process can be characterized for analytic purposes as an interaction between two competing normative models, the Crime Control Model and the Due Process Model.[17]

The Crime Control Model stresses efficiency in repressing criminal conduct, as well as related values of speed, finality, and informality. It is primarily concerned with the issue of *factual* guilt, and since it has a high degree of "confidence in the reliability of informal administrative fact-finding activities that take place in the early stages of the criminal process" (by the police, for example), those suspects not screened out in the early stages are presumed on this model to be factually guilty.[18] The Crime Control Model sees the formal judicial stage of the criminal process as largely superfluous at best, or, at worst, as a major hindrance to that model's primary task of efficiently repressing criminal conduct. Reduced to its barest essentials the Crime

17. Herbert L. Packer, "Two Models of the Criminal Process," *University of Pennsylvania Law Review,* 113 (1964), 1–68. The discussion below of these two models is based upon this fine article.

One problem with Professor Packer's treatment of the American criminal process is his slighting of the function of the Due Process Model in crime control itself. Because notions and symbols of due process in our culture are imbedded in the very legitimacy of government, a crucial degree of compliance with the law is induced by the ideal and assumed operation of the Due Process Model. I am indebted to Professor Edmund W. Kitch of the University of Chicago Law School for this point. Presumably, the increasing awareness today of the limited impact of this model in practice is not unrelated to rising doubts concerning the legitimacy of some of our institutions and to rising crime rates.

In focusing on Packer's two analytic models, I do not mean to imply that various organizations, such as the police, are free of political and other pressures affecting behavior of members. If in this broader perspective some positions taken in this article suggest a lack of sympathy for complex problems faced by police, to some degree this is attributable to my primary concern here with the quality of effective justice, whatever circumstances may be pled in extenuation. For a very recent and partial survey of the quality of effective justice in Chicago, see Jay Miller, "Verdict: Guilty — Racism Marks Chicago Police," *Focus Midwest,* 6 (1968), 10–15.

18. Packer, "Two Models," p. 12.

Control Model consists of two elements: "(a) an administrative fact-finding process leading to exoneration of the suspect, or to (b) the entry of a plea of guilty." [19]

The Due Process Model, on the other hand, incorporating Western liberal values of equality, individualism, and limited governmental power, is primarily concerned with *legal* rather than factual guilt.[20] It is not concerned simply with the reliability of administrative determinations of factual guilt. Thus, "the factually guilty may nonetheless be legally innocent," and one can assert defenses "that have nothing to do with factual guilt . . ." [21]

Rather than trying to maximize efficiency in repressing criminal conduct, the Due Process Model subjects the criminal process to controls — in the United States, especially judicial controls — that prevent it from operating at maximum efficiency. In this antiauthoritarian manner, the Due Process Model employs the judicial sanction of nullity to invalidate determinations of guilt when the procedures employed in reaching those determinations, such as unreasonable searches or coerced confessions, violate the model's values.

While the trend of the last decade or so has favored an increasing role for the Due Process Model in the United States, today our criminal process still tends by and large to resemble the Crime Control Model.[22] Insofar as this is true, this model focuses attention on similarities rather than on differences between the criminal processes in America and in Communist China, for China's criminal process may be characterized almost exclusively in terms of the Crime Control Model.

In the United States, the criminal process typically is a system of justice without trial, in which

> conviction is by the accused's plea of guilty, with no trial required. In the federal courts, the guilty plea receives the heaviest use, 86 percent [of the cases] in the fiscal years 1960 through 1963, while in the state courts, the use of the plea trails by [only] 5 to 10

19. *Ibid.*, p. 13.
20. Due process in this sense is not synonymous with legality, understood as rule-following. Due process, as used here, involves rule-following plus a commitment to substantive positions that epitomize the entire development of Anglo-American liberal culture.
21. Packer, "Two Models," p. 17.
22. *Ibid.*, p. 23.

percent . . . [Thus,] routine decision-making in the administration of criminal justice is hidden from public view . . . The case is often "tried" in an informal setting.[23]

The implications of this fact are endless, and from the perspective of the Due Process Model they are negative. Under that model, "the arraignment [at which the accused enters his plea] is the fulcrum of the entire criminal process. It is at this point that one of two things happens: either the possible errors and abuses at the earlier, largely unscrutinized stages of the process are exposed to judicial scrutiny, or they are forever submerged in a plea of guilty." [24] Since appeals from a judgment based on a guilty plea are highly improbable, the determination of the issue of guilt by plea is likely to be final. This is significant, because the "fewer appeals . . . the likelier it is that Crime Control norms will prevail." [25]

This likelihood is enhanced by the fact that guilty pleas frequently have been made without effective aid of counsel, or, if the accused is indigent, wholly without aid of counsel, since at least until recently the state has been under no obligation to provide counsel at this stage of the criminal process. Without even the form of an adversary proceeding in the determination of the issue of guilt, assertion of the infringement of the accused's rights and vindication of those rights have not been common.

The system of justice without trial in the United States severely violates principles of legality and due process. While the influence of the judiciary in favor of both reaches to some extent into all organizations within the criminal law enforcement community, it is certainly strongest in the formal adjudicatory process itself. To the extent that cases do not go to trial, the concern with legality and due process tends to be replaced by an acceptance of "bargain justice," which essentially reflects the criminal law community's dominant concern with efficient law enforcement. All organizations within the community acquiesce to varying degrees in this system of bargain justice that undermines legality. Under the system the defendant, his attorney, the prosecution, and frequently the judge engage in a process of negotiation that, within a broad range, determines the specifics of the disposition of the case under a bargained-for plea of guilty.

23. Skolnick, *Justice Without Trial*, p. 13.
24. Packer, "Two Models," p. 49.
25. *Ibid.*, p. 56.

Recognizing this community of interests, Fuller writes that one reason why sole reliance on courts to control "the lawless administration of the law" has proved "relatively ineffective" is that the lower courts tend "to identify their mission with that of maintaining the morale of the police force." [26] The consequence of this system of justice in the United States is that "although the ideals of the law emphasize individual rights and protections, the everyday mass-processing of offenders takes place under conditions which increasingly invite systematic violations, denials, and evasions of these rights and protections." [27]

As I have indicated above, the impact of the Crime Control Model is clearest in the early stages of the criminal process. The process begins with discretionary acts of the police.[28] The police in all criminal law enforcement communities have enormous power to halt the legal process at the outset. In addition, police discretion involves the systematic manner in which police deal with suspects:

In contrast to the criminal law presumption that a man is innocent until proved guilty, the policeman tends to maintain an administrative presumption of regularity, in effect a presumption of [factual] guilt. When he makes an arrest and decides to book a suspect, the officer feels that the suspect has committed the crime as charged. He believes that as a specialist in crime, he has the *ability to distinguish between [factual] guilt and innocence.*[29]

Moreover, "the policeman is offended by judicial assumptions running contrary to probabilistic fact — the notion of due process of law staunchly maintains a rebuttable presumption of innocence in the face of the policeman's everyday experience. . . ." [30]

The extent of police initiative and ingenuity in pursuit of efficient repression of criminal conduct in the United States is reflected in the organizational demand within police departments for "a type of

26. Fuller, *The Morality of Law*, pp. 81–82.
27. Jerome H. Skolnick, "The Sociology of Law in America: Overview and Trends," *Law and Society*, a supplement to *Social Problems*, 13 (Summer 1965), 17.
28. In this regard, see Joseph Goldstein, "Police Discretion Not to Invoke the Criminal Process: Low Visibility Decisions in the Administration of Justice," *Yale Law Journal*, 69 (March 1960), 543–94. For a revealing case study of the problem of judicial control of police, see Herman Schwartz, "Stop and Frisk," *Journal of Criminal Law, Criminology and Police Science*, 58 (1967), 433–64.
29. Skolnick, *Justice Without Trial*, p. 197.
30. *Ibid.*, p. 233.

'professional' police practice in which the concern for legality is minimal." [31] For example, responding to an intra-organizational control mechanism aimed at measuring the efficiency of the police, policemen follow a policy of selective enforcement of the law in order to appear efficient according to the controlling standard. That standard is the clearance rate, which is the percentage of crimes *known* to the police that the police organization *treats as* having been solved. By this standard, solving a crime does not require a conviction; knowledge of who the offender is appears to be sufficient if the offender already is in the hands of the police. Inducing detained suspects to confess to prior offenses thus raises the clearance rate. In order to induce such confessions, policemen offer three basic commodities in a bargained-for exchange: "reduction of charges and counts [in the instant case], concealment of actual criminality, and freedom from further investigation of [confessed] prior offenses." As a consequence of this practice, "criminality becomes [the suspect's] commodity for exchange . . . [and] under certain conditions the attention paid by working detectives to clearance rates may *reverse the hierarchy of penalties* associated with the substantive criminal law . . . In some cases defendants who confess to large numbers of crimes will tend to be shown more leniency in prosecution than those who are in fact less culpable." [32]

Another example of the weakness of the ideal of legality in American police practice is the exercise of initiative by police in crimes, such as prostitution and narcotics violations, that typically are without citizen complaints, "crimes without victims." For the solution of such crimes the need for police initiative is very great,[33] and that initiative is reflected in police-sustained informer systems. In the case of prostitutes, police often try to transform the prostitute, who is not considered a "good pinch" since prostitution is only a misdemeanor, into an informant. To accomplish this feat police treat as discretionary the mandatory quarantine requirements for girls arrested on prostitution charges, thereby creating "commodities of exchange" that can be used to bargain with prostitutes for information.[34]

31. *Ibid.*, p. 110.
32. *Ibid.*, pp. 174–76.
33. The broader applicability of the concept of "crimes without victims" to China — involving, for example, black-market transactions or, generally, crimes against the state — is one way of accounting for China's high levels of police initiative and all the practices associated therewith.
34. Skolnick, *Justice Without Trial*, pp. 112–138.

Police ingenuity in undermining legality and due process is also reflected in their efforts to substantially neutralize such judicial controls as the exclusionary rule. The purpose of the exclusionary rule is to discourage illegal searches and seizures, which are especially prevalent in the investigation of crimes without victims. In practice, to evade the bite of the rule while achieving literal compliance with it, police may rely on thinly related events (such as a suspect's prior parole violation) that constitute grounds for legal arrest, which in turn validates any search made "incident" to such an arrest.

Even more subtly, the police develop evasive strategies to make their behavior appear legal. They fabricate probable cause for arrest, reconstructing "a set of complex happenings in such a way that, subsequent to the arrest, probable cause can be found according to appellate court standards." [35]

At best, the exclusionary rule has had an uneven effect on police practice. Its maximal impact is purely a function of police concern with a loss of possible conviction. Even where the police are concerned with getting a conviction, the likelihood that the conviction may be attained by a guilty plea, in which the element of the illegal search is only one factor in a complex bargain, further undermines the effectiveness of the rule. Moreover, in the early stages of a case or in general patrolling activities, the risk of losing a conviction is too remote to serve as an effective deterrent in any event. Similarly, where prosecution is not even contemplated, as in the "small pinch" where the police are primarily interested in creating an informant, the exclusionary rule has little or no effect on police behavior.

The picture that emerges, then, of this functioning community of organizations is in startling contrast to idealized images of the American criminal process. The judiciary is in fact substantially less autonomous, particularly in the courts of first instance, than the ideal suggests. Indeed, if one can speak of the American criminal process as a judicial one, it is only with an awareness of the severe limitations and unevenness of the influence of the judiciary on the entire process. While organizational perspectives within the community vary, as evidenced by the increasing concern for legality and due process as one proceeds sequentially from organization to organization in the criminal process, these different perspectives tend to be resolved in concrete instances through informal bargaining, which often involves

35. *Ibid.*, p. 215.

elements of expediency, rather than through the application of formal rules. The concern for efficient enforcement of the law, epitomized in the police organization, appears to dominate the concern for individual treatment of offenders according to notions of legality or due process.

The Chinese Criminal Process in Perspective

In this light, a number of features of the Chinese Communist criminal process may be re-examined, again not to deny the differences between that process and its counterpart in the United States, but to put these differences in perspective. For purposes of comparison I use Professor Jerome A. Cohen's sophisticated, recent book on the Chinese criminal process, *The Criminal Process in the People's Republic of China, 1949–1963: An Introduction*,[36] in which the outlines of patterned processes have begun to emerge.

First, a few words about the book itself. The book focuses, as it should, on the patterns of action and interaction among the individual, the police, the procuracy, the courts, and the Communist Party. It goes beyond the sterile listing of relevant institutions and the statement of their official hierarchical positions and their roles in formal organizational charts — so common to earlier studies in this field — and deals instead with behavior at the operational level. However, the book — especially the introductory essay — does not explicitly set forth the comparative perspectives necessary to understand the Chinese criminal process relative to the criminal process in other countries. Notwithstanding a few scattered, muted comments, such as "Other standard tactics [of the Chinese Communists] also have a familiar ring to a student of criminal law" (p. 30), the bare-bones nature of the argument of the essay may well lead non-specialists to compare the Chinese process with the idealized and misleading images of the American process that they formed in high-school civics classes. Specialists such as Professor Cohen himself, who has had experience as a prosecutor, will immediately draw many parallels to their own experience in the United States and will see the inferences to be drawn from the essay's many subtle descrip-

36. (Cambridge: Harvard University Press, 1968).

tions.[37] The nonspecialist, I fear, will tend as before to understand the American and Chinese systems as a dichotomy only slightly more refined than that of good and evil.

I have selected four points from Professor Cohen's book for purposes of comparison with actual practice in the United States. First, the police, procuracy, and judiciary in China really "serve as constituent units of a single administrative structure" (p. 48). Second, the suspect in China lacks a meaningful chance to defend himself, and most of the criminal law process is carried on *ex parte* (p. 49). Third, the "inherently coercive environment" in China inhibits the defendant "from utilizing even the limited opportunities to defend himself that do exist" (p. 50). And fourth, the criminal process in China tends to judge the man at least as much as the act.

First, although in the United States the police, the prosecution, and the courts preserve their organizational identities sufficiently to make it inappropriate to treat them as "constituent units of a single administrative structure," it is nonetheless true, as I have argued above, that these organizations tend to cooperate as a community in emphasizing the efficient repression of criminal conduct. On the other hand, as Cohen points out, in China the hierarchical structure of the "units" and the separation of functions among police, procuratorial, and judicial "units" provide an institutionalized basis for reviewing and limiting the exercise of arbitrary discretion by law enforcement officials. So to some degree, despite the existence of "a police-dominated, highly integrated system of judicial and extrajudicial sanctions" (p. 47), there is even in China a measure of organizational integrity.

These organizations in China form a tightly-knit community precisely because of the relative absence of the competing Due Process

37. Perhaps it should be made clear here how narrowly the category "specialists" must be defined. For example, many graduates of this country's foremost law schools probably would be excluded from the category. On the basis of personal experience, I can attest that at least as late as 1961 it was possible, because of the extreme emphasis of the case method on judicial elements and judicial perspectives, to graduate from the Harvard Law School without a realistic conception of how the criminal process operates in the United States.

It might seem that my criticism of Professor Cohen for not accomplishing what he did not attempt to do is gratuitous. However, because of the prevalence of myths and biases about our own and the Chinese processes, I feel that my comments are justifiable. In this context comparative perspectives must be explicitly stated if communication is to be successful.

Model. In the United States that model is institutionalized in the judiciary, particularly in the appellate courts, and there provides the tension within the community that sharpens the definition of organizational boundaries. In China the organizations are bound together by a nearly exclusive preoccupation with efficient enforcement. While, as I have stated above, this preoccupation necessarily implies at least a minimal concern with rule-following, it does not imply a like concern with substantive due process.

Second, with regard to the defendant's lack of opportunity to defend himself, two points should be made. The inquisitorial system — which is not unique to Communist nations — generally offers the defendant less opportunity to defend himself than does the adversary system. The inquisitorial system ideally relies primarily upon official initiative to protect a defendant's interests. In many phases of the legal system in the United States — and especially in the dominant criminal procedure of justice without trial — the adversary nature of the process is substantially diluted.[38] Frequently the defendant's formal right to defend himself appears in practice to be compromised and transformed into a "right" to bargain about the charges and the prospective sentence.

Third, the United States is not without its own coercive environment that inhibits the assertion of formally existing rights. To a substantial degree, suspects who anticipate repeated future encounters with the police, such as prostitutes and addicts, are inhibited from asserting their legal rights by the fear of having the book thrown at them the next time.[39] Indigent defendants, furthermore, appear to be inhibited by their entire life situation from asserting their rights.[40] In addition, "a large proportion of poor defendants (particularly in misdemeanor cases) are not represented [by counsel] at all. Moreover, when counsel is provided he frequently has neither the resources,

38. For a relevant discussion of the public defender office, see David Sudnow, "Normal Crimes: Sociological Features of the Penal Code in a Public Defender Office," *Social Problems*, 12 (1965), 255–276. Qualifying some of Sudnow's points, Jerome H. Skolnick deals with the problem more generally in "Social Control in the Adversary System," *Journal of Conflict Resolution*, 11 (1967), 52–70.

39. Skolnick, *Justice Without Trial*, p. 146. Again, if only because in China the category of persons who anticipate repeated future encounters with the police may be broader than in the United States, inhibitions among suspects and defendants there may tend to be more generalized than in the United States.

40. Ironically, the counterpart in China to indigents in the United States probably is the bourgeoisie, who are inhibited increasingly from asserting their rights by their entire life situation since 1949.

the skill, nor the incentive to defend his client effectively, and he usually enters the case too late to make any real difference in the outcome. Indeed, the generally higher rate of guilty pleas and prison sentences among defendants represented by assigned counsel or the public defender suggests that these attorneys may actually undermine their clients' position." [41]

Fourth, all criminal law systems try to reconcile two standards for judging crime, the man and the act. While it appears true that the Chinese at least explicitly place comparatively more weight on the man, the American criminal law process seems to focus on the man at the beginning and end of the process. At the beginning, the police as part of their working personality develop "a perceptual shorthand to identify certain kinds of people as symbolic assailants," men who the police presume are inclined as a class or a group to criminality.[42] Police are trained to observe "departures from the 'normal' [and] . . . this disposition to stereotype is an integral part of the policeman's world." [43] The result of stereotyping often may be that an act committed by a man who does not fit the stereotype (for example, a white man, middle-class in appearance, running out of a house in a "nice neighborhood") is likely to be presumed to be normal, while the same act committed by a man who conforms to the stereotype (such as an apparently lower-class black) may be taken as an attempted theft or burglary and will initiate the criminal process.

Similar stereotypes appear to operate during a trial when the trier of fact tries to ascertain whether intent requisite for guilt was present: "The required intent is so little susceptible of definite proof or disproof that the trier of fact is almost inevitably driven to asking, 'Does he look like the kind who would stick by the rules or one who would cheat on them when he saw the chance?' This question, unfortunately, leads easily into another, 'Does he look like my kind?' " [44]

Finally, the whole man is explicitly taken into account in the

41. Jerome E. Carlin and others, "Civil Justice and the Poor," *Law and Society Review*, 1 (1966), 56. This article provides a devastating critique of the *de facto* and *de jure* class bias of the entire American legal system. In fact, it is not altogether clear to me that the class or status (or race) of a suspect or defendant is less relevant to the probable disposition of his case in the United States than in China. Only the good guys and bad guys are changed to protect the respective systems. In this regard, see also Sudnow.

42. Skolnick, *Justice Without Trial*, pp. 45, 105.

43. *Ibid.*, p. 83.

44. Fuller, *The Morality of Law*, pp. 72–73.

judge's determination of sentence and in subsequent parole proceedings.

Conclusion

A focus on organizational imperatives here has led to an emphasis on similarities between Chinese and American criminal processes. This emphasis has been intensified by an effort to distinguish sharply between stated ideals of the American system and its operational reality. Yet the operational reality of a criminal process itself is influenced by stated ideals, particularly to the degree that such ideals are institutionalized or embodied in concrete organizational form.

The stated ideal of due process in the United States has a tremendous normative impact. Policemen, for example, in the light of widely held societal values generally are not willing to flout due process ideals openly. Precisely for this reason, evasions and violations of due process restraints normally occur in areas of low public visibility. Moreover, due process ideals are afforded an organizational protector, the appellate courts. In so far as these courts can make their influence felt throughout the system, concerns with individual rights, fair trial, and so on shape the criminal process.

In China the situation is different. The dominant concern, as one would expect of a still revolutionary government, is with substantive justice rather than with due process. China's stated ideals have reflected a high degree of confidence in the Party's certain knowledge of good and evil, of who should be punished and for what. Such confidence implies less concern for due process than is shown in the United States system, less agnosticism regarding the positive value of governmental exercise of power against suspected deviants. Even to the degree that China may be said to be concerned about problems of due process, the ideal of due process, as suggested above, has not been embodied in any organization. Thus, in the competition within the community of organizations constituting the criminal process, due process ideals regularly lose out.

Ongoing processes are inextricably complex, involving shared and competing stated ideals, communities of competing organizations and individuals, and interaction between ideals and concrete "reality." Comparisons of criminal processes require a sophisticated awareness of the problematic nature of our understanding of the familiar component of the comparison as well as a healthy skepticism of previous descriptions of the strange component. Professor Cohen, I am sure, would be the first to agree that the criminal process in China is neither as unlike its American counterpart as a comparison of our stated ideals with China's operational reality would indicate, nor as similar as a comparison of the regularized abuses of our process with the Chinese process would suggest. Truth, as usual, elusively lies somewhere between these poles.

10 Chinese Attitudes Toward International Law — and Our Own

Jerome Alan Cohen

A century ago Peking was in crisis. A series of wars had humiliated China and shattered its millennial isolation. Western force had rudely awakened the "Central Realm" to the fact that, beyond the tributary peoples of East Asia, lay powerful nation-states with a vastly different view of society, government, and international relations. Moreover, the Western "barbarians" seemed bent on further opening up China and compelling it to participate in the Western state system. How should China meet this challenge? A small group of modernizers, who wanted to use barbarian techniques to check the barbarians, advocated engrafting the new Western learning upon traditional Confucian ideology and institutions.

Western demands were often couched in terms of the Westerners' system of international law. Having witnessed China's need for knowledge of this subject, an American missionary named Martin had just translated Wheaton's *Elements of International Law* into Chinese. The mandarins at first suspected this book "as the Trojans did the gift of the Greeks," but, after successfully invoking its principles in a dispute with Prussia, certain Chinese officials recognized that international law could be a useful defensive weapon. Yet, should the Chinese Emperor, the Son of Heaven, abandon the pretensions of his universal overlordship of the hierarchically-organized sinocentric world in favor of a system premised on the sovereign equality of many states? Should he concede that the Western powers had been right in seeking to have their representatives reside in Peking? Should he agree to station Chinese diplomats in foreign capitals? Should Chinese students be sent abroad to study international law and should that subject be injected into the Confucian curriculum at home? Such actions were scarcely conceivable to

Note: Adapted from American Society of International Law *Proceedings* (1967).

Chinese traditionalists, and, amid the antiforeign atmosphere of the era, die-hard obscurantists waged a bitter struggle against the modernizers whom they called "sinners against the Confucian heritage."

Opinion among Westerners concerned with China policy was in an equal state of ferment. Although all wanted to end China's isolation, they varied greatly in both motives and preferred methods. Some diplomats condemned missionary Martin's attempt to introduce international law, arguing that it would lead the Chinese to recognize how greatly the recently imposed "unequal treaties" had taken advantage of them. As the French chargé d'affaires put it: "Who is this man who is going to give the Chinese an insight into our European international law? Kill him — choke him off; he will make us endless trouble." The Western trading community also was apprehensive about supplying an instrument that might curb newly acquired commercial privileges and prevent the exaction of further concessions. Missionary Martin, on the other hand, saw international law as a vehicle for bringing the heathen to Christ. And many diplomats, including Americans and Englishmen, approved of Martin's effort in the belief that it would show the Chinese that force was not the West's only law and would help them understand and deal with the outside world, to the mutual benefit of China and the West.[1]

Today Peking is again in crisis, its elite badly divided over whether and how to bring China out of isolation. Again, spokesmen for "rationality" claim that the prevailing Chinese ideology — no longer Confucianism but Maoism — must be adapted to meet the demands of modernization. And the outcome of the current struggle for power will inevitably affect the degree to which China accepts the rules and institutions of the world community.

Western opinion also remains in ferment over China policy. Some voices call for the continuing isolation of the Communist regime and emphasize evidence of its open hostility to the international status quo. Others argue for an end to China's isolation and take comfort from those words and deeds that indicate the Communists' willingness to accept aspects of the existing international system. It is inevitable and proper that scholars of international law contribute to this de-

1. For the above quotations and details of this fascinating story, see Immanuel Hsü, *China's Entry into the Family of Nations: The Diplomatic Phase, 1858–1880* (Cambridge, Mass.: Harvard University Press, 1960), chaps. 8, 9.

284 | Jerome Alan Cohen

bate. Indeed, it is surprising that there have thus far been so few studies of the twenty-year record of the People's Republic (PRC) in international law.

A perusal of those studies that have appeared leads me, as an area specialist, to make a few suggestions for consideration by international lawyers who come fresh to the China field.

1. I would, first of all, urge scholars to take account of the extent to which Chinese Communist attitudes toward international law are related to the breakdown of China's imperial tradition. I do not insist upon an acquaintance with China's pre-imperial history, despite the fact that during that period (from the eighth to the third centuries B.C.) a number of contending Chinese states developed recognizable rules to govern their interrelations. Although that ancient experience may in the nineteenth century have helped a historically conscious elite to understand the multi-state system of the West, its relevance to contemporary Chinese attitudes is marginal. Nor do I maintain that contemporary attitudes are substantially the product of the hierarchically organized East Asian tribute system over which Chinese emperors ruled throughout most of the period from 221 B.C. until the Revolution of 1911. Some observers note traces of the tribute tradition in the style of Communist diplomacy: the special emphasis on exchange of visits and gifts; the inaccessibility and glorification of the supreme ruler; and the sense of uniqueness, righteousness, and superiority that appears to inhibit friendly relations on the basis of equality. But these are resonances the existence and significance of which are the subject of academic dispute.[2]

What is beyond dispute and what is of overriding importance is not the impact of the imperial tradition but the impact of its destruction. By the early years of the twentieth century the succession of humiliations that began with the Opium War (1839–1842), and that was symbolized by the stigma of extraterritoriality, had created Chinese nationalism out of Confucian culturalism. It had instilled in a proud and once powerful people the determination to end their country's status as a semi-colony and to achieve its recognition as a sovereign equal. The Chinese Communists drove to power by capturing this nationalist sentiment. Upon gaining control of mainland China in 1949, they promptly abolished the vestiges of imperialist

2. See, e.g., J. K. Fairbank, *China: The People's Middle Kingdom and the USA* (Cambridge, Mass.: Harvard University Press, 1967); and B. Schwartz, "The Maoist Image of World Order," *Journal of International Affairs,* 21 (1967), 92.

exploitation and sought international acceptance of their sovereign status. Yet, two decades later, they are still outsiders in a world community that is willing to admit them only on terms they deem incompatible with national self-respect. Moreover, because of renewed American intervention in the Chinese civil war in 1950, they have been prevented from attempting to establish their authority over what they deem to be China's island province of Taiwan. And they have not been very successful in preventing other humiliations, such as American violations of China's airspace.

Is it any wonder that Chinese leaders maintain a "vivid sense of outrage"[3] and manifest an almost obsessive concern with vindicating and preserving national sovereignty? To condemn them, as some writers have done, for retaining the nineteenth-century notions of sovereignty that they were taught by the West is like condemning American Negroes for being obsessed with achieving the equality that they have been promised — and that the rest of us have enjoyed — for a century. In both cases, the average white observer is almost totally unable to conceive of what long-imposed second-class citizenship means.

2. Historical perspective is useful in other respects. What makes the China problem especially complex is the continuing existence on Taiwan of the pre-Communist regime, the Republic of China (ROC), with which the U.S. is allied. In these circumstances, appraisal of the Communist record has often involved, at least implicitly, comparison with that of the ROC. If such comparisons are to be made, they should be comprehensive and should take into account the history of Chinese nationalism rather than focus exclusively on recent legal and political positions.

For example, it is true, at least from the American viewpoint, that the ROC has "an enviable record in the United Nations and in the international community."[4] Yet it is helpful to remember that when in 1928 Chiang Kai-shek's Kuomintang Party (KMT) seized control of the ROC it was, as the Communist regime is now, a vigorous challenger of the international status quo. Much of its political support rested upon its promise to restore Chinese dignity by recovering

3. See M. Mancall, "The Persistence of Tradition in Chinese Foreign Policy," *The Annals,* 349 (September 1963), 14, 23.

4. M. McDougal and R. Goodman, "Chinese Participation in the United Nations: The Legal Imperatives of a Negotiated Solution," *American Journal of International Law,* 60 (1966), 671, 698.

China's lost rights and ending foreign domination. Although in 1943 the ROC formally succeeded in abolishing extraterritoriality, its deteriorating political condition after World War II led it to abandon anti-imperialism and become more closely allied to the West, thereby forfeiting to Communism much of the political legitimacy that derives from Chinese nationalism. History suggests that the ROC's "enviable record" may in part be the product of weakness rather than virtue, and that any government strong enough to rule the China mainland will be ardently nationalistic for some time to come and unwilling to promote world order on other people's terms.

Similarly, critics who seek to establish the wickedness of the Peking government frequently seize upon Mao Tse-tung's famous aphorism — an incomplete statement of his political philosophy — that "political power grows out of the barrel of a gun." But Mao is not the only Chinese patriot to have learned this lesson from the West; he simply has been more candid than others in articulating it. Chiang Kai-shek, after a four-month visit to the Soviet Union during the KMT's romance with the Comintern, returned to China in 1923 to forge a strong party-army that proceeded to use force to bring a semblance of unity to the country. Indeed, Chiang's subsequent defeat by the Communists has been attributed to his excessive reliance on militarism and failure to appreciate the explosive potential of peasant nationalism and the social and economic needs of Chinese society.

Knowledge of modern Chinese history also brings into focus the image of "Free China" that is often presented to justify exclusion of the Communists from the world community. We ought to recall that, during the era of Soviet influence, the KMT became a Leninist-style dictatorship; that political repression was a prominent feature of its tenure on the mainland; that, in re-establishing Chinese control over Taiwan after Japan's defeat, this dictatorship destroyed the flower of Taiwanese leadership in a blood bath that took thousands of lives; and that during the past two decades it has quietly violated the "rule of law" by using secret police and secret military tribunals to imprison large numbers of persons, both Mainlanders and Taiwanese, who have actively sought democratic self-government. I do not mean to imply that other governments, including our own, have had spotless records in dealing with self-determination or other aspects of political freedom, but I simply want to emphasize the value of giving an historical dimension to any comparisons of the rival Chinese regimes.

3. We must not only take account of the nineteenth- and twentieth-century background of Chinese Communist attitudes toward international law, but we must also recognize that those attitudes themselves are already part of history. This is true not only of the Communists' record during their decades of struggle to achieve nation-wide power prior to 1949, but also of the post-'49 era. Although some scholars underemphasize the fact, Peking's views on many aspects of international law have been far from static. To be sure, there have been certain constants, such as the enduring emphasis upon sovereignty that has consistently led Communist writers to denounce all schemes for "world law" as neo-colonialist subterfuges designed to subject China to the rule of an adverse majority. But on so important a matter as its relation to the United Nations, for example, the attitude of the People's Republic has gone through a number of distinct stages that began with hopeful expectation of participation and evolved into frustrated antagonism that in turn led to the recent noisy search for a substitute.[5] Scholars are superfluous if their only task is to do a scissors and paste job on current Chinese statements, for clipping services and propaganda organizations bombard us with reminders of Peking's recent hostility. Scholarship, after all, should tell us how the past became the present and why. Otherwise we may mistake the PRC's present attitudes as eternally fixed and be deterred from attempting to encourage moderation of those attitudes.

4. In examining the evolution of Chinese Communist attitudes toward international law we must be alert to the large extent to which they represent reactions rather than initiatives. For example, contrary to the view of some observers, a major reason why "Communist China has either ignored or challenged virtually every activity of the United Nations" in recent years may well be that it bitterly resents being excluded from participation.[6] One should also note that many of the PRC's severely censured actions appear to have been acts of retaliation against felt injustice. Was it a coincidence that the PRC seized United States' compounds in Peking in 1950 the day after the U.S. defeated a Soviet effort to unseat the ROC representative in the

5. See Byron Weng, "Communist China's Changing Attitudes toward the United Nations," *International Organization*, 20 (1966), 677.
6. The quotation is from McDougal and Goodman, "Chinese Participation," p. 711. On page 713 they attribute Peking's refusal to cooperate in U.N. disarmament efforts not to its exclusion from the U.N. but to its perception that the U.S. manipulates the U.N. and has no intention of disarming.

Security Council? And was there no connection between the Red Guards' abuse of a French diplomat in the winter of 1967 and the arrest of Chinese students who had been demonstrating in Paris the day before?

Moreover, if, as it appears, the Chinese Communists regard international law as an instrument of policy to be used when useful, to be adapted when desirable, and to be ignored when necessary, we should not overlook the extent to which this attitude reflects their perception of how others play the game. The topic deserves detailed treatment, but brief reference to a few of the PRC's legal experiences with the so-called leader of the imperialist camp should illustrate the point.

Until the outbreak of the Korean War the U.S. position was that Taiwan had been restored to China under the 1943 Cairo Declaration, that the Allied Powers had accepted the exercise of Chinese authority over the island since V-J Day, that the widely anticipated Communist invasion of Taiwan would thus constitute continuation of a civil war, and that the United States would not become involved in that civil conflict. The North Korean attack on June 25, 1950, reversed all this. The United States promptly dispatched the Seventh Fleet to "neutralize" the Taiwan Strait and, what was even more upsetting to the Communists, it reopened the question of the legal status of the island by declaring that "the determination of the future status of Formosa must await the restoration of security in the Pacific, a peaceful settlement with Japan or consideration by the United Nations." [7]

In the fall of 1950, in an effort to frustrate the consequences of Soviet vetoes in the Security Council, the United States persuaded the General Assembly to adopt the Uniting for Peace Resolution, a significant departure from the original understanding of the United Nations Charter and one which could not square with the PRC's fundamentalist principles of constitutional interpretation.

What had been distrust of Western legalism became cynicism in February 1951 when the General Assembly found that the PRC had engaged in aggression by aiding North Korea after the U.N. Command had ignored repeated Chinese warnings against implementing its plan to bring down the North Korean regime by driving to the Chinese border. To the Chinese Communists, who had yet to con-

7. Statement of President Truman, June 27, 1950, *Department of State Bulletin,* 23 (1950), 5.

solidate their power at home and who were cognizant of Western intervention in the Soviet Union in 1918, American action in Korea appeared to be a repetition of Japan's design to conquer China via Korea and Manchuria. Thus it constituted a grave threat to China's security and created a sense of immediate danger that impelled China to send "volunteers" to meet what was perceived to be aggression by the United States.[8]

Negotiation of the Korean armistice further confirmed the Chinese in their belief that their opponents regarded international law merely as a tool of foreign policy. Although neither the United States nor the People's Republic had yet adhered to the 1949 Geneva Convention Relative to the Treatment of Prisoners of War, by mid-1952 each had stated that for purposes of the conflict it would, with certain reservations, be bound by provisions of the Convention. One of those provisions, Article 118, stated that "Prisoners of war shall be released and repatriated without delay after the cessation of active hostilities." This language was in contrast to that used in Article 109, which provided for the obligatory return of seriously sick or injured prisoners prior to cessation of hostilities but which went on to state that no such prisoner "may be repatriated against his will during hostilities."

The Chinese argued for what they claimed to be a literal construction of Article 118, taking the position that after cessation of hostilities all prisoners were to be returned without exception. Again the Americans adopted a "policy-oriented" interpretation, claiming that humanitarian considerations required an interpretation of the article that would authorize states to refuse to repatriate a prisoner against his will.

Secretary Dulles proved even more willing than Secretary Acheson to suit international law to American convenience. For example, in 1950, when the United States was confident of its voting strength in the Security Council, it had maintained that the question of Chinese representation was procedural; by 1954, however, the United States' view was that this had become a substantive matter subject to a veto.

What must have been especially infuriating to the Chinese was Dulles's sanctimonious posturing about international law. In 1954,

8. For authoritative interpretation of these events, see Tang Tsou, *America's Failure in China, 1941–1950* (Chicago: University of Chicago Press, 1963), chap. 13, and Allen Whiting, *China Crosses the Yalu: The Decision to Enter the Korean War* (New York: Macmillan, 1960), chap. 8.

for example, the PRC announced that two Americans, John Downey and Richard Fecteau, had been convicted of espionage and sentenced to life imprisonment and twenty years, respectively. According to the opinion of the Supreme People's Court and the evidence subsequently displayed, the Americans had been CIA agents whose plane had been shot down in northeastern China in late 1952 while they had been making contact with Chinese anti-Communists whom they had previously organized and dropped into China. The United States responded to the Chinese announcement with a strong note of protest, and, in the Dulles tradition, an even harsher press release that branded the convictions "a most flagrant violation of justice" based upon "trumped-up charges." These men, it was claimed, were civilian personnel, employed by the Department of the Army in Japan, who had been lost on a flight from Korea to Japan. Their "continued wrongful detention," the release said, "furnishes further proof of the Chinese Communist regime's disregard for accepted practices of international conduct." [9]

Apparently on the assumption that the best defense is a good offense, even though the United States had never announced that these "civilian personnel" were missing, the note accused the PRC of practicing deception by having failed to include their names on a list of Americans remaining in China. And, incredible though it may seem a decade later, in February 1957, Mr. Dulles delivered the *coup de grâce* to the affair by telling a press conference that, although the PRC had indicated that it would release the prisoners if the United States would allow American newsmen to visit China, he would not approve such an arrangement because it would constitute yielding to Chinese "blackmail." [10] The United States has never admitted the truth of the PRC's assertions, even though it has been an open secret that Downey and Fecteau were actually CIA agents, [11] and even though such an admission, coupled with an expression of regret, would give them what would seem to be their only chance of immediate release.

Space precludes discussion of the legal dispute to which the 1955 Sino-American agreement on the repatriation of civilians gave rise,

9. *Department of State Bulletin*, 31 (1954), 856f.
10. *New York Times*, Feb. 6, 1957, p. 1.
11. See, *e.g.*, D. Wise and T. Ross, *The Invisible Government* (New York: Random House, 1964), pp. 106–108; *New York Times*, Sept. 9, 1957, p. 7.

but suffice it to say that the Chinese were careful to link their own incomplete performance under the agreement to antecedent acts of bad faith by the Americans. It is also not possible to linger over our sponsorship of U-2 overflights by the ROC, our Vietnam intervention, and other recent American actions toward China that have done little to moderate the PRC's jaundiced view of international law. Nor can I do more here than emphasize the PRC's sensitivity to the dexterity with which the United States applies international law elsewhere in the world, especially in its own bailiwick, as exemplified by overthrow of the Arbenz regime in Guatemala, organization of the Bay of Pigs fiasco, and intervention in the Dominican Republic in 1965.

5. Plainly, if the process of integrating China into the family of nations is ever to be completed, students of international law will have to empathize rather than moralize, and give the PRC's words and deeds a fair hearing. It is not enough merely to quote Chinese Communist statements, such as those asserting that the United States and the Soviet Union dominate the United Nations, or that the United States has no intention of disarming, as though these assertions carry their own refutation; we should inquire in each instance to what extent there is evidence to support the Chinese belief. If we trace the Communists' contemporary attitudes back to their scorn of the League of Nations, we might ask whether the League's abject failure to come to China's assistance provided a reasonable basis for disillusion. If we condemn the Communists for refusing to accept a "two China" policy and to renounce the use of force in the Taiwan Strait, what should we say about the Chiang Kai-shek regime for sharing this position? Similarly, Communist claims to Tibet and to territory on the Indian border may take on a different hue if we know that the ROC position is fundamentally the same.

If we castigate the PRC for preferring to settle the Indian boundary dispute by negotiation rather than adjudication, we should inquire how many issues the United States has submitted to the ICJ of late. If we sermonize about the PRC's rejection of a U.N. rôle in Vietnam, should we not point out that the 1954 and 1962 Geneva Conferences demonstrate that the PRC has not been unwilling to participate in international conferences in which it enjoys equal status with other powers? If we criticize the PRC for insisting on the unanimity principle at international conferences, should we not ask what great power has been willing to do without a veto over important matters? If we censure the PRC for pronouncing its readiness to transfer nuclear weapons information to other countries, should we not acknowledge that it has never made such a transfer? If we recognize, as many political observers do, that China's behavior has been cautious, though its rhetoric has been hostile, is it fair to characterize that behavior as "guerrilla-type caution"? [12]

At times American international lawyers appear to teeter on the brink of self-deception. Recently, for example, in an effort to demonstrate the proposition that the PRC's performance at past multinational conferences "belies the possibility that it will act constructively at the United Nations," two writers soberly noted that "Communist China has sought to manipulate the membership and timing of international conferences to insure that the conferences produced preferred results." [13] Is there a foreign office in the world that is not guilty of such a charge?

What I have said is intended not as an apologia but as a plea for understanding. According to the Chinese classics, when the superior man is treated in an unreasonable manner, he is supposed to attribute the difficulty to his own personal failings and to examine his own behavior to find the source of the problem. Although hardly a panacea, were we to adopt such an attitude toward the Chinese, we might make a modest contribution to ameliorating present international tension. Of course, no amount of empathy can erase the fact that the Chinese Communists devoutly preach their own version of the Marxist-Leninist challenge to the bourgeois state system and, within the limits of China's capabilities, seek to translate this revolutionary ideology into action. Yet, as Benjamin Schwartz has pointed out, there is more than one level to China's international relations.[14] Even in the throes of the Cultural Revolution, except for a period in the spring and summer of 1967 when the Foreign Ministry fell into the hands of extremists, the PRC has by and large continued to carry on conventional diplomatic and commercial relations within the bourgeois nation-state framework. And, as the Sino-Soviet dispute has deepened, it has increasingly invoked principles of international law in its relations within the Communist orbit. The strands of Chinese theory and

12. See McDougal and Goodman, "Chinese Participation," p. 708.
13. *Ibid.*, p. 717 (text and note 233).
14. See Schwartz, "The Maoist Image," p. 101.

practice are many. China is Communist, to be sure, but it is also an aspiring great power, a chauvinistic "new nation" and the heir to a distinctive history and cultural style. Our task is to assess these complex strands as objectively and comprehensively as possible in order to facilitate what must inevitably be the slow and painful process by which China and the world adjust their demands upon each other. We should not caricature the Chinese demands. It will be difficult enough to deal with reality.

11 Some Characteristics of Japanese Studies on Contemporary Chinese Law

Yasuhei Taniguchi

Despite the fact that Communists have been in control of at least part of China since the 1930's, Japanese studies on Chinese Communist law began only after the end of World War II due to the suppression of the study of Communist law by the Japanese government.[1] Although academic freedom was restored in 1945, economic conditions in occupied Japan and the civil war in China made it impossible for Japanese scholars to study Chinese Communist law until the establishment of the People's Republic of China in 1949. Since then, however, a number of articles and books have been written about various aspects of Chinese Communist law. Approximately 280 articles, essays and translations by about 100 authors have appeared in more than 100 different magazines, and about 20 books have been published. The subjects treated therein range from the philosophy of law to the law of maritime insurance. If quantity is any indication, then, the study of the law of the People's Republic seems to be a flourishing field in Japan.

Published material has not been limited to studies on Chinese law. Other aspects of China — politics, economics, culture — have also been the subject of extensive writings. This situation gives rise to a need, on the one hand, for a complete bibliography,[2] and on the

1. Some studies may have been made by the military or by certain secret agencies of the government, but as yet none have been made public. A study of the history of the Chinese Communist Party which had been secretly undertaken by the Information Service of the Foreign Ministry was made public after the war. Hatano Kanichi, *Chūgoku kyōsantō shi* (History of the Chinese Communist Party), Tokyo, Jiji tsūshin sha, 1961.

2. See the following bibliographies, albeit incomplete: Ishikawa Tadao, "A List of Articles on Modern China Published in Japan, 1946–1955," [Keiō University] *Hōgaku kenkyū* (Journal of law, politics and sociology), 29 (1956), 1121–1128, and Hirano Katsuaki, "A List of Post-War Materials on Chinese Law," [Hōsei University] *Hōgaku shirin* (Review of law and political science), 3–4 (1961), 178–199, which covers the years up to 1960. See also Asian-African Comprehensive Studies Group, *Nihon ni okeru Ajia-Afurika kenkyū no genjō to kaidai — bunken mokuroku kaidai Chūgoku: hōritsu* (Present conditions and problems of Asian-African studies in

other, for a guide for beginners in Chinese studies. To meet the latter need two young students of China recently published a book entitled "Introduction to China Today: What to Read," in the preface of which they state,

> Japan may rank first in the world in the amount of publications on China . . . But naturally quantity does not necessarily coincide with quality. We cannot help admitting that there is much poor stuff. Readers, then, should have a selective eye, and if possible, know how to use good material and bad. This book was written to meet the demands of readers. It aims to provide them with a dependable guide . . .[3]

The following discussion is designed to serve a similar purpose. It will be concerned with certain characteristics of Japanese studies on Chinese law and provide information which may be helpful to foreign students of Chinese law in their use of Japanese materials.

Characteristic I: Popularity of Study

As is obvious from the number of authors who have written about the subject, numerous Japanese jurists are interested in Communist Chinese law. Although there are no more than ten specialists in the field,[4] a number of nonspecialists have on occasion published works on Chinese law. In 1955, for example, a well-known constitutional lawyer wrote a long article entitled "Constitution of the People's Republic of China."[5] And in 1960 a civil law professor wrote his sole

Japan. Bibliography and bibliographic introduction. China: law), Tokyo, Asian-African Comprehensive Studies Group, 1966 (private publication), which contains a list and brief summaries of selected articles and books in Japan and of all the articles in the Chinese magazine, *Cheng-fa yen-chiu* (Political-legal research), and of most of the articles in the Chinese journal, *Fa-hsüeh* (Legal studies).

3. Niijima Atsuyoshi and Nomura Kōichi, *Gendai Chūgoku nyūmon: nani o yomubeki ka* (Introduction to China today: what to read), Tokyo, Keisō shobō, 1965, p. 1.

4. The relative scarcity of "specialists" as contrasted with the abundance of nonspecialist writers may seem strange in view of the popularity of Chinese studies. This phenomenon is attributable to the Japanese system of professorships. In most universities there are no positions for professors of contemporary Chinese law, although there are for German, Anglo-American, French, and sometimes Soviet law. Chinese law must thus be studied as an avocation by professors occupying seats in other fields. In short, it is practically impossible to make a living solely by doing research on Chinese law.

5. Tabata Shinobu, "Constitution of the People's Republic of China," *Dōshisha hōgaku* (The Dōshisha law review), 6 (1955), 95–128.

work on China, "Introduction to Chinese Conciliation Law." [6] There are many other such cases, indicating that a great many jurists are interested in Chinese law and are willing to study and write about it when the proper opportunity or stimulus appears.

A busy market for such articles exists. Among one hundred legal journals and other magazines a number of prosperous ones are published on a commercial basis: one for law students, one specializing in comments on recent Supreme Court cases, one aimed at legal practitioners in general, and so forth. These all offer articles on Chinese law from time to time, and this in turn stimulates interest in the subject among jurists.

Tradition is a major reason for the popularity of Chinese legal study. In prewar Japan there was virtually no academic research on contemporary China, but there was a firmly established tradition of historical study. Because of China's domestic and international circumstances in the late nineteenth and early twentieth centuries, modern China was not considered worthy of academic research. The few existing studies tended to be tools for militaristic ambition and colonial policy.[7] Ancient China, on the other hand, was considered most worthy of scholarship. The study of Chinese dynastic history and philosophy began when Japanese students entered middle school (that is, at age 12). Reading Chinese classics (in Chinese) was compulsory. Japanese intellectuals over the age of 40 are products of this education, and the younger generation has also been exposed to this kind of cultural environment.

Intellectuals originally had complex feelings toward things Chinese: on the one hand, a veneration of ancient Chinese culture which so fundamentally influenced their mode of life and thinking, while on the other, a feeling of Japan's present superiority to China which was the result of Japan's apparently successful modernization. They were startled to see the People's Republic of China emerge out of a period which had not been regarded as a worthwhile subject of serious academic research. In addition, these intellectuals had a special feeling for Marxism which influenced their attitude toward the People's Republic. Thus, a tradition of study of Chinese history but of ignor-

6. Miyazaki Toshiyuki, "Introduction to Chinese Conciliation Law," *Hōgaku kenkyū*, 33 (1960), 507–525.

7. The complete "estrangement" of studies of contemporary China from those of Chinese history has been pointed out in Niijima Atsuyoshi and Nomura Kōichi, *Gendai Chūgoku nyūmon*, p. 6.

ing contemporary China plus the emergence of the People's Republic gave rise to Japanese intellectual interest in Communist China.

The postwar interest in Communist Chinese law among non-specialists must be interpreted against this background. But at the same time the increased interest among specialists was a reaction to the suppression of socialist or Communist legal studies during the war.

A certain passivity toward research in depth on China exists among many Japanese legal scholars who are not "specialists" on Chinese law. They do not actively seek materials for research but rather wait until some interesting material appears. Studies are occasioned solely by outside events. A professor of civil law, for instance, has written:

> In the summer of the year before last I had the opportunity to obtain through a book-importing firm a Chinese book entitled "Basic Problems of Civil Law in the People's Republic of China." But up to today I have not had time to go into it in detail. I here present a part of the book.

With that, he published three articles on succession, ownership, and tort, almost exclusively relying on that one book.[8] This is not an isolated case, as a glance at the subject-matter of the articles on Chinese law will indicate. My investigation has revealed the following tabulation of writings which appeared roughly from 1949 through early 1969. More than sixty articles and translations, for example, were written about the Constitution of the People's Republic of China solely on the basis of the text of that document and of other related materials. Other favorite subjects are the judicial system (about thirty items), marriage and divorce law (about thirty-five items), labor law (about twenty items), and criminal law (about fifteen items). It is true that these subjects are of general interest, but it is also true that in these areas there are relatively more Chinese statutes, drafts, Chinese-authored articles, and Japanese eyewitness reports available. Recently, however, the scarcity of materials has resulted in fewer of these "occasional" writings. Since 1965 I have seen almost none of them.

8. Kurata Ayao, "On the Inheritance System in the People's Republic of China," *Kōnan hōgaku* (Kōnan law review), 1 (February 1961), 318; "On Ownership in the People's Republic of China," *ibid.*, 2 (December 1961), 331–356, and 3 (December 1962), 255–275; "On the Concept of Tort in the People's Republic of China," *ibid.*, 5 (October 1964), 147–176.

Japanese jurists are always ready to react to Chinese legal material. As a result, most available material has been introduced to Japanese readers in the form of translations or summaries as well as through articles in which authors advance their own views based on the material.[9] The general interest in China means that these writings, placed before the general public, are actually read by many. Thus what happens in China forms, to a certain extent, a part of the common knowledge of Japanese jurists. Therefore, the legal situation in China is generally much better understood by jurists in Japan than by those anywhere else in the world, including the Soviet Union and the East European countries.[10]

It is inevitable, however, that the writings of nonspecialists are rather poor in description and analysis. Many articles on Chinese law, when compared with those on other legal subjects, do not meet the general standards of Japanese legal writing.

Characteristic II: Marxian-Oriented Approach

Chinese Communist law in Japan is studied almost exclusively by a group of lawyers identified as "Marxist jurists" who subscribe to "Marxian legal science." [11] They are mostly law professors who advocate Marxist-Leninist rather than "capitalist" legal institutions.[12]

This phenomenon appears to pervade the study of socialist law in general. Since the 1920's the study of Soviet law has been pursued mainly by Marxist students of law. The same tendency continued with even greater intensity after the end of the government's wartime suppression. When the People's Republic of China emerged as another socialist country, students of Soviet law turned their attention to China and the Marxian method was applied to Chinese law.

9. Whether or not Japan has imported more original material than any other country, cannot be answered. It is generally doubted. A leading scholar in socialist legal studies, Hirano, is said to have remarked that China was reluctant to export documentary material to Japan because it would immediately be handed over to the United States.

10. Kida Junichi, "Sino-Soviet Conflict and Criminal Justice in China," *Hōritsu jihō* (Legal journal), 37 (January 1965), 72–77.

11. See, for example, Numata Inejirō, "Tasks of Marxian Legal Science in Japan," *Hōritsu jihō*, 37 (April 1965), 12–19.

12. They form the legal section of the *Minshu shugi kagakusha kyōkai* (Association of Democratic Scientists) founded about twenty years ago. Some are members of the Japanese Communist Party.

An explanation of the reasons behind the exclusively Marxian approach of Japanese students of Chinese law must begin with the fact that, in the absence of a Christian tradition in Japan, Marxism was readily accepted as the only complete doctrine which could successfully explain the facts of society.[13] Marxism has had a profound effect upon intellectuals since it was introduced to Japan during the Meiji era.[14] After academic freedom was restored in 1945, there was an even greater inclination on the part of Japanese intellectuals to accept Marxist doctrine.[15] It is even likely that in the post-war turmoil many intellectuals actually thought that a domestic revolution was imminent. In this atmosphere, interest in Chinese Communist law was more than mere dilettante curiosity. Interestingly enough, the situation has until recently remained more or less the same, despite the fact that circumstances have changed radically in the intervening years. Until very recently, it seemed almost taboo for intellectuals to doubt (at least openly) the correctness of Marxist doctrine. Faced with what to them were the reactionary policies of the Japanese government, their anti-authoritarian attitude and their distrust of government (another tradition of Japanese intellectuals)[16] compelled adherence to Marxism. But today the situation is gradually changing. The so-called "progressives" (that is, the Marxists) have become conservative. And within the socialist law field criticism has begun to be directed at the approach to the study of Soviet law. One comparativist, for instance, recently remarked:

Japanese study [of Soviet law] has been done predominantly from the Marxian point of view. The relation between Marxism and law is a controversial problem. The question of what is Marxian legal science cannot be easily answered. Thus, discussion has tended to become a fruitless scholasticism. Soviet law in practice has changed constantly. These changes cannot be thoroughly

13. Maruyama Masao, *Nihon no shisō* (Thought in Japan), Tokyo, Iwanami shoten, 1961, p. 51.
14. See Herbert Passin, "Modernization and the Japanese Intellectual: Some Comparative Observations," in Marius B. Jansen, ed., *Changing Japanese Attitudes Toward Modernization* (Princeton: Princeton University Press, 1965), p. 473. For the role of intellectuals in socialist movements, see Robert A. Scalapino and Masumi Junnosuke, *Parties and Politics in Contemporary Japan* (Berkeley: University of California Press, 1962), pp. 17, 61, 77, 118, 138, 146.
15. Cases of rightists becoming eager Marxists were not infrequent.
16. See Herbert Passin, "Modernization," p. 449.

explained by the Marxian point of view. It is hoped that a more "sachlich" attitude, like that of contemporary Western students will be adopted.[17]

Even more severe criticism could be directed against students of Chinese law. While some students of Soviet law now take a non-Marxian approach, such is not yet the case in the Chinese legal camp. As a result of their Marxist orientation, students of Chinese law adhere to the official Chinese view and defend the Chinese legal system. They look at Chinese legal institutions and official views thereon not only with full approval but often with adoration. They do not criticize, for example, the lack of personal liberty in China or the absence of the rule of law. Such criticism is said to be based on "bourgeois" concepts of law and thus utterly groundless. According to one writer:

> Since the law of socialist countries has a social background which is entirely different from that of capitalist countries, the judicial system of these countries must be properly understood within the socialist social organization. In comparing legal principles, it is unscientific to condemn those of the socialist countries by applying such mythical tests of monopolistic capitalist states as "rule of law" or "Rechtsstaat" . . .
>
> In reading Chinese articles the first task of academicians is to analyze and understand the peculiarly Chinese characteristics exclusively from what Chinese say. Attacks from bourgeois concepts of law cannot be accepted except as political statements which have no meaning within the academic world.[18]

Japanese students of Chinese law generally accept without question the statements of Chinese officials and as a result they appear to be mere spokesmen or Japanese agents of the Chinese government rather than analytical outside observers. Their mode of expression sometimes even tends to become emotional. One nonspecialist, for example, concluded that the "People's Republic of China is not an aggressive state," because the preamble of the Chinese Constitution

17. Igarashi Kiyoshi, "Comparative Law and Japanese Legal Studies," in Itō Masami, ed., *Gaikoku hō to Nihon hō* (Foreign law and Japanese law), Tokyo, Iwanami shoten, 1966, p. 352.
18. Hariu Seikichi, "Some Theoretical Problems of the Law of the People's Republic of China," *Tōyō bunka kenkyūjo kiyō* (Bulletin of the Oriental Research Institute), 39 (1965), 93.

states that "[o]ur firm and consistent policy is to strive for the noble cause of world peace and the progress of humanity." [19] And a specialist, explaining the antirightist struggle in 1957, stated:

> Rightists, under the guise of socialist legal theory and on the basis of Western bourgeois culture, willfully tried to utilize a temporary occurrence in the Soviet Union [de-Stalinization and its impact in other Communist states]. In short, they shot a poisoned arrow against the basic structure and line of movement of the new China. This was an extremely aggressive criticism of the people's democratic government as it was then.[20]

The same author in another article says that the rightists' writings "betrayed, when closely examined, their own slovenliness and an underlying wicked conspiracy." [21]

This type of naiveté pervades most "academic" articles and books on Chinese law despite the fact that the same authors show a great deal of sophistication in commenting on Japanese legal institutions and problems.

It may be recalled that Japanese Marxist students of Soviet law were very much embarrassed when de-Stalinization occurred in the Soviet Union.[22] Since then, although they have not discarded their belief in Marxism, they have changed their attitudes and have tried to establish themselves as independent observers. Unfortunately, this has not been the case with students of Chinese law. Although some of them, after the "Hundred Flowers" period, allowed that there were failings or inadequacies in Chinese policy,[23] most still maintained an attitude similar to that of the students of Soviet law before de-Stalinization. A firm belief that "de-Stalinization" in China is impossible seems to underlie their position. It is assumed that the Chinese government regards de-Stalinization and the Hungarian in-

19. Tabata Shinobu, "Constitution of the People's Republic of China," p. 109.

20. Fukushima Masao, Chūgoku no jinmin minshu seiken (People's Democratic Government of China), Tokyo, Tokyo University Press, 1965, p. 561.

21. Fukushima Masao, "Legal Theory and the Sino-Soviet Conflict," Hōritsu jihō, 37 (November 1965), 47.

22. A Marxist frankly admits their embarrassment and dismay at that time: Yokoyama Kōichirō, "Past and Present Japanese Study of Socialist Law: A Lecture at Friedrich Schiller University," Hōritsu jihō, 38 (November 1966), 32. Another writer said: "All Japanese Marxists were placed at the crossroads." See Numata Inejirō, "Tasks of Marxian Legal Science in Japan," p. 13.

23. Fukushima Masao, Ubukata Naokichi, and Hasegawa Ryōichi, Chūgoku no saiban (Chinese justice), Tokyo, Tōyō keizai shimpō sha, 1957.

cident as lessons and has solved, through the doctrine of "two kinds of contradictions," [24] all relevant problems. A Soviet law specialist of the new school, after a short trip to China, suggested in a comparison between late-1960's China and the Soviet Union of the 1930's that China would not repeat the Soviet Union's mistakes.[25]

Most students of Communist law have not entered the field to understand their neighbors better or to improve Japan's performance in trade negotiations with Communist countries.[26] They are interested in it primarily as a tool for the criticism of Japanese law in particular and capitalist law in general. This purpose is openly declared [27] and is evident in writings which contrast Japanese or capitalist law with Chinese law. For example, one writer footnoted his discussion of China's judicial reform and the replacement and reeducation of judges from the old regime with the comment that Japan's "new Constitution has been construed with old sense" because judges who served under the old Constitution were permitted to serve under the new.[28]

Another writer, in explaining the Chinese concept of "independence of adjudication," criticized the bourgeois principle of separation of powers:

> As a matter of fact, a historical condition which gave the separation of powers doctrine certain progressiveness has disappeared in the capitalistic states. When the bourgeois class grasps all three powers, the mutual check by those powers cannot but become a formality. . . . The judiciary is subordinated to the bourgeois class and becomes "independent" from the people.[29]

24. Fukushima Masao, Chūgoku no jinmin minshu seiken, p. 552 ff; Kida Junichi, "Sino-Soviet Conflict and Criminal Justice in China," p. 77, states, "The socialism of the Soviet Union and of East European countries is in danger."

25. Fujita Isamu, "Socialist Reformation and Law: Impressions of Travel in China and Some Remarks," Hōgaku seminā (Jurisprudence seminar), 119 (February 1966), 52–53.

26. There are, of course, exceptions. For example, see Sakamoto Tsuyoshi, Soren to Chūkyō no kaijō hoken (Maritime insurance in the Soviet Union and Communist China), Tokyo, Bungadō shoten, 1961.

27. Fukushima Masao, Chūgoku no hō to seiji (Chinese law and politics), Tokyo, Nihon hyōron sha, 1966, pp. 1–2; Asai Atsushi, "Tasks of Research on Socialist Law in Japan," Hōritsu jihō, 38 (November 1966), 23; Numata Inejirō, "Tasks of Marxian Legal Research in Japan," p. 15.

28. Ubukata Naokichi, "History and Outline of the Chinese Judicial System," in Fukushima Masao, ed., Shakai shugi kokka no saiban seido (Judicial systems of socialist countries), Tokyo, Tokyo University Press, 1965, p. 273.

29. Takahashi Yūji, "Principle of 'Independent Adjudication,'" in Fukushima, ed., Shakai shugi kokka no saiban seido.

Reports of travelers in China often go to extremes in making comparisons with conditions in Japan. Thus, a recognized civil law specialist who was highly moved by posters and an excited scene on National Day (October 1) asked himself whether the Japanese people might become more willing to pay taxes if a portrait of the Japanese prime minister were posted on the wall of tax offices.[30]

If one purpose of comparative legal study is to furnish information and material on which to improve one's own legal system, the method employed by Japanese students of Chinese law can be called "comparative." Believers in Western democracy may have doubts about the comparability of Communist law with capitalist law;[31] but for Japanese Marxist students who have a "socialist outlook" there can be a good "comparison." They regard their study as a step, however small, toward a socialist revolution. One Marxist who has criticized the tendency of adherence to every Soviet and Chinese official announcement and who has emphasized "independent" research feels that the ultimate difference between Marxist and non-Marxist studies on socialist law lies in the fact that the Marxist students have a "socialist outlook." [32]

It may be easily inferred from the foregoing that the Marxist students' acceptance of the Chinese or Marxian doctrine that the law is a mere tool by which the government governs makes them invariably emphasize the importance of including the study of politics in the study of Chinese law.[33] But apart from such methodological necessity, their partisan approach leads at times to their actual involvement in international and domestic politics.

The situation was relatively simple when relations between the Communist Parties of the Soviet Union, China, and Japan were

30. Kainō Michitaka, "Laborers in China," *Hōritsu jihō*, 26 (November 1954), 3.
31. John N. Hazard, "Socialist Law and the International Encyclopedia," *Harvard Law Review*, 79 (1965), 278–302.
32. Nakayama Kenichi, "A Soviet v. American Discussion on the Nature of Soviet Law — On Berman's Book," *Hōritsu jihō*, 38 (November 1966), 35, where the author acknowledges Berman's "objective" attitude despite Tumanov's criticism and defines Berman's position as lacking a "socialist outlook" but as embodying the "ideology of peaceful coexistence."
33. In the preface to Fukushima Masao, *Chūgoku no hō to seiji*, p. 1, the author states that the title "signifies that the book was written from the standpoint of the inseparability of law and politics" and that "this is the very key for understanding Chinese law." See also Asai Atsushi, "Characteristics of Chinese Law — On the Political Nature of Law," [Aichi University] *Hōkei ronshū* (Journal of law and economics), nos. 51, 52 (November 1966), pp. 165–187.

harmonious. Marxist students of Soviet and of Chinese law had only to juxtapose socialist law with bourgeois law and attack the latter. This position which holds to a simple dichotomy of world legal systems, although still basically maintained, had to be qualified when the Sino-Soviet conflict arose. Since then the study of the differences between Soviet law and Chinese law has attracted considerable attention. The Chinese law specialists have sided with China, and they emphasize the uniqueness of Chinese law as distinguished from Soviet law and even the socialist superiority of the former over the latter. It is more accurate today to talk about contemporary Japanese study of Chinese law in terms of Maoism rather than of broader Marxism.

It is common knowledge that the Japanese Communist Party is in a severe conflict with the Chinese government.[34] The resulting international and domestic political situation has affected "academic" research on Chinese law. The antagonism recently culminated in the ousting of the old pro-Soviet and pro-Japanese Communist leader of Japanese Marxian studies, Hirano Yoshitaro, from his position as president of the Institute of Chinese Studies by the pro-Chinese members who constituted a majority. Hirano was later deprived even of his membership in that Institute, a private association.[35] These incidents demonstrate that Chinese studies in Japan have in the past been under Communist Party influence.

Characteristic III: The Use of Eye-Witness Reports

Jurists have been among the thousands of Japanese people who have for various purposes traveled to China. Although no accurate figures can be cited, Japan probably has sent the largest number of jurists to China.[36]

34. Editorial Staff of "Ajia keizai jumpō" of the Institute of Chinese Studies, "Research on Contemporary China and Its Impediment — Communist Party of Japan," Chūgoku kenkyū geppō (China research monthly), no. 227 (1967), pp. 26–35.

35. "Special General Meeting of the Institute of Chinese Studies Decides Membership Deprivation of Those Who Obstruct Contemporary Chinese Studies," Chūgoku kenkyū geppō, no. 228 (1967), p. 31.

36. The number is well over three hundred, according to Miyauchi Hiroshi, "Legislation: Present Conditions and Basic Principles," in Seinen Hōritsuka Hōchū Daihyō-dan, ed., Hōritsuka no mita Chūgoku (China as seen by jurists), Tokyo, Nihon hyōron sha, 1965, p. 189.

Four groups of Japanese jurists have visited China since 1955: February 6–23, 1955; August 7–September 4, 1959; May 23–June 19, 1963; and August 15–September 11, 1965.[37] These visits were the result of invitations from the Chinese Political-Legal Association in Peking. With the exception of the first visit, the Japanese International Jurists Liaison Association (*Kokusai Hōritsuka Renraku Kyōkai*), an association of "progressive" jurists formed for the purpose of establishing contact with jurists of socialist countries, was the recipient of the invitations and organized the trips. The first trip was made under rather special circumstances: when a delegation of Japanese jurists, including practitioners, law professors, and judges, attended the Asian Lawyers Conference held in Calcutta in January 1955, they received through the Chinese representatives to the conference an invitation to visit China. The first trip is therefore not usually considered as a visit of normal course, and the last is more commonly referred to as the third visit.

The visiting missions consisted of ten to twenty-five jurists, mostly practicing attorneys but also some professors of law or political science.[38] Chinese law specialists such as Niida Noboru, Fukushima Masao, and Kida Junichi saw Communist China for the first time as members of the second group.

There is no formal procedure for selection. It is said that upon receiving an invitation from China, the president of the Liaison Association, Nagano Kunisuke, a former president of the Federation of Japanese Bar Associations, contacts local agents of the Liaison Association, who are leading "progressive" jurists in their respective areas, and they get in touch with suitable persons. As a result, the members selected are always "progressive" people: professors who believe in Marxism, union lawyers, and members of the Free Lawyers Association,[39] who are usually engaged in litigation involving political issues.

37. Some jurists have joined groups consisting of members of other professions. For example, the 1954 "Academic Cultural Delegation to National Day Celebrations," consisted of "men of culture" and included some jurists. See Sugawara Masato, "Glance at Justice in New China," *Jiyū to seigi* (Liberty and justice), 6, no. 2 (1955), p. 30. There was also the 1957 "Peace Delegation from Okayama." See Terada Kumao, "People and Revolution in New China," *ibid.*, 9, no. 5 (1958), pp. 11–15.

38. In Japan professors of political science are usually members of the law faculty.

39. For information about this organization, see Jiyū Hōsōdan, ed., *Jiyū hōsōdan monogatari* (Tale of the Free Lawyer's Association), Tokyo, Rōdō jumpō sha, 1966.

Some individual members of these groups have written about their experiences for various legal and other periodicals. The last three missions were so well organized that the collected essays of the individual members were published: "Chinese Law and Society" (1960), "China as Seen by Jurists" (1965), and "China in Revolution" (1966)[40] were the products, respectively, of the 1959, 1963 and 1965 trips. According to the authors, they all visited universities, factories, people's communes, courts, prisons, and they were lectured by, and exchanged questions and answers with, the personnel of those institutions and other responsible government officials. They also met ordinary citizens. What to see and whom to meet were arranged by agreement. According to a member of the 1963 group:

> There are many people who say that visitors to socialist countries are shown only good things. But the Chinese were frank enough to meet all our requests insofar as time allowed. The leaders of China did not try to conceal the fact that contemporary China is still backward in development. To satisfy our wishes to see back streets and the residences and way of life of workers and peasants, they took us to such places and showed us old slums where the poorest people still lived. We were perfectly free to take pictures, except at military facilities and in planes.[41]

The number of jurists who have traveled individually to Communist China is unknown. Although the Japanese government has sometimes rejected applications for passports for trips to China on the ground that it would prejudice the national interest, many people have nevertheless gotten into China. As far as can be determined from publications, however, it appears that few jurists have individually visited there. Considering the passive attitude of the nonspecialists toward research in Chinese law, it is likely that there are many jurists willing to join a group tour when the opportunity presents itself, but only a few venturous enough to attempt an individual

40. Nihon Hōritsuka Hōchū Daihyōdan and Kokusai Hōritsuka Renraku Kyōkai, ed., *Chūgoku no hō to shakai* (Chinese law and society), Tokyo, Shin dokusho sha, 1960; *Hōritsuka no mita Chūgoku*; Daisankai Hōchū Hōritsuka Daihyōdan, ed., *Kakumei no naka no Chūgoku 1965* (China in revolution, 1965), Tokyo, Rōdō jumpō sha, 1966.
41. Watanabe Yōzo, "China as Seen by a Jurist," *Sekai* (World), no. 220 (1964). To the same effect is Toshitani Nobuyoshi, "From a Trip to China: A Jurist's Image of China," *Hōgaku seminā*, 91 (October 1963), 61–64.

trip to a China where real conditions are not well known. Since the beginning of the 1950's there have been occasional reports of seemingly individual travelers: some were invited to attend the celebration of National Day;[42] others visited China enroute from the Soviet Union or Eastern European countries;[43] and still others attended the Peking Science Symposium in August 1964.[44] However, it is hard to learn from the reports whether the reporters really traveled individually or as members of some kind of group. Most of these travelers apparently took a tour similar to that of the groups, visiting courts, prisons, and so forth.

No Japanese jurist, however, has ever lived in China for a long period of time in order to study Chinese law, as many have done in the United States and in Europe. As a matter of fact, until recently no Japanese jurist had stayed at length in any of the socialist countries, despite great interest in their legal systems, since these countries did not offer scholarships and in some cases did not even permit entry for such purposes. But it is also true that Japanese students have not eagerly sought the opportunity because they have not felt it necessary. The situation is, however, slowly changing. In recent years Japanese students of Soviet law have begun to acquire experience through a period of study in the Soviet Union.[45]

The most prominent feature of the writings of those who have traveled in China is, as might be expected, the Marxist orientation. These writings usually are informal essays rather than academic articles and the authors have greater freedom to express unrestrainedly their admiration for China, but critical observations of the Chinese legal system do occur. An older practicing attorney, a member of the 1959 group, wrote:

42. Kaino Michitaka, "Laborers in China," p. 2. This was in fact a group tour. Sugawara Masato, "Glance at Justice in New China," p. 32.
43. Aoyagi Morio, "People's Justice in the Soviet Union and China," *Hanrei jihō* (Journal of leading cases), 82 (1956), 1–2. Kida Junichi, "Sino-Soviet Conflict and Criminal Justice in China," p. 72.
44. Hariu Seikichi, "Some Theoretical Problems of the Law of the People's Republic of China," *Tōyō bunka kenkyūjo kiyō*, 39 (1965), 93.
45. One student was an attaché in the Japanese embassy in Moscow. Details on the visits of others are unknown. Presumably, they were arranged through personal connections and financed privately. Besides these, it is noteworthy that some of the younger Japanese who studied in Lumumba University in Moscow have recently begun careers of scholarship in law. A personnel exchange agreement exists between Moscow University and Ritsumeikan University (Kyoto), but no law professor has yet gone to Moscow. The program, unique in Japan, is handicapped by Ritsumeikan's financial difficulties.

I cannot accept the Chinese [judicial] system with approval. I cannot help having doubts and fears. Conceding that China is still in a period of transition and has no complete statutes, I have doubts about the fairness of judicial decisions because the participation of the masses in settling disputes makes these decisions susceptible to various irrational factors such as time, place, circumstances, emotion, chance and deliberate action [sic].[46]

This kind of observation, however, is exceptional. More typical is this statement by another member of the 1959 group:

I regret that there is not enough space to write everything. What I want to say about my impression of a one-month trip to China is simply as follows: "Long live socialism! Long live the union of Chinese people! Long live peace! And long live the union of all people in the world!" [47]

More recently, some writers have tried to couch their statements in a way that is more acceptable to the reader. For example, one article introduced the Chinese adjudication process by quoting an explanation of a Chinese official, and then continued:

A counter argument can be made to the foregoing explanation to the effect that it describes nothing short of a "kangaroo court" by the manipulated masses. But to explain Chinese court practice in this way would make it difficult for us to explain other related aspects of the Chinese legal system in action. For example, the actual conditions of prison life in Peking, which we ourselves witnessed, could not be explained as an extension of a "kangaroo court" . . . [Mention of other facts] . . . These facts indicate something different from the use of power for arbitrary mass manipulation.[48]

Another writer stated:

My impression is that the Japanese people still have too little knowledge about China. By knowledge I do not mean that of the general Japanese public who read only newspaper reports based on

46. Mizuno Tōtarō, "Judicial system," in *Chūgoku no hō to shakai*, p. 55.
47. Hashimoto Atsushi, "Labor Union Movements," in *Chūgoku no hō to shakai*, p. 142.
48. Tanaka Tadabumi and Kawaguchi Tadashi, "Proletarian Dictatorship and the Mass Line," in *Kakumei no naka no Chūgoku 1965*, pp. 41–42.

Hong Kong information. I find that even the image of China which intellectuals and scholars have obtained through books is equally superficial. It seems to me that more than half of the comments written about the Sino-Soviet conflict are based on an incorrect or inaccurate view of China; that if the information was correct the basic point of view on China was in some way wrong . . .

I could not really understand from books what the mass line actually meant. But by seeing and hearing things in China I felt that I understood it . . .[49]

He concluded that in China the role of law is small; that is, that the degree of the state's reliance on law in enforcing its policies is minimal.

Despite their subjective or impressionistic approach, these eye-witness reports contain vivid pictures of what their authors saw and heard, providing useful information for students of Chinese law. Descriptions of civil and criminal trials have been repeatedly presented with photographs of those trials. Discussions of marriage law practice have included copies of the marriage registration form, pictures of the marriage certificate, and even the score of a song entitled "Song of Free Marriage." [50]

Statements made by responsible Chinese officials to the travelers are important and some of the travelers' reports record almost verbatim what the Chinese said.[51] But unfortunately most reports include only fragmentary quotations. The following is representative:

How then is an investigation by way of adhering to the people conducted? According to the explanation by the . . . Messrs. Ch'in P'ing and Wu Te-feng, the judge, upon receiving a complaint, always makes an on-the-spot investigation. If necessary he brings his own sleeping mats and continues the investigation for many days. He first meets persons related to the case. Then he walks around to see people not related to the case to elicit their judgments and opinions. He does this in such a way and at such a time that the production activities of those interviewed are not disturbed. In [a] . . . divorce case the judge stayed for a considerable period first

49. Watanabe Yōzo, "China as Seen by a Jurist," pp. 222, 225, 227.
50. Kuroki Saburō, "Basic Characteristics of the New Marriage Law of China," *Kokusai seikei jijō* (Journal of international affairs), 20 (1955), 1–10.
51. Kuroki Saburō, "Legal, Political and Other Kinds of Education in China: Extract Memorandum During Travel in the New China," *Kokusai seikei jijō*, 21 (1955), 127–150.

in the factory where the husband worked and then in the people's commune of which the wife was a member. During working hours he was engaged in labor in order to experience the living conditions of both parties, and in his leisure time he elicited facts and opinions from many persons. We were told that "he could thus grasp the accurate facts of the case." This story impressed us very much . . .[52]

In response to Chinese invitations to Japanese jurists, Japan invited Chinese lawyers to visit Japan in 1958 and in 1961.[53] The Chinese gave lectures at local bar associations, attended receptions, and so on. Unlike the Japanese delegates to China, they were not at all eager to "learn" from Japan. Their lectures consisted mostly of talk about "American imperialism."[54] Obviously they were not interested in contributing useful information for the benefit of Japanese scholarship.

Conclusion: Present Trends and Future Prospects

Up to early 1969, few articles had been published in Japan on the impact of the Cultural Revolution on the Chinese legal system,[55] although other aspects of China in "revolution" have been reported almost daily in Japanese newspapers and in almost every issue of various magazines. This is mainly due to the fact that no new material has been imported; in fact, new legal material that is more than fragmentary is probably difficult to obtain even in China. A more important consideration is the probability that fluctuating conditions in China have perhaps deterred most students of Chinese law from expressing any definite view.[56]

52. Ōkawa Shūzo, Sawa Katsumi, and Ueki Norio, "Chinese Justice and Conciliation," in *Kakumei no naka no Chūgoku 1965*, pp. 269, 281–282.
53. In addition, the "Chinese Academic Representatives Delegation," which included some jurists, visited Japan in 1964.
54. "Lecture of the Chinese Jurists Delegation at the Tokyo Bar Association," *Hōritsu jihō*, 33 (June 1961), 92–101.
55. Asai Atsushi's "Some Issues in the Cultural Revolution," in *Aichi daigaku kokusai mondai kenkyūjo kiyō* (Papers of the Aichi University International Questions Research Institute), no. 42 (December 1967), pp. 81–108, is political rather than legal but was written by a Chinese law specialist who traveled in China from September to October, 1967. See also his "The Cultural Revolution as Seen by a Lawyer," in *Hōgaku seminā*, 142 (January 1968), 74–77, which is more legal although brief.
56. The Red Guard movement, wall posters, and other such occurrences have had a profound impact on Japanese intellectuals. China's Cultural Revolution redounded to the benefit of the Liberal Democratic Party in the Lower House election in January 1967 — revolutionary excesses disillusioned voters whose affinity for China had in the past made them partisans of other more "pro-China" parties.

It is unlikely that substantial new material on law will appear in the near future, even if the present turmoil ceases. For the time being, Japanese students will continue to pursue their study of the theoretical aspects of Chinese law, discussing the "legality" principle, the "all people's state" as opposed to the "proletarian dictatorship," the "withering away" of the state, and so forth. Such work can probably be done without new material.[57] Yet as long as the present adherence to the Chinese "line" continues, this discussion will be too limited to have any influence on the academic world.

The new trend in Japanese study of Soviet law toward a more objective and analytical approach may eventually be duplicated in the field of Chinese law, enabling Japanese studies on Chinese law to rival Western ones. The fact that many Japanese students are Marxists with a "socialist outlook" should not make it impossible for them to communicate with Western students if they at least share a common methodology. Two fighters can fight in the same ring under the same rules though one fights for prize money and the other simply to test his skill.

Assuming that the general standard of Japanese studies on Chinese law is elevated[58] and that Japanese Marxists can learn to communicate with Westerners, Japanese studies can make significant contributions to the field.

First, the deep-rooted tradition of study of Chinese history and Chinese legal history will be extremely helpful in the study of contemporary Chinese law. At present, students of Chinese law adhering to the Chinese line completely reject the suggestion of continuity with the past and emphasize the "special Chinese characteristics" of the Chinese legal system as contrasted with the Soviet. However, they do not mean the traditional Chinese legal system. They refer solely to the Maoist influences on that system and do not ask whether there is anything traditional in Maoism itself. When Japanese legal scholars begin to explain China's present in terms of its past, as some see traditional Russian elements in contemporary Soviet law, Japanese studies on Chinese contemporary law combined

57. "A volume of work is left to be done on the materials we already have," Fukushima Masao, *Chūgoku no hō to seiji*, p. 1. Compiling and reorganizing work started in the past can usefully be done under the present conditions. A recent publication of this sort is Mukōyama Hiroo's *Chūgoku rōdō hō no kenkyū* (A study of labor law in China), Tokyo, Chūō keizai kenkyūjo, 1968.

58. For this to happen it will first be necessary to provide full-time professors on law faculties or in research institutes of major universities.

with the long tradition of historical studies of China will make a great contribution.[59]

Second, the geographical and cultural affinity of Japan to China should not be underestimated here. Chinese influence on Japanese culture has been tremendous and is still felt with considerable force. Yet Japan has modernized at a much faster pace than China and is now in many ways moving closer to the Western world. Japan could thus be China's interpreter to the Western world. Japan is obviously in a position to be a leader in the study of Chinese law, as it has been in the study of Chinese history and art.

59. An eminent historian, the late Niida, seemed to take such an approach. See Niida Noboru, *Chūgoku shakai no hō to rinri* (Law and ethics in Chinese society), Tokyo, Kōbundo, 1955. Niida was not a Marxist but simply a humanist and a believer in the sociology of law, according to Fukushima Masao, "Chinese Studies of Dr. Niida," *Hōritsu jihō*, 38 (September 1966), 91.

12 Soviet Perspectives on Chinese Law

Harold J. Berman

When we study our own law, we carry over from our general education and from our daily experience a feeling, at least, of the underlying philosophy upon which it is based, of the processes by which it has developed over time, and of the relationship which it bears to our political, economic, religious, and other social institutions. We may refrain from a systematic analysis, or indeed, from any mention, of these philosophical, historical, and sociological foundations of our law, but nevertheless, we are aware of them, and this awareness provides the context of our teaching and our research.

In contrast, when we study a foreign legal system we cannot count on any similar awareness — either in ourselves or in those whom we address through our teaching and writing — of its intangible interconnections with the social values, the social memory, and the social institutions of the people whose law it is. Lacking an intuition of the "inarticulate major premises" — in Holmes's famous phrase — of the foreign law, we are in danger of uncritically transferring to it the assumptions which we make about the underlying foundations of our own law. For this reason alone, in analyzing a foreign law we have the responsibility of seeking to articulate its basic philosophical, historical, and sociological presuppositions. Moreover, it is this very necessity of articulating the major premises of foreign legal systems — and hence indirectly, at least, of our own legal system — that makes the science of comparative law exciting and illuminating.

Comparative law has suffered, however, from a narrowness of perspective in this regard. Like its sister disciplines legal history and legal philosophy, comparative law has been largely Western in its orientation — and not only Western, but nineteenth-century Western, which means nationalistic, rationalistic, and individualistic. It has taken for granted certain nineteenth-century Western presuppositions about the nature of law: that each national legal system develops more or less autonomously; that private law can be studied more or less independently of public law and of the Great Revolutions which have successively transformed public law; that law is an expression of the will of legislative, administrative, and judicial officers; that the main purpose of law is to enable private persons to calculate the consequences of their conduct; and so forth.

Such presuppositions as these are reinforced by the traditional focus of comparatists upon the comparison of the so-called Anglo-American and continental European legal systems. Within this focus much attention has been given to the greater influence of Roman law upon the continental European systems, their reliance upon codes as contrasted with judicial precedent, their greater use of inquisitorial as contrasted with adversary techniques, and their emphasis upon doctrinal consistency as contrasted with historical continuity. In interpreting and explaining such differences, the better scholars are able to derive insights into the social functions of law, the relationship of legal to political and social institutions, the extent to which law reflects various concepts of justice and freedom. But these insights, as valuable as they are, fall within the framework of a single legal culture. They presuppose a common core of legal categories, rooted in a common history. For English and American law, no less than the legal systems of continental Europe, have emerged out of the experience of the Catholic Middle Ages, the Renaissance and Reformation, the rise of Parliamentary government, and nineteenth-century liberal democracy.

The term "Western" is one that is becoming increasingly important in comparative law as the study of non-Western legal systems forces us to recognize the strong family likeness of European legal systems, including the English. "Western" is a name which points to the inarticulate major premises that underlie our own (Western) law. It means a certain separation of law from other political institutions and, in another sense of the term "law," from other scholarly disciplines. It means a professional class of jurists; an independent judiciary; a system of rules; a striving to make the rules meet the demands of conscience; a conception of an organically growing body of doctrine and institutions continuous over long periods of time. And it means all these things reflected in categories of contract, property, delict, crime, legal personality, representation, and a host of other basic legal categories created over the past nine centuries, in part out of the older Roman law of Byzantium.

Yet the term "Western" hardly helps in the analysis of non-Western legal systems. "Non-Western" law is simply law in which a substantial number of the basic characteristics of Western law are absent. But what is present? The term "non-Western" does not tell us. Ultimately, it is not fruitful — though we may perhaps begin this way — to study "non-Western" legal systems solely in terms of the extent to which they do or do not contain elements of Western law.

In studying the legal system of Communist China, we may be aided by viewing it from the perspective of Soviet law, since Soviet law is closely related both to Chinese law and to Western law. To draw a metaphor from kinship relations, one might say that Soviet law is an illegitimate son of Western law, now grown to maturity, and Chinese law is a wayward daughter of Soviet law, still walking the streets.

Soviet law is, in part, a continuation of prerevolutionary Russian law — although the Soviets do not like to admit this. The prerevolutionary Russian lawyers and legal scholars survived the Revolution and were at hand in the 1920's when Lenin (who, indeed, was himself a lawyer) called for new codes. The Soviet procuracy, "created" (as the Soviets say) by Lenin, has the same functions — and especially the important function of general supervision of the legality of administrative acts — which were exercised by the old Russian procuracy of Peter the Great and his successors. Even the most recent Soviet civil and criminal codes were written by jurists who were trained before the Revolution or who were trained by jurists who themselves were trained before the Revolution; in any event, they bear many marks of their Russian ancestry.

Prerevolutionary Russian law was both within and without the Western legal tradition. Russia, historically, is Christian; but Russian Christianity did not undergo the Papal Revolution of the late eleventh century, which produced a revival of Roman legal learning throughout the West and a systematic body of canon law. Nor did Russia experience — after two-and-a-half centuries of Mongol domination — undergo the Renaissance and Reformation, which laid the foundations of our modern Western national legal systems. Prior to the nineteenth century, Russia had her own type of legal order, which was more diffuse than Western law; there was no professional judiciary (although there were courts presided over by administrative officials), no professional bar (although certain persons could represent others in litigation), and no legal scholarship (although law was discussed by writers on religious and political themes)· However, in the one hundred years preceding the Bolshevik Revolution, and especially after the great reforms of the 1860's, Russian law became increasingly Westernized. A brilliant class of jurists emerged and sought to take from all the Western legal systems those features which would be best suited for Russia. Yet the Western influence had to compete with the strong antilegal tendencies of Russia's Byzantine, Mongol, and Russian Orthodox heritage.

In the first years after 1917, the Bolsheviks, imagining that they were about to enter paradise, tried to eliminate not only prerevolutionary law but law all together. Several years later, in the NEP period, they restored the "bourgeois" law — temporarily. In fact, the "temporary" NEP codes lasted until the 1960's. Yet Communist one-party rule (which was Lenin's unique contribution to political science) and a centrally planned economy (which was Stalin's unique contribution to economics) challenged the capacity of Russia's relatively recently acquired Western legal concepts to provide a framework of order and of justice for Soviet society. One can, indeed, view Soviet law — as many Westerners have viewed it — as a mockery of law, as failing to be "law" (that is, Western law) at all. One can also view it — as the Chinese Communists now view it — as a typical example of a "bourgeois," that is, a Western, legal system.

The Soviets do have a professional class of jurists (more than 100,000 in number); their law is embodied in a system of rules; they have an abundant legal literature; they claim, at least, to have an independent judiciary and a separation of law from other political institutions; they seek to make their legal rules and procedures meet the demands of conscience; they conceive of their legal system as an organically growing body of doctrine and institutions continuous since 1917; their law is expressed in categories of contract, property, delict, crime, legal personality, representation, and other basic familiar categories of the Roman tradition. In these respects, Soviet law is an example of a Western legal system.

At the same time, Soviet law is characterized by at least four features which distinguish it from Western systems and which relate it to the law of Communist China. Two of these I have already mentioned: the one-party state — that is, the control of the entire political life of the society by a unified, disciplined elite corps, the Communist Party; and the centrally planned economy — that is, the management of the entire economic life of the society by state officials operating under a unified, centrally determined plan. A third feature of Soviet law which distinguishes it from Western law and relates it to Communist Chinese law is what I have called elsewhere its "parental" character — that is, its emphasis upon the role of law in educating a new type of man, characterized, above all, by his consciousness of his social responsibilities and by his desire to cooperate in building the Communist society.[1] The Soviet conception of the subject of law, legal man, as a youth to be guided and trained, and of the lawmaker or judge as a parent, also has, I am told, a strong resemblance to certain aspects of traditional Chinese law.

A fourth feature of Soviet law which must be mentioned in this connection is its conception of historical time. First, Soviet legal theory makes a sharp division between prerevolutionary and revolutionary law; second, it sees revolutionary law as developing through successive transitional stages of proletarian dictatorship and socialism before achieving Communism. This periodization provides a certain continuity and a certain integration in any given period. At the same time, it introduces an added factor of instability. Especially the apocalyptic vision of classless Communism as a time when law itself will wither away and be supplanted by love casts some doubt not only on the permanence but also on the ultimate validity of existing legal regulation.

Viewed from the Soviet perspective, China started in 1949 along the same historical path upon which Russia started in 1917. China would undoubtedly have to undergo the birth pangs of revolution; she would have to crush her class-enemies and attempt to eliminate the survivals of the past in the mentality of her people. However, China was fortunate in having the Soviet experience to build on. She would not have to repeat the mistakes made by the Soviet leaders. In particular, China could find in the more mature Soviet example the kind of governmental and legal structure — worked out during more than thirty years — that could provide a framework of stability and at the same time a framework for progress toward the common ultimate goal. More particularly, China could receive the Soviet

1. See H. J. Berman, *Justice in the USSR*, 2nd ed. rev. (New York: Vintage Books, 1963), p. 277 ff.

system of criminal, civil, labor, and family law; could train a judiciary, a procuracy, and a bar on the Soviet model; and could use these and other Soviet-type legal institutions to foster the one-party state, the centrally planned economy, the education of the people to be socially conscious, and the transition through proletarian dictatorship to socialism and thence to classless, law-less communism.

This view of Chinese law is clearly reflected in the writings of Soviet jurists during the period from 1950 to 1960. The Soviet authors glowed with the pride of parenthood. A Soviet jurist in 1951 congratulated the Chinese for using the courts, the procuracy, and the criminal law — all modelled on the Soviet example — for "the merciless suppression of active counterrevolutionaries" as well as for the punishment and education of offenders generally.[2] He stated that Chinese jurists were working on codes of criminal law and procedure, and that they had set up legal consultation offices to give legal assistance to those who need it. Another Soviet jurist in 1954 stressed that in drafting new family legislation, the Chinese government had "paid close attention to Soviet legislation on family and marriage relations, and especially the decrees of the early years of Soviet power."[3]

Writing in 1956, the Soviet jurist Lunev, who was himself an adviser to the Chinese Ministry of Justice in Peking during the mid-1950's, stated glowingly:

With the transition of the People's Republic of China to expanded planned socialist construction, the Communist Party of China, proceeding from the experience of socialist construction in the USSR, has pointed out that in the new conditions it is necessary even more firmly and stubbornly to introduce legality, it is necessary daily and decisively to struggle against the slightest manifestation of illegality, arbitrariness, bureaucratism, and naked administrativeness.[4]

2. Z. M. Chernilovskii, *Gosudarstvennyi Stroi Kitaiskoi Narodnoi Respubliki* (State structure of the People's Republic of China), Moscow, Gosyurizdat, 1951, p. 83. *Cf.* V. F. Kirichenko, "Legislative Acts of the People's Republic of China Concerning the Struggle Against State Crimes," SGP, no. 2 (1952), p. 69.
3. N. S. Sudarikov, "The Democratization of Family and Marriage Legislation of the People's Republic of China," SGP, no. 7 (1954), p. 35.
4. A. E. Lunev, *Sud, prokuratura i gosudarstvennyi kontrol' v Kitaiskoi Narodnoi Respublike* (Court, procuracy, and state control in the People's Republic of China), Moscow, Gosyurizdat, 1956, p. 22.

Lunev did note certain features of Chinese law that a Soviet reader might find strange. Whether a criminal case should be sent to trial was decided by a committee which included not only judges but also the procurator and the chief of police.[5] Prior to 1954 there was no legal profession to represent defendants, and since 1954 colleges of advocates had been created experimentally on a very small scale, although "all possible measures are being taken in the People's Republic of China for strengthening and vitalizing the work of the bar." [6] In the PRC there was "thus far" no state *arbitrazh* to decide disputes between state enterprises,[7] and courts did not try labor cases.[8] The Chinese daughter looked like her Soviet father, but she still had a lot of growing up to do. At the same time, she seemed to have adopted certain family characteristics in an exaggerated form. Lunev gave a good deal of attention to, although he did not comment on, the people's mediation committees, through which "hundreds of thousands of workers, peasants, worker intelligentsia, householders, and other members of the population are drawn into active state and social work." He also discussed the "people's tribunals" formed to carry out land reform and enforce campaigns of various kinds, with power to impose death sentences without right of review by higher courts. He also wrote of the establishment of a system of "correspondents of the procuracy," which, he stated, bring masses of people into contact with the work of the procuracy, uncovering bureaucrats, embezzlers of state property, speculators, and so on.[9]

As early as 1957, one detects in Soviet writings on Chinese law a certain impatience. The codes were still not written, which led to the making of decisions "on an *ad hoc* basis." The writers were nevertheless "confident" that the Chinese jurists would succeed in bringing their work on codification to fruition.[10] Also attention was paid to the Chinese criticism of the presumption of innocence, to the absence of a right of appeal by the accused, the use of indictments by enterprises and organizations, and so forth.[11] Soviet authors

5. *Ibid.*, p. 9.
6. *Ibid.*, p. 32.
7. *Ibid.*, p. 36.
8. *Ibid.*, p. 39, n. 2.
9. *Ibid.*, p. 59.
10. S. N. Bratus', A. N. Mishutin, and N. K. Morozov, "Certain Problems of the Structure and Forms of Activity of the Agencies of Justice of the People's Republic of China," SGP, no. 2 (1957), pp. 53–60.
11. V. E. Chugunov, *Ugolovnoe sudoproizvodstvo Kitaiskoi Narodnoi Respubliki* (Criminal procedure of the People's Republic of China), Moscow, Gosyurizdat, 1959.

stated, somewhat condescendingly, that various of these features of Chinese law "correctly express the relative positions of the forces in the class struggle," [12] or are "needed in China to completely wipe out those survivals of the old ideology which still remained after the victories of the building of socialism in 1956–57." [13] It was understood that the People's Republic of China was still in "the transition period from capitalism to socialism." [14]

There is another aspect of Soviet literature on Chinese law in the period 1957–1960. It was at this time that the Soviet legal system itself was beginning to experiment with social courts and with the enlistment of the masses in the administration of justice. Soviet writings on Chinese law discussed at some length — albeit noncommittally — the extensive Chinese use of traveling courts, mass-discussion techniques, social accusers, social courts, mediation committees, socialist patriotic contracts, and the like.[15] It is quite possible that the Soviet antiparasite laws of 1957–1961, the revival of Soviet comrades' courts in 1959, and the systematic participation of representatives of social organizations in Soviet judicial proceedings since 1960–1961, reflect Chinese influence. All of these phenomena have roots in earlier periods of Soviet history, but these roots had appeared to wither after 1936.

It is of some interest that the last article on Chinese law in the Soviet legal press in this period of Soviet-Chinese relations, in March 1961, was a translation of an article by the deputy director of the Chinese Institute of Law.[16] For Soviet readers, the references in this article to the struggle against "bourgeois-rightist" elements among Communist Chinese jurists, and the purging of them from the ranks of legal scholars, must have been a chill reminder of their own Stalinist past.

12. A. E. Lunev, "The Socialist Essence of the People's Republic of China," *SGP*, no. 9 (1959), p. 15.

13. G. S. Ostroumov, "A New Form of Drawing the Public Into the Struggle for the Observance of the Rules of Socialist Communal Life," *SGP*, no. 5 (1960), p. 73.

14. A. E. Lunev, *Sushchnost' konstitutsiya Kitaiskoi Narodnoi Respubliki* (Essence of the constitution of the People's Republic of China), Moscow, Gosyurizdat, 1958, p. 159.

15. G. Ostroumov, "What Is New in the Work of the Courts of the People's Republic of China," *Sovetskaya yustitsiya* (Soviet justice), no. 9 (1959), pp. 64–66; and Ostroumov, "A New Form," p. 73.

16. Chou Hsin-min, "Organizatsionnye voprosy razvitiya pravovoi nauki v Kitaiskoi Narodnoi Respublike" (Organizational problems of the development of legal science in the People's Republic of China), *SGP*, no. 3 (1961), pp. 64–72.

Thereafter a long silence in Soviet legal periodicals prevailed until November 1966, when another Chinese article, in Russian translation, was published.[17] In this article, four graduates of the Peking Law School stated: "We have studied at Peking University for five years, and never has a single person in a single class systematically and thoroughly told of the works of Chairman Mao. What have we studied? Soviet Civil Law, Soviet Criminal Law [and] Criminal Procedure, Bourgeois Public Law, the History of State and Law of Foreign Countries, the History of State and Law of China, etc. . . . Several years have passed since we finished our studies, but we have not seen that any sort of 'Soviet criminal and civil law' has helped to decide a single case . . ."

By 1966, of course, Soviet readers of legal literature were already well aware, through the daily newspapers, of the break between the Soviet and Chinese Communist Parties, and of the new Soviet Party line on Chinese law. In 1964 an unsigned article in *Isvestiya* denounced Chinese disrespect for legality both in theory and in practice.[18] The Chinese, according to the article, believe that a continuation of the dictatorship of the proletariat can lead directly to Communism, that the socialist stage can be bypassed, and that the illegal repression of many hundreds of thousands of people can be justified as a "Great Leap Forward" to the classless society. "Things have come to a strange pass," the writer stated, "when the secretary of a district party committee ousts the judge, sits at the bench himself, and starts to decide cases. And such instances are presented in the press as positive experience." Also the article stressed that nowhere in Chinese literature is democracy mentioned. In light of these developments, "it is understandable that the Chinese leaders have construed the dethroning of the Stalin cult by our [Soviet] party as something directed against them, against their theories and practices . . ."

Again in February 1967, in an article by a prominent Soviet jurist, *Isvestiya* attacked the Chinese for violations of socialist legality and socialist democracy.[19] "Without legality there can be no genuine

17. " 'Cultural Revolution' and the Teaching of Law in China," *SGP*, no. 11 (1966), pp. 138–140.
18. "Revolutionary Theory Is a Guide to Action," *Isvestiya*, May 17, 1964, p. 3, translated in *Current Digest of the Soviet Press*, 16 (1964), 3–4.
19. E. Kalinychev, "Democracy and Legality," *Isvestiya*, February 12, 1967, p. 4, translated in *Current Digest of the Soviet Press*, 19 (March 1, 1967), 8–9.

democracy," said the author. He attacked the vagueness and inconsistency of Chinese criminal law and procedure and castigated the Chinese for the absence of criminal and civil codes. He pointed out that in the first years of the Soviet Union Lenin directed that a labor code and a family code be drawn up and that subsequently in 1922–1923 seven new codes were adopted.

And so the father casts his rebellious daughter out of the house until she mends her ways.

To many Westerners, it must seem the height of irony for Soviet writers to denounce the Chinese for the absence of legality. As recently as May 22, 1967, one could read in an American magazine the following comment by a prominent American Sovietologist reviewing Sir William Hayter's book *The Kremlin and the Embassy*:

> Illustrative of [Sir William's] ability to convey much with a few sure strokes is this account of dinner with his former philosophy tutor at Oxford on his return from the Soviet Union in the '30s: "I was airing my famous open mind to him when he asked me: 'Is there a rule of law there?' On reflection I saw that this was the right question and that the unquestionably correct negative answer told one nearly all one needed to know of Stalin's Russia." [20]

Sir William Hayter's "few sure strokes" are now duplicated in Soviet writings about Communist China. Yet surely the Soviets know as well as the Chinese (and as well as the less self-righteous among Westerners) that to say of a nation that it lacks the rule of law does *not* tell one "nearly all one needs to know" about that nation, or, indeed, about its legal system.

Here Jerome A. Cohen's account of his conversation with a spokesman of Communist China is very pertinent.

> "The trouble with you Westerners," the man said, wagging his finger at me before I could sit down, "is that you've never got beyond that primitive stage you call the 'rule of law.' You're all preoccupied with the 'rule of law.' China has always known that law is not enough to govern a society. She knew it twenty-five hundred years ago, and she knows it today." The man, interestingly enough, was a London-educated Chinese barrister who practices in Hong

Kong and is known there as a principal, if unofficial, spokesman of the People's Republic of China . . . One should note that the barrister's formulation was that "law" is "not enough" to govern Chinese society, and not that it is unimportant or irrelevant in that task.[21]

If we view Chinese law from the perspective of Soviet experience — and not merely from the perspective of the present Soviet denunciations — we may be able to gain some deeper insights both into the importance and relevance of law in the task of governing Chinese society and into the "something more" that is needed in that task.

A Soviet perspective on Chinese law would require us to ask, first, whether the present Chinese "nihilistic" attitude toward law, as the Soviets characterize it,[22] is simply a temporary stage in the development of the Chinese Revolution — just as the nihilistic attitude toward law which prevailed in the Soviet Union in the initial period of War Communism and again in the early 1930's was a temporary stage in the development of the Russian Revolution. It must be recalled, in this connection, that the Marxist-Leninist science of revolutions postulates the development of revolutions through stages. Also Soviet experience testifies to the existence of such stages, although the stages of the Russian Revolution do not conform to the original Leninist theory. In fact, the Russian Revolution, like the French Revolution of 1789–1815, the English Revolution of 1640–1689, and the German Reformation of 1517–1555, has ultimately "settled down." [23] The "permanent revolution," originally conceived as a revolution of the international proletariat, has become a national revolution, a Russian revolution, and has been embodied in more or less stable legal institutions. Indeed, the phrase "permanent revolution" has been abandoned in the Soviet Union, and the Soviet writers refer with some hostility to the use of that phrase by the Chinese.[24] It is, of course, a mistake to attempt to impose some rigid pattern of revolutionary stages upon the Chinese experience; history always defies such preconceived patterns. Yet the very example of Soviet experience during the past fifty years, coupled with the intense

21. Jerome A. Cohen, "The Criminal Process in the People's Republic of China: An Introduction," *Harvard Law Review*, 79 (1966), 469–471.
22. F. Kalinychev, "Democracy and Legality," p. 4.
23. Cf. E. Rosenstock-Huessy, *Out of Revolution: Autobiography of Western Man* (New York: W. Morrow, 1938).
24. F. Kalinychev, "Democracy and Legality," p. 4.

Chinese interest in that experience and in the Marxist-Leninist doctrine used by the Soviets to interpret it, compels us to reconstruct the development of Chinese law from the perspective of a theory of revolutions.

Second, the comparison of Soviet and Chinese law makes it clear that Marxist-Leninist doctrine may move in alternative directions. Without the lessons of Soviet experience, it would be tempting to view Chinese law — as the Chinese Communist Party theoreticians would have us view it — as a manifestation of the "true" Marxist-Leninist teaching. We know, however, that Chairman Mao's version of Marxism-Leninism is not necessarily the only authentic version; the Khrushchev-Brezhnev version has at least equal claim to authenticity. Moreover, the Khrushchev-Brezhnev version is not the Stalin version. Thus Soviet experience helps us, when we approach Chinese law, to understand the flexible dimensions of the doctrine which the Chinese have proclaimed to be the chief source of their political and legal ideas.

Third, by the same token, Soviet experience teaches us that "ideology" alone does not make a legal system. The Soviets, like the Chinese after them, began by casting out all prerevolutionary law. They thought that they were creating a new heaven and a new earth. However, in order to govern they needed law, and in order to create law they were compelled to resort to the legal language of the past, for it was that language which the people to be governed understood and respected. In the Soviet case, as we have seen, there was available in the legal language of the Russian past a host of terms, concepts, grammatical and stylistic constructs, techniques, and institutions, which could be adapted to the needs of the Revolution — and which helped to shape the operative thought of the leaders of the Revolution. Inevitably, therefore, Soviet law contains a strong "Russian" component, and it follows that from the perspective of Soviet experience one would distrust any explanation of Chinese Communist law which did not search for its "Chinese" (as contrasted with its "Marxist-Leninist") component. Law by its very nature is rooted in the history and language of the community whose law it is; if we did not know this before the Russian Revolution, we know it now, since the Russian Revolution launched perhaps the most powerful attack ever made against the legal institutions of the past but was ultimately forced to return to them. It would be surprising, to say the least, if the Chinese Revolution does not repeat this experience.

Fourth, Soviet experience helps us to overcome narrow nineteenth-century Western concepts of law and legality as having an existence independent of the convictions and passions which ultimately give non-Western idea, that law is "not enough" to govern a people. If any community its basic character. It is not only a Chinese idea, or a we go behind the Age of Enlightenment in our own Western tradition, we have abundant testimony of the close ties between law and faith, and, indeed, of the subordination of law to faith. It was not a Chinese who said, "The law was given by Moses, but grace and truth come by Jesus Christ." The genius of the West has been to maintain connections between secular law and spiritual faith, without sacrificing either. These connections have rested basically on religious beliefs which may not be widely accepted today, especially in the academic community, but which unquestionably have exerted a profound influence historically on all Western legal systems. Indeed, it is not too much to say that if Christianity is taken out of the Western tradition there is no Western law.

It is necessary to stress these "nonrational" elements of Western law in order to evaluate properly the dynamism and the apocalypticism of Soviet and Chinese law. In a profound sense, Marxism, both as a social science and as an eschatological faith, has exerted a Westernizing influence in Russia and possibly also in China, although in each case Marxism has itself undergone a transformation.

Finally, the language of Soviet law, together with our own experience in translating that language into Western terms and concepts, provides a better foundation than we would otherwise have for comprehending Chinese legal language. This is especially true of those parts of Chinese legal language that are themselves translations into Chinese from the Russian, but it is also true of Chinese legal terms and concepts that are of independent Chinese origin. The comparison of Soviet law with Western legal systems has made us aware that our language, at least, need not be wholly "culture-bound." The word "law," for example, exists both inside and outside our own tradition; that is, it is broad enough in its connotations to convey meanings other than those which we attach to it traditionally. If we can translate the Russian term *pravo* as "law," we can also translate the

Chinese term *fa* as "law," although in both cases we must be careful not to identify the translation too closely with the original. Other Western legal terms are also susceptible of expansion of meaning — it may be said, for example, that the Chinese "socialist patriotic contract" is not *really* a contract. At the same time we must be mindful that our word "contract" itself has many meanings. In a junior high school in the city of Newton, Mass., pupils are asked to sign "contracts" pledging themselves to work diligently and imaginatively at certain subjects for a period of time. In 1967 this practice was hailed at a national conference of public school personnel as one of the major creative innovations in American elementary school education! Are these pledges *really* "contracts"? They lack consideration, they are entered into under duress, the children lack the capacity to contract, they are not intended to be legally binding, and so forth and so on. Yet efforts to eliminate the term "contract" at the school in question met with staunch resistance.

Apart from questions of translatability or nontranslatability of technical legal terms, there are basic legal ideals which have counterparts in many, most, and possibly all, languages: all societies make a distinction between just and unjust rules, and in all societies those who govern attempt to do so in part, at least, according to rules that they hope will be considered just. "Just," "rules," and "govern" are English words; however, they have almost equivalent counterparts in other Western languages, and they also have counterparts, though not always quite so equivalent, in non-Western languages.

Similarly, all major modern languages have some word for "command," for "obey," for "regulate," for "agree," for "possess," for "offense," for "harm," for "compensate," for "claim," and so on. There are dangers, of course, in compiling glossaries of such terms, because their connotations differ in different languages. Several years ago, at a conference of American and Soviet dignitaries, the final American report stated that the American delegation consisted of "private citizens"; this was rendered in Russian translation as *obshchestvennye deiateli*, which upon retranslation into English appeared as "public figures." The important Soviet term *obshchestvennyi*, which has been translated variously as "social," "public," and "civic," has no exact English equivalent, just as the English word "private" has no exact Soviet equivalent, at least when joined with the word "citizen." (Indeed, even in English it may be asked whether a citizen, a *cives*, should be called private in the original sense of that term, which meant "separated from the state." The Russian term for "private," *chastnyi*, signifies a separate part, but in Soviet terminology it has come to mean something akin to anti-social.)

This short excursion into linguistic problems is intended only to emphasize, first, that without descending into the dark pit of cultural relativism, it is necessary to analyze and evaluate a non-Western legal system in terms of its own basic premises and not merely in terms of the ideas, history, and social functions of Western legal systems; second, that despite all difficulties, the gift of translation, and the gift of language itself, is a basis for hope that a person trained in Western legal systems can grasp the distinctive features of a non-Western legal system; and third, that an approach to Chinese law through Soviet law, which has both Western and non-Western elements, and which was "received" in China, can help to make us more sensitive to the nuances of meaning in Chinese legal language and, therefore, to the philosophical, historical, and sociological foundations — the "inarticulate major premises" — of Chinese law.

13 Soviet Sources on the Law of the People's Republic of China

George Ginsburgs

The study of Communist Chinese law is fraught with many difficulties. Not the least of these is the problem of getting enough reliable data on what the law is and how the legal system operates on the mainland. Under the circumstances, watchers of the China scene have tried by various means to supplement the meagre fund of available information. Those able to visit China on more or less protracted jaunts have brought back personal impressions from conversations with ordinary Chinese citizens as well as officials and Party cadres. Some have even managed to obtain permission to observe sessions of the local people's courts at work and have shared their experiences with their less fortunate colleagues. Systematic interviewing of Chinese refugees in Hong Kong and Macao has also contributed to the sum total of our knowledge of legal life behind the so-called Bamboo Curtain. Finally, perusal of what has been published on legal developments in Communist China in foreign languages has helped further flesh out the picture.

A special place in the latter literature must be accorded to the output of Soviet authors and that for several reasons: first, given the close ties which once prevailed between the USSR and the PRC, the Soviets are sure to have had freer access in those days to Chinese legal materials than almost anyone else; second, since for a while the Chinese regime was consciously borrowing from the Soviet jurisprudential repertoire in constructing its own legal universe, the Soviets might have a better insight into and understanding of the way in which these principles and formulas were adapted to and utilized in their new environment; third, until quite recently a number of Soviet professors and practitioners of law went to China on extended trips and a few were posted in China for considerable periods as technical advisers or expert consultants to assorted ministries and departments

Note: Reprinted from the *University of Toronto Law Journal*, 18, no. 2 (1968), 179–197.

associated with legislative affairs, matters of law enforcement, and the actual administration of justice, so that they had the opportunity to familiarize themselves with what was happening in the field and many of them, of course, dealt with these issues in their writings.

The present paper, then, is an attempt to assess the whole of Soviet literature on Communist Chinese law since the promulgation of the People's Republic of China on October 1, 1949, to determine what can be learned from it. It is, in short, a quick Cook's tour of the Chinese Communist legal landscape as perceived through Soviet eyes, undertaken for the express purpose of appraising, both quantitatively and qualitatively, the merits of the collection as a source of enlightenment on the state of the law in the PRC.

Two hundred and sixty-eight titles printed in the USSR treating of diverse aspects of law in Communist China have been identified. In volume alone the record is indeed impressive. To date, less seems to have been produced on the subject in the rest of the world put together. In the Soviet Union itself, none of the other "people's democracies" has attracted comparable attention for its accomplishments in the legal domain, which indicates the relative importance of China in the Soviet scheme of things and the real interest in Soviet quarters in the pattern of events in that country.

The items range from brief news reports to imposing scholarly monographs. The bulk consists of medium-length journal articles. Size means little in terms of the substantive value of a particular piece. Often, a significant bit of fact will be buried in a bleak feature story describing the itinerary of a Soviet lawyers' delegation to the PRC or, conversely, of a Communist Chinese lawyers' group in the USSR, or hailing the successes of a library exchange program. By the same token, lengthier papers have frequently turned out to be mere glosses, clumsily paraphrasing the original language of some key legislative measure, with no element of either analysis or criticism to justify the effort.

The total can be broken down into major categories as follows: Constitutional law, 152; Civil law, 8; Criminal law, 16; Family law, 6; Fiscal law, 12; Labor law, 6; Land law, 10; Procedural law and judicial organization, 32; Miscellaneous, 26; for a total of 268.

Roughly four-fifths of the gross amount falls under the general heading of public law (constitutional law, criminal law, fiscal law, procedural law, and judicial organization). This is not too surprising.

Marxist ideology has traditionally emphasized the public sector, in law as in every sphere of human endeavor. Added to that, for many years the Chinese Communist leadership devoted much time and energy to the question of the proper institutional mechanism for the exercise of power. In that respect, Soviet scholars may simply have followed suit, automatically echoing in their own approach to the topic the dominant theme in Chinese official pronouncements. Besides, it is only normal for constitutional phenomena and matters connected with the fundamental structure of political authority to figure more prominently in bibliographies than will other areas of the law which are, by definition, not as crucial for the future of the entire community.

Table 13.1 gives the distribution of publications by year according to the above categories. The numerical profile in this table calls for some clarification. To begin with, the statistics for the early years (pre-1954) are somewhat deceptive in that a large percentage of the works published at that stage were surveys of the whole spectrum of the initial social and economic transformations wrought by the Chinese revolution. The metamorphosis of the law constitutes but one facet of this mass process and for the most part it was discussed in the context of the land reform campaign, the revised tax rules, the destruction of the old bureaucratic apparatus, and so on. A good deal of space was allotted to extolling the virtues of the common program of the Chinese People's Political Consultative Conference. If this category is not included in computing the annual totals, then the 1949–1959 period represents a steadily rising curve, except for a dip in 1952 for which no satisfactory explanation readily comes to mind and a drop in 1958 the reasons for which can be traced to the internal situation in China. Assuming a year's lag between the time of writing and actual publication, the decline in 1958 would have had to have its roots in the events of 1957.

Two possibilities thus suggest themselves. First, expectations were rife that the current codification projects would soon bear positive fruit and Soviet academicians may have paused in their labors until they had something concrete to explore; second, the antirightist drive which exploded in 1957 and spilled over into the Great Leap Forward, with its antilegalist and antiexpertise orientation, may have caused the Russian specialists on China to wait until the dust settled before voicing any opinions on what was transpiring in their big

Table 13.1. Annual Distribution of Publications.

Category

Year	Constitutional law	Civil law	Criminal law	Family law	Fiscal law	Labor law	Land law	Procedural law	Miscellaneous	Total
1949	8									8
1950	23				2	1	2			28
1951	13				4	1	4	1		23
1952	5		1	2	3	1		1		13
1953	13		1		2	2	1	1		20
1954	15	1		2				2	1	21
1955	8	1	1			1		6	3	20
1956	11	1					1	4	4	21
1957	11	1	3				1	8	9	33
1958	12	1	1	1			1	3	2	21
1959	19	2	3	1				3	6	34
1960	5		4					1		10
1961	5	1						1		7
1962					1			1		2
1963										0
1964	1									1
1965										0
1966									1	1
1967	1									1
1968			2							2
1969	2									2
Total	152	8	16	6	12	6	10	32	26	268

neighbor's backyard and what the future held in store for the still embryonic local legal system. In combination or separately, these factors may account for the curious incident.

After 1959 the mounting ideological dispute between Moscow and Peking took its toll on the academic front too. The learned profession was a thought slow in responding to the changing mood and, for a while, was about a year behind the politicians in its attitude toward Chinese affairs. In 1962 it finally caught up with the latest developments and since then only seven "scholarly" pieces on Chinese law have appeared in the Soviet press, all violently critical of China's "new course," needless to say.

The character and tone of Soviet writing in this realm have thus far passed through three distinct phases. Between 1949 and 1954 what Soviet commentators had to tell about the Communist Chinese experiment in the legal field sounded uniformly and blandly complimentary. In other words, whatever the mainland Chinese turned their hand to Soviet sources greeted as a constructive application of the Soviet model, evidence of "proletarian solidarity," and proof that the Chinese were making rapid advances in "building socialism" at home by drawing on the Soviet experience. Rarely did the Soviet spokesmen venture into specific details or dissect the technical differences between the emergent pattern in Red China and the Russian blueprint or say why the Chinese sample should deviate from the Russian edition. The Chinese specimen was treated as a junior variant of the Russian version. Its discernible features were noted, to be sure, but prompted no conclusions about the likelihood of their crystallizing into a peculiarly Chinese answer to some of these questions and ultimately, perhaps, competing with the Russian original. The *leitmotiv* in those days was "creative adaptation" of Soviet practices to prevalent Chinese conditions but what the phrase implied in objective terms was not spelled out.

A much more sophisticated approach marked the next chronological segment, 1954–1962. China was treated as an equal, an autonomous power within the "fraternal camp." The Chinese "road to socialism" gained acceptance as a recognized offshoot of the parent tree. Soviet authors at this point became engaged in true comparative law analysis (on a regional scale), contrasting Chinese, Soviet, and East European solutions to particular problems, striving to isolate the environmental forces responsible for such divergences, attempting to predict how these issues would be handled in the long run and, in the meantime, evaluating, albeit very cautiously, the relative merits of each method of regulating human conduct. Indeed one even finds occasional references to Chinese accomplishments which might also serve a useful purpose if transplanted to the domestic soil: for instance, the "mass-line" policy in the work of judicial organs, the norm that all top government institutions must report to the legislature on their activities between sessions, the frequent resort to nation-wide discussions of proposed major items of legislation, the device of provisional enactment of statutory measures under which a draft of a law is approved in the assembly and sent out to the competent agencies for spot testing to see how it functions and whether modifications may be required, whereupon an amended bill is submitted in the chamber for a final vote, met with open appreciation.

Verbal endorsement only conveyed half of the picture, however. For, at this juncture, the Soviet authorities consummated a series of revisions in the legal sector which strongly resembled some of the legal stratagems here invented by the Chinese. Thus, the procuratorial committees in the PRC suddenly acquired a counterpart in the collegia of the procuracy of the USSR. The volunteer correspondents attached to the PRC procuracy were matched by the public assistants who helped its Soviet opposite. The Soviets introduced the people's guards, reinvigorated the comrades' courts, inaugurated social tribunals in an effort to broaden the citizenry's role in the maintenance of law and order, just as the Chinese had done previously. Some of the parallels may have been pure coincidence, of course, but it is quite safe to state that to a degree the Soviet hierarchy was in effect inspired by the Chinese innovations and either borrowed what seemed to fit its own plans, modifying it in the process if need be, or was subconsciously influenced by China's example to strike out in the same direction. At any rate, outwardly it looked as though on several counts the Soviet regime was following the Chinese lead.

Furthermore, seen in retrospect the 1954–1957 interlude represented the golden age of law in Communist China. The concern in that country with due process and normal, stable, juridical relations impressed the Soviet legal clan favorably. The net result was that the number of articles attempting to capture the Chinese legal panorama increased, and since the raw material lent itself to serious treatment it generated a superior brand of literature in every sense. By the same token, effective juxtapositions can be assayed when common grounds exist, producing meaningful contrasts and stimulating suggestive conceptual associations. Clearly, the paths of Soviet and Chinese law were converging and under the circumstances it was quite logical that there should be increased mutual scholarly interest, as well as a deeper appreciation and understanding of each other's hopes and expectations.

After 1962 Soviet sources have little to offer on the subject of Chinese Communist law. The old enthusiasm is largely replaced by abuse and vituperation. Proper perspective is lost again and henceforth the Chinese can no longer do anything right in the eyes of their former allies. In short, emotional one-sidedness continues to dominate this branch of the sciences, but whereas hitherto the sentiments had been all favorable now they are all unfavorable. Still, it is possible to differentiate between newspaper vignettes with their bloodcurdling tales of "Red Guard" terror and shrill attacks on the reign of violence and arbitrariness allegedly sweeping the nation and the more sober timbre of the few articles appearing in journals catering to a more specialized audience. It goes without saying that the latter also unequivocally indict the excesses of the so-called "Cultural Revolution," but they manage to carry out the assignment without being guilty of the grating stridency and repellent crudeness so characteristic of the coverage of similar episodes in the mass media. For example, a recent essay published in a Soviet law review on the legal situation in China in the early days of the Cultural Revolution is in many respects a remarkably good, thorough study of what has been happening in that country.[1] The author is avowedly opposed to the events he describes, yet provides considerable factual information on the travails of the legal profession in the state of crisis which grips the land and, while he flatly condemns the Chinese leadership for its course, he at least has reasoned out his position and furnished a sufficient basis for his conclusions.

Not surprisingly, the quality of Soviet writing on Chinese Communist law is very uneven. Much of it runs to straight expository narrative, devoid of creative thought or searching analysis; here even the documentation is sparse or, often enough, altogether absent, and recorded practice is simply ignored. On the other hand, a number of

1. G. S. Ostroumov, "Politico-legal Ideology and the Crisis of Political Authority in China," SGP, no. 6 (1967), pp. 59–66.

Soviet publications display the standard academic paraphernalia: footnotes, ample use of formal references that testifies to earnest research, bibliographies, and so on. To one not conversant with the Chinese materials, these are indispensable tools for further enquiry. Their value on that score to a scholar who has access to and can read Chinese legal literature, however, is rather doubtful. The data cited is gathered from sources which are available abroad and can be consulted in the original. The work done makes it easier for the rest of the academic community and can serve as a guide to newcomers to the field, but it is no substitute for going back to the primary treatises and compilations, if one possesses the requisite linguistic equipment.[2]

Thus, the chief Soviet contribution to the study of Chinese Communist law lies elsewhere: in the unique opportunity enjoyed by Soviet jurists for many years to observe in person the internal functioning of the Chinese governmental apparatus, to acquaint themselves with its *modus operandi*, in brief, to penetrate the official facade and check theory against reality. These visual impressions, inside knowledge picked up from conversations with Chinese colleagues, private experiences, an occasional stray fact not generally advertised but no secret to the initiated, infuse the scene with a breath of life, pointing out unsuspected discrepancies between the letter of the law and the manner in which it is applied, quoting the rules as they appear on the books and explaining how they are actually executed, distinguishing between paper schemes and substantive performance. These elements, no matter how marginal their message, offer a vital corrective by bringing into sharper focus the outer world's image of China's legal evolution, otherwise shaped to a large degree by heavy

2. Soviet authors dealing with the law of the PRC do not seem bothered by the problem of terminological equivalence in rendering Chinese jural language into Russian. The review by O. A. Arturov of the volume *Zakonodatelnye akty Kitaiskoi Narodnoi Respubliki*, published in SGP, no. 4 (1953), pp. 172–174, and the review by G. V. Ignatenko of the compilation *Konstitutsiya i osnovnye zakonodatelnye akty Kitaiskoi Narodnoi Respubliki*, printed in SGP, no. 7 (1956), pp. 130–134, both collections of statutory documents, criticize the editors for many errors, inaccuracies, and oversimplifications in textual translation as well as carelessness and inconsistency in the use of various counterparts for Chinese words. However, the broader methodological issue of whether certain Chinese legal expressions can be adequately translated into Russian is never raised, and Soviet writers do not appear to be aware of the question's importance. Or perhaps, knowing the sources from which the Chinese borrowed these concepts and being more familiar with the style of Communist legal composition, they have less trouble finding the proper formulas to communicate ideas couched in the same tradition.

dependence on reports composed and circulated by the regime itself.

To sum it up, an individual fluent in Chinese and within reach of a comprehensive collection of mainland publications could certainly get a good picture of Chinese Communist legal affairs without the aid of Soviet sources. Though such an approach might easily cost him a few significant details, the risk of missing some essential bit of intelligence is low. One who relied solely on the English-language translations produced by various organizations either in Hong Kong or in Washington, D.C., would find the going tougher. The job would not be impossible and, for that matter, a high proportion of the current scholarly output in this area belongs to that category. This type of enterprise would greatly benefit from the extra data contained in the Russian texts. In both cases, the principal merit of Soviet literature is that it sheds light on how the norms are ultimately interpreted and enforced and whether the legal machinery can fulfill its statutory duties and in what fashion: in short, it succeeds in projecting the basic human ingredient onto the master-screen which otherwise would tend to become cluttered up with inanimate objects.

The Russian material itself is more suited to some purposes than others. On constitutional issues, the organization of the legal branch, the mechanics of judicial administration, the procedural aspects of court, procuracy, and police activity, Soviet publications are extremely helpful, indeed indispensable. But it would be foolhardy to count on them alone in trying to discover, for instance, what has happened since 1949 in the sphere of civil law, or marriage law, or even criminal law.

Ideally, a person interested in writing on some facet of Chinese Communist law should first exhaust every available source of information. Few people have the chance, the time, the energy, and the tools for the task. Most will have to be content to stake out a small claim and mine it diligently. Their findings, when eventually pooled with whatever their fellow investigators have gathered, will, hopefully, furnish an accurate map of Communist China's legal topography. Until then, however, each will continue to dig on his own, trusting that his efforts will profit the common cause. The Soviet share must be included if all are to derive maximum benefit from this eminently worthwhile venture.

Bibliography

This bibliography does not include newspaper items. Although it lists Chinese titles translated into Russian and published in the USSR, it omits anything published in the Russian language in China proper (for instance, articles from the Russian-language edition of *People's China* printed in Peking). An attempt has been made, whenever possible, to transliterate Chinese names into English according to the accepted rules. In several cases, however, the only thing that could be done was to transcribe phonetically their rendition in Russian.

1. Constitutional Law

Anuchin, V. A., "Concerning the New Administrative Division in the People's Republic of China," *Geografiya v shkole* (Geography in school), no. 1 (1951), pp. 25–31.

Artemiev, S. and F. S. Tsaplin, *Material k lektsii na temu "Natsionalnyi vopros v Kitaiskoi Narodnoi Respublike"* (Material for lecture on the topic "The national question in the People's Republic of China"), Moscow, 1957, 33 pp. (Vsesoyuznoe obshchestvo po rasprostraneniyu politicheskikh i nauchnykh znanii.)

Arturov, O. A., "Bases of the State Law of People's China: On the Occasion of the Approval of the Constitution of the People's Republic of China," *Pyataya nauchnaya konferentsiya Tomskogo gosudarstvennogo universiteta im. V. V. Kuibysheva, posvyashchennaya 305-letiyu Tomska,* sektsiya yuridicheskikh nauk (Tomsk, 1957), pp. 25–40.

Arturov, O. A., *Gosudarstvennyi stroi Kitaiskoi Narodnoi Respubliki* (State structure of the People's Republic of China), stenogramma publichnoi lektsii (Moscow: Izd. "Znanie," 1951), 24 pp.

Arturov, O. A., "The People's Republic of China," in *Gosudarstvennoe pravo zarubezhnykh sotsialisticheskikh stran* (State law of the foreign socialist countries), ed. V. F. Kotok (Moscow: Gosyurizdat, 1957), pp. 358–395.

Arturov, O. A., "Review of *Zakonodatelnye akty Kitaiskoi Narodnoi Respubliki,* edited by E. F. Kovalev, Moscow, Gosinoizdat, 1962, 423 pp.," *Sovetskoe gosudarstvo i pravo* (Soviet state and law), no. 4 (1953), pp. 172–174.

Arturov, O. A., and M. A. Shafir, "State Construction of the People's Republic of China," *Voprosy filosofii* (Problems of philosophy), no. 2 (1953), pp. 39–56.

Astafiev, G., "Construction of the People's Republic of China," *Novoe vremya* (New Times), no. 30 (1950), pp. 8–14.

Avarin, V. Ya., "The Chinese Proletariat in the Struggle for the Victory of the People's Revolution," *Bolshevik Sovetskoi Latvii* (Bolshevik of Soviet Latvia), no. 17 (1950), pp. 48–56; no. 18, pp. 55–65.

Avarin, V. Ya., "Great Victory of the Chinese People," *Sovetskaya kniga* (The Soviet book), no. 11 (1949), pp. 3–14.

Avarin, V. Ya., "The People's Republic of China," *Pogranichnik* (Border guard), no. 22 (1949), pp. 70–76.

Avarin, V. Ya., "State and Economic Construction of the People's Republic of China," *Voprosy ekonomiki* (Problems of economics), no. 2 (1950), pp. 44–64.

Avarin, V. Ya., *Uspekhi Kitaiskoi Narodnoi Respubliki* (Successes of the People's Republic of China), stenogramma publichnoi lektsii, prochitannoi v Tsentralnom lektorii Obshchestva v Moskve, Moscow, "Pravda," 1950, 30 pp. (Vsesoyuznoe obshchestvo po rasprostraneniyu politicheskikh i nauchnykh znanii).

Bereznyi, L. A., "Concerning the Main Stages of the Formation and Development of the People's Democratic Dictatorship in China: On the Occasion of the 10th Anniversary of the People's Republic of China," *Istoriya i filologiya Kitaya* (Chinese history and philology), Uchenye zapiski Leningradskogo gosudarstvennogo universiteta, seriya vostokovedcheskikh nauk, no. 281, vyp. 10 (Leningrad, 1959), pp. 19–34.

Bobotov, S. V., A. I. Lukyanov, and E. P. Gavrilov, "Synthesis of the Experience of the Masses in Legislative Activity in the People's Republic of China," *Sovetskoe gosudarstvo i pravo*, no. 5 (1959), pp. 96–107.

Ch'en Po-ta, "Stalin and the Chinese Revolution," *Bolshevik*, no. 17 (1950), pp. 53–62.

Chernilovskii, Z. M., *Gosudarstvennyi stroi Kitaiskoi Narodnoi Respubliki* (State structure of the People's Republic of China), Moscow: Gosyurizdat, 1951, 96 pp.

Chernilovskii, Z. M., "The People's Republic of China," in *Istoriya gosudarstva i prava* (History of state and law), Moscow: Gosyurizdat, 1961, pp. 388–429.

Chirkin, V. E., *Osnovy gosudarstvennogo prava Kitaiskoi Narodnoi Respubliki* (Bases of state law of the People's Republic of China), lektsii po gosudarstvennomu pravu stran narodnoi demokratii (Sverdlovsk, 1958), 63 pp. (Sverdlovskii yuridicheskii institut im. A. Ya. Vyshinskogo).

Chkhikvadze, V. M., "Concerning the Nature of Democracy, Legal Ideology, and Legality in the PRC," in *Za chistotu Marksizma-Leninizma* (For the purity of Marxism-Leninism), Moscow: "Mysl," 1964, pp. 284–299.

Chou En-lai, *O rabote pravitelstva Kitaiskoi Narodnoi Respubliki* (Concerning the work of the government of the People's Republic of China), dok-lad na pervoi sessii Vsekitaiskogo sobraniya narodnykh predstavitelei v Pekine 23 sentyabrya 1954g. (Moscow: Gospolitizdat, 1954), 48 pp.

Chou Fang, *Gosudarstvennye organy Kitaiskoi Narodnoi Respubliki* (State organs of the People's Republic of China), tr. from the Chinese by L. M. Gudoshnikov and G. S. Ostroumov, edited and with a foreword by M. A. Shafir (Moscow: Inlitizdat, 1958), 223 pp.

Chou Hsin-min, "Organizational Questions of the Development of Legal Science in the PRC," *Sovetskoe gosudarstvo i pravo*, no. 3 (1961), pp. 64–72.

"Constitution of the People's Republic of China," *Sotsialisticheskaya zakon-nost* (Socialist legality), no. 10 (1954), pp. 1–4 (editorial).

"Constitution of the People's Republic of China," *Novoe vremya*, no. 39 (1954), Supplement, pp. 2–12 (text).

"Constitution of the People's Republic of China," in *Konstitutsii stran narod-noi demokratii* (Constitution of the countries of people's democracy), ed. V. N. Durdenevskii (Moscow: Gosyurizdat, 1958), pp. 163–196.

"Construction of the New Democratic China," *Kultura i zhizn* (Culture and life), no. 22 (1950), pp. 3–4.

Denisov, A. I., "The People's Republic of China — State of a Socialist Type," *Vestnik Moskovskogo universiteta* (Journal of the Moscow University), seriya ekonomiki, filosofii, prava (1956), 1:111–120.

Denisov, A. I., "State Structure of the People's Republic of China," *Tezisy dokladov yuridicheskogo fakulteta yubilennoi sessii MGU* (Moscow, 1955), pp. 13–15.

Dubinskii, A. M., *Kitai 1918–1949 godov* (China of the years 1918–1949), stenogramma lektsii, prochitannoi v Vysshei partiinoi shkole pri TsK VKP (b), (Moscow, 1950), 117 pp.

Dyatlenko, N., "The Chinese People Advance on the Leninist-Stalinist Path," *Kommunist Ukrainy* (Communist of the Ukraine), no. 3 (1953), pp. 39–56.

Efimov, G., "Construction of New China," *Propaganda i agitatsiya*, no. 17 (1950), pp. 58–64.

Efimov, G., "Formation of the People's Republic of China," *Propaganda i agitatsiya* (Propaganda and agitation), (Leningrad), no. 19 (1959), pp. 27–36.

Efimov, G., "Great Successes of the People's Republic of China," *Propa-gandist*, no. 6 (1953), pp. 40–49.

Efimov, G. V., "Great Victory of the Chinese People," *Vestnik Leningrads-kogo universiteta* (Journal of the Leningrad University), no. 12 (1949), pp. 55–78.

Ermashev, I., *Svet nad Kitaem* (Light over China), Moscow: "Molodaya gvardiya," 1950, 468 pp.

"First Anniversary of the People's Republic of China," *Za prochnyi mir, za narodnuyu demokratiyu* (For a lasting peace, for a people's democracy), no. 39 (1950), p. 1.

Gavrilov, I., "A Weapon of the Despotism of the Maoists," *Sovety deputatov trudyashchikhsya* (Soviets of working people's deputies), no. 6 (1969), pp. 108–110.

Glunin, V. I., *Sotsialisticheskaya revolyutsiya v Kitae* (The socialist revolution in China), Moscow: Sotsekgiz, 1960, 247 pp.

Gorbacheva, Z. I., "National Construction in the Southwestern Regions of the People's Republic of China," *Sovetskaya etnografiya* (Soviet ethnography), no. 4 (1952), pp. 101–113.

Gosudarstvennyi stroi stran narodnoi demokratii Azii (State structure of the countries of people's democracy in Asia), uchebnoe posobie dlya studentov VYuZI, ed. N. T. Samartseva (Moscow, 1956), 203 pp. (includes section on the state structure of the PRC, written by M. A. Shafir).

"Grandiose Prospect," *Novoe vremya*, no. 31 (1955), pp. 15–16 (second session of the National People's Congress).

"Great Historic Victory of the Chinese People," *Vneshnyaya torgovlya* (Foreign trade), no. 10 (1950), pp. 1–5.

"Great Democratic Transformations in China," *Za prochnyi mir, za narodnuyu demokratiyu* (For a lasting peace, for a people's democracy), no. 31 (1950), p. 3.

"Great China," *Novoe vremya*, no. 17 (1953), pp. 1–3 (on the occasion of elections to the local and national people's congresses).

Gudoshnikov, L. M., "Competence and Order of Work of the National Congress of People's Representatives," in *Voprosy gosudarstva i prava stran narodnoi demokratii* (Questions of state and law of the countries of people's democracy), ed. V. F. Kotok and N. P. Farberov (Moscow: Gosyurizdat, 1960), pp. 107–134.

Gudoshnikov, L. M., "Development of the System of Local Organs of State Government and State Administration in the People's Republic of China," *Sovetskoe gosudarstvo i pravo*, no. 10 (1957), pp. 13–25.

Gudoshnikov, L. M., *Mestnye organy gosudarstvennoi vlasti i gosudarstvennogo upravleniya Kitaiskoi Narodnoi Respubliki* (Local organs of state government and state administration in the People's Republic of China), Moscow: AN SSSR, 1958, 186 pp.

Gudoshnikov, L. M., "Organization of State Control in the PRC," *Vestnik gosudarstvennogo kontrolya* (Journal of state control), no. 5 (1954), pp. 55–59.

Gudoshnikov, L. M., "The People's Republic of China," in *Gosudarstvennoe pravo stran narodnoi demokratii* (State law of the countries of people's democracy), ed. V. F. Kotok (Moscow: Gosyurizdat, 1961), pp. 330–372.

Gudoshnikov, L. M., "Review of *Lektsii po konstitutsionnomu pravu Kitaiskoi Narodnoi Respubliki*, Pekin, Kitaiskoe izdatelstvo yuridicheskoi literatury, 1957, 304 pp.," *Sovetskoe gosudarstvo i pravo*, no. 6 (1959), pp. 158–160.

Gudoshnikov, L. M., *Vysshie organy gosudarstvennoi vlasti i gosudarstvennogo upravleniya Kitaiskoi Narodnoi Respubliki* (Supreme organs of state government and state administration in the People's Republic of China), Moscow: AN SSSR, 1960, 109 pp.

Gudoshnikov, L. M., and B. N. Topornin, "Crisis of the Political-Legal Development in China," *Sovetskoe gosudarstvo i pravo*, no. 5 (1969), pp. 11–20.

Gureev, P., "Concerning the State of the Dictatorship of the People's Democracy in China," *Sbornik nauchnykh rabot slushatelei Akademii* (Collection of scientific works of auditors of the Academy), (Voenno-yuridicheskaya Akademiya Sovetskoi Armii), 3 (Moscow, 1950), 13–44.

Ignatenko, G. V., "The National People's Congress — Supreme Organ of State Power in the People's Republic of China," *Sovetskoe gosudarstvo i pravo*, no. 2 (1957), pp. 61–72.

Ignatenko, G. V., "Review of *Konstitutsiya i osnovnye zakonodatelnye akty Kitaiskoi Narodnoi Respubliki*, ed. by N. G. Sudarikov, Moscow, IL, 1955, 690 pp.," *Sovetskoe gosudarstvo i pravo*, no. 7 (1956), pp. 130–134.

Ignatenko, G. V., *Sistema predstavitelnykh organov Kitaiskoi Narodnoi Respubliki* (The system of representative organs of the People's Republic of China), Moscow: Gosyurizdat, 1959, 212 pp.

Izbiratelnye sistemy stran mira, spravochnik (Electoral systems of the countries of the world, handbook), Moscow: Gospolitizdat, 1961, pp. 31–34.

Kalinov, I., "In the Great Family of Equal Nations of China," *Svet nad Baikalom* (Light over Baikal), no. 1 (1955), pp. 123–128 (National autonomy in the PRC).

Kasatkin, V. F., "Solution of the National Question in the PRC," *Sovetskoe vostokovedenie* (Soviet Oriental studies), no. 4 (1956), pp. 16–27.

Kireev, G. V., "Review of A. E. Lunev, *Sushchnost Konstitutsii Kitaiskoi Narodnoi Respubliki*, Moscow, Gosyurizdat, 1958, 159 pp.," *Sovetskoe gosudarstvo i pravo*, no. 2 (1960), pp. 162–163.

Kitaiskaya Narodnaya Respublika: Vsekitaiskoe sobranie narodnykh predstavitelei. Materialy pervoi sessii (The People's Republic of China: National People's Congress, materials of the first session), Moscow: "Pravda," 1954, 168 pp.

Kondratiev, R. S., and L. A. Grachev, *Gosudarstvennyi stroi Kitaiskoi Narodnoi Respubliki* (State structure of the People's Republic of China), Moscow, Gosyurizdat, 1959, 124 pp.

Konstitutsiya i osnovnye zakonodatelnye akty Kitaiskoi Narodnoi Respubliki (Constitution and basic legislative acts of the People's Republic of China), ed. and with a foreword by N. G. Sudarikov (Moscow: Inlitizdat, 1955), 690 pp.

Konstitutsiya i osnovnye zakonodatelnye akty Kitaiskoi Narodnoi Respubliki

(1954–1958), (Constitution and basic legislative acts of the People's Republic of China, 1954–1958), ed. and with a foreword by A. G. Krymov and M. A. Shafir (Moscow: Inlitizdat, 1959), 727 pp.

Konstitutsiya Kitaiskoi Narodnoi Respubliki (Constitution of the People's Republic of China), Moscow: "Pravda," 1954, 32 pp.

Kotov, K. F., "Construction of Local National Autonomy in Sinkiang," *Uchenye zapiski yuridicheskogo fakulteta Kazakhskogo gosudarstvennogo universiteta* (Scientific notes of the law faculty of Kazakh state university), no. 4 (1957), pp. 83–101.

Kotov, K. F., *Mestnaya natsionalnaya avtonomiya v Kitaiskoi Narodnoi Respublike: na primere Sintszyan-Uigurskoi avtonomnoi oblasti* (Local national autonomy in the People's Republic of China: On the example of the Sinkiang-Uighur national region), Moscow: Gosyurizdat, 1959, 196 pp.

Kovalev, E. F., "Concerning Democratic Transformations in the People's Republic of China," *Voprosy istorii* (Problems of history), no. 4 (1951), pp. 26–43.

Kovalev, E. F., "Development of People's Democracy in China," *Novoe vremya,* no. 16 (1953), pp. 3–8 (On the occasion of elections to local and national people's congresses).

Kovalev, E., "The People's Republic of China on the Rise," *Bolshevik,* no. 17 (1950), pp. 63–72.

Kovalev, E., "Political and Economic Transformations in the People's Republic of China," *Planovoe khozyaistvo* (Planned economy), no. 1 (1950), pp. 74–91.

Kovalev, E. F., "Review of *Obrazovanie Kitaiskoi Narodnoi Respubliki: Dokumenty i materialy,* Moscow, Gospolitizdat, 1950, 136 pp.," *Sovetskaya kniga,* no. 10 (1950), pp. 69–74.

Kozhokhin, B. I., "Inception and Development of the Socialist State in China: On the 10th Anniversary of the Proclamation of the People's Republic of China," *Pravovedenie* (Jurisprudence), no. 3 (1959), pp. 17–26.

Kuznetsov, A., *Novyi Kitai* (New China), Moscow: Gospolitizdat, 1952, 150 pp. (State structure of the People's Republic of China: pp. 9–30).

Liu Shao-ch'i, *O proekte konstitutsii Kitaiskoi Narodnoi Respubliki* (On the draft constitution of the People's Republic of China), doklad na pervoi sessii Vsekitaiskogo sobran'iya narodnykh predstavitelei v Pekine 15 sentyabrya 1954g. (Moscow: Gospolitizdat, 1954), 56 pp.

Liu Shao-ch'i, "On the Draft Constitution of the People's Republic of China: Report at the First Session of the National People's Congress in Peking, September 15, 1954," *Kommunist,* no. 14 (1954), pp. 15–45.

Liu Yung-an, *Demokraticheskoe i sotsialisticheskoe stroitelstvo v Severo-Vostochnom Kitae* (Democratic and socialist construction in north-eastern China), Moscow: Gospolitizdat, 1957, 238 pp.

Lozyuk, N., "Socialist Transformations in the PRC and Their Peculiarity," *Kommunist Ukrainy,* no. 9 (1956), pp. 52–64.

Lunev, A. E., "Forms of Participation by the People's Masses in the Work of the State Organs of the People's Republic of China," *Sovetskoe gosudarstvo i pravo*, no. 1 (1958), pp. 71–79.

Lunev, A. E., "Organs of State Control of the People's Republic of China," *Vestnik gosudarstvennogo kontrolya*, no. 6 (1955), pp. 52–56.

Lunev, A. E., "Socialist Essence of the Constitution of the People's Republic of China," *Sovetskoe gosudarstvo i pravo*, no. 9 (1959), pp. 15–23.

Lunev, A. E., *Sushchnost Konstitutsii Kitaiskoi Narodnoi Respubliki* (Essense of the Constitution of the People's Republic of China), Moscow: Gosyurizdat, 1958, 159 pp.

Makogon, S. O., "Solution of the National Question in the European Countries of People's Democracy and People's China," *Uchenye zapiski* (Scientific notes), (Kievskii gosudarstvennyi universitet im. T. G. Shevchenko), t. XVI, vyp. XIII, sbornik yuridicheskogo fakulteta, no. 10 (Kiev, 1957), pp. 43–56 (in Ukrainian).

Martynov, A., "National Elections in the People's Republic of China," *Otvety na voprosy trudyashchikhsya* (Answers to workers' questions), vyp. 40 (1953), pp. 55–60.

Maslennikov, V., "Concerning the Nature of People's Democracy in China," *Voprosy ekonomiki*, no. 3 (1953), pp. 54–69.

Maslennikov, V., "Historic Victory of the Chinese People," *Voprosy ekonomiki*, no. 11 (1949), pp. 44–58.

Maslennikov, V. A., *Sotsialno-ekonomicheskie preobrazovaniya v Kitaiskoi Narodnoi Respublike* (Social and economic transformations in the People's Republic of China), stenogramma publichnoi lektsii, prochitannoi v Tsentralnom lektorii Obshchestva v Moskve (Moscow: "Znanie," 1950), 30 pp.

Maslennikov, V., "Two Years of the People's Republic of China," *Voprosy ekonomiki*, no. 11 (1951), pp. 66–81.

Maslennikov, V., "A Year of Great Transformations in the People's Republic of China," *Voprosy ekonomiki*, no. 9 (1950), pp. 40–55.

Materialy tretiei sessii Vsekitaiskogo sobraniya narodnykh predstavitelei (Materials of the third session of the National People's Congress), Moscow: Gospolitizdat, 1956, 247 pp. (June 15–30, 1956).

Materialy vtoroi sessii Vsekitaiskogo sobraniya narodnykh predstavitelei, 5–30 iyulya 1955g. (Materials of the second session of the National People's Congress July 5–30, 1955), Moscow: Gospolitizdat, 1956, 440 pp.

Meliksetov, A. V., *Material k lektsii na temu "Edinyi narodno-demokraticheskii front Kitaya, ego rol i znachenie v sotsialisticheskom stroitelstve"* (Material for lecture on the topic "United popular democratic front of China, its role and significance in socialist construction"), Moscow: "Znanie," 1957, 38 pp.

Menzhinskii, V. I., and L. D. Voevodin, "The People's Republic of China — State of the People's Democratic Dictatorship," in *10 let Kitaiskoi Narodnoi Respubliki* (Ten years of the People's Republic of China), Moscow: IMO, 1959, pp. 32–59.

Mikhailov, N., "China Reborn," *Molodoi Bolshevik* (Young Bolshevik), no. 13 (1950), pp. 33–48.

Mikheev, V., "The Forces of the People's Republic of China Are Growing and Solidifying," *Kommunist*, no. 15 (1953), pp. 85–93.

Mikheev, V., "Program of Construction of the New China," *Bolshevik*, no. 8 (1950), pp. 67–72.

Muzachev, V., "A Historic Session (2nd)," *Novoe vremya*, no. 32 (1955), pp. 23–25 (Second session of the National People's Congress).

Obrazovanie Kitaiskoi Narodnoi Respubliki, dokumenty i materialy (Formation of the People's Republic of China, documents and materials), Moscow: Gospolitizdat, 1950, 135 pp.

Obshchaya programma Narodnogo politicheskogo konsultativnogo Soveta Kitaya (prinyata 1-i sessiei Narodnogo politicheskogo konsultativnogo Soveta Kitaya 29 sentyabrya 1949g.), (Common program of the Chinese People's Political Consultative Conference, adopted at the 1st session of the Chinese People's Political Consultative Conference, September 29, 1949), Moscow: Gospolitizdat, 1950, 22 pp.

"On the Nature and Particularities of People's Democracy in the Countries of the East," *Izvestiya Akademii Nauk SSSR* (USSR Academy of Sciences News), seriya istorii i filosofii, 1952, t. IX, no. 1, pp. 80–87 (Report of a conference).

Orlovskii, P. E., "Constitution of the Great Chinese People's Democratic State," *Sovetskoe gosudarstvo i pravo*, no. 7 (1954), pp. 19–26.

Ostroumov, G. S., "Politico-Legal Ideology and the Crisis of Political Authority in China," *Sovetskoe gosudarstvo i pravo*, no. 6 (1967), pp. 59–66.

Osnovnye normativnye akty o mestnykh organakh gosudartsvennoi vlasti i gosudarstvennogo upravleniya Kitaiskoi Narodnoi Respubliki: sbornik dokumentov (Basic normative acts concerning local organs of state government and state administration in the People's Republic of China: collection of documents), Moscow: Gosyurizdat, 1959, 504 pp.

Ovchinnikov, V., "At the First Session of the National People's Congress," *Novoe vremya*, no. 40 (1954), pp. 11–15 (from the meeting hall).

Ovchinnikov, V., "Deputy Pu Chung-chih," *Novoe vremya*, no. 6 (1955), pp. 24–27.

Patyullin, V. A., "Destruction of the Kuomintang State Machine in China," *Sovetskoe gosudarstvo i pravo*, no. 10 (1959), pp. 47–59.

Patyullin, V. A., "On the Question of the Inception of the Socialist State in China," *Sovetskoe gosudarstvo i pravo*, no. 10 (1958), pp. 36–47.

Perevertailo, A. S., "The People's Republic of China: State of People's Democracy," *Uchenye zapiski Instituta vostokovedeniya* (Scientific notes of the Institute of Oriental Studies), vyp. 2 (1951), pp. 95–115.

Petrov, V. S., "Type and Form of the State of the People's Republic of China," *Vestnik Leningradskogo universiteta*, no. 11, seriya ekonomiki, filosofii i prava, vyp. 2 (1957), pp. 150–161.

Plashevskii, Yu., "Great Transformations in the People's Republic of China," *Bolshevik Kazakhstana* (no. 8), (Alma-Alta, 1951), pp. 45–48.

Rachkov, O., "Successes of People's China in Solving the National Question," *Kommunist Kazakhstana* (Communist of Kazakhstan), no. 10 (1954), pp. 16–21.

Radvogin, A. V., "Development of Autonomy in the People's Republic of China," *Uchenye zapiski otdeleniya pravovedeniya* (Scientific notes of the sector of jurisprudence), (Kirgizskii gosudarstvennyi universitet), vyp. 1, *Voprosy sovetskogo prava* (Frunze, 1958), pp. 75–103.

Rakhimov, T. R., "Successes of the People's Republic of China in Solving the National Question," *Voprosy istorii*, no. 1 (1954), pp. 43–59.

"Scientific Session Dedicated to the People's Republic of China," *Vestnik Akademii Nauk SSSR* (Journal of the USSR Academy of Science), no. 2 (1950), pp. 66–68.

Seifulin, M. M., "National State Construction in the People's Republic of China," in *Nauchnaya konferentsiya aspirantov VIYuN Ministerstva Yustitsii SSSR* (Scientific Conference of Candidates of the National Institute of Juridical Sciences of the Ministry of Justice of the USSR), Tezisy dokladov (1953), pp. 16–20.

Sergiev, A., *Rol demokraticheskoi diktatury naroda v stroitelstve sotsializma v Kitae* (The role of the people's democratic dictatorship in the construction of socialism in China), Moscow: Gospolitizdat, 1958, 389 pp.

Shafir, M. A., "A Book on the Local Organs of Government of People's China," *Sovety deputatov trudyashchikhsya*, no. 8 (1958), pp. 90–93. (Review of L. M. Gudoshnikov, *Mestnye organy gosudarstvennoi vlasti i gosudarstvennogo upravleniya Kitaiskoi Narodnoi Respubliki*, Moscow, 1958, 187 pp.)

Shafir, M. A., "Consolidation and Improvement of the State Apparatus in the People's Republic of China," *Sovetskoe gosudarstvo i pravo*, no. 11 (1959), pp. 38–47.

Shafir, M. A., *Demokratischeskaya diktatura naroda v Kitae: odna iz form diktatury proletariata* (The people's democratic dictatorship in China: one of the forms of the dictatorship of the proletariat), Moscow: "Znanie," 1959, 47 pp.

Shafir, M. A., "Legislative Work in the People's Republic of China," *Sovety deputatov trudyashchikhsya*, no. 4 (1959), pp. 86–88.

Shafir, M. A., "The People's Republic of China," in *Gosudarstvennoe pravo stran narodnoi demokratii* (State law of the countries of people's democracy), ed. A. Kh. Makhnenko (Moscow, 1959), pp. 319–350.

Shafir, M. A., *Ustanovochnye lektsii po gosudarstvennomu pravu stran narodnoi demokratii* (Introductory lectures on state law of the countries of people's democracy), dlya studentov VYuZI. Lektsiya 3 (Gosudarstvennyi stroi KNR), Moscow, 1951, 36 pp. (VYuZI).

Shafir, M. A., and G. S. Ostroumov, "Concerning Improvement of the Organizational Forms of Management of Industry in the PRC," *Sovetskoe gosudarstvo i pravo*, no. 5 (1958), pp. 111–116.

Shcherbakov, I., "China: A People's Republic," *Molodoi Bolshevik*, no. 22 (1949), pp. 60–65.

Shchetinin, B. V., "The Representative System in the People's Democratic States of Asia," *Sovetskoe gosudarstvo i pravo*, no. 2 (1955), pp. 33–41.

Shevel, I. B., "National Construction in the Sinkiang Uighur Autonomous Region of the PRC," *Sovetskaya etnografiya*, no. 2 (1956), pp. 95–105.

Shumilov, O., "First National Elections in China," *Novoe vremya*, no. 33 (1953), pp. 7–11.

Sokolov, P., "Concerning the Essence and Form of State Power in the Countries of People's Democracy, the German Democratic Republic and in China," *Propaganda i agitatsiya*, no. 5 (1951), pp. 23–29.

Sudarikov, N. G. "Constitution of Peace, Progress, and Democracy," *Novoe vremya*, no. 44 (1954), pp. 8–13.

Sudarikov, N. G., "Construction and Consolidation of Organs of State Power in the People's Republic of China," *Sovetskoe gosudarstvo i pravo*, no. 8 (1951), pp. 23–42.

Sudarikov, N. G., "Creation and Consolidation of Local Organs of Government of the People's Republic of China," *Sovetskoe gosudarstvo i pravo*, no. 11 (1951), pp. 53–63.

Sudarikov, N. G., "Electoral System of the People's Republic of China," *Sovetskoe gosudarstvo i pravo*, no. 5 (1953), pp. 114–128.

Sudarikov, N. G., *Gosudarstvennyi stroi Kitaiskoi Narodnoi Respubliki* (State structure of the People's Republic of China), Moscow: "Znanie," 1956, 48 pp. (Vsesoyuznoe obshchestvo po rasprostraneniyu politicheskikh i nauchnykh znanii).

Tadevosyan, E., "Successes of the PRC in Solving the National Question," *Moskovskii propagandist* (Moscow propagandist), no. 4 (1957), pp. 67–72.

"Ten Years of the State of Proletarian Dictatorship in China," *Sovetskoe gosudarstvo i pravo*, no. 9 (1959), pp. 3–14.

Tesselman, I. *Kitaiskaya Narodnaya Respublika* (The People's Republic of China), Kiev: Gospolitizdat USSR, 1951, 100 pp. (in Ukrainian).

Tsao Tzu-tan, Wan Chieh, and Ko Shen-shen, "Doctrine of the Two Types of Contradictions in the Legal Science of the PRC," *Pravovedenie*, no. 2 (1959), pp. 185–186.

Ukrainstev, M., "Creation of the People's Republic of China," *Bloknot agitatora* (Agitator's notebook), no. 30 (1949), pp. 38–48.

Valiakhmetov, G. M., "Internal Organization of Tibet," *Sovetskoe gosudarstvo i pravo*, no. 7 (1956), pp. 113–118.

Valiakhmetov, G. M., *Organy vlasti i upravleniya Tibeta* (Organs of government and administration of Tibet), Moscow: Gosyurizdat, 1958, 45 pp.

Voevodin, L. D., "Bases of State Law of the People's Republic of China," in

L. D. Voevodin, D. L., Zlatopolskii, and N. Ya. Kuprits, *Gosudartsvennoe pravo stran narodnoi demokratii* (State law of the countries of people's democracy), (Moscow: IMO, 1960), pp. 161–217.

Voevodin, L. D., *Gosudarstvennyi stroi Kitaiskoi Narodnoi Respubliki* (State structure of the People's Republic of China), Moscow: Gosyurizdat, 1956, 270 pp.

Voevodin, L. D., "On the Solution of the National Question in the State Construction of the People's Republic of China," *Sovetskoe gosudarstvo i pravo*, no. 6 (1953), pp. 104–119.

Vysshie organy gosudarstvennoi vlasti stran narodnoi demokratii: sbornik normativnykh aktov (Supreme organs of state power of countries of people's democracy: collection of normative acts), vyp. 2: Strany Azii, ed. L. M. Gudoshnikov (Moscow: Gosyurizdat, 1961), PRC, pp. 45–88.

Yakovlev, A. G., "The Economic Policy of the Central People's Government of the People's Republic of China with Regard to the National Border Regions in the Example of Sinkiang," *Kratkie soobshcheniya Instituta vostokovedeniya* (Brief reports of the Institute of Oriental Studies), 1952, t. VII, pp. 41–55.

Yakovlev, A. G., *Reshenie natsionalnogo voprosa v Kitaiskoi Narodnoi Respublike*, (Solution of the national question in the People's Republic of China), Moscow: Izd. vostochnoi literatury, 1959, 111 pp.

Yakovlev, V., "National Elections in China: Letter from Peking," *Novoe vremya*, no. 13 (1954), pp. 24–27.

Yuriev, M., "Consolidation of People's Democracy in China," *Novoe vremya*, no. 29 (1954), pp. 4–8 (on the occasion of the publication of the draft Constitution).

Yuriev, M. F., "Review of Z. M. Chernilovskii, *Gosudarstvennyi stroi Kitaiskoi Narodnoi Respubliki*, Moscow, Yurizdat, 1951, 96 pp.," *Sovetskaya kniga*, no. 11 (1951), pp. 68–70.

Zakonodatelnye akty Kitaiskoi Narodnoi Respubliki (Legislative acts of the People's Republic of China), tr. from the Chinese, ed. and with a foreword by E. F. Kovalev (Moscow: Inlitizdat, 1952), 423 pp.

Zhukov, F., "The Great October Socialist Revolution and China," *Novoe vremya*, no. 46 (1949), pp. 14–18.

2. Civil Law

Belyakova, A. M., *Nekotorye voprosy grazhdanskogo prava Kitaiskoi Narodnoi Respubliki* (Certain questions of civil law of the People's Republic of China), Moscow: Izd. Moskovskogo universiteta, 1961, 49 pp.

Chzhan Die and M. Kirillova, "Questions of Inheritance in the People's Republic of China," *Sovetskaya yustitsiya*, no. 6 (1959), pp. 31–34.

Dzhorbenadze, S. M., "Particularities of Inception of State Socialist Ownership in the People's Republic of China," *Sovetskoe pravo* (Soviet law), no. 5 (Tbilisi, 1959), pp. 25–33 (in Georgian).

Karavaikin, A., "Property Right in People's China," *Sotsialisticheskaya zakonnost*, no. 4 (1956), pp. 43–46.

Lunev, A. E., "Certain Questions of the Law of State Socialist Ownership in the People's Republic of China," *Sovetskoe gosudarstvo i pravo*, no. 7 (1954), pp. 27–32.

Lunev, A. E., "Law of Co-operative Ownership in the People's Republic of China," *Sovetskoe gosudarstvo i pravo*, no. 8 (1955), pp. 74–81.

Nikolskii, M. M., "Particularities of the Execution of Socialist Nationalization in the People's Republic of China: Concerning the Question of the Creation and Consolidation of the State Sector in the Economy of the PRC During the Reconstruction Period," in *Voprosy ekonomiki i mezhdunarodnykh otnoshenii: sbornik statei* (Questions of economics and international relations: collection of articles), Moscow: IMO, 1957, pp. 3–20.

Pozdnyakov, V. S., "Civil Law of the People's Republic of China," in *Grazhdanskoe pravo stran narodnoi demokratii* (Civil law of the countries of people's democracy), ed. D. M. Genkin (Moscow: Vneshtorgizdat, 1958), pp. 47–121.

3. Criminal Law

Chugunov, V., "Combination of Punishment with Magnanimity in the Law of the People's Republic of China," *Sotsialisticheskaya zakonnost*, no. 4 (1960), pp. 54–56.

Chugunov, V., "Legislation and Practice in the Area of Struggle Against Criminality in the PRC," *Sovetskaya yustitsiya* (Soviet justice), no. 9 (1959), pp. 35–37.

Delyusin, L., "Two Paths: Concerning the Policy of the People's Government Toward Counterrevolutionary Elements," *Novoe vremya*, no. 13 (1957), pp. 20–22.

Domakhin, S. A., "Questions of Development of Criminal Legislation of the People's Republic of China," *Pravovedenie*, no. 3 (1959), pp. 71–77.

Domakhin, S. A., "The Struggle Against State Crimes in the People's Republic of China," *Vestnik Leningradskogo universiteta*, seriya ekonomiki, filosofii, prava, 1957, no. 5, vyp. 1, pp. 116–128.

Gelfer, M. A., "Criminal Law of the People's Republic of China," in *Sovetskoe ugolovnoe pravo, Obshchaya chast* (Soviet criminal law, general part), ed. V. M. Chkhikvadze (Moscow: Gosyurizdat, 1959), pp. 388–400.

Gelfer, M. A., *Uchebnoe posobie po ugolovnomu zakonodatelstvu stran narodnoi demokratii* (Study aid on the criminal legislation of the countries of people's democracy), odobreno Sovetom i utverzhdeno direktorom VYuZI (Moscow, 1953), 129 pp. (Includes section on the criminal law of the PRC).

Gelfer, M. A., *Ugolovnoe zakonodatelstvo Kitaiskoi Narodnoi Respubliki* (Criminal law of the People's Republic of China), uchebnoe posobie dlya studentov VYuZI, (Moscow, 1955), 58 pp.

Kalinychev, F., "Violation of Democracy and Legality in the PRC," *Sotsialisticheskaya zakonnost*, no. 2 (1968), pp. 32–34.

Kirichenko, V. F., "The Legislative Acts of the People's Republic of China on the Struggle with State Crimes," *Sovetskoe gosudarstvo i pravo*, no. 2 (1952), pp. 65–69.

Kitaiskaya Narodnaya Respublika, Koreiskaya Narodno-Demokratischeskaya Respublika, Mongolskaya Narodnaya Respublika, Demokraticheskaya Respublika Vietnam (The People's Republic of China, the Korean People's Democratic Republic, the Mongolian People's Republic, The Democratic Republic of Vietnam), ed., M. A. Gelfer (Moscow: Gosyurizdat, 1957), 92 pp. (Criminal legislation of foreign democratic countries).

Koldin, V. Ya., "Certain Questions of Criminal Law Policy of the People's Republic of China," *Vestnik Moskovskogo universiteta*, seriya ekonomiki, filosofi, i prava, no. 4 (1958), pp. 153–172.

Ostroumov, G. S., "New Form of Involvement of the Public in the Struggle for the Observance of Rules of Socialist Co-living in the PRC," *Sovetskoe gosudarstvo i pravo*, no. 5 (1960), pp. 73–81.

Perlov, I. D., "Deviations from Democratic Principles of Administration of Justice in the PRC," *Sovetskoe gosudarstvo i pravo*, no. 1 (1968), pp. 75–82.

Shafir, M. A., "Concerning Certain Forms of Involvement of the Public in the Struggle for the Observance of Legality and Public Order in the People's Republic of China," in *Rol obshchestvennosti v borbe s prestupnostyu* (The role of the public in the struggle against criminality), materialy mezhvuzovskoi nauchnoi konferentsii s uchastiem prakticheskikh rabotnikov (Voronezh: Izd. Voronezhskogo universiteta, 1960), pp. 133–142.

Wan Chieh, "Outline of the Development of Responsibility for Complicity in the Criminal Legislation of the People's Republic of China," *Pravovedenie*, no. 3 (1960), pp. 59–65.

4. Family Law

Petrov, N. A., "Questions of Marriage and Family in New China," *Sovetskaya etnografiya*, no. 1 (1954), pp. 85–96.

Ryasentsev, V. A., "Basic Traits of Family Law in the People's Republic of China," in V. I. Boshko, ed. *Ocherki sovetskogo semeinogo prava* (Essays on Soviet family law), Kiev, 1952, pp. 358–366.

Sudarikov, N. G., "Democratization of Family and Marriage Legislation in the People's Republic of China," *Sovetskoe gosudarstvo i pravo*, no. 7 (1954), pp. 33–40.

Sverdlov, G. M., *Sovetskoe semeinoe pravo* (Soviet family law), Moscow: Gosyurizdat, 1958, "Transformations in the Family Law in the People's Republic of China and the Other Socialist States of Asia," pp. 288–295.

U Chan-chzhen and M. Ya. Kirillova, "Grounds and Procedure for the Dissolution of Marriage in the People's Republic of China," *Pravovedenie*, no. 2 (1959), pp. 142–150.

Yaichkov, K., "Marriage and Family Law of the People's Republic of China," *Sotsialisticheskaya zakonnost*, no. 1 (1952), pp. 52–58.

5. Fiscal Law

Boldyrev, B. G., "Consolidation of Currency Circulation in the People's Republic of China," *Dengi i kredit* (Money and credit), no. 4 (1951), pp. 40–45.

Boldyrev, B. G., "Consolidation of the Currency and Credit System of the People's Republic of China," *Dengi i kredit*, no. 10 (1951), pp. 40–47.

Boldyrev, B. G., "Construction of a Currency and Credit System in the People's Republic of China," *Dengi i kredit*, no. 8 (1950), pp. 33–42.

Boldyrev, B. G., "Finances and Credit: Powerful Lever for the Development of the Economy of the People's Republic of China," *Finansy i kredit SSSR* (Finance and credit), no. 2 (1952), pp. 50–59.

Boldyrev, B. G., *Finansy Kitaiskoi Narodnoi Respubliki* (Finances of the People's Republic of China), ed. V. A. Maslennikov (Moscow: Gosfinizdat, 1953), 197 pp.

Boldyrev, B. G., "The State Budget in the Service of Economic Construction of the People's Republic of China," *Sovetskie finansy* (Soviet finances), no. 7 (1951), pp. 22–30.

Boldyrev, B. G., *Uspekhi Kitaiskoi Narodnoi Respubliki v stroitelstve novoi denezhnoi i finansovo-kreditnoi sistemy* (Successes of the People's Republic of China in the construction of a new currency and financial-credit system), Moscow: "Znanie," 1952, 39 pp. (Vsesoyuznoe obshchestvo po rasprostraneniyu politicheskikh i nauchnykh znanii).

Borisov, S., "The Budget of the People's Republic of China: Important Weapon of Peaceful Construction," *Finansy i kredit SSSR*, no. 5 (1953), pp. 47–57.

Chekhutov, A. I., *Nalogovaya sistema Kitaiskoi Narodnoi Respubliki* (The tax system of the People's Republic of China), Moscow: Izd. vostochnoi literatury, 1962, 205 pp.

Doroshin, I., "Consolidation of Currency Circulation in People's China," *Sovetskie finansy* (Soviet finances), no. 10 (1951), pp. 22–28.

Lavrov, V., "Organization and Construction of the Fiscal System of the People's Republic of China," *Sovetskie finansy*, no. 11 (1950), pp. 17–27.

Novak, L., "The Currency Regime of the People's Republic of China," *Vneshnyaya torgovlya*, no. 11 (1952), pp. 32–36.

6. Labor Law

Acharkan, V., "The Trade Unions of China on Guard in the Interests of the Workers," *V pomoshch profsoyuznomu aktivu* (The trade union activists' aid), no. 10 (1951), pp. 36–38.

Galegin, V., and I. Markov, "Trade Union Construction in People's China," *Professionalnye soyuzy* (Trade unions), no. 10 (1950), pp. 34–37.

Krasavchikov, O. A., "Basic Traits of Labor Insurance in the People's Republic of China," *Sovetskoe gosudarstvo i pravo*, no. 7 (1953), pp. 114–122.

Pasherstnik, A. E., *Trudovoe pravo stran narodnoi demokratii* (Labor law of the countries of people's democracy), uchebnoe posobie (Moscow: Gosyurizdat, 1955), 140 pp. ("The Labor Law of the PRC," ch. 2, pp. 87–112).

Pentkovskii, V., "Labor Legislation in the People's Republic of China," *Professionalnye profsoyuzy*, no. 4 (1952), pp. 38–44.

"Tasks of the Chinese Trade Unions: Interview with the Chairman of the All-China Federation of Trade Unions, Lai Jo-yü," *Novoe vremya*, no. 25 (1953), pp. 16–17.

7. Land Law

Kazantsev, N. D., "Transformation of Land Relations in the People's Republic of China: Report from the Chair of Land and Collective Farm Law of the Leningrad University on November 28, 1950," *Vestnik Leningradskogo universiteta*, no. 2 (1951), pp. 145–148.

Kazantsev, N. D., "Transformation of Land Relations in the People's Republic of China on the Basis of the Law of 1950," *Izvestiya Akademii Nauk SSSR, Otdelenie ekonomiki i prava*, no. 2 (1951), pp. 108–122.

Kovalev, E., "Land Reform and the Consolidation of the Alliance of Workers and Peasants in China," *Kommunist*, no. 13 (1953), pp. 120–128.

Liu Shao-ch'i, "Concerning the Land Reform in China," *Za prochnyi mir, za narodnuyu demokratiyu*, no. 29 (1950), pp. 3–4.

Osnovnye zakonodatelnye akty po agrarnym preobrazovaniyam v zarubezhnykh sotsialisticheskikh stranakh, ed. N. D. Kazantsev (Moscow: Gosyurizdat, 1958), vyp. 1: The People's Republic of China, the Korean People's Democratic Republic, the Mongolian People's Republic, the Democratic Republic of Vietnam, 290 pp.

Pavlov, I. V., "Certain Questions of the Legal Position of Agricultural Producers' Co-operatives in the People's Republic of China," *Sovetskoe gosudarstvo i pravo*, no. 7 (1957), pp. 32–42.

Rogov, V., "Land Transformations in the Province of Chekiang: Letter from China," *Novoe vremya*, no. 19 (1951), pp. 14–17.

Shvetsov, N., "Land Reform and the Successes of the Rural Economy of Democratic China," *Sotsialisticheskoe selskoe khozyaistvo* (Socialist agriculture), no. 3 (1951), pp. 54–60.

Sun Ya-ming, "Model Charter of the Agricultural Production Co-operative of the People's Republic of China," *Sovetskoe gosudarstvo i pravo*, no. 3 (1956), pp. 92–102.

Tu Kuo, "The Peasants of New China," *Za prochnyi mir, za narodnuyu demokratiyu*, no. 41 (1950), p. 2.

8. Procedural Law and Judicial Organization

Aparnikova, Ts., "Preliminary Processing of Civil Cases in the Courts of the People's Republic of China," *Sovetskaya yustitsiya*, no. 8 (1957), pp. 59–60.

Bratus, S. N., A. N. Mishutin, and N. K. Morozov, "Certain Questions of Structure and Forms of Work of the Judicial Organs of the People's Republic of China," *Sovetskoe gosudarstvo i pravo*, no. 2 (1957), pp. 53–60.

Chang Chih-jang, "The People's Courts of China after the Proclamation of the Constitution," *Sovetskoe gosudarstvo i pravo*, no. 4 (1955), pp. 32–40.

Chang Tzu-p'ei and V. E. Chugunov, "Basic Traits of the Criminal Procedure of the People's Republic of China," *Sovetskoe gosudarstvo i pravo*, no. 2 (1957), pp. 73–81.

Chou Hsin-min, "Nature of the People's Procuracy of the People's Republic of China and Its Tasks," *Sovetskoe gosudarstvo i pravo*, no. 6 (1956), pp. 44–51.

Chugunov, V. E., "Brief Outline of the Development of the Judiciary and the Procuracy in the People's Republic of China," *Uchenye zapiski* (Rostovskii na-Donu gosudarstvennyi universitet), t. 68, vyp. 4, ch. 2 (Rostov-na Donu, 1957), pp. 37–61.

Chugunov, V. E., "Inception of the Legal Procedure of the People's Republic of China," in *Rol obshchestvennosti v borbe s prestupnostyu* (The role of the public in the struggle against criminality), materialy mezhvuzovskoi nauchnoi konferentsii s uchastiem prakticheskikh rabotnikov (Voronezh: Izd. Voronezhskogo universiteta, 1960), pp. 296–308.

Chugunov, V. E., *Ugolovnoe sudoproizvodstvo Kitaiskoi Narodnoi Respubliki: ocherki* (Criminal procedure of the People's Republic of China: essays), Moscow: Gosyurizdat, 1959, 285 pp.

Chugunov, V. E., and I. F. Ryabko, "The Principle of People's Democratic Legality in the Criminal Procedure of the People's Republic of China," *Uchenye zapiski Rostovskogo na-Donu gosudarstvennogo universiteta* (Scientific notes of the Rostov-on-the-Don State University), t. 59, trudy yuridicheskogo fakulteta, vyp. 3 (1957), pp. 143–153.

Grobovenko, Ya. V., "The Court and the Procuracy of the People's Republic of China," in *Organizatsiya suda i prokuratury v SSSR* (Organization of the court and the procuracy in the USSR), ed. D. S. Karev (Moscow: Gosyurizdat, 1961), pp. 263–268.

Gudoshnikov, L. M., "The Judicial Reform of 1952–1953 and the Further Democratization of the Judicial System of the People's Republic of China," *Sovetskoe gosudarstvo i pravo*, no. 8 (1954), pp. 56–62.

Gudoshnikov, L. M., "The Role of the Judicial Organs of the People's Republic of China in Carrying Out the Land Reform," *Sovetskoe gosudarstvo i pravo*, nos. 2–3 (1953), pp. 102–107.

Gudoshnikov, L. M., *Sudebnye organy Kitaiskoi Narodnoi Respubliki* (The judicial organs of the People's Republic of China), Moscow: Gosyurizdat, 1957, 134 pp.

Koldin, V., "Participation of the People's Masses of China in the Struggle Against Criminality," *Sotsialisticheskaya zakonnost*, no. 11 (1958), pp. 53–54.

Kolmakov, V. P., "Development of Criminology and Court Expertise in the People's Republic of China," *Voprosy kriminalistiki* (Problems of criminology), no. 3 (1962), pp. 112–124.

Kolmakov, V. P., "The Method of 'Mass Line' in Procuracy and Court Work in the People's Republic of China," *Sovetskoe pravo*, Kiev, no. 3 (1959), pp. 119–123 (in Ukrainian).

Lebedinskii, V. G., and Yu. A. Kalenov, *Prokurorskii nadzor v SSSR: ocherki po kursu* (Procuracy supervision in the USSR: course outlines), Moscow: Gosyurizdat, 1957, (The Procuracy of the People's Republic of China, pp. 270–272).

Lunev, A. E., *Sud, prokuratura i gosudarstvennyi kontrol v Kitaiskoi Narodnoi Respublike* (The courts, the procuracy and state control in the People's Republic of China), Moscow: Gosyurizdat, 1956, 71 pp.

"Organization and Activity of Judicial Organs in the People's Republic of China," *Sovetskoe gosudarstvo i pravo*, no. 8 (1955), pp. 116–120. (Abridged statement of two reports given by the Minister of Justice of the PRC, Shih Liang, during the stay in the USSR of a delegation of Chinese jurists.)

Ostroumov, G., "New Elements in the Work of the Courts of the People's Republic of China," *Sovetskaya yustitsiya*, no. 9 (1959), pp. 64–66.

Shih Liang, "Answers of the Minister of Justice of the PRC, Shih Liang, to Questions from the Editors of the Journal, 'New Times,'" *Novoe vremya*, no. 29 (1955), pp. 13–14.

Shih Liang, "Organization and Activity of Judicial Organs of the People's Republic of China," *Sovetskoe gosudarstvo i pravo*, no. 8 (1955), pp. 116–120.

Shih Wei-chao and V. Chugunov, "Organization of the Bar in the People's Republic of China," *Sotsialisticheskaya zakonnost*, no. 10 (1956), pp. 52–56.

Stepanova, M., and M. Tulisov, "Thirty Days in People's China," *Sovetskaya yustitsiya*, no. 1 (1957), pp. 44–48 (organization and activity of the organs of justice of the PRC).

Strogovich, M. S., *Kurs sovetskogo ugolovnogo protsessa* (Textbook of Soviet criminal procedure), Moscow: AN SSSR, 1958, 703 pp. (The Criminal Procedure of the PRC, pp. 572–576).

Sudarikov, N. G., "Judicial Organs of the People's Republic of China," *Sotsialisticheskaya zakonnost*, no. 10 (1951), pp. 47–54.

Sudarikov, N. G., "Organization of the Courts and the Procuracy of the People's Republic of China," *Sotsialisticheskaya zakonnost*, no. 5 (1952), pp. 50–57.

Tadevosyan, V., "Legislation on the Procuracy in the People's Republic of China," *Sotsialisticheskaya zakonnost*, no. 12 (1954), pp. 39–42.

Ugolovno-protsessualnoe zakonodatelstvo zarubezhnykh sotsialisticheskikh gosudarstv (Criminal-procedural legislation of foreign socialist states), sbornik, ed. D. S. Karev (Moscow: Gosyurizdat, 1956), PRC, pp. 695–705.

Wang Hou-li, "Organization and Activity of the Judicial System of the People's Republic of China," *Sovetskaya yustitsiya*, no. 1 (1958), pp. 47–51.

Zakon ob organizatsii narodnogo suda Kitaiskoi Narodnoi Respubliki (Law on the organization of the people's courts of the People's Republic of China), Moscow: Gosyurizdat, 1955, 14 pp.

Zakon ob organizatsii prokuratury Kitaiskoi Narodnoi Respubliki (Law on the organization of the procuracy of the People's Republic of China), Moscow: Gosyurizdat, 1955, 10 pp.

354 | George Ginsburgs

9. Miscellaneous

"Chinese Legal Literature, 1955," *Sovetskoe gosudarstvo i pravo*, no. 8 (1956), pp. 154–156.

Chou Hsin-min, "Concerning the Creation of the Institute of Law of the Academy of Sciences of China," *Sovetskoe gosudarstvo i pravo*, no. 4 (1959), pp. 136–138.

"The 'Cultural Revolution' and Legal Instruction in China," *Sovetskoe gosudarstvo i pravo*, no. 11 (1966), pp. 138–140.

"Gift of the Chinese Political-Legal Association to the Institute of Law of the Academy of Sciences of the USSR named after A. Ya. Vyshinskii," *Sovetskoe gosudarstvo i pravo*, no. 3 (1955), p. 131.

Gudoshnikov, L. M., "The Chinese Law Journal 'Cheng-fa Yen-chiu' Nos. 4–6 for 1955 and Nos. 1–3 for 1956," *Sovetskoe gosudarstvo i pravo*, no. 2 (1957), pp. 144–148.

Gudoshnikov, L. M., "Chronicle of Scientific Life in the People's Republic of China," *Sovetskoe gosudarstvo i pravo*, no. 9 (1959), p. 135.

Gudoshnikov, L. M., "In the People's Republic of China," *Sovetskoe gosudarstvo i pravo*, no. 5 (1957), p. 146.

Gudoshnikov, L. M., "Journal of the Central Political-Legal Cadre School of the PRC," *Sovetskoe gosudarstvo i pravo*, no. 10 (1957), p. 145.

Gudoshnikov, L. M., "Second General Meeting of the Chinese Association of Political and Legal Sciences," *Sovetskoe gosudarstvo i pravo*, no. 6 (1956), pp. 141–142.

Gudoshnikov, L. M., "Third Meeting of the Chinese Association of Political Science and Law," *Sovetskoe gosudarstvo i pravo*, no. 1 (1959), p. 143.

Gudoshnikov, L. M., and Yu. N. Gradov, "The Chinese Law Journal 'Cheng-fa Yen-chiu'; Survey of Nos. 1–3 for 1955," *Sovetskoe gosudarstvo i pravo*, no. 1 (1956), pp. 157–160.

Gudoshnikov, L. M., and Yu. N. Gradov, "Through the Pages of the Chinese Law Journal 'Cheng-fa Yen-chiu' (Nos. 3 and 4 for 1954)," *Sovetskoe gosudarstvo i pravo*, no. 2 (1955), pp. 155–158.

Ilichev, L., "Soviet Legal Literature in the People's Republic of China: Chinese Legal Literature in the USSR," *Sovetskoe gosudarstvo i pravo*, no. 9 (1959), pp. 132–135.

"In the People's Republic of China," *Sovetskoe gosudarstvo i pravo*, no. 2 (1957), pp. 142–143 (signed with initials M.K.).

"Legal Literature of the People's Republic of China, 1956–1958," *Sovetskoe gosudarstvo i pravo*, no. 2 (1959), pp. 158–159.

Lunev, A. E., "A Book on the Visit of Chinese Jurists to the USSR: Review of *Sbornik zapisei kitaiskikh yuristov o prebyvanii v SSSR i opyte raboty sovetskikh organov yustitsii*," Peking, 1955, Vol. 1, *Sovetskoe gosudarstvo i pravo*, no. 4 (1956), pp. 153–154.

Mishutin, A., and V. Andreevskii, "Delegation of Soviet Jurists in the People's Republic of China," *Sotsialisticheskaya zakonnost*, no. 2 (1957), pp. 45–51 (on the work of the organs of justice of the PRC).

Ostroumov, G. S., and G. V. Lilie, "The Chinese Legal Journal 'Cheng-fa Yen-chiu' (Nos. 4–6 for 1956 and Nos. 1–6 for 1957)," *Sovetskoe gosudarstvo i pravo*, no. 7 (1958), pp. 144–148.

Ostroumov, G. S., and G. V. Lilie, "The Chinese Legal Journal 'Cheng-fa Yen-chiu'," *Sovetskoe gosudarstvo i pravo*, no. 12 (1959), pp. 123–126.

"Political-legal Research, Theoretical Journal of the Jurists of the People's Republic of China," *Sovetskoe gosudarstvo i pravo*, no. 7 (1954), pp. 146–147 (signed with initials A.L.).

"Scientific Conference in the Political-Legal Institute of Eastern China," *Sovetskoe gosudarstvo i pravo*, no. 5 (1958), pp. 154–155 (signed with initials V.P.K.).

"Second Scientific and Theoretical Conference of the Peking Political-Legal Institute," *Sovetskoe gosudarstvo i pravo*, no. 10 (1957), p. 145.

"The State of Scientific Research Work in the Political-Legal Institutes and the Legal Faculties of Universities of the People's Republic of China in 1956," *Sovetskoe gosudarstvo i pravo*, no. 8 (1957), pp. 144–145 (signed with initials Sh. V.).

"Stay in the Soviet Union of a Delegation of Chinese Jurists," *Sovetskoe gosudarstvo i pravo*, no. 6 (1955), pp. 107–108.

Tulisov, M. P., "Guests of the Chinese Jurists," *Sovetskoe gosudarstvo i pravo*, no. 1 (1957), pp. 121–124 (work of the judicial organs of the PRC).

Wang Shu-wen, "Discussion of the Chinese Jurists on the Right of Ownership of Capitalists to the Means of Production in Mixed State-Private Enterprises," *Sovetskoe gosudarstvo i pravo*, no. 7 (1957), pp. 142–145 (Survey of articles from the journals "Cheng-fa Yen-chiu," nos. 2, 4 and 6, 1956, and "Hua-tung Cheng-fa Hsüeh-pao," no. 1, 1956).

Glossary
Chinese- and Japanese-Language Books

Glossary

act (n.); t'iao-li 條例

act (v.); hsing-wei (kōi) 行爲

act of killing a person; sha-jen hsing-wei 殺人行爲

adjudication; shen-p'an 審判

adjudication division; shen-p'an-t'ing 審判庭

adjustment, arrangement, mediation [archaic]; t'iao-ch'u 調處

adultery; t'ung-chien 通姦

alimony; shan-yang-fei 贍養費

all; chün 均, tou 都

allocate; tiao-po 調撥

already; i 已, i-ching 已經

already punished [Ch'ing code]; i-chüeh 已決

ambassador [current usage]; ta-shih 大使, ti-i-teng ch'in-ch'ai 第一等欽差

and; yü 與

animals; tung-wu 動物

arbitration; chung-ts'ai (chūsai) 仲裁

assistant professor; fu-chiao-shou 副教授

at; yü 於

authority; minken 民權

based on; chi-yü 基於, ni motozuite に基いて

based on the above discussion; chi-shang lun-chieh 基上論結

bear responsibility; tse-jen 責任

beer; bīru ビール

believe a coerced statement; pi-kung-hsin 逼供信

belligerency; chiao-chan t'uan-t'i 交戰團體

bill of prosecution; ch'i-su-shu 起訴書

blockade; feng-kang 封港, feng-so 封鎖

bring; ch'ü 取

bring up [a case] for examination; t'i-ch'i shen-ch'a 提起審查

bring up [an accused] for questioning; t'i-ch'i shen-wen 提起審問

buy; mai 買

cabotage [PRC]; yen-an hang-yün 沿岸航運

cabotage [ROC]; yen-an mao-i ch'üan 沿岸貿易權

cadre; kan-pu 幹部

cadre's meeting; kan-pu-hui (kambukai) 幹部會

can, may, shall; te 得

candid; t'an-pai-ti 坦白的

capitulation [PRC]; wai-jen t'e-ch'üan t'iao-k'uan 外人特權條款

capitulation [ROC]; ling-shih ts'ai-p'an t'iao-k'uan 領事裁判條款

care for [support]; shan-yang 贍養

case discussed by three members; san-yüan t'ao-lun 三員討論

celestial body; t'ien-t'i 天體

central country, middle kingdom, China; Chūgoku 中國

Chinese technique for reading Japanese; ho-wen han-tu-fa (wabun kandoku hō) 和文漢讀法

civil law; minpō 民法

clausula rebus sic stantibus [PRC]; ch'ing-shih pu-pien t'iao-k'uan 情勢不變條款

clausula rebus sic stantibus [ROC]; ch'ing-shih pien-ch'ien t'iao-k'uan 情勢變遷條款

code, Taihō; taihō ritsuryō 大寶律令

code, Tokugawa; osadamegaki 御定書

code, Yōrō; yōrō ritsuryō 養老律令

collective security; chi-t'i an-ch'üan 集體安全, shūdan teki anzen hoshō 集團的安全保障

competence theory; ch'üan-hsien shuo 權限說

complaint by injured party; kao-su 告訴, k'ung-su 控訴

compulsive settlement; ch'iang-chih chieh-chüeh 強制解決

comrades' court, comrades' adjudication committee; t'ung-chih shen-p'an-hui 同志審判會

confession; t'an-pai 坦白, tzu-pai 自白

confession [before discovery]; tzu-shou 自首

conspiracy; kung-mou 共謀

conspiratorial murder, secretly-planned murder; yin-mou sha-jen 陰謀殺人

conspire, secretly plan; yin-mou 陰謀

constitute; chü-pei 具備

constitution; hsien-fa (kempō) 憲法

constitutional government; kensei 憲政

consul; ling-shih 領事

consultation [PRC]; hsieh-shang 協商

consultation [ROC]; tzu-shang 諮商

contiguous zone [PRC]; p'i-lien ti-tai 毗連地帶

contiguous zone [ROC]; lin-chieh ch'ü 鄰接區

continental shelf [PRC]; ta-lu chia 大陸架

continental shelf [ROC]; ta-lu p'eng 大陸棚

contraband; chin-chih-p'in 禁制品, chin-wu 禁物

control; kuan-chih 管制, kuan-shu 管束

corporation; fa-jen (hōjin) 法人

counsellor [PRC]; ts'an-tsan 參贊

counsellor [ROC]; ts'an-shih 參事

courier [PRC]; wai-chiao hsin-shih 外交信使

courier [ROC]; wai-chiao hsin-ch'ai 外交信差

court; fa-yüan 法院, fa-t'ing 法庭

crime of killing a person; sha-jen-tsui 殺人罪

decided purchase contract; p'ai-kou 派購

decision; chieh-chüeh 解決

decision on a case made by the three chiefs; san-chang ting-an 三長定案

decisions approved by the Party ccm-mittee; tang-wei p'i-chun 黨委批准

decree; fa-ling 法令

defendant; pei-kao 被告

democracy; min-chu (minshu) 民主, te-mo-k'o-la-hsi 德謨克拉西

deprivation [of political rights]; po-to 剝奪, ch'ih-to 褫奪

detain; chü-liu 拘留

diplomacy; wai-chiao 外交

diplomatic relations; wai-chiao kuan-hsi 外交關係

disarmament; ts'ai-chün 裁軍, gumbi shukushō 軍備縮小

dispute; chiu-fen 糾紛

"dispute, quarrel, or disagreement"; chiu-fen, ch'ao-chia huo i-chien pu-t'ung 糾紛, 吵架或意見不同

doctrine of continuous voyage [PRC]; chi-hsü hang-ch'eng chu-i 繼續航程主義

doctrine of continuous voyage [ROC]; chi-hsü hang-hai chu-i 繼續航海主義

dualism; erh-yüan lun 二元論

economy; keizai 經濟

edict; yü 諭

education-and-rehabilitation through labor; lao-tung chiao-yang 勞動教養

enemy character; ti-hsing 敵性

enforce; tu-ts'u 督促

escape from prison; yüeh-yü t'o-t'ao 越獄脫逃

examine, investigate; shen-ch'a 審查

exchange of notes; huan-wen 換文, kōkan kōbun 交換公文

exequatur [PRC]; ling-shih wei-jen-shu 領事委任書

exequatur [ROC]; ling-shih cheng-shu 領事證書

explanation; setsumei 說明

extradition [current usage]; yin-tu 引渡

extradition; chiao-ch'u 交出

extradition [return]; chiao-huan 交還

fabricate evidence; wei-tsao cheng-chü 偽造證據

family; chia-t'ing 家庭

fight, brawl; tou-ou 鬪毆
five generations; wu tai 五代
fixed purchase contract; ting-kou 訂購
foreign policy; wai-chiao cheng-ts'e 外
交政策
forget it!; suan-le 算了
four withs; ssu-t'ung 四同

gas; wa-ssu 瓦斯, gasu ガス
general provisions; tsung-tse (sōsoku)
總則
genocide; mieh-chüeh chung-tsu 滅絕種
族
genocide [PRC]; mieh-chung-tsui 滅種
罪
genocide [ROC]; ts'an-hai jen-ch'ün-
tsui 殘害人群罪
genocide [to cause harm to or to destroy
human groups in a ruthless manner];
ts'an-hai jen-ch'ün 殘害人群
genocide [to cause harm to or to destroy
racial groups]; wei-hai chung-tsu 危
害種族
go (v.); hsing 行, yuku 行く
good offices [current usage]; wo-hsüan
斡旋

habeas corpus [ROC]; t'i-shen 提審
handle; ch'u-li 處理
heir; hsiang-hsü-jen (sōzokunin) 相續人
homicide, murder; sha-jen 殺人
homicide case, murder case; sha-jen-an
殺人案
horse; ma (uma) 馬
human rights; jen-ch'üan 人權

if; ju 如, ju-kuo 如果
incite; chiao-so 教唆
individuals; ko-jen 個人
individuals [residents]; chü-min 居民
ineffective; wu-hsiao 無效
injure by beating; ta-shang 打傷
instructions; chih-shih 指示
insurgency [PRC]; wu-chuang pao-
tung t'uan-t'i 武裝暴動團體
insurgency [ROC]; p'an-luan t'uan-t'i
叛亂團體

international comity; kuo-chi li-jang 國
際禮讓
international custom; kuo-chi kuan-li 國
際慣例
international law; wan-kuo kung-fa 萬
國公法, wan-kuo lü-li 萬國律例
international law [current usage]; kuo-
chi fa 國際法
international practice; kuo-chi t'ung-li
國際通例
intervention, interference; yü-wen t'o-
kuo cheng-shih 與聞它國政事, kan-yü
干預
investigation; chen-ch'a 偵查, tiao-ch'a
調查

joint office for three chiefs; san-chang
lien-ho pan-kung 三長聯合辦公
judge; fa-kuan 法官, shen-p'an-yüan 審
判員, t'ui-shih 推事
judge [officer of the court]; yü-shen-
yüan 預審員
juror, [people's] assessor; p'ei-shen-
yüan 陪審員

labor union; rōdō kumiai 勞動組合
law; lü-li 律例
laws; fa 法, fa-lü 法律
law-making treaties; li-fa t'iao-yüeh 立
法條約
laws and orders; fa-lü yü ming-ling 法律
與命令
laws and regulations; fa-lü yü kuei-tse
法律與規則
lecturer; chiang-shih 講師
letter of recall; chao-hui kuo-shu 召回
國書
letter of recall [current usage]; tz'u-jen
kuo-shu 辭任國書
literature; bungaku 文學
litigation issue; sung-cheng 訟爭

make trouble; sheng-shih 生事
manage; torishimaru 取り締る
maritime prize statute; hai-shang pu-
huo t'iao-li 海上捕獲條例
meaning translation [free translation];

iyaku 意譯
measures; pan-fa 辦法
mediate; t'iao-chieh 調解
mediation; chung-pao 中保
mediation [current usage]; t'iao-t'ing 調停
memorial; tsou 奏
ministry of foreign affairs; wai-chiao pu 外交部
mobilize; dōin 動員
monopoly; dokusen 獨占
murder; mou-sha 謀殺
mutual nonintervention in internal affairs; hu pu kan-she nei-cheng 互不干涉內政

necessary; hsü 須
negotiated contract; i-kou 議購
negotiation; shang-i 商議
neutrality; chü-wai 局外, chung-li 中立
not as it ought to be; shih pu-ying-kai-ti 是不應該的
not satisfactory; pu t'uo-tang 不妥當
not yet punished [Ch'ing code]; wei-chüeh 未決
note sent by one state to another; kuo-shu 國書

object theory; k'o-t'i-shuo 客體說, tui-hsiang shuo 對象說
occasion; baai 場合
occupation; yüan-shih chan-yu 原始占有
offender; fan-jen 犯人
offender whose case has already been adjudged; i-chüeh-fan 已決犯
offender whose case has not been adjudged; wei-chüeh-fan 未決犯
open [to the public]; kung-k'ai 公開
order contract; i-kou ho-t'ung 議購合同
orders; ming-ling 命令
outer space; yü-chou k'ung-chien 宇宙空間
outer space [PRC]; wai-ts'eng k'ung-chien 外層空間
outer space [ROC]; t'ai-k'ung 太空

parental officials; fu-mu-kuan 父母官
peace treaty; ho-yüeh 和約
peaceful coexistence [PRC]; ho-p'ing kung-ch'u 和平共處
peaceful coexistence [ROC]; ho-p'ing kung-ts'un 和平共存
pencil; empitsu 鉛筆
people; min 民
people's money, i.e., currency of the PRC; jen-min-pi 人民幣
people's tribunal; fa-t'ing 法庭
people's tribunal head, chief judge of an adjudication division; t'ing-chang 庭長
perjury; wei-cheng 偽證
philosophy; tetsugaku 哲學
pirate; hai-tao 海盜
plaintiff; yüan-kao 原告
plan, try; ch'i-t'u 企圖
political-legal institutions of higher learning; cheng-fa yüan-hsiao 政法院校
power; ken 權
pre-indictment examination or investigation; yü-shen 預審
preliminary; yü-hsien 預先
preparatory; yü-pei 預備
preparatory examination; yü-pei shen-ch'a 預備審查
preparatory hearing; yü-pei shen-li 預備審理
preparatory interrogation; yü-pei shen-hsün 預備審訊
prescription; lao-ku 牢固, nien-chiu shou-yung 年久收用
private relationship; p'ing-tu 砰度
privilege; ch'üan-li 權利
privilege [PRC]; t'e-ch'üan 特權
privilege [ROC]; yu-li 優例
prize court; pu-huo shen-chien t'ing 捕獲審檢廳
prize tribunals; chan-li fa-yüan 戰利法院; pu-huo shen-chien so 捕獲審檢所
prize tribunals [current usage]; pu-huo fa-yüan 捕獲法院
procedure; shou-hsü (tetsuzuki) 手續
professional; chuan 專

professional discipline; chuan yeh 專業

professor; chiao-shou 教授

proletarian internationalism; wu-ch'an chieh-chi kuo-chi chu-i 無產階級國際主義

propriety; li 禮

provide with shelter [also used for a coercive roundup of undesirables]; shou-jung 收容

province of mankind; jen-lei ch'üan-t'i chih shih 人類全體之事

provisions; kuei-ting 規定

proviso; tadashi-gaki 但書

pursue and capture; chui-chi 追緝

pushed away [their] work; t'ui-ch'u liao-shih 推出了事

questioning, interrogation; shen-wen 審問

ratification; chun 准, chun-hsing 准行

ratification [current usage]; p'i-chun 批准

readjudication; tsai-shen 再審

recognition of belligerency; chiao-chan t'uan-t'i ti ch'eng-jen 交戰團體的承認

red; hung 紅

re-examination of a case; t'i-shen 提審

reform; chiao-hua 教化, kai-tsao 改造

regulations; fa-kuei 法規, kuei-tse 規則

rehabilitation-through-labor; lao-tung chiao-yang 勞動教養

reimburse; ch'ang-fu 償付

relationship of living together; t'ung-chü kuan-hsi 同居關係

reporting an official's unlawful conduct or dereliction of duty [denunciation]; chien-chü 檢舉

reprisal; ch'iang-ch'ang 強償

residual sovereignty [PRC]; ts'an-ch'üeh ti chu-ch'üan 殘缺的主權

residual sovereignty [ROC]; sheng-yü chu-ch'üan 剩餘主權

right of angary [PRC]; chan-yung chung-li ts'ai-ch'an ch'üan 占用中立財產權

right of angary [ROC]; fei-ch'ang cheng-yung ch'üan 非常徵用權

rights [civil, human, etc.]; ch'üan-li (kenri) 權利

rights of the person; jen-shen ch'üan-li 人身權利

seize [a suspect]; chü-t'i 拘提

self-defense; tzu-hu 自護

self-defense [current usage]; tzu-wei 自衞

sell; mai 賣

send down; hsia-fang 下放

settlement or placement [of vagrants or ex-convicts]; an-chih 安置

"seven doctors" incident (1903); shichi hakushi 七博士

shall, should, ought to; ying 應

six codes; roppō zensho 六法全書

socialist international law; she-hui chu-i kuo-chi fa 社會主義國際法

sound translation [transliteration]; onyaku 音譯

sovereignty; chu-ch'üan 主權

space law; t'ai-k'ung fa 太空法, uchū kūkan hō 宇宙空間法

space theory; k'ung-chien shuo 空間說

subject; chu-t'i 主體

supplement; fu-tse 附則

suspect (n.); hsien-i-fan 嫌疑犯

system; t'i-hsi 體系

take a wife; ch'ü 娶

tale; monogatari 物語

talk around a subject; man-t'an 漫談

teaching assistant; chu-chiao 助教

telegram; tien-pao (dempō) 電報

territory; ling-t'u 領土, ling-yü 領域

theory of competence; kuan-hsia shuo 管轄說

third party complaint [accusation]; kao-fa 告發

tien; tien 典

"to rebel is justified"; tsao-fan yu-li 造反有理

treaty; meng-yüeh 盟約, t'iao-yüeh 條約, yüeh 約

trees, flowers, and other plants; chih-wu 植物

trial; shen-p'an 審判

trial preparation; yü-pei shen-p'an 預備
審判

two parties; liang-tsao 兩造

unequal treaty; pu-p'ing-teng t'iao-
yüeh 不平等條約

unified; t'ung-i 統一

usage; li 例

vassal state [PRC]; fu-yung kuo 附庸國

vassal state [ROC]; shu-kuo 屬國

veto power; fou-chüeh-ch'üan 否決權,
kyohi ken 拒否權

voluntary surrender; tzu-shou 自首

war criminal; chan-fan 戰犯, sensō
hanzai jin 戰爭犯罪人

Chinese- and Japanese-Language Books

Asai Torao 淺井虎夫. *Shina ni okeru hōten hensan no enkaku* 支那に於ける法典編纂の沿革.

Asakura 朝倉治彦 et al., eds. *Meiji sesō hennen jiten* 明治世相編年辭典. Tokyo: Tōkyōdō, 1965.

Chan-kuo ts'e 戰國策. Shanghai: Shang-wu yin-shu kuan, 1935.

Chang Ch'i-kuang 張緝光. *Han-i hsin fa-lü tz'u-tien* 漢譯新法律辭典. Translated by Hsü Yung-hsi 徐用錫. Tokyo: Ching shih i-hsüeh-kuan, 1905.

Chang Chih-tung 張之洞. *Chang Wen-hsiang kung ch'üan chi (ch'üan hsüeh p'ien)* 張文襄公全集 (勸學篇). Peking: Ch'u-hsüeh ching-lu, 1937.

Chang Ch'un-t'ao 張春濤, Kuo K'ai-wen 郭開文, and Ch'en Chieh 陳傑. *Han-i fa-lü ching-chi tz'u-tien* 漢譯法律經濟辭典. Tokyo: Keibunkan shokyoku, 1907.

Chang Jo-yü 張若愚. *Fa-hsüeh chi-pen chih-shih chiang-hua* 法學基本知識講話. Peking: Chung-kuo ch'ing-nien ch'u pan she, 1963.

Ch'ang-k'uang ch'i-yeh shih-yung fa-kuei shou-ts'e 厰礦企業實用法規手冊. Peking: Fa-lü ch'u pan she, 1958.

Ch'en Ku-yüan 陳顧遠. *Chung-kuo kuo-chi fa su yüan* 中國國際法溯源. Shanghai: Shang-wu yin-shu kuan, 1934.

Ch'en Lü-chieh 陳履潔. *P'ing-shih kuo-chi kung-fa* 平時國際公法. N.p., 1907.

Cheng Ching-i 鄭競毅. *Fa-lü ta-tz'u-shu* 法律大辭書. Shanghai: Shang-wu yin-shu kuan, 1936.

Ch'ien Hsün 錢恂, and Tung Hung-wei 董鴻禕. *Jih-pen fa-kuei chien-chu* 日本法規簡註. Shanghai: Shang-wu yin-shu kuan, 1907.

Chien-fei ssu-fa chih-tu 奸匪司法制度. Nei-cheng-pu tiao-ch'a-chü 內政部調查局. Taipei, 1950.

Chien-wei Su-Huan pien-ch'ü jen-min ts'ai-ch'an-ch'üan pao-chang t'iao-li 奸偽蘇皖邊區人民財產權保障條例. Kuo-min-tang chung-yang tang-pu tiao-ch'a t'ung-chi-chü 國民黨中央黨部調查統計局. Taipei, n.d.

Chin-Chi-Lu-Yü pien-ch'ü fa-ling hui-pien 晉冀魯豫邊區法令彙編. Chin-Chi-Lu-Yü pien-ch'ü cheng-fu 晉冀魯豫邊區政府.

Chou Chia-ch'ing 周家清. *Hun-yin-fa chiang-hua* 婚姻法講話. Peking: Chung-kuo ch'ing-nien ch'u pan she, 1964.

Chou Keng-sheng 周鯁生. *Kuo-chi fa ta-kang* 國際法大綱. Shanghai: Shang-wu yin-shu kuan, 1929.

Ch'üan-kuo kao-teng hsüeh-hsiao chao-sheng wei-yüan-hui 全國高等學校招生委員會. *I-chiu-wu-ssu nien shu-ch'i kao-teng hsüeh-hsiao chao-sheng sheng-hsüeh chih-tao* 一九五四年暑期高等學校招生升學指導. Peking, 1954.

Chung-hua jen-min kung-ho-kuo fa-kuei hui-pien 中華人民共和國法規彙編. Kuo-wu-yüan fa-chih-chü 國務院法制局. 13 vols. Peking: Fa-lü ch'u pan she, 1956–1964.

Chung-hua jen-min kung-ho-kuo hsing-fa tsung-tse chiang-i 中華人民共和國刑法總則講義. Chung-yang cheng-fa kan-pu hsüeh-hsiao hsing-fa chiao-yen-shih 中央政法幹部學校刑法教研室. Peking: Fa-lü ch'u pan she, 1957.

Chung-hua jen-min kung-ho-kuo hun-yin-fa chi-pen wen-t'i 中華人民共和國婚姻法基本問題. Peking, 1958.

Chung-hua jen-min kung-ho-kuo kao-teng chiao-yü-pu 中華人民共和國高等教育部. *Kao-teng hsüeh-hsiao chao-sheng sheng-hsüeh chih-tao (chuan-yeh chieh-shao pu-fen) 1958* 高等學校招生升學指導（專業介紹部分）1958. Peking: Kao-teng chiao-yü ch'u pan she, 1958.

Chung-hua jen-min kung-ho-kuo min-fa chi-pen wen-t'i 中華人民共和國民法基本問題. Chung-yang cheng-fa kan-pu hsüeh-hsiao 中央政法幹部學校. Peking, 1958.

Chung-hua jen-min kung-ho-kuo t'iao-yüeh chi 中華人民共和國條約集. Chung-hua jen-min kung-ho-kuo wai-chiao-pu 中華人民共和國外交部. Peking: Fa-lü ch'u pan she, 1961.

Chung-hua jen-min kung-ho-kuo yu-hao t'iao-yüeh hui-pien 中華人民共和國友好條約滙編. Chung-hua jen-min kung-ho-kuo wai-chiao-pu 中華人民共和國外交部. Peking: Shih-chieh chih-shih ch'u pan she, 1965.

Chung-hua jen-min kung-ho-kuo yu-kuan kung-an kung-tso fa-kuei hui-pien 中華人民共和國有關公安工作法規彙編. Peking: Ch'ün-chung ch'u pan she, 1957.

Chung-kuo jen-min ta-hsüeh fa-lü-hsi kuo-chia yü fa-ch'üan li-lun chiao-yen-shih, ed. 中國人民大學法律系國家與法權理論教研室. *Lun jen-min min-chu chuan-cheng ho jen-min min-chu fa-chih* 論人民民主專政和人民民主法制. Peking: Chung-kuo jen-min ta-hsüeh ch'u pan she, 1958.

Chung-kuo jen-min ta-hsüeh kuo-chia ho fa-ch'üan li-shih yen-chiu-shih, ed. 中國人民大學國家和法權歷史研究室. *Chung-kuo kuo-chia ho fa-ch'üan li-shih ts'an-k'ao tzu-liao (Ti-san-tz'u kuo-nei ko-ming chan-cheng shih-ch'i chieh-fang-ch'ü ti cheng-ts'e fa-ling hsüan-chi)* 中國國家和法權歷史參考資料（第三次國內革命戰爭時期解放區的政策法令選集）. Peking, 1958.

Chung-kuo jen-min ta-hsüeh min-fa chiao-yen-shih, ed. 中國人民大學民法教研室. *Chung-hua jen-min kung-ho-kuo min-fa ts'an-k'ao tzu-liao* 中華人民共和國民法參考資料. Peking: Chung-kuo jen-min ta-hsüeh ch'u pan she, 1956.

Chung-kuo jen-min ta-hsüeh min-fa chiao-yen-shih, ed. 中國人民大學民法教研室. *Chung-hua jen-min kung-ho-kuo min-fa tzu-liao hui-pien* 中華人民共和國民法資料彙編. Peking: Chung-kuo jen-min ta-hsüeh, 1954.

Chung-kuo jen-min ta-hsüeh shen-p'an-fa chiao-yen-shih, ed. 中國人民大學審判法教研室. *Chung-hua jen-min kung-ho-kuo min-shih su-sung ts'an-k'ao tzu-liao (Ti-i chi)* 中華人民共和國民事訴訟參考資料（第一集）. Peking, 1958.

Chung-kuo jen-min ta-hsüeh t'u-shu-kuan, ed. 中國人民大學圖書館. *T'u-shu fen-lei fa* 圖書分類法. Peking, 1962.

Chung-kuo k'o-hsüeh-yüan fa-hsüeh-yen-chiu-so jen-min kung-she yen-chiu hsiao-tsu, ed. 中國科學院法學研究所人民公社研究小組. *Kao-chü jen-min kung-she ti hung-ch'i sheng-li ch'ien-chin* 高舉人民公社的紅旗勝利前進. Peking: Fa-lü ch'u pan she, 1960.

Chung-yang jen-min cheng-fu fa-ling hui-pien 中央人民政府法令彙編. 7 vols. Peking, 1952–1955.

Dai kanwa jiten 大漢和辭典.

Daisankai Hōchū Hōritsuka Daihyōdan, ed. 第三回訪中法律家代表團. *Kakumei no naka no Chūgoku 1965* 革命のなかの中國 1965. Tokyo: Rōdō jumpō sha, 1966.

Fan-kung yu-chi-tui t'u-chi fu-chien lien-chiang lu-huo fei-fang wen-chien hui-pien 反共游擊隊突擊福建連江鹵獲匪方文件彙編. Kuo-fang-pu ch'ing-pao-chü 國防

部情報局. Taipei, 1966.

Fei-ch'ing yen-chiu tsa-chih-she, ed. 匪情研究雜誌社. *I-chiu-liu-ch'i fei-ch'ing nien-pao* 一九六七匪情年報. Taipei, 1967.

Fei-ch'ü ssu-fa chih-tu N 1 匪區司法制度 N 1. Kuo-min-tang chung-yang wei-yüan-hui ti-liu-tsu 國民黨中央委員會第六組. Taipei, 1958.

Fei-wei fa-kuei chi-yao 匪偽法規輯要. Ssu-fa hsing-cheng-pu tiao-ch'a-chü 司法行政部調查局. Taipei, 1961 (vols. I, II); 1962 (vol. III).

Fei-wei "Hsien-fa ts'ao-an" ti p'ou-shih 匪偽"憲法草案"的剖視. Hsing-cheng-yüan she-chi wei-yüan-hui 行政院設計委員會. Taipei, 1954.

Fei-wei ti-fang ssu-fa chih p'ou-shih 匪偽地方司法之剖視. She-k'ao-hui 設考會. Taipei, 1954.

Fukushima Masao 福島正夫. *Chūgoku no hō to seiji* 中國の法と政治. Tokyo: Nihon hyōron sha, 1966.

——*Chūgoku no jinmin minshu seiken* 中國の人民民主政權. Tokyo: Tokyo daigaku shuppan kai, 1965.

——, ed. *Shakai shugi kokka no saiban seido* 社會主義國家の裁判制度. Tokyo: Tokyo daigaku shuppan kai, 1965.

——, Ubukata Naokichi 幼方直吉, and Hasegawa Ryōichi 長谷川良一. *Chūgoku no saiban* 中國の裁判. Tokyo: Tōyō keizai shimpō sha, 1957.

Han-ying shih-shih yung-yü tz'u-hui 漢英時事用語詞滙. Hsin-hua t'ung-hsün she wai-wen kan-pu hsüeh-hsiao 新華通訊社外文幹部學校. Peking: Shang-wu yin-shu kuan, 1964 (preliminary edition).

Hatano Kanichi 波多野乾一. *Chūgoku kyōsantō shi* 中國共產黨史. Tokyo: Jiji tsūshin sha, 1961.

Heibonsha 平凡社. *Jimmei jiten* 人名辭典.

Hozumi Nobushige 穗積陳重. *Hōsō yawa* 法窗夜話. Tokyo, 1932.

Hsien-hsing fa-ling hui-chi 現行法令彙集. Chin-Ch'a-Chi pien-ch'ü hsing-cheng wei-yüan-hui 晉察冀邊區行政委員會.

Hsien-tai kuo-chi fa shang ti chi-pen yüan-tse ho wen-t'i 現代國際法上的基本原則和問題. Peking: Fa-lü ch'u pan she, 1956.

Hsing-chao chih-chang 星軺指掌. 1876 [?].

Hsing-fa tsung-tse fen-chieh tzu-liao hui-pien 刑法總則分解資料彙編. Ch'üan-kuo jen-min tai-piao ta-hui ch'ang-wu wei-yüan-hui fa-lü shih 全國人民代表大會常務委員會法律室. Peking: Fa-lü ch'u pan she, 1957.

Hsü Shih-tseng 徐師曾. *Wen-t'i ming-pien* 文體明辨. N.p.: Shou kuai t'ang, 1580.

Huang Ta 黃達. *Wo kuo she-hui chu-i ching-chi chung ti huo-pi ho huo-pi liu-t'ung* 我國社會主義經濟中的貨幣和貨幣流通. Peking: Chung-kuo ts'ai-cheng ching-chi ch'u pan she, 1964.

Itō Masami 伊藤正己, ed. *Gaikoku hō to Nihon hō* 外國法と日本法. Tokyo: Iwanami shoten, 1966.

Jen-min ssu-fa kung-tso shih wu-ch'an chieh-chi chuan-cheng ti jui-li wu-ch'i (k'o-hsüeh yen-chiu yüeh-chin ts'ung-shu) 人民司法工作是無產階級專政的銳利武器(科學研究躍進叢書). Peking, 1958.

Jih-pen hsing-fa 日本刑法. Edited by Suekawa Hiroshi 末川博. Peking: Fa-lü ch'u pan she, 1956.

Jiyū Hōsōdan 自由法曹團, ed. *Jiyū Hōsōdan monogatari* 自由法曹團物語. Tokyo: Rōdō jumpō sha, 1966.

K'ang-Jih ken-chü ti cheng-ts'e t'iao-li hui-chi, Shen-Kan-Ning chih pu 抗日根據地政策條例彙集陝甘寧之部. 1942.

Kao Ming-k'ai 高名凱, and Liu Cheng-t'an 劉正埮. *Hsien-tai han-yü wai-lai tzu yen-chiu* 現代漢語外來字研究. Peking: Wen-tzu kai-ke ch'u pan she, 1958.

Ko-kuo chiao-she kung-fa lun 各國交涉公法論. Shanghai: Hsiao ts'ang shan-fan, 1896.

Kung-an kung-tso yüeh-chin chi 公安工作躍進集. Fa-lü ch'u pan she 法律出版社. Peking, 1958.

Kung-fa hui-t'ung 公法會通. Peking: Pei-yang shu-chü, 1898.

Kung-fa pien-lan 公法便覽. Peking: T'ung wen kuan, 1877.

Kung-fei fa-chih wen-t'i ti fen-hsi 共匪法制問題的分析. Ssu-fa hsing-cheng-pu tiao-ch'a-chü 司法行政部調查局. Taipei, 1959.

Kung-fei fa-ling kuei-chang hui-pien 共匪法令規章彙編. Kuo-min-tang chung-yang tang-pu tiao-ch'a t'ung-chi-chü 國民黨中央黨部調查統計局. Taipei.

Kung-fei i-nien lai ssu-fa kung-tso ti ch'ing-k'uang fen-hsi 共匪一年來司法工作的情況分析. Nei-cheng-pu tiao-ch'a chü 內政部調查局. Taipei, 1957.

Kung-fei ssu-fa chih yen-chiu 共匪司法之研究. Ch'en Shan 陳珊. Taipei: Yang-ming-shan chuang, 1957.

Kung-fei ssu-fa chih-tu chih yen-chiu 共匪司法制度之研究. Ssu-fa hsing-cheng-pu tiao-ch'a-chü 司法行政部調查局. Taipei, 1958.

Kung-fei ssu-fa hsien-k'uang 共匪司法現況. Kuo-chia an-ch'üan-chü 國家安全局. Taipei.

Kung-fei ssu-fa kai-ko chih yen-chiu 共匪司法改革之研究. Kuo-fang-pu ti-erh-t'ing 國防部第二廳. Taipei, 1953.

Kung-fei ti ssu-fa kung-tso 共匪的司法工作. Ssu-fa hsing-cheng-pu tiao-ch'a-chü 司法行政部調查局. Taipei, 1956.

Kuo-wu-yüan fa-chih-chü fa-chih-shih yen-chiu-shih 國務院法制局法制史研究室. *Ch'ing-shih-kao hsing-fa-chih chu-chieh* 清史稿刑法志註解. Peking: Fa-lü ch'u pan she, 1957.

Kuo-wu-yüan fa-chih-chü fa-chih-shih yen-chiu-shih 國務院法制局法制史研究室. *Chung-kuo fa-chih-shih ts'an-k'ao shu-mu chien-chieh* 中國法制史參考書目簡介. Peking: Fa-lü ch'u pan she, 1957.

Lao-tung pao-hu fa-kuei hsüan-pien 勞動保護法規選編. Peking: Fa-lü ch'u pan she, 1961.

Lei Sung-sheng 雷崧生. *Kuo-chi fa yüan-li* 國際法原理. Taipei: Cheng chung shu-chü, 1960.

Li Ch'eng-jui 李成瑞, and Tso Ch'un-t'ai 左春台. *She-hui chu-i ti yin-hang kung-tso* 社會主義的銀行工作. Peking, 1964.

Liang Ch'i-ch'ao 梁啓超. *Yin-ping-shih wen-chi* 飲冰室文集. Shanghai: Chung-hua shu-chü, 1926.

Lin Ch'i 林棨. *Kuo-chi fa ching-i* 國際法精義. Fukien: Min-hsüeh hui, 1903.

Liu Ling-yü 劉令輿. *Liu-fa ch'üan-shu t'ung-shih* 六法全書通釋. Taipei, 1965.

Lu-ti chan-li hsin hsüan 陸地戰例新選. Shanghai: Shen chi shu chuang, 1897.

Mao Tse-tung 毛澤東. *Mao Tse-tung hsüan chi* 毛澤東選集. Peking: Jen-min ch'u pan she, 1964.

Maruyama Masao 丸山眞男. *Nihon no shisō* 日本の思想. Tokyo: Iwanami shoten, 1961.

Meiji bunka zenshū: gaikoku bunkahen 明治文化全集外國文化編. Meiji bunka ken-kyū kai 明治文化研究會. Rev. ed. Tokyo: Nihon hyōron shin sha, 1955.

Minpō goi kōhon 民法語彙講本. Tokyo: Hōmushō, 1886.

Min-tsu kung-tso shih-yung fa-kuei shou-ts'e 民族工作實用法規手冊. Peking: Fa-lü ch'u pan she, 1958.

Miyazaki Kōjirō 宮崎孝治郎, ed. *Shin hikaku konyinhō* 新比較婚姻法. 4 vols. Tokyo: Keisō shobō, 1960–62.

Mukōyama Hiroo 向山寛夫. *Chūgoku rōdō hō no kenkyū* 中國勞働法の研究. Tokyo: Chūō keizai kenkyūjo, 1968.

Murakami Sadakichi 村上定吉. *Shina rekidai no keisei enkaku to genkō keihō* 支那歴代の形成沿革と現行刑法. Tokyo, 1932.

Nakajima Hanjirō 中島半次郎. *Nisshin kan no kyōiku kankei* 日清間の教育關係. Tokyo, 1909.

Nihon Hōritsuka Hōchū Daihyōdan 日本法律家訪中代表團. *Chūgoku no hō to shakai* 中國の法と社會. Tokyo: Shin dokusho sha, 1960.

Nihon ni okeru Ajia-Afurika kenkyū no genjō to kaidai—bunken mokuroku kaidai Chūgoku: hōritsu 日本におけるアジア・アフリカ研究の現状と解題―分見目綫解題中國：法律. Ajia-Afurika sōgō kenkyū soshiki アジアアフリカ綜合研究組織. Tokyo, 1966.

Niida Noboru 仁井田陞. *Chūgoku hōseishi kenkyū, kazoku hō* 中國法制史研究家族法. Tokyo: Tokyo daigaku shuppan kai, 1962.

—— *Chūgoku shakai no hō to rinri* 中國社會の法と倫理. Tokyo: Kōbundo, 1954.

Niijima Atsuyoshi 新島淳良, and Nomura Kōichi 野村浩一. *Gendai Chūgoku nyū-mon: nani o yomubeki ka* 現代中國入門―何を讀むべきか. Tokyo: Keisō shobō, 1965.

Nung-ts'un shih-yung fa-kuei shou-ts'e 農村實用法規手冊. Peking: Fa-lü ch'u pan she, 1958.

Okada Asatarō 岡田朝太郎. *Hikaku keihō* 比較刑法. 2 vols. Tokyo, 1936.

—— *Keihō kakuron* 刑法各論. Tokyo, 1925.

—— *Keihō sōron* 刑法總論. 2nd ed. Tokyo, 1932.

—— *Nihon keihō ron (kakuron no bu)* 日本刑法論（各論の部）. Tokyo, 1896.

——, ed. *Shin keiritsu* 清刑律. Tokyo, 1912.

Osatake Takeshi 尾佐竹猛. *Ishin zengo ni okeru shisō* 維新前後に於ける思想. Tokyo, 1925.

Ōtsuki Fumihiko 大槻文彦. *Mitsukuri Rinshō kunden* 箕作麟祥君傳. Tokyo: Maruzen, 1907.

Pei-ching shih jen-min fa-yüan pi-shu-ch'u 北京市人民法院秘書處. *Jen-min ssu-fa kung-tso chü-yü* 人民司法工作舉隅. Peking: Hsin-hua shu-tien, 1950.

P'u-t'ung pai-k'o ch'üan-shu 普通百科全書. Tokyo: Hui wen-hsüeh she, 1904.

Sakamoto Tsuyoshi 坂元毅. *Soren to Chūkyō no kaijō hoken* ソ連と中共の海上保險. Tokyo: Bungadō shoten, 1961.

Sanetō Keishū 實藤惠秀. *Chūgokujin Nihon ryūgakushi* 中國人日本留學史. Tokyo: Kuroshio, 1960.

—— *Chung-i jih-wen shu-mu-lu (Chūyaku nichibunsho mokuroku)* 中譯日文書目錄. Tokyo: Zaidan hōjin kokusai bunka shinkō kai, 1945.

San-nien fei-ch'ing (Ssu-fa pu-fen) 三年匪情（司法部分）. Ssu-fa hsing-cheng-pu tiao-ch'a-chü 司法行政部調查局. Taipei, 1953.

Seinen Hōritsuka Hōchū Daihyōdan 靑年法律家訪中代表團. *Hōritsuka no mita Chūgoku* 法律家のみた中國. Tokyo: Nihon hyōron sha, 1965.

Shang-yeh shih-yung fa-kuei shou-ts'e 商業實用法規手册. Peking: Fa-lü ch'u pan she, 1958.

Shen K'o-ch'in 沈克勤. *Kuo-chi fa* 國際法. Taipei: Hsüeh-sheng shu-chü, 1964.

Ssu-fa-hsing-cheng-pu tiao-ch'a-chü so ts'ang Chung-kung fa-lü wen-chien 司法行政部調查局所藏中共法律文件. 28 vols. (available at the Library of Congress).

Stalin (Ssu-ta-lin) 斯大林. *Ma-k'o-szu chu-i yü yü-yen hsüeh wen-t'i* 馬克思主義與語言學問題. Peking, 1950.

Su-lien k'o-hsüeh yüan fa-lü yen-chiu so, ed. 蘇聯科學院法律研究所. *Kuo-chi fa* 國際法. Peking: Shih-chieh chih-shih ch'u pan she, 1959.

Ta ch'ing lü-li hui-t'ung hsin-tsuan 大清律例會通新纂. Taipei: Wen-hai ch'u pan she, 1964. Reprint.

Tabata Shigejirō 田畑茂二郎. *Kokusai hō I* 國際法 I. Tokyo: Yūhikaku, 1957.

Takayanagi 高柳眞三 et al., eds. *Nihon hōseishi jiten* 日本法制史辭典. Tokyo, 1967.

Ting Wei-liang 丁韙良. *Wan-kuo kung-fa* 萬國公法. Peking: T'ung wen kuan, 1864.

Toriyabe Sentarō 鳥谷部銑太郎. *Seijigaku teikō* 政治學提綱. Tokyo: Yakusho ihen sha.

Ts'ui Shu-ch'in 崔書琴. *Kuo-chi fa* 國際法. Shanghai: Shang-wu yin-shu kuan, 1947.

Tsui-hsin liu-fa ch'üan-shu 最新六法全書. Chang Chih-pen 張知本. Taipei: Ta Chung-kuo t'u-shu kung-ssu, 1956.

Wai-Meng wei "Meng-ku jen-min kung-ho-kuo" hsien-fa 外蒙偽 "蒙古人民共和國" 憲法. Meng-Tsang wei-yüan-hui tiao-ch'a-shih 蒙藏委員會調查室. Taipei, 1954.

Wang Ch'iang-sheng 王強生. *Hai shang kuo-chi fa* 海上國際法. Peking: Fa-lü ch'u pan she, 1957.

Wang Fu-yen 汪馥炎. *Kuo-chi kung-fa lun* 國際公法論. Shanghai: Fa-hsüeh pien i she, 1933.

Wang Jung-pao 汪榮寶, and Yeh Lan 葉瀾. *Hsin erh ya* 新爾雅. Shanghai: Kuo hsüeh she, 1903.

Wang Li 王力. *Chung-kuo hsien-tai yü-fa* 中國現代語法. Shanghai: Shang-wu yin-shu kuan, 1947.

——— *Chung-kuo yü-fa li-lun* 中國語法理論. Chungking: Shang-wu yin-shu kuan, 1944.

Wang Nai-ts'ung 王迺聰. *Hsin hun-yin-fa wen-t'i chieh-ta hui-pien* 新婚姻法問題解答彙編. Peking: Wen-hua kung-ying she, 1951.

Wei "Chung-hua-jen-min-kung-ho-kuo hsien-fa ts'ao-an" chi fu-chien 偽 "中華人民共和國憲法草案" 及附件. Yang-ming-shan chuang 陽明山莊. Taipei, 1954.

Wei hun-yin-fa chi fei-ch'ü hun-yin chiu-fen 偽婚姻法及匪區婚姻糾紛. Nei-cheng-pu tiao-ch'a-chü 內政部調查局. Taipei, 1950.

Wei-cheng-wu-yüan fa-pu fei-chih li-yung pan-fa 偽政務院發佈廢紙利用辦法. Nei-cheng-pu tiao-ch'a-chü 內政部調查局. Taipei.

Wei-cheng-wu-yüan kung-pu pao-chang fa-ming-ch'üan yü chuan-li-ch'üan chan-hsing t'iao-li 偽政務院公佈保障發明權與專利權暫行條例. Nei-cheng-pu tiao-ch'a-chü 內政部調查局. Taipei, 1950.

Wu Nien-tzu 吳念慈, K'o Pai-nien 柯柏年, and Wang Shen-ming 王愼名. *Hsin shu yü tz'u-tien* 新術語辭典. Shanghai: Nan-ch'iang shu-chü, 1929.

Yokota Kisaburō 橫田喜三郎. *Kokusai hōgaku* 國際法學. Tokyo: Yūhikaku, 1955.

Index

Index

OH

O| I83 TFC
Cohen

AS
WW